FLORIDA STATE
UNIVERSITY LIBRARIES

FEB 18 1998

TALLAHASSEE, FLORIDA

REBEL
ON
THE RIGHT

Henry Page Croft (1881–1947) as he began his parliamentary career in 1910.

REBEL ON THE RIGHT

Henry Page Croft
and the Crisis of British
Conservatism,
1903–1914

Larry L. Witherell

Newark: University of Delaware Press
London: Associated University Presses

© 1997 by Associated University Presses, Inc.

All rights reserved. Authorization to photocopy items for internal or personal use, or the internal or personal use of specific clients, is granted by the copyright owner, provided that a base fee of $10.00, plus eight cents per page, per copy is paid directly to the Copyright Clearance Center, 222 Rosewood Drive, Danvers, Massachusetts 01923. [0-87413-622-9/97 $10.00+8¢ pp, pc.]

Associated University Presses
440 Forsgate Drive
Cranbury, NJ 08512

Associated University Presses
16 Barter Street
London WC1A 2AH, England

Associated University Presses
P.O. Box 338, Port Credit
Mississauga, Ontario
Canada L5G 4L8

The paper used in this publication meets the requirements
of the American National Standard for Permanence of Paper
for Printed Library Materials Z39.48–1984.

Library of Congress Cataloging-in-Publication Data

Witherell, Larry L., 1949–
  Rebel on the right : Henry Page Croft and the crisis of British Conservatism, 1903–1914 / Larry L. Witherell.
    p. cm.
  Includes bibliographical references and index.
  ISBN 0-87413-622-9 (alk. paper)
  1. Croft, Henry Page, 1881–1947. 2. Conservatism—Great Britain—History—20th century. 3. Great Britain—Politics and government—1901–1910. 4. Great Britain—Politics and government—1910–1936. 5. Conservative Party (Great Britain)—History. I. Title.
DA566.9.C76W58   1997
941.084′092—dc21   97-13256
                                                                      CIP

PRINTED IN THE UNITED STATES OF AMERICA

Contents

List of Abbreviations	7
Acknowledgments	9
Introduction	15
1. Birth of an Imperialist	23
2. A Crack Begins to Show (1904–1906)	36
3. From Lincoln to the Confederacy (1906–1907)	53
4. Croft, the Confederates, and the Balfour Question (1907)	69
5. Croft, the Confederates, and Political Cannibalism (1908–1909)	85
6. Imperial Mission, Reveille, and the Call to Action (1910)	110
7. Croft, the Reveille, and the Fight against Humdrum Toryism (1910)	131
8. Croft, Conservative Party Politics, and the Balfour Question (1911)	146
9. Militant Unionism or a National and Imperial Party (1911)	165
10. Croft, Bonar Law, and the Betrayal of the Imperial Idea (1912–1913)	181
11. All for Naught (1912–1914)	196
Conclusion	208
Appendix 1: Confederate Membership	214
Appendix 2: Membership of Reveille	221
Appendix 3: Manifesto of the Unionist Reveille (1910)	226
Appendix 4: Members of the Imperial Mission (1911–1913)	229
Notes	234
Bibliography	274
Index	285

Abbreviations

BL	British Library
Bodl Lib	Bodleian Library
CAC	Churchill Archives Centre
HLRO	House of Lords Record Office
Hatfd Hse	Archives held by the Marquess of Salisbury, Hatfield House
Herts RO	Hertfordshire Record Office
NLS	National Library of Scotland
PRO	Public Record Office
SRO	Scottish Record Office
UBL	University of Birmingham Library
UTL	University of Texas Library
WSRO	West Sussex Record Office

Acknowledgments

At the conclusion of a long but most enjoyable adventure, it is now a pleasure to convey my sincere appreciation to the very many individuals who provided support and encouragement as this project sprang to life.

I am indebted to Professor J. K. Munholland for his unfailing support, encouragement, and confidence in this project and whose counsel and friendship I will always value. I must also record my gratitude for the advice, support, and encouragement that Professor John D. Fair was always prepared to offer and provide, as well as to Professor R. J. Q. Adams, who likewise was always ready to share his knowledge and insights. He was also very kind to permit me to read chapters from his forthcoming biography, *Andrew Bonar Law: A Life in Politics.* Many other individuals have provided assistance and support, mostly by sharing their thoughts and ideas or enduring my endless discussions about Henry Page Croft and Edwardian politics, including Professor J. L. Altholz, Dr. Derek Blakeley, Professor Robert Cole, Mr. Joseph Coohill, Dr. Nick Crowson, Dr. S. M. Ellwood, Professor Thomas Kennedy, Professor S. E. Lehmberg, Professor T. O. Lloyd, Professor Peter Mellini, Professor Roy Matthews, Professor Rainer Praetorius, Professor J. A. Ramsden, Dr. D. F. Steele, Dr. John Swanson, Dr. Michael Taylor, Mr. Richard Thurlow, and Professor Carolyn White.

A major contribution that a project such as this provides is the many wonderful friends made during the many research trips. I wish to make special mention of four such friends: Professor Martin and Rosalie Alexander, who were always ready to extend an English welcome to me; Dr. Roger Griffin, whose assistance and hospitality during my visits to Oxford were invaluable; and Dr. Roger Eatwell, who not only shared his thoughts and knowledge about British politics but took time to introduce me to the wonderful city of Bath.

I need also to acknowledge the many kind archivists, librarians, and their institutions who helped in so many different ways to put this book together: Colin Harris, Helen Langley, Steven Ellison, Katherine Bligh, and Robin Harcourt Williams, whose patience and knowledge made my visits to Hatfield so pleasant, productive, and instructive. I also thank The Bodleian Library; University of Birmingham Library; Bristol University Library; British Library; British Library of Political and Economic Sciences; University of Cambridge Library; Churchill Archive Centre; Colindale Newspaper Archives; Hatfield House; Hertfordshire Record Office; House of Lords

Record Office; University of Leeds Library; Liverpool City Library; Mitchell Library, Glasgow; Mitchell Library of the State of New South Wales; Modern Record Centre, University of Warwick; Northumberland Record Office; National Library of Scotland; University of Reading Library; Scottish Record Office; University of Sheffield Archives; Harry Ransom Humanities Research Center, University of Texas; and West Sussex Record Office.

I should also thank the following for permission to quote from material for which they hold copyright: Lady Elizabeth Gass (Alexander Acland-Hood); Nigel Arnold-Forster (Hugh Oakley Arnold-Forster); Earl of Balfour (Arthur James Balfour); Lady Juliet Townsend (F. E. Smith); Clerk of Records, House of Lords Record Office, and the Beaverbrook Foundation Trustees (Andrew Bonar Law and Patrick Hannon); University of Birmingham (Austen and Joseph Chamberlain); the Marquess of Salisbury (Lord Hugh Cecil and the 4th Marquess of Salisbury); Professor Ann Lambton (Lord Robert Cecil); Dowager Countess of Bessborough (Lord Duncannon); Harry Ransom Humanities Research Center, University of Texas (J. L. Garvin), Sir Lingard Goulding, Bt (Edward Goulding); Lord Coleraine (Richard Law, 1st Lord Coleraine); Lord Egremont (3d Lord Leconfield); Earl of Malmesbury (5th Earl of Malmesbury); Viscount Long, C. B. E. (Walter Long); West Sussex Record Officer (Leopold S. Maxse); John A. Maxton, MP (James Maxton); Earl of Portland (Lord Henry Cavendish-Bentinck and the 6th Duke of Portland); Viscount Ridley (2d Viscount Ridley); Edward Sandars (J. S. Sandars); Samuel Houldsworth, Major, and Ralph Abel Smith (Abel Henry Smith); Mrs. R. M. Stafford (Arthur Steel-Maitland); Lord Willoughby de Broke (19th Lord Willoughby de Broke), and David Donald Turnour, 8th Earl Winterton (6th Earl Winterton). I have diligently tried to identify, locate, and contact the owners of all copyright materials, and I hope those whom I could not identify or locate will accept my sincere apologies for my use of any copyrighted materials in the writing of this history. I also thank Oxford University Press for permitting me to use material from my article on the Confederacy, which appeared in *Twentieth Century British History*. In addition to permitting me to use and quote extensively from his father's papers, I am greatly indebted to Michael Henry Glendower Croft, 2d Baron Croft, whose knowledge of British politics, encouragement, assistance, and hospitality made this book an exciting and enjoyable adventure. I enjoyed our many evenings during which we discussed his father, family, and politics, both past and present, over wonderful dinners and fine wine, and I had hoped to have had many more. However, it is with great sadness that I learned that Lord Croft passed away on 11 January 1997 while this book was being prepared. He was very interested in seeing that his father was not forgotten by history. I am also pleased to thank Richard Page Croft, Hon. Mrs. Diana Uhlman, and Hon. Bernard

Croft, now 3d Baron Croft, for their assistance and hospitality during my researches.

My most sincere gratitude and expression must be reserved for my wife, Sherry, and daughter, Kerry, for their patience, support, encouragement, without which this book would never have come to fruition.

REBEL
ON
THE RIGHT

Introduction

> Although he was a strong Conservative, he cared more for the defence of the nation and the Empire than for Conservative Party allegiance, and in supporting the Imperial cause he constantly displeased political leaders who were taking shorter views than he took and who definitely preferred malleable placemen as colleagues to uncompromising patriots with strong views and powerful arguments.
>
> —Viscountess Milner, 1948

On 7 December 1947, at the age of sixty-six, Brigadier-General the Rt. Hon. Sir Henry Page Croft, PC, CMG, TD, DL, 1st Baronet Croft of Knole, and 1st Baron Croft of Bournemouth, died suddenly and unexpectedly. As befitted his life and political career, he died in harness, on his way to a session of the House of Lords. He had sat in the upper chamber only since May 1940 when Winston Churchill, soon after becoming prime minister, selected Sir Henry Page Croft as one of his joint parliamentary undersecretaries of state for war and secured a peerage for him from King George VI. Previously Croft had sat in the House of Commons without interruption since the general election in January 1910.

Shortly after Churchill became Britain's war leader in May 1940, he telephoned Croft at his home in Bournemouth. Churchill informed Croft of his new assignment in the War Office and announced that Croft would be going to the House of Lords. Croft tried to decline the honor, pleading that he "loved the House of Commons" and did not want to leave. The issue was settled quickly when the prime minister responded, "Henry, you must, it's your duty."[1] The next day, with newspapers packed with reports about the government reorganization, Jimmy Maxton, the socialist Clydesider and Independent Labour MP, wrote to Croft with congratulations. He noted that "our proximity on the bench has led me to appreciate your qualities, your personal courage, your independence of thought, and your steadfastness in sticking to your own principles."[2] Being in the extreme wings of their respective parties, Maxton and Croft spent nearly eighteen years together in the gangway at the House of Commons, and Maxton's description is most revealing.

Just before his death, Croft had completed another article on imperial affairs, an issue that had been at the center of his ideas, politics, and passion for nearly a half century.³ As evidenced by the hundreds of articles and thousands of speeches promoting the importance of the British empire, he devoted his entire public career, which spread across five decades, to the British empire and the goal of imperial unity. Leo Amery, a long-time friend, who perhaps was the only living politician to rival Croft's dedication to the empire, noted that Croft's "whole life was, indeed, given to that task which Mr. Churchill has recently defined as 'the most honoured of all, to unite and combine our Commonwealth of Nations and Empire, without which the safety of this island cannot endure nor its prosperity return.'" Croft, Amery declared, was unshakable in his conviction that the goal of imperial unity "could only be fulfilled if the economic aspect of that unity received due recognition."⁴ Brendan Bracken wrote that Croft "was more of a crusader than a politician. He strived with all his heart and soul to strengthen the spiritual and material resources of the British Empire."⁵ As most of the memorials observed, Croft "gave up a great part of his political life to champion Imperial Preference." One of Croft's constituency newspapers, the *Bournemouth Daily Echo,* noted that although the leaders of the Conservative party "were sometimes inclined to compromise . . . not so Lord Croft. He was an unwearying and resourceful fighter. Lord Croft never changed, tired or faltered in advocating the causes in which he believed."⁶ Richard Law, son of Croft's early leader, Andrew Bonar Law, noted, "I cannot think of any men in political life whose character I respect more. . . . I remember, too, (although they were not always in agreement) how much respect my father had for him—indeed, the name Henry Page Croft is among my earliest political memories."⁷

The tributes to Croft suggest "that no one in the Conservative party . . . has been a more consistent advocate of the cause of Empire trade and Empire unity than Lord Croft."⁸ Croft held firm to an unshakable promotion of the British nation and defense of the empire. His uncompromising nationalism made him a radical Conservative early in his career. Although he may have been one of the last remaining diehards, he was by all accounts the most prominent member of the Conservative party's extreme right wing during the first half of the twentieth century. This was the view held by the Conservative prime minister, Stanley Baldwin. In the summer of 1935, Baldwin confided to a young and ambitious R. A. Butler that to rise as party leader he must be capable of steering a path between Harold Macmillan on the left and Henry Page Croft on the right. Only "then you will be on a path to leader of the Conservative party."⁹

Lord Leconfield wrote that his long-time friend and political ally "was a great fighter for the Conservative party and it was a real pity that there were not any others like him in the party."¹⁰ With the passage of forty years, Croft's good friend forgot that Croft's earliest political activities were as a rebel on the right, a position from which he often found himself at odds with the party and its leadership. Notwithstanding his long-standing association with the Conservative party, Croft was never hesitant to direct his rhetorical and political artillery against his own leaders. Although a fixture on the party's extreme right flank, Croft always considered himself "an Imperialist first before all those other questions."[11] It followed from this posture that Croft perhaps viewed himself as another William Pitt "the Younger," seeking to salvage the British state from what he perceived to be parliamentary stalemate and corruption. For Croft, the party, and even the state, existed for the purpose of promoting and defending the nation and empire. Accordingly, at the end of the First World War, he abandoned the Conservative party for what he believed to be its neglect of the national interests. In September 1917 he took the dramatic step of establishing a rival, the National party, which existed until 1923.[12] Although he eventually returned to the Conservative fold, he nevertheless continued his effort to influence party and government policy through another political experiment, the Empire Industries Association, a substantial body of Conservative back-bench MPs and representatives of Britain's business interests, which he controlled from 1924 to his death.

Although Croft usually is noted by historians for his involvement with these two organizations, his political development began during the crisis years of British conservatism, 1903–14. It was during these years that we find the emergence of a substantial political discontent and development of his radical conservatism. During the Edwardian period, Croft launched a series of radical conservative movements, which pivoted around his determined nationalism and imperial politics. It was here that he became the ultimate imperialist, perhaps one of the last remaining unapologetic imperialists, whose own passing in 1947 corresponded with the passing of the empire itself. Inasmuch as his imperial views were the product of his intense nationalism, Croft considered the empire as the principal instrument with which to protect and promote the British nation and race. As Britain entered the twentieth century with a new set of social, economic, political, and international challenges, Croft's political activities were generally developing in response to these challenges. His activities and development also coincided with crisis within the Edwardian Conservative party, as it, too, struggled to face the new century.

Recently, a scholar of early twentieth-century Britain bemoaned that "the Edwardian Conservative party remain[s] the Cinderella of Edwardian historiography, languishing in the shadows while its ugly sisters, the Liberal and Labour parties, hog the limelight."[13] For sixty years the character of Edwardian political historiography has been virtually determined by George Dangerfield's *The Strange Death of Liberal England,* as historians have followed the Liberal party's retreat into the mist of political irrelevance and subsequently focused on the sequential rise of the British Labour party. It has only been recently that scholars have begun to examine the condition of the Edwardian Conservatives. It now may be argued that it was in fact the Conservative party that experienced the most obvious and serious difficulties in the decade prior to the First World War. The party lost three consecutive elections, including the humiliating defeat in 1906; ousted its own leader in 1911; was generally divided into several factions; and was out of power for seventeen years.[14]

In light of the developing interest in conservatism and the Conservative party, historians are being charged to explore the hinterland of the Edwardian party to provide a more detailed picture of the political and ideological dynamics during this crucial period.[15] Excavation reveals an instability caused by a series of coincidental transitions. The Edwardian Conservative party experienced a generational transition, a shift in leadership from the aristocratic tradition of Salisbury and Balfour to the meritocracy of Bonar Law and Baldwin. There was a corresponding ideological transition as the party struggled to construct a set of cardinal principles more appropriate for the new century. These were accompanied by political and institutional adjustments as Conservatives faced new political struggles within a new political atmosphere. This overall period of party evolution produced a temporary vacuum, the manifestation of which was an anemic leadership, a paucity of ideas and programs, and an exceedingly cautious political strategy. The youthful, frustrated, and radicalized sector of the party, in which we find young Henry Page Croft championing major campaigns, attempted to rush into this vacuum in an effort to define the party's ideological orthodoxy and influence the construction of a more dynamic, aggressive, and modern party. The political ambiguity and instability that resulted from the evolutionary transition as the party progressed through this period, as well as from the stress of economic, social, political, and international challenges, produced a dysfunctional party in the decade prior to the First World War. This dysfunction pushed a new generation of conservatives toward a political aggressiveness, or radical conservatism, with which the party was unaccustomed. It even provoked near cannibalistic behavior in certain quarters of the party.

The process in which the radicals sought to develop a new ideological orthodoxy and construct a more modern party occurred with little intellectual intercourse or dialogue between the party's youth and the incumbent political elite; soon serious tensions developed. These tensions rose to distrust and then to estrangement as the radicalized right wing saw a failure of intellectual creativity, political will, and determined leadership. The party's right wing feared that continued impotence under such conditions would not only sacrifice the party but would eventually forfeit Britain's future. Burdened by such apocalyptic visions, Croft and his associates within the tariff reform organizations, the Confederacy, the Reveille, and the Imperial Mission were pushed to excommunicate and exterminate wobblers and even to seek the overthrow of their leader. They abandoned the gentlemanly politics of the nineteenth-century style and turned to a radical conservatism.

The unexplored hinterland can be found in the membership and activities of the radicalized right wing that has not received any scholarly treatment. By reconstructing the political career of one of the more interesting, active, and controversial members of the Conservative party's radical sector, this study hopes to excavate some of the party's previously disregarded territory. An examination of the political development and activities of Henry Page Croft, a prominent member of this militant wing, provides insight into the condition of Edwardian conservatism during this era of transition.

Croft, if considered at all by historians, is usually remembered as a caricature of ultraconservatism during the interwar period. More important is what he is not remembered for: his flirtation with alternative and radical political movements, particularly his right-wing National party (1917–23) and the Empire Industries Association (1924–47). Both were the natural legacies of the discontent and determination found within his Edwardian political activities, which included an extremely impressive association of local tariff reform groups; the Confederacy, a subterranean movement that sought to purify the party; the Reveille, a political strike force that unleashed the campaign that brought down Arthur Balfour as party leader in 1911; and the Imperial Mission, an early attempt to supersede the existing party arrangement with an alternative imperial and national party.

It was during the decade prior to the First World War that a young and ambitious Henry Page Croft began to experiment with his own current of alternative politics. In doing so he steadily flirted with an embrace of an independent imperial and national party. The nineteenth-century character of the Conservative party was rapidly disintegrating as the tenor and approach to both intra- and extraparty politics undertook a markedly different turn during the years leading up to 1914. Croft also represented a new set of political and nationalist ideas that he articulated and promoted through his own extraparliamentary movements, his local tariff reform groups, the Confederacy, the Reveille, and the Imperial Mission. No longer was the state viewed in nineteenth-century terms as a passive institution. Instead, Croft viewed the state as an activist institution that had the authority and responsibility to forward constructive and aggressive programs, particularly those which contributed to social and political stability, economic prosperity, and national and imperial security. Although such constructive programs helped preserve the position and authority of those in power, the overall goal was to defend, strengthen, and advance the British state, nation, and empire.

Croft came of age at a time when the position of Britain was being politically and economically challenged abroad and when the social conditions and arrangements were breeding discontent at home. As a result, in 1903, Croft was swept away by the appeal of Joseph Chamberlain's program of tariff reform and the images it held out: optimism for the future by providing an albeit simplistic answer to the need for economic prosperity, social reform, and contentment, and political, military and diplomatic security. In 1906 Croft made his first attempt to translate his commitment to the empire into a political opportunity with a seat in Parliament. Encouraged by Joseph Chamberlain, Croft entertained the idea of challenging the prominent Conservative free trader in Croft's home territory of East Hertfordshire. Instead he traveled to Lincoln where, as a Tariff Reform and Unionist candidate, he challenged his party's sitting free trade MP in the 1906 general election. The episode exposed not only the generational shift but the ideological schism within the Conservative party as it struggled over the issue of fiscal and imperial politics. It also documented the political risks that Croft was prepared to take in pressing his political program.

In the wake of the Conservative party's 1906 electoral debacle, Croft and several other young conservatives who shared his disposition became increasingly frustrated over the anemic condition of the Conservative party and its inability to articulate and promote a militant and constructive program that revolved around the reconstruction of the empire. This condition was blamed on apathetic and ineffective party leadership as well as the presence of a contingent of free traders. Croft acted on this frustration and established the Confederacy, a surreptitious and rebellious movement of determined young conservatives whose objective was to purge the party of wobblers. In an effort to put the party on a new road to political victory and imperial reform, Croft's Confederacy first needed either to push or pull Balfour into accepting tariff reform as "the first constructive policy of the Conservative and Unionist Party." Soon a seriously dangerous schism appeared within the party.

With the leadership subscribing to fiscal and imperial reform after Balfour's lukewarm conversion at the Birmingham conference in November 1907, the Confederates unleashed a devastating campaign against the remaining free traders, including such prominent figures as Lord Robert Cecil, son of the late prime minister, Lord Salisbury. Croft's all-out attack against and destruction of Abel Henry Smith, the Conservative free trade MP for East Hertfordshire, provides an important case study of the determination of the radical wing of the Conservative party. The episode also provides the first study of the extent to which tariff and imperial reform had taken root among the constituencies and their local associations, and the extent this momentum contributed to the conversion of the national party leadership and apparatus. Controlling the Confederacy as well as an extensive tariff reform organization throughout East Hertfordshire, Croft's political, organizational, and campaigning skills had now become quite evident. They were joined by his unrestrained determination to advance fiscal and imperial reform with a puritanical, "take no prisoners" policy.

In January 1910 Croft was elected to Parliament from Christchurch. Notwithstanding his personal accomplishment, he remained seriously disenchanted over the lack of constructive programs, fortitude, and leadership within the Conservative party in the face of the Liberal government's attack on the constitution and its neglect of the British empire. In August 1910, he gave voice to this discontent with a call to action and the creation of the Reveille movement. The Reveille movement, supported by a committee of one hundred right-wing rebels, represented the beginning of a direct and open challenge to the leadership of Arthur Balfour. At the same time, Croft established the Imperial Mission with which to provide organizational substance to his imperial idea. Although the Confederacy and Reveille represented one shape of Croft's approach to alternative politics, the Imperial Mission represented the beginnings of a national and imperial party. Neither the Reveille nor the Imperial Mission has been the subject of any historical examination.

As 1910 drew to a close, Croft and the Reveille became irreversibly estranged from Balfour after the party leader backed away from the "first constructive policy" of the Conservative party. For purely tactical reasons, owing to the December 1910 general election, Balfour promised not to impose food taxes, a crucial component of Croft's imperial idea, without first submitting the issue to a referendum. Croft and his Reveille responded with a full-scale challenge against Balfour and played a major but unexamined role in forcing the party leader's retirement in late 1911.

Croft was encouraged by the ascendancy of Andrew Bonar Law to the leadership of the Conservative party in November 1911, and as a result he voluntarily scaled back the activities of the Reveille. After initially making strong tariff reform statements, Bonar Law, under pressure from a nervous backbench, soon betrayed the imperial idea by abandoning food duties. This precipitated another party leadership crisis in 1912–13, during which Croft was prepared to resurrect the Confederacy with a campaign against an indecisive Bonar Law.

However, by 1913 the betrayal had been completed, and it was impossible for Croft to resurrect his alternative political movements, either the Confederacy or the Reveille. The nation and the Conservative party were engulfed by the great crisis over Ireland, Ulster, and the preservation of the Union. Croft, the ultimate imperialist, was faced with the Conservative party's position that suggested a willingness to sacrifice the empire to save the Union with Ireland. The paradox of such a position was not lost on Croft. Although he did not play a highly visible or prominent role in the party's resistance to home rule, he was compelled to reconcile his Conservative party politics and his imperial politics. The result produced some unnoticed attempts to secure a compromise. Although it generally is considered that the events at Sarajevo in June 1914 delayed the demise of the Liberal party, it might be suggested with equal weight that the outbreak of the First World War also prevented the self-destruction of the Conservative party. The party was then given the necessary pause in which to continue its transition from the nineteenth to twentieth centuries.

Perhaps relieved at the fact that Britain had avoided the catastrophe of civil war, Croft promptly went to France in August 1914, where he could fight for king, country, and empire. The reconstruction of Croft's early political career provides a look at the dynamics, crises, and controversies of Edwardian conservatism through the activities of an unorthodox but principled nationalist who, staunchly positioned on the party's right flank, was dedicated to defending Britain and her empire.

1
Birth of an Imperialist
(1903)

The fact is the party to which I belong is the greatest party in the world—the British Empire; and I consider on a National Question like this we should rise superior to a petty party strife.
—Henry Page Croft, 14 December 1903

Don't be deceived by the puny, pithy, pandering, prattle of prehistoric, party-mad pessimists.
—Henry Page Croft, 14 December 1903

Britain entered the twentieth century suffering from a degree of nervous anxiety yet seeming oblivious to what a new age held in store. At the same time, the future for a young Henry Page Croft, as he entered into his own adulthood, appeared unmistakably clear and well defined. In June 1902, removed from Britain's political debates and controversies, Croft celebrated his twenty-first birthday and left Trinity Hall, Cambridge, although without taking a degree. His departure from Cambridge took him only a short distance, back to the family seat at Fanhams Hall, Ware, in East Hertfordshire, where he returned to pursue a business career in the family enterprise, Henry Page & Co., Maltsters.

To understand the personal as well as the political deportment of Henry Page Croft, one must be given a glimpse of his ancestry, thus appreciating its burden. Lord Wedgwood, the former Liberal and Labour MP, believed that the Croft "family could claim more representatives in the House of Commons than is the case with any other family in England."[1] Beginning in 1296, members of the Croft family have sat in at least sixty Parliaments and in every century.[2] The family descended from Bernard de Croft in the time of William the Conqueror and is listed in the *Domesday Book* as having held the lands now occupied by Croft Castle, near Leominster, in Herefordshire.

In addition to parliamentary services, Croft's various ancestors served Prince Edward, son of Henry III; fought at the battles of Mortimer's Cross, Tewkesbury and Stoke; served Henry VII; served the duke of Northumberland and the earl of Leicester under Edward VI; had been imprisoned by Mary I; served as comptroller of the royal household under Elizabeth I; died in the service to Charles I; had been made bishop of Hereford by Charles II; and served as physician to Princess Charlotte, daughter of the prince of Wales, later George IV, at her tragic death in 1817.

Croft's father, Richard Benyon Croft (1843–1912), was educated at the Royal Naval College and then joined the Royal Navy in 1858, serving over fifteen years. He later became a major and honorary lieutenant-colonel in the Hertfordshire Yeomanry and a lieutenant (retired) in the Royal Navy. In 1869 he married Anne Elizabeth Page (1843–1921), the only child and heiress of Henry Page of Ware, in East Hertfordshire. Henry Page had built up a very prosperous grain trade and a maltster business, Henry Page & Co. Maltsters of Ware. R. B. Croft was persuaded to leave the navy and enter business with Henry Page, in which he was engaged until his death in January 1912.

In 1880 Fanhams Hall, a large country house and estate located in Ware, was given to Elizabeth Page Croft by her father, and it became the seat for the Crofts of Ware. Here they raised their two sons, Richard Page Croft (1872–1961) and Henry Page Croft (1881–1947), and six daughters in relative luxury. As a child Croft was first sent to St. David's School, Reigate, thereafter to Eton, where he did not particularly excel, and finally to Shrewsbury where he continued his interest in rowing. Even Croft confessed astonishment when he passed on to Trinity Hall, Cambridge. It was orthodoxy at Fanhams Hall that a degree in chemistry would benefit the family's malting business. It was the same belief that only a few years earlier had sent Croft's older brother, Richard, to Trinity Hall to study chemistry but with little precedent-setting success.

As may be gleaned from the brief pages on his "Cambridge Days" in his autobiography, it was neither scholarship nor intellectual curiosity that consumed his time, energy, and passion but instead was rowing. Croft had achieved a distinguished rowing career having won races at Eton at age thirteen, been captain of boats at Shrewsbury, twice won the Thames Cup at the Henley Regatta, and been captain of the Trinity Hall Boat Club. Interestingly, Croft's earliest venture into the arena of national public debate was a 1901 defense of the Englishness of rowing, which he issued against the call to internationalize the competition at the Henley Regatta.[3] This desire to preserve England and Englishness from the contamination of a foreign intrusion remained a consistent theme in his political and social thought.

Reaching a certain level of maturity on the edge of the twentieth century, one might easily construct an image of both Croft and Britain coming to the end of their respective "splendid isolation" in the summer of 1902. After having come down from Cambridge, Croft entered the family business. Any hesitancy that he may have entertained during his university days was eliminated on 5 September 1901 when his brother was severely wounded in the South African war. Richard Page Croft's experience and suffering had a great impact upon the younger Croft. In 1900 Henry joined the First Hertfordshire Volunteer Battalion of the Bedfordshire Regiment, and during his university vacations, he trained with regular regiments, including the Highland Light Infantry which he would meet again in 1914. Notwithstanding an intense desire to follow his brother to South Africa, the request for his father's permission was never fully pressed since, as Croft explained, they believed the relief of Kimberly, Ladysmith, and Mafeking marked the winding down of any serious fighting. The South African war served to introduce Croft to Britain's empire in a profound and dramatic fashion.

Richard's military service, his tragic injuries in South Africa, and his lengthy convalescence resulted in an immediate imposition on Croft. It required his entering the family business as soon as practicable and immediately assuming responsibilities for its operation and management. Here the young Croft came into contact with an array of businessmen and merchants and developed considerable knowledge of the corn trade as well as the brewing industry. Within a very short period of time, Croft mastered all aspects of the business, that is, financial, operational, and labor relations. He boasted that he "learned thus early the sorrows of the capitalists and the extraordinary ups and downs in trade for which our Socialist brethren never make any allowance."[4] Although it is not his business apprenticeship of 1902-5 in which we are primarily interested, we must recognize the role it played in these politically formative years. His experience in the operation of the firm provided him with a critical appreciation of and insight into the problems of British industry and commerce. This is particularly significant given the agri-industrial character of the malting and brewing business. Equally important his hands-on experience gave him his own empirical basis with which to approach political and economic questions. Perhaps more important since we are concerned about the development of politics and a politician, his business experience enveloped him with a claim of credibility when he addressed the economic questions circulating within the political arena.

Liberated from the arduous demands of academic challenges and separated from the frivolity of youth, Croft was captured by the debate developing on the national political scene, and which, as with Croft's own thoughts, was increasingly focusing on questions of imperial unity, defense, and fiscal policy. For Croft the empire represented the greatness, invincibility, and perpetuality of Britain; and to an ambitious and energetic youth, it offered the requisite charge of excitement. The question was how the opportunity to pursue a new direction was to present itself. Where was it to be found? In whom would it be embodied? The occasion, individual, and opportunity were soon to become obvious.

Having been raised in East Hertfordshire, in the shadow of the great Cecil family, it would have been easy to look to Hatfield. Lord Salisbury, the prime minister, however, was tired and unexciting and had become the personification of caution at a time when a new age and century were opening, new visions were appearing, and new ideas circulating. On 7 May 1902, Salisbury, in his last major public speech and as if with a sense of anticipation, prophetically admonished Britain not to push imperial integration.[5]

Croft, however, soon found himself pulled in other political and intellectual directions. On 16 May 1902, only a few weeks before Croft departed Cambridge, the colonial secretary, Joseph Chamberlain, declared that "the question" facing Britain as it proceeded into an anxious and complex future "was whether the British Empire is to continue strong, powerful, and united, or whether it is to fall to pieces by disruption or by tolerated secession." Accordingly, he urged, "let us raise our thoughts to the transcendent possibilities of a federation of the British race." Chamberlain's biographer, Julian Amery, considered the speech to be "the prologue to the Tariff Reform campaign."[6] Chamberlain's ideas were soon embraced by a collection of young conservatives, for whom the call for a "federation of the British race" represented the promise of a new economic, political, and cultural nationalism founded on the reconstruction of the empire.

In April 1902, the Chancellor of the Exchequer, Sir Michael Hicks Beach, made a minor dent in Britain's free trade tradition by introducing a corn duty in an attempt to raise revenue needed by wartime exigencies. It was to be, Hicks Beach insisted, only temporary and should not be considered as any prelude to protectionism. Chamberlain nevertheless seized the initiative and set forth the elements of a new fiscal policy, within which were the foundations of an advanced imperial policy. Chamberlain claimed that Britain's overall security was precarious as her commercial rivals resorted to hostile tariffs and trading practices in an effort to cut her off from profitable trade, which was her lifeblood. However, he pointed out, Britain cannot combat hostile rivals by clinging on to the antiquated economic theory of free trade. Inasmuch as Britain and her empire were subjected to attack at all corners, he urged that Britain "must draw closer our internal relations, the ties of sentiment, the ties of sympathy, yes and the ties of interest."[7]

Years later Croft recalled that "the Chamberlain idea . . . appealed to me as something really constructive and the most attractive of his proposals was the idea of Imperial Preference that I hoped and believed might lead to . . . ultimate federation."[8] The importance of imperial unity was no longer an abstraction. It had been given form and substance in the bush of South Africa and by the thousands of British and colonial soldiers, such as Richard Croft, who had served there. In 1912 Croft wrote that the South African war obliged Britain to "appreciate the meaning of Empire." He further described that the nation had been moved by "the spectacle of the manhood of the younger countries coming spontaneously to the assistance of the Mother-country." He concluded with near melodramatic flare, that the war, if it had accomplished nothing else, "made the world listen to the call of the blood of the British race, and it found a place in the hearts of Britons at home for the grown brothers overseas."[9]

In June 1902 Britain and the empire prepared for the coronation of Edward VII and in doing so symbolically closed the curtain on Victorian England, now a past and tired age. In the wake of such imagery, Britain was soon to shake itself loose from the age of Salisbury. The prime minister, seventy-two years old and in ill health, retired on 11 July 1902; he passed the helm of the government to his nephew, Arthur James Balfour. The ease and calm with which the transfer was accomplished belied the turmoil and crisis that would soon erupt within the Conservative party. Balfour's new government revealed little change and was perhaps nothing more than a caretaker ministry, while the party, and the country as a whole, prepared to face the challenges of a new century.

As a result of Chamberlain's new imperial and fiscal ideas, there were now factions in and out of Westminster for whom the colonial secretary "was the man of tomorrow and the day after tomorrow."[10] Accordingly, it is not difficult to understand how from very early on Croft embraced Joseph Chamberlain as being the leader and tariff reform as being the idea with which to construct a dynamic, confident, and modern imperial Britain. Chamberlain represented the excitement and strength of the British empire; for Croft these ideas were the source of a nearly spiritual optimism for the country's future.

While the implications of Chamberlain's fiscal and imperial suggestions ignited enthusiasm within Croft and others, they concurrently struck horror in the hearts of such orthodox free traders as C. T. Ritchie, Balfour's new Chancellor of the Exchequer, who immediately began defensive actions in various forums of political opinion. The events involving Chamberlain, Balfour, and the cabinet are well known and may be abbreviated here.[11] A conference of the colonial premiers had been meeting throughout the summer of 1902, having been brought together for the coronation. The colonial conference convinced the colonial secretary that commercial preference for the colonies would produce the imperial unity that had long been his dream. In his opening speech to the premiers, Chamberlain's vision became clear: "Our paramount objective is to strengthen the commercial, political and strategic bonds between Britain and her Dominions."[12] Believing he had accurately gauged the colonial temperament, in October 1902 Chamberlain raised the issue of remitting the corn duty for Canada with the cabinet. Notwithstanding a vigorous and heated opposition from Ritchie, Chamberlain eventually secured the cabinet's endorsement on 19 November. In early December, Chamberlain departed on a tour of South Africa, which in itself was an integral part of his promotion of imperial unity. During the colonial secretary's absence, Ritchie, who was preparing the government's budget for submission in April 1903, continued to press his objections to colonial preference, which he backed with a threat to resign should the cabinet's decision of 19 November be implemented. Ritchie claimed the preference policy would result in a substantial loss of revenue and precipitate the need to impose or raise domestic taxes. With Chamberlain unable to counter the chancellor, Ritchie's position gained the cabinet's support by the end of March. On 23 April, Ritchie introduced his budget, which not only abandoned the corn duty in particular but denounced food tariffs in general. Chamberlain had been dealt a major blow. The Conservatives were now divided into three factions: the free traders, Chamberlain's protectionists, and Balfour, who was desperately trying just to hold his ministry intact.

Frustrated, Chamberlain turned to his Birmingham loyalists on 15 May with a critical address, a virtual declaration of war.[13] As Julian Amery suggests, "no one speech in British history has ever caused such a sensation . . . or led to such momentous consequences."[14] Elie Halévy wrote that Chamberlain's "declaration came as a thunderbolt" to Balfour and the government. On the very day of the speech, Balfour admonished a deputation of protectionists, led by Henry Chaplin, not to push for colonial preferences, as the occasion was not a propitious one.[15] Leo Amery, a contemporary who eventually became a close friend and associate of Croft, proclaimed Chamberlain's speech to be "as direct and provocative as the theses which Luther nailed to the church door at Wittenberg."[16]

The speech struck a responsive chord in the sleepy East Hertfordshire village of Ware as young Croft read of Chamberlain's proclamation: while the "feeling of Imperial patriotism was checked for a generation . . . it was never extinguished. The embers were still alight. . . . The Empire is new. The Empire is in its infancy. Now is the time when we can mould that Empire, and we and those who live with us can decide its future destinies."[17] For Croft the method of promoting such ideas was logically seductive, and Chamberlain's simplistic eloquence took deep root within the young Croft. Imperial unity rested on the question of trade and commerce. Accordingly, Chamberlain proclaimed, "it is the business of British statesmen to do everything they can, . . . to keep the trade of the colonies with Great Britain; to increase the trade, to promote it." The first stroke is to offer preferential tariffs to the empire.[18]

Croft was impressed by the implications that Chamberlain's proposal suggested for Britain and the empire. "If this country were in danger," declared the colonial secretary, "it is my conviction that there is nothing within the power of these self-governing colonies that they would not do to come to our aid. . . . their resources, in men and money, would be at the disposal of the mother country in such an event."[19] The significance of the Birmingham speech was the fact that it occurred during a vacuum of imperialist and fiscal ideas but also within a period absent of political and ideological leadership within the party. Chamberlain's speech constituted a unilateral declaration for the new century and for a Conservative party that appeared to be without energy or vision. It was a declaration that Croft promptly embraced and promoted for the rest of his life. The promotion and success of British nationalism rested on the success of the new imperialism.

The speech set off an avalanche of enthusiasm as well as opposition both inside and outside the houses of Parliament. The divisions and turmoil were so great within the cabinet that Balfour was forced to arrange a truce between his ministers in an effort to save his government from disintegrating. The truce, however, merely postponed the inevitable and transferred the struggle outside of Parliament as partisans began to spread their respective gospel. As Chamberlain's biographer noted, "the movement thus developed a dynamic of its own which would never quite be brought under control."[20]

In mid June, Chamberlain initiated the process that eventually led to the formation of the Tariff Committee of the Birmingham Liberal Unionist Association, although it was to remain of limited importance for all practical purposes. On 22 June 1903 a meeting of Conservative MPs was held to promote Chamberlain's views on preferential trade within the empire. Six days later negotiations commenced for the creation of a national, extraparliamentary tariff reform organization. The momentum toward the establishment of a protectionist organization did not escape the notice of the party's free traders, as they responded by founding the Free Food League on 13 July with sixty MPs. On 21 July the Tariff Reform League officially came into existence at a dinner party held at Stafford House, the London residence of the duke of Sutherland.

Back in East Hertfordshire, Croft seemed to be isolated. He did not move in the London circles and had no known links with any of national political, academic, or journalistic cadres. In addition virtually over the hill from Ware was Hatfield, ancestral home of the Cecils and the bastion of free trade. One of the more vocal free trade proponents, Abel Henry Smith, East Hertfordshire's long-time MP, often teamed up with the locally influential *Hertfordshire Mercury* to ensure that the constituency was well fed on a diet of free trade ideology.[21] Nevertheless, Croft still felt the energy generated by Chamberlain's Birmingham speech. The precise date of contact between Croft and a national tariff reform organization remains elusive. Inasmuch as the Croft family exercised considerable influence within the Ware Conservative association and wielded a major presence in the East Hertfordshire Conservative and Liberal Unionist Association, it is quite probable that contact may have been established shortly after mid-July 1903. That is when the Birmingham Tariff Reform committee contacted local party agents and associations.[22] Regardless, it appears that at the time the Tariff Reform League was organized or shortly after the publicity of its establishment, Croft "leapt into the fray and immediately started an organisation of the Tariff Reform League in East Herts."[23] By October 1903 he was referring to the organization as the Ware Branch of the Tariff Reform League.[24]

Although opponents recognized that tariff reform could not prevail without the support of the working classes, supporters often doubted whether Chamberlain had the commitment to do what was needed to popularize tariff reform; some believed that his rigid priorities for imperial preference and unity constituted an intellectual obstruction to the practical necessity of working-class support.[25] Chamberlain "was frankly contemptuous of the trade union leaders and never made any serious effort to win over individuals among them or give them a permanent place in his movement."[26] In an apparent effort to rehabilitate Chamberlain in the eyes of working men, in August 1903 Henry Chaplin vigorously urged Chamberlain to commence a direct dialogue with labor leaders.[27] Chaplin also had important connections with trade union leaders in Lancashire and was quite concerned that working men were exceedingly sensitive on the issue of food taxes. Chaplin continued to press on with the issue, arguing that it was imperative for Chamberlain to meet the trade union leaders. Notwithstanding Chaplin's efforts, Chamberlain did not want to meet with any trade union leaders because, he said, "the difficulty of working with working-men representatives, if they are not of our party is the probability of a distorted account getting into the newspapers. But I do not dislike the idea of having a talk with some of the principal men."[28]

Within a matter of days of Chaplin's advice to Chamberlain urging the latter to be more sensitive to assuaging the concerns of the working classes and Chamberlain's unsatisfactory response, Henry Page Croft began his own campaign for tariff reform in East Hertfordshire. Not truly appreciating the formidability of his task, Croft initiated his battle for tariff reform with a series of articles under the title of "Considerations for Working Men." The articles were clearly intended to enlist the support of the working class of East Hertfordshire.

In mid-December 1903, Croft organized an impressive tariff reform rally at which Henry Chaplin, affectionately known in Lincolnshire as the "squire" and elder statesman of protectionism, was the principal speaker. It follows that sometime during autumn 1903, Croft and Chaplin entered into an alliance. What is known is that Croft met Chamberlain early in the campaign, and it appears that the occasion can be narrowed to the same time period during which Croft was engaged in publishing his articles (August through October). Croft records meeting Chamberlain at a London party at the age of twenty-two. "Happily the lady with whom I was sipping lemonade was well acquainted with the great man and I was speedily introduced. I was immensely impressed from the first, . . . and told him I was prepared to serve the cause in any way he might suggest."[29] This chance meeting over lemonade probably resulted in an introduction between Croft and Chaplin. It was a most significant introduction given Chaplin's subsequent contribution to Croft's political career. Nevertheless, without more evidence we may proceed with the conclusion that Croft's articles were not the product of any national tariff reformer's conscious suggestion but the beginning of Croft's own political acumen.

Croft was frustrated by what he believed to be an issue of national interest being treated in an entirely partisan manner. From his very first articles, Croft appealed to the "readers to disregard the selfish party attacks . . . for surely in a great national question like this we should rise superior to petty feeling, and unite in an endeavour to thrash the matter for the good of the country."[30] Croft then began to weave his view of empire, and the means by which it must be protected and promoted, into a direct appeal to the working class. He argued that free trade within the empire will increase profits and wages at home and produce prosperity among the colonies, which in turn will benefit Britain.[31] In addition, it is Britain's moral responsibility to hold the empire together and not permit the colonies "to slip gradually from all family ties." Britain was obligated to hold the empire together not merely for Britain's grandeur but in satisfaction of the demands of the empire itself, "for every member of this huge family is asking you for Free Trade within the Empire." Building on his interpretation of the South African war, Croft reminded his readers that the colonists "came in thousands to your aid, from every part of the world, in your darkest hours of 1900 and 1901." All they want in return "is that the Empire shall protect its trade from the rest of the world, to the benefit of all within it." He scoffed at the "bread tax" argument put forward by Liberals and such Conservative free traders as Lord Hugh Cecil. Rather, he pointed out that three million British jobs had been created since the Canadian policy of preference had been initiated in 1896. With the sound of a political battle cry, Croft urged that Britain "save your trade, and above all keep your colonies."[32]

Subjected to intense criticism from the *Hertfordshire Mercury,* Croft began to view himself as a David against Goliath, which, given the particular circumstances in Hertfordshire at the time, was not such an unreasonable image. Nevertheless, he still managed to give as well as he received, and he did so with a good bit of humor and smug satisfaction. He argued that Cobden's free trade argument was no longer relevant to the twentieth century and that it had been smashed by the political and economic realities of increasingly complex and dangerous international dynamics.[33] Cobden's theory did not produce an international trading community of free trade states as he predicted would emerge within five years after Britain embraced free trade.

Croft further attacked what he viewed as the significant inconsistency in free trade orthodoxy. To the working men of Hertfordshire, he noted that the price of bread did not rise when Hicks Beach imposed the shilling corn tax in 1902. Any increase in the price of foreign food will be mitigated by the supply of affordable food from the empire. If the empire had expanded in the nineteenth century under Cobden's free trade theories, then it would expand even more, in terms of economic trade, under a reciprocal free trade arrangement with all the colonial components. Croft suggested that a united free trade empire would not only produce all that was needed within the empire but would force foreign countries "to reduce their tariffs to a reasonable amount" so that the trading world would begin to approach Cobden's reciprocal free trade system. Indicating the development of his political thinking, Croft argued that the debate should be neither partisan nor political, but one that sought to promote the empire while concurrently protecting the nation. It was a debate within which the nation's interests must above all else remain supreme.[34]

In the meantime, critical events had transpired at Westminster. On 14 September 1903, Chamberlain resigned from the government, followed by free traders C. T. Ritchie, Lord Balfour of Burleigh, Lord George Hamilton, and eventually the duke of Devonshire. Now unencumbered by membership in the cabinet, Chamberlain launched the campaign for tariff reform with his famous Glasgow speech of 6 October 1903. At Glasgow, Chamberlain declared that his objectives were the "maintenance and increase of the national strength and prosperity of the United Kingdom" and "the creation of an Empire such as the world has never seen . . . [by] cement[ing] the union of the states beyond the seas." He sought "to consolidate the British race; we have to meet the clash of competition" against British commerce and Britain's physical existence.[35] He gave substance to the later description of "imperial preference as being first and foremost, a matter of sentiment."[36]

Chamberlain's autumn campaign produced a national standoff between the tariff reform campaign and the labor movement, which Chamberlain was content to ignore. It also frustrated Croft in his attempts to make local inroads into the working classes. Croft did not, however, become discouraged as a new development within the free trade movement was about to change his approach to the tariff reform campaign, a change that could easily be characterized as the transition from rhetoric to action. It brought him into the arena of rough-and-tumble politics, an arena that he was always to relish and enjoy and for which he ultimately became well known. During the autumn campaign, the national strategy was integrally linked to the personal promotion of tariff reform by Chamberlain as well as the personal promotion of the great Joe himself. The free trade strategy seemed to be one of subjecting Chamberlain to an onslaught of critics as speakers would, in sandwich style, precede and follow Chamberlain on his speaking circuit.

Although Croft attended at least Chamberlain's Birmingham rally, which was 4 November 1903, he soon was consumed by his own tariff reform campaign. After establishing the Ware Branch of the Tariff Reform League during the summer of 1903, Croft "proceeded to form branches in every town and village in the constituency." He was excited by the response, and soon he began to link up all the branches into the East Hertfordshire Tariff Reform League of which his father became president. Almost immediately Croft's "little army grew until it numbered over 1,500 members."[37]

1: Birth of an Imperialist (1903)

The first major tariff reform rally or demonstration of any significant proportion which did not involve Chamberlain's personal participation was organized by Croft and the Ware branch of the Tariff Reform League. As Croft described, "at the height of the row between Mr. Chamberlain and the Duke of Devonshire we arranged a mass meeting in the Drill Hall in Ware" for Monday, 14 December 1903. Henry Chaplin, "our heavy artillery," was the featured speaker before an assembly of thirteen hundred, which was an impressive accomplishment given the modest size of Ware.[38] The event further introduced Croft to the national tariff reform movement and its leaders, particularly the "squire."

Croft's tariff reform rally would have enjoyed greater national exposure had it not been overshadowed by the duke of Devonshire's provocative letter of 11 December 1903. Due to the death of their MPs, the London constituencies of Dulwich and Lewisham, which had been held by substantial Conservative majorities, were in the midst of by-election campaigns in early December. On 11 December 1903, the duke of Devonshire, the president of the Unionist Free Food League, in a letter to the constituencies' voters, declared "that an elector who sympathises with the objects of that league would be well advised to decline to give his support, at any election, to a Unionist candidate who expresses his sympathy with the policy of Mr. Chamberlain and the Tariff Reform League."[39] It was promptly described as being the views of the Unionist Free Food League.[40] This provoked the Liberal press to editorialize about the "breakup of Unionism," asserting that the duke's exhortation would manifest itself in Conservative defeats at Dulwich and Lewisham.[41]

Regardless of the results at Dulwich and Lewisham, the letter announced the outbreak of civil war within the Conservative party. A few days later at East Hertfordshire, Henry Chaplin and Henry Page Croft spoke to a crowd of thirteen hundred. Chaplin could not resist the opportunity, and he became the first tariff reform leader to point to the storm clouds gathering as a result of the duke's potentially devastating pronouncement. Chaplin trashed the duke's "unsettled opinions and constant changes of mind," calling his letter not only a declaration of war against Chamberlain but also against Balfour and his ministry. As if he was relieved at having broken the tension and exposed the issue, Chaplin made his stand and declared that he "always preferred an open foe to a faint-hearted friend."[42] Chaplin then sent a shot across the bow of the Conservative free traders: "Did it ever occur to the Duke of Devonshire that two parties could play at that game?" As he had no intention of lying down, Chaplin saw no reason why free trade Conservatives should not be singled out for retribution as well.[43]

Chaplin sat down and was followed by the twenty-two-year-old Henry Page Croft. Within a few short years, Croft became well known for his dynamic and moving platform speeches, and he was to be in constant demand by parliamentary candidates who sought his assistance during campaigns. His success perhaps stemmed from his ability to weave his view of historical greatness with a logical simplicity. As may be gleaned from his first national speech made at the beginning of a great historical controversy, he spoke with intensity and sincerity.

The essence of tariff reform, for Croft, was a new imperial arrangement, which meant that the names of Rhodes and Salisbury—"the two greatest Hertfordshire men in history"—found their way into his address. Croft then revealed his soul. He explained how tariff reform was not only essential for the country but essential for the future prosperity of the British working classes. Referring to Liberals as well as to the Conservative free traders who were a force in the constituency, he conceded his unpopularity "with all existing parties in East Hertfordshire." He revealed the core of his political beliefs and principles when he dismissed such concerns: "the fact is the party to which I belong is the greatest party in the world—the British Empire; and I consider on a National Question like this we should rise superior to a petty party strife." He expressed admiration not only for those men "who have left the Government in a body" but even more for those members of the Opposition "who have left their party not in a body but singly, because they believe their erstwhile opponent, Mr. Chamberlain, is working for the good of the country."[44]

Although even Chamberlain had avoided the agricultural areas during his autumn campaign, Croft suffered from no such hesitancy: "Now you agriculturalists, how does this system affect you?" He promptly sullied the Cobden theories by noting that England had experienced a decrease in acres under grain cultivation since conversion to free trade, contrary to Cobden's prediction. In a revealing look at his view of imperial economics, with a hint of xenophobia as well as a romantic nineteenth-century rural prejudice, he rhetorically inquired, "Where do the men who reap and plough go to . . . ? They go to the towns, where they crowd others out of England; but where in turn do these men go to? Some to the Colonies but by far the greatest number . . . to foreign countries, where they help the foreigner to compete against you." He continued, "men whom you drive out of England, since there is no work owing to your system of trade, go to help the foreigner to dump goods into England." Under a system of imperial preference, however, "this is the stream of emigrants which you will divert to your Colonies . . . and make it possible for your Colonies to compete with the foreigner." He engaged his audience in a less-than-subtle treatise in British nationalism:

> Who are your Colonists? Are they not British-born, men of your own blood, your kith and kin? Do you wish to discard them? Or do you wish to strengthen the links that bind them to you? We have seen Englishmen lay down their lives by thousands in the past for the Colonies. Since the days of Elizabeth we have been proud to give our money and our lives for the Colonies. You have seen them rush to the flag in the nation's darkest hour, and yet when they ask us to negotiate with them, to give them a slight preference, we do not give them. If we refuse this, if

our Colonies make friendly arrangements with foreigners which the motherland has refused, can we hope that a mere bond of sentiment will for ever bind them to us?[45]

Continuing his appeal to the working class, Croft denied that tariff reform would tax the working class but that instead it taxes "the rich man's champagne, the rich man's piano, the rich man's motorcars." Whether it is the foreigner or the wealthy who is being taxed, Croft declared without equivocation, tariff reform "is certainly going to give the British workman more settled work, and in consequence higher wages." Noting that he had been an eyewitness, Croft claimed that Chamberlain was not standing alone: six thousand working men of Birmingham were there with him. If the basis of the free-trader argument was that the British economy was prospering, well, asked Croft, "Who are you going to believe—the duke of Devonshire or the captains of industry; Sir Henry Campbell-Bannerman or the British workman who has lost his job?" With the crowd now cheering with every sentence, Croft drove them to a roar of supportive laughter when he urged them to "think well; don't be deceived by the puny, pithy, pandering, prattle of pre-historic, party-mad pessimists!" For this energized and excited young man, tariff reform represented a program with which Britain could maintain an economic and international preeminence. It would provide employment, preserve domestic industry and commerce, strengthen the empire, and ensure world peace. Tariff reform was the cornerstone of a new imperial idea.

In a move that was significant for its prophecy of future political developments, Croft offered a resolution that not only endorsed Chamberlain and his fiscal reform proposals but denounced the duke of Devonshire's provocative act and those who supported it.[46] The resolution, which was the first public response by the tariff reform movement to the duke's letter, passed by near-unanimous acclamation.

The impact and importance of the meeting did not go unappreciated by Chaplin or unnoticed by Chamberlain.[47] With the meeting successfully concluded, Henry Page Croft clearly experienced a significant transformation. Although the speech of this novice had little national import, it did, however, signal the birth of an unabashed imperialist. Croft, for whom imperialism was the crucial instrument of his nationalism, now embarked on an unorthodox political journey that pivoted around these synergistic ideas of tariff reform and imperial unity. In their pursuit he would refuse to submit himself or his ideas to the traditional political paradigm. Instead, he was soon willing to take whatever political course was necessary to promote the empire and defend the nation. This he would do even if it meant waging a war within the Conservative party in an effort to purify the party's political thinking. He soon found it would be necessary to purge the party of wobblers before tariff reform and imperial unity could successfully be promoted to the country.

2
A Crack Begins to Show (1904–1906)

> I told him I was prepared to serve the cause in any way he might suggest. Before I knew what was happening he had extracted a promise from me to fight a constituency and from that movement I became one of Chamberlain's men.
> —Henry Page Croft, *My Life of Strife*

Croft was quickly swept up by the imperial idea that he found within Chamberlain's program, but the aspiring politician needed to forge his ideas and determination under the fire of a political contest. However, his opponents were not to be Liberals but were to be found among Balfour's own colleagues. Croft thus embarked on a journey during which he eventually came to challenge the party's leadership itself. He did so, however, to create a more dynamic and aggressive party, one that was needed by Britain to meet the challenges of the twentieth century.

The day following the Ware tariff reform rally the voters of Dulwich and Lewisham remained steady, although the Conservative majority in Dulwich was reduced from 3,042 to 1,437 and in Lewisham from 2,414 to 2,012. Although local contests were complicated affairs, it could be suggested that the duke of Devonshire's admonition had not had time to take hold, having been made public only three days before the elections. However, in the five succeeding elections from 15 December 1903 to 15 February 1904, the Conservative candidates were not so fortunate.[1]

The party's loss in the mid-Hertfordshire constituency of St. Albans was particularly disappointing for Croft. The Conservative member, Vicary Gibbs, had held the seat since 1892, most recently with a twenty-five hundred–vote majority, and was forced to stand in a by-election when he accepted a government contract in January 1904. What had excited Chamberlainites such as Croft was the fact that the contest was waged unmistakably over tariff reform. It was expected that Gibbs should have had little trouble with the challenger, John Bamford Slack, a political newcomer and unequivocal free trade advocate.[2] Even Sir Henry Campbell-

2: A Crack Begins to Show (1904–1906)

Bannerman, leader of the Liberals, viewed the contest as a political barometer for future developments.³ The resulting Liberal victory, although with only a meager 132–vote majority, stunned the tariff reformers.

In the wake of the mid-Hertfordshire by-election, following so close on the heels of the duke of Devonshire's betrayal of the Conservative party, Croft intensified his efforts on behalf of tariff reform with a hardened determination. In his own constituency of East Hertfordshire, the Hertford division of Hertfordshire, he was faced with a prominent and active Conservative free trader, Abel Henry Smith.⁴ Gradually but steadily, Croft began to circle Smith.⁵ In February 1904 the Croft family further extended tariff reform influence over the Ware Conservative association when Henry Page Croft was elected to the executive committee. He now joined his father, R. B. Croft, who had served as its vice president ever since he cofounded the association in 1898.

At the same annual meeting, the association also brought up with disapproval the vote that Smith had given against Balfour's government on Chamberlain's tariff reform proposals. The association's executive committee then voted twenty to six to summon Smith before the next committee meeting on 17 March 1904, at which time they intended to secure an explanation for his voting record.⁶ Seeing how the battle lines were rapidly falling into place, Smith made a preemptive move. On 4 March he ventured before the East Hertfordshire Working Men's club and secured a vote of confidence.⁷ Although the documentary evidence fails to disclose the maneuvering that surely went on between Smith and the Ware Conservatives during 1904, the report of the executive committee for 1904 states, "we are glad to say that questions with regard to the proposals of Mr. Chamberlain and Fiscal Reform . . . were settled in a satisfactory manner and the possibility of a secession of any supporters of our Members has been, it is hoped averted."⁸ After gaining effective control over the Ware Conservative association, Croft and the tariff reformers decided to gain control of the local East Hertfordshire Conservative association. As Croft recorded, "this took a lot of doing because, of course, we were up against the national party machine."⁹

By summer 1904 Croft, demonstrating the overconfidence and eagerness of youth, but nevertheless being assuredly premature, began to entertain serious notions of challenging Smith. Croft reflected on his first conversation with Joseph Chamberlain in 1903. "I told him I was prepared to serve the cause in any way he might suggest. Before I knew what was happening, he had extracted a promise from me to fight a constituency and from that moment I became one of Chamberlain's men."¹⁰ In late June or early July 1904, he wrote to Chamberlain, seeking his approbation more than anything else, but informing the great politician of Croft's intent to take up the charge and to fight a constituency for tariff reform. Croft intended to make his formal announcement as soon as Parliament adjourned for the summer. With encouraging warm wishes, Chamberlain agreed that Croft was "right to wait till the close of the session before making your announcement."[11]

Croft was now in frequent communication with politicians and others associated with the tariff reform groups in London. It did not take long before rumors of his intentions circulated among the political and social clubs, particularly that premier London club, Parliament. Croft's unsuccessful secret was thrust into the public domain on 1 August in rather awkward and somewhat embarrassing circumstances, that is, during the debate on Sir Henry Campbell-Bannerman's motion of censure. It was ironic that the debut of Croft's political career was proclaimed publicly during a parliamentary debate that exposed the intensity, frustration, and animosity between the Conservative free traders and the tariff reformers. The event also prophetically warned of a rapidly widening schism within the Conservative party.

Campbell-Bannerman sought to embarrass Balfour by pointing out that certain of his ministers had accepted official positions in the Tariff Reform League, "a political organisation which has formally declared its adherence to a policy of preferential duties involving the taxation of food."[12] He was then followed by Lord Hugh Cecil, Conservative MP, who also happened to be a notable member of the duke of Devonshire's Unionist Free Food League.[13] Rising to attack the government's policy of ambiguity, Cecil promptly proceeded to the issue that had divided the Conservative party into two hostile camps ever since the duke of Devonshire's letter of December 1903. While the Conservative tariff reformers suggested that the "fiscal controversy was only an academic discussion to educate the public mind," Cecil argued that the "free traders did not object to discussion," but they were not permitted to do so without fear of political retribution. "If they were only sitting round the fireside talking over the fiscal question it was not desirable that some of them should be violently taken by the shoulders and thrown into the passage." Then in an undisguised query directed to Chamberlain, he asked "how were they to have a fair, open-minded discussion on a great Imperial question if they were not to be secure of their seats in Parliament." In a less-than-subtle swipe at Chamberlain, Cecil claimed that what the government was doing was so disreputable that he could not bring himself to accuse them of it. He nevertheless was compelled to describe it for the benefit of the other members. The government, he claimed, through its policy of ambiguity and uncertainty over fiscal reform and preference, was "keeping the matter nominally open while they allowed underground efforts to be made to turn their own supporters who did not agree with the new fiscal policy out of Parliament, and then, when that had been done, the machine would go on to carry out the dictates of . . . the Member for West Birmingham."[14]

As an overture of hollow conciliation, Cecil demurred that "he was quite honest in saying he did not suspect the right hon. friend the Prime Minister of any such intention." With intentional provocation, he nevertheless stated that "he was not quite sure that he did not suspect his right hon. friend the Member for West Birmingham." What had angered Cecil was promptly revealed as he turned to the issue of Croft. He explained that he understood that Chamberlain had encouraged Croft, a protectionist, to challenge Abel Henry Smith. Such action, Cecil asserted, was not calculated "to create an atmosphere suitable for the discussion of this 'academic' question." Chamberlain was then heard to interject, "well, I encouraged it."[15]

Interestingly, *The Times*'s report of the debate omitted any reference to Cecil's last two sentences and to Chamberlain's muffled response. Understandably, Cecil wrote to correct the omission. "In the course of my speech I mentioned that I had heard that Mr. Chamberlain had an interview with a gentleman (a Mr. Croft) and had pressed him to stand as a Protectionist against the member for East Hertfordshire, Mr. Abel Smith. I said that I had only heard it as gossip, and that if Mr. Chamberlain denied the story I should, of course, entirely accept his denial." Cecil pointed out that "on this implied appeal Mr. Chamberlain very frankly interjected (in reference to pressing Mr. Croft to stand), 'Well, I encouraged it.'"[16]

Clearly there had been no love lost between Cecil and Chamberlain. Cecil suggested that "Chamberlain is not genuinely trying to unite the whole Unionist Party nor is he intending to abandon his fiscal policy. He is rather trying to strengthen himself by a union—real or apparent—with the Prime Minister, and so isolate the Unionist Free Traders."[17] He believed that anyone who had the courage to stand up to Chamberlain and his political machine "run[s] the risk of political extinction."[18] The East Hertfordshire affair was more than likely an outburst of frustration; since July 1904 Cecil had been subjected to an aggressive campaign in his own constituency of Greenwich.[19] Tempers and nerves were frayed as Parliament approached the summer recess. As a result, some of the prominent players believed that to "wipe out Joe & and all his work would be the best thing for the party and country."[20] There was also a recognizable level of anger toward Balfour's tolerance of Chamberlain and the tariff reformers.[21]

When Chamberlain formally responded, he noted that Cecil had "put it to me that I had advised a certain gentleman to stand for a constituency now occupied by a Unionist Member. I do not think I need go into the details of a conversation which I thought entirely idle at the time; but I admit that I did advise and even encouraged what I thought to be the gentlemanly, laudable intention."[22] During the brief and somewhat innocuous meeting between Croft and Chamberlain, the latter applauded that "I am glad to hear you are endeavouring to educate East Herts." Croft responded, "if the Government come into line with you, I shall oppose or assist in opposing Mr. Abel Smith."[23] Chamberlain quickly turned the table on Cecil, a supporter of the duke of Devonshire's retaliation policy as set forth in the "Dulwich letter" of December 1903.[24] Chamberlain pointed out that Conservative free traders had "issue[d] manifestoes praying all Unionist electors to withdraw support from any Unionist Member" who subscribed to fiscal reform. The former colonial secretary now revealed his own frustration as he rhetorically inquired of Cecil, "what is to be said of the Free Food League, of which I believe my noble friend is a distinguished member, which goes down to Birmingham and opens an office there with the express object of defeating . . . the present Member for South Birmingham who stood as a Unionist candidate."[25] The censure motion failed 210 to 288; Cecil abstained and Smith thought it wiser to stand by the government on this occasion.

Croft experienced a rather uncomfortable feeling at putting the "chief" in such an embarrassing position. Nevertheless, Chamberlain consoled Croft not to be alarmed that he was "quite ready to take full responsibility for any advice [he] may have given" Croft.[26] Perhaps due to his regret or, as may be considered with equal plausibility, because of the wise counsel of one of his seniors, after the disconcerting publication of his political ambitions, Croft paused over any direct attack on Smith.[27] While tempers in Hertfordshire and within Conservative circles cooled, Croft thought it better to focus his attack on the Liberals and particularly C. R. Buxton, an unabashed free trader and Liberal candidate for the East Hertfordshire seat.[28] This is not to suggest that Croft had dismissed his intentions to challenge Smith, for not far below the surface tensions in Hertfordshire were pushing the factions toward an eventual confrontation.[29] Croft merely needed an opportune issue with which to maneuver Smith into a position of political vulnerability. He did not have long to wait because Chamberlain was constructing the very issue that Croft could appropriate and easily apply against Smith.

Chamberlain had designs for maneuvering Balfour into a position where the prime minister would be forced to succumb to the sheer weight of public opinion and be obliged to make considerable concessions to the tariff reform program. Chamberlain was attempting to force Balfour into accepting the idea of a colonial conference that Chamberlain had proposed on 1 August 1904. Of course Balfour was working with equal diligence and skill not to be outmaneuvered.[30] By mid-October the prospect of a colonial conference had been placed on the tariff reformers' strategic horizon. Croft was now provided the issue to use in his local struggle against Smith.

As the nation slipped into the new year, the atmosphere was charged with an anxiety about the coming session of Parliament. The national press and London circles were teeming with speculation as to when the present Parliament would be dissolved.[31] Reports circulated about Chamberlain's supporters being hard at work in preparation for an election, well aware that seventy-nine Conservatives had already announced their intention to retire at the next general election; they were also excited about the possibility of targeting several troublesome Conservative free traders.[32] Even some of Chamberlain's closest associates believed that if he did not force a general election by July he most likely was politically finished.³³ Such anxious times made Croft's designs much more critical and urgent. As Croft later suggested, the tariff reformers of East Herts thought that "the air ought to be cleared" and that it was only right they should have a voice in the future policy of the district's member of Parliament.³⁴ Accordingly, on 9 January 1905, the Ware Working Men's Unionist Association held a special meeting to consider initiating an inquiry into Smith's lack of support for a colonial conference, which has an impact on any policy of imperial preference and tariff reform.³⁵

Described in polite terms as having a "decidedly lively character," the heated meeting brought about the confrontation that the tariff reformers had sought. Smith's supporters, however, were prepared and had assembled a sufficient number of backers should any challenge prove to be a threat to Smith's position. Admiral Hastings, Smith's election agent and proxy, read a letter from the MP wherein he stated "that if at any time he felt himself unable to support the Government he would take his constituents into his confidence, but he could not pledge himself to support a thing which at present he knew nothing about."³⁶ Given his refusal to make any concession of support toward the government, the meeting was then pressed for a resolution requiring a pledge from Smith on the tariff reform questions. Croft knew that Smith would refuse, and this would provide the political position and argument that he needed to challenge Smith. Croft would then be in a position to argue that Smith had refused to support the government and, thus, had betrayed the government, the Conservative party, and the electors who had sent him to Westminster as a Conservative. The first vote produced a nineteen to seventeen majority in support of the tariff reform resolution and against Smith. However, a successful challenge over a technicality caused a second poll to be conducted which then provided the MP with a thirty-four to eighteen majority, a serious but tactical defeat for Croft, who had labored so hard to bring the free trader to the political dock. In the wake of this result, Croft was reported to have remarked "that after doing his best to smooth over their difficulties, he was afraid there was nothing now to look forward to but a three-cornered fight in East Herts."³⁷ Nearly identical accounts promptly made their way into the London dailies, and in one report it was suggested that Richard Page Croft would challenge Smith as a tariff reform candidate.³⁸

Notwithstanding a desire to banish free traders, under the present circumstances Croft could not afford to be perceived as a destructive or troublesome element within the party. Such a characterization would render the neutralization of Smith immaterial because the advantage could not be exploited. Croft prudently and swiftly attempted to correct the reports in the London papers, explaining that during a private meeting of the Ware Unionist Working Men's Club a discussion resulted over whether Smith would support the government after the colonial conference. Although Smith's letter of minimal support was read, Croft contended that "there was no question of free trade versus tariff reform before the Club and as regards the report of a split in the Unionist ranks it does not exist." He explained that the ultimate vote was in effect merely a technical recognition that the issue of Smith's support should be addressed through the constituency association and not through a social club, which was the true character of the Working Men's Unionist association.[39] However, it was not as clear as might be suggested because Croft's response concluded with a rather ambiguous statement that the Ware Conservative association "still hope to be able to support" Smith.[40]

Fortunately for Smith, the free traders were able to shield him when the executive committee of the East Hertfordshire Conservative and Liberal Unionist Association met on 18 January 1905. Under the presidency of Sir George Faudel-Phillips, a free trader, the committee resolved to "do its utmost to secure the return of Mr. Abel Smith." By providing their own interpretation to Smith's letter—not unlike the approach taken by Chamberlain after Balfour's acceptance of the colonial conference subject to the two-election condition—the tariff reformers who were present were then able to join the resolution and avoid any criticism for splitting the party.[41]

In Chamberlain's case, Balfour accepted the idea of a colonial conference to discuss tariffs and imperial preference only if the conference would be preceded and succeeded by an election, thus giving the voters a chance to sanction both the actual conference as well as its product. Notwithstanding intense negotiations through his son, the Chancellor of the Exchequer, Austen Chamberlain, the elder Chamberlain was unable to push Balfour away from the two-election condition. Chamberlain decided just to make "the best of the new position. He would disregard Balfour's reservations and concentrate on the proposal for a conference."[42]

Croft and the tariff reformers of East Hertfordshire decided to take a similar tack with Smith. Thus they were able to avoid any charge of splitting the party, but their position allowed them to continue to prod the free trade MP on the issue of the conference. The tariff reformers took the position that Smith "was in favour of an Imperial Conference, and that he would continue to be a supporter of the Prime Minister." Although this was not Smith's position, it was not difficult for Croft to make the claim. He then announced that the members of the East Hertfordshire branch of the Tariff Reform League would be advised to extend their support.[43] Of course, given the fact that the Liberal candidate, Charles Roden Buxton, was an adamant free trader, Croft had few alternatives other than to make the best of the Smith situation.[44] In a display of political astuteness, Croft proceeded to convince local tariff reform associations that Smith was a tariff reform supporter. Under his guidance the branches of the Tariff Reform League responded with a resolution to assist the Conservative candidate who, the tariff reformers claimed, supported Balfour's policy of retaliation as well as the colonial preference.[45]

2: A Crack Begins to Show (1904–1906)

Because Smith's letter setting out his position had been published in the local and London papers, it was quite obvious to all concerned that the Tariff Reform League's resolution did not accurately reflect his position. However, because he could only make himself politically vulnerable by challenging the Croft interpretation, Smith remained silent.[46] Croft nevertheless was not content to permit Smith to stray too far from the tariff reformer's interpretation as Croft warned that support from the tariff reformers was extremely tenuous.[47] His retreat from a challenge to the free trade MP for East Hertfordshire was merely to be temporary. Croft and Smith would meet again.

Although Croft was eager to translate his energy and commitment for tariff reform and imperial unity into a political strategy, he discovered very early in 1904 that the most serious opposition was to be found within his own political party. Croft soon accepted the fact that if tariff reform and a new imperial idea were to be promoted to and embraced by the country, then a major reconstruction of the Conservative party would be a prerequisite.

After it appeared that Smith had slipped out of the grasp of the tariff reformers, Croft could not give pursuit. During his maneuvering against Smith, Croft also was engaged in discussions with local Conservative officials at Lincoln about the possibility of contesting the Lincoln City seat as a tariff reformer. Given the friendship and political allegiance that had developed between Henry Chaplin and Croft and the endearing embrace with which Lincolnshire held Chaplin, it was not surprising that Croft had been invited to meet the local party officials. Many years later, Croft recorded that Chamberlain had "arranged with Mr. Chaplin to send me up to fight Lincoln city." However, Chamberlain cautioned that Croft "had no chance whatever of winning." Instead, his objective was to block the return of the incumbent free trade Unionist. Chamberlain said he preferred "an open enemy as a Member for Lincoln than a protesting friend who will stab me in the back."[48] The object of Chamberlain's scorn was Charles Hilton Seely, a wealthy coal owner, who had sat for Lincoln city as a Liberal Unionist since 1895. They first crossed in 1902 when Seely was only one of two government MPs to vote against the corn duty in Sir Michael Hicks Beach's budget.

On 24 January 1905, Croft met with several leading Lincoln Conservatives, and on the next day, he met with the chairman of the Lincoln and Bracebridge Conservative and Liberal Unionist Association. Croft then rushed back to Cambridge where on 28 January he supported Henry Chaplin at a large rally being held for the inauguration of the Cambridge Tariff Reform League. He returned north for Chamberlain's impressive assembly at Gainsborough on 1 February where Chamberlain was accompanied on the platform by Croft and several others who were identified as prospective candidates for Lincoln constituencies in the general election, which everyone believed was very near.[49]

This was a period of intense activity for Croft, who was now being called on to campaign in Lincoln as well as to maintain pressure on Smith in East Hertfordshire. He also continued his speeches and writings on behalf of tariff reform, but perhaps more important, Croft was now intimately involved in crucial organizing activities both in East Hertfordshire and, as we shall see, on the national level. He was not oblivious to the risk to his political career that would result from challenging a sitting MP from his own party.

However, Croft remained thoroughly convinced that political momentum leaned in the direction of Chamberlain and that the future of Britain rested with the new and energetic view of the British empire now being promoted on several fronts. Further, he felt immense gratitude to Chamberlain for his very public and gracious defense of Croft's activities in Hertfordshire. In face of the risk at Lincoln, he was reassured by Chamberlain: "I know you are making a sacrifice and taking a risk; but I promise you this—you will never regret it as long as I live."[50] Equally important to his decision to contest Lincoln was Croft's conviction for tariff reform. As someone who relished action, he also wanted his opportunity to bat. He was not content merely to pen letters and articles for the local East Hertfordshire press. Being what Croft considered as "one of Mr. Chamberlain's purging brigade," he now believed it was time to be done with it. Chamberlain had once said to Croft: "I would far rather have a Liberal Free Trader in the House than [Seely] who fawns on me and stabs me in the back." Croft was soon subscribing to such rather severe views with the frequency and flexibility that "history will show that any Party which has a main creed and yet allows enemies of that faith to remain in its ranks does itself untold harm. One opponent on your own side," Croft continued, "is more damaging than ten of the enemy."[51]

Croft's involvement at Lincoln as a tariff reform candidate would be seen as part of an overall campaign against the party's free traders. They had been excessively nervous since a letter on 13 January 1904 from Ratcliffe Cousins, secretary of the Tariff Reform League, threatened that the league intended to commit its entire organization to oppose all free traders, whether Conservative or Liberal.[52] As Parliament convened for the 1905 session, Lord Robert Cecil advised Balfour that nearly thirty seats had been subject to attack by the Tariff Reform League and its supporters. Cecil clearly suggested that the actors involved enjoyed the personal sanction of Chamberlain.[53]

The most prominent battle was fought at Greenwich where Hugh Cecil had been subjected to a relentless attack since the summer of 1904. As a result, Croft's challenge at Lincoln escaped close scrutiny by the national press, which was preoccupied with Cecil's problems at Greenwich, a seat he had held since 1895. Several Conservative free traders avoided a fight by converting to protectionism and preference; others announced their intention to retire; still others, such as Cecil, when faced with the withdrawal of support from the local Conservative association, declared they would stand as an independent free trade candidate. Cecil's response provoked a nervous Balfour to plead with him "to remain in the party."[54]

It was within the confusion caused by multiple internal tensions as well as the anxiety of an anticipated, but unannounced, general election that Croft continued his tariff reform organizing and began his campaign in Lincoln. He quickly came to the conclusion that he had nothing to lose, and, therefore, he actively sought to convince the Lincoln Conservative association to adopt him. On 14 March 1905, he embarked on his journey to Parliament with a direct attack against Seely. The prerequisite for a successful campaign would be to discredit Seely in the eyes of the Conservative electorate. While recognizing his position "was not one of all beer and skittles," Croft promptly denounced Seely for abandoning Balfour during a critical division, particularly when Balfour had made a specific appeal for the party to hold tight.[55]

Although Croft continued to make the obligatory comments in support of working men, he generally focused his campaign on that sector of the economy and English society that, in his view, was responsible for Britain's greatness—the land. "Agriculture," he argued, "had been responsible for keeping the physical strength of this country continually renewed. We find from the countryside and towns that depended upon agriculture the best recruits for the British Army."[56] This led to his routine savaging of Cobden, a ritual during these early years. Croft proceeded on to the empire. Although he considered the question of empire as being above partisan politics, and he appealed for such deference, it remained difficult to promote the romantic notion of empire in isolation. Representing the vigor and character of the budding Conservative politician, Croft appealed on behalf of the sensibility of British commerce. He argued that "the colonies had proved themselves our best customers" and given that they will continue to grow and expand, it was imperative to maintain the trade. For instance, he noted, "11 million colonists have purchased more manufactured goods from us in the last ten years than the rest of Britain's trading partners." This translated into colonists purchasing nearly £6 per capita while the other countries were spending only shillings on British goods. He also reminded the voters that the colonies made great sacrifices supporting Britain during the South African war.[57]

Croft was concerned with the argument, that is, the intellectual composition of its logic, as well as the rhetorical appeal and the presentation. The press on both sides of the issue were favorably impressed by Croft's youthful style. The *Sheffield Daily Telegraph* congratulated the Lincoln Conservatives for securing "so fitting a gentleman to champion their cause." He was recognized early as "a champion of Empire. . . . He is different," wrote the *Lincolnshire Chronicle,* "because every word he utters upon it is the impress of deep thought and sincere conviction, and these are qualities all too rare in the present day. It is not too much to say he made a great impression upon his hearers."[58]

Eagerness and youthful imprecision quickly pushed him into a political controversy. Proud of the urging and support for his challenge at Lincoln, which he believed came from Chamberlain, Croft allowed the credit of this endorsement to circulate within the local Conservative association. Within no time Seely brought the issue to Sir Alexander Acland Hood, the government's chief whip. In a letter to Croft dated 6 April 1905, Seely's agent, Reginald Stephens, pointed out that Acland Hood was unable to confirm Croft's boast that he "had been approached by a Minister of Cabinet rank to come down and contest Lincoln" against the sitting MP. Accordingly Seely's agent demanded to know by what authority Croft had made the statement. Croft responded on 8 April with his characteristic austerity, that is, he did not feel obliged "to answer questions as to statements [he] may have made at private meetings." Croft assured the correspondent, "I have never in public stated that I was approached by a Minister of Cabinet rank to come down and contest Lincoln against Mr. Seely." Croft coyly added, "I have never suggested to anyone that I had received the support of a Minister of the present Government." In fact, Croft was confirming the true identity of his most important supporter. Stephens continued the futile exercise on 12 April, offering to publish the full correspondence. By a final letter of 13 April, Croft mooted Stephen's protest with unadulterated election propaganda, suggesting he had no objection to the publication of their correspondence. Croft came "at the invitation of the Executive Committee of the official Conservative and Liberal Unionist Association" inasmuch as he could claim to be an absolute supporter of the party's fiscal policy. It was Seely, Croft reminded the public, who ignored party policy and betrayed the party's leader.[59]

Seely responded by circulating a letter among the Lincoln press, in which Acland Hood stated that no other candidate for Lincoln would be recognized "so long as the present Member supported the Government." Croft parried, sarcastically noting that "it seemed to him that the precise reason why the Committee [of the Lincoln Conservative association] came to their decision was because the member [Seely] did not support the Government." He then suggested a certain interpellation of the chief whip as to "what he meant by 'supporting the Government,' because apparently he had not been made acquainted with the votes which Mr. Seely had registered on various occasions." At a campaign rally, Croft asked whether or not the people of Lincoln were to be denied the freedom of choice in their decision, to which the audience cried "No!" "Was Lincolnshire to be dictated to by a gentleman in London, however distinguished?" Again the crowd answered "No!" Croft then assured his audience that "so long as he had an Association at his back, and two working men to propose and second him, he should not give in." He concluded with the cry of "British trade, British employment, and British wages for British working men," which provoked huge applause.[60] Finally, on 11 January 1906, only a few days before the polling began, Croft received an official blessing from Acland Hood and the Central Office.[61]

Having lost the endorsement of the Lincoln and Bracebridge Conservative and Liberal Unionist Association, Seely attempted to confuse the identities through the creation of an alternate Liberal Unionist organization and, then, claiming its support. In late June 1905, however, the council of the national Liberal Unionist Association declared that local constituencies were within their rights to determine their own candidates. After examining the dispute that arose over Croft's adoption by Lincoln, the council held the Lincoln and Bracebridge Conservative and Liberal Unionist Association to be the properly constituted association. Therefore the committee considered itself bound to support Croft who had been properly selected as the candidate by the association.[62]

Seely next tried to blunt Croft's challenge by trying to gain control of the Constitutional Club and the Primrose League, both important institutions of Conservative support in Lincoln. In the end Seely gained neither.[63] For his part Croft gained the endorsement of the Lincolnshire Farmer's Union.[64] Although no election had yet been called, Croft viewed the summer as a campaign. He battled day after day, speaking or appearing at any event or gathering where he could promote tariff reform and imperial unity. Although Croft claimed to have called on four thousand voters, he nevertheless accepted putting the "true valuation on the promises of electors as . . . I did not poll nearly as many votes as I received promises in my personal canvass."[65]

Chamberlain was also in the midst of a campaign of sorts, with his own concerns. Not only did tariff reform have to struggle against free traders, be they Liberals or Conservative free fooders, but it was severely hobbled within the Conservative party by the tension between the Chamberlainites and Balfour's policy of ambiguity. It was this tension that Chamberlain believed contributed to the East Finsbury defeat in June 1905, where the Tory candidate crawled away from Chamberlain's "whole hog" position in favor of Balfour's more ambiguous and perhaps palatable pronouncements. In the wake of the East Finsbury loss, Chamberlain believed that "a little more of this and there will be an insurrection which, indeed, would probably be as good for the Conservative party as it would be for the people of Russia. . . . I think there ought to be another meeting of Conservatives to consider the whole question of their organisation."[66] Both Croft and Chamberlain received encouraging news on 5 July 1905 when Captain Henry Staveley Hill, a tariff reformer, won a by-election at Kingswinford division of Staffordshire with the support of the Birmingham organization.[67] Croft extended a most positive interpretation to the Kingswinford results.

On 5 January 1906, Chamberlain wrote Croft, congratulating the young candidate on the progress he was making at Lincoln on behalf of the tariff reform cause at Lincoln and stating that he "shall be delighted . . . to welcome you as a colleague in the next House of Commons." Understanding that the letter was more for propaganda purposes than anything else and that Croft would promptly release the letter to the press, Chamberlain continued. "The policy of tariff reform, which you are advocating, should appeal to all working men, industrial and agricultural alike, as it is calculated to make easier the lot of those who know only too well how hard the struggle for existence is." He concluded by soliciting "the support of all Unionists and . . . all those Liberals who put the interests of their countrymen and the welfare of their fellow-countrymen before those of party in your endeavour to secure fair play for British trade and increased employment for the British worker." As expected the letter was promptly released to the local newspapers for distribution.[68]

Croft was selfless with his own support. In the midst of his campaign, he took time to run down to Hampstead where he supported the candidacy of John S. Fletcher, who was fighting a tight contest. Fletcher succeeded in keeping the seat for the Conservatives and tariff reform.[69] Always possessive about developments in Hertfordshire, Croft urged Chamberlain and the Tariff Reform League to provide assistance to Thomas F. Halsey, who held a seat in Hertfordshire since 1874. Croft's concerns contained substance as Halsey was nevertheless defeated in the 1906 election.[70]

In early November, George Hudson, the sitting Conservative MP for the Hitchin division (North) of Hertfordshire, announced he would retire at the next general election. Friends and allies in East Hertfordshire immediately urged Croft to withdraw from Lincoln and stand for Hitchin. In all likelihood Croft would have been a successful favorite son. Nonetheless, he felt it would not be honorable to abandon Lincoln at this stage.[71] Having waived his claim to stand for the North Herts seat, Croft became equally concerned about a prospective candidate who was considering standing for it. The prospective candidate, a Mr. Priestley, had approached Croft about support from the Tariff Reform League or, in the alternative, a declaration of neutrality from the league. Croft thereafter wrote to Chamberlain, who responded that "the situation seems to me very unsatisfactory." Chamberlain considered Priestley "to be a very weak-kneed supporter of tariff reform."[72] Croft concurred with the leader's assessment, and Priestley was forced to abandon any thought of contesting North Herts.[73]

Within Chamberlain's letter of 5 January 1906 was the suggestion that success depended on tariff reform being accepted by the working class. This was, however, a realization to which Croft had returned early in his campaign. This may have been due to the damage perceived to have been inflicted by Seely's attacks, which accused protectionism as being antiworking class. It motivated Croft to make certain rhetorical adjustments; these adjustments, which clearly sought to embrace the working class, also revealed a slight wandering from Chamberlain orthodoxy. Although not actually violating the integrity of the Chamberlain program, Croft more and more began to stress "fair trade" as being the essence of the overall program. He stressed the importance of protecting the British working man. He pointed out that decades of free trade had brought 13 million to verge of hunger and put eight hundred thousand on relief. In May 1905 Croft reminded workers that free trade had permitted dumping on the British market that promoted sweating by their rival producers.[74] Shifting the emphasis of his argument to appeal to both workmen and masters, he now argued that all he wanted was fair trade.

Croft always seemed to have had a difficult time grappling with the concept of class, expressing more of a populist or, at times, even a corporatist notion as it was reflected in his charge that the present free trade policy was one of utter selfishness. Free trade "was the policy of the rich, and meant that the rich man wanted to buy his champagne, his motor cars and pianos a little cheaper, and that by buying foreign motor cars and pianos he was throwing hundreds and thousands of British working men out of employment."[75] Because the wealthy "save a penny here and there," he continued, "the British factory must close down, families must starve, misery and ruin must fall on thousands." Croft would cry in his speeches, "This is free trade." He argued that tariff reformers "believe that the employment of the masses is the first necessity and we say give your own people 'fair trade.'"[76]

As he amplified his attack against unfair trade, he targeted foreigners and Germans in particular. Inasmuch as Germany had installed a hostile trade barrier that prevented access to British goods, Britain needed to arm herself with defensive tariffs. Such tariffs, Croft argued, would grant Britain the power to bargain with her economic and international rivals. Free trade could only be achieved with tariffs, protection, and the power to retaliate. Fair play and fair trade now became his cry.[77] Fair trade must be pursued, by bargaining if possible, but retaliation if necessary.[78]

Croft was not only pained by the social misery that followed unemployment, but he was haunted by a vision of the national waste that resulted; he saw a catastrophic hemorrhage of economic vitality and opportunity draining Britain of its imperial greatness and national future. It becomes understandable why he was equally hurt by the criticism that tariff reform would further injure working men and women of Britain. Accordingly, he sought to push the question of the condition of British workers above the fray of partisan squabbles. Yet he continually found himself frustrated by the inaction of the traditional political debate and political elites. He believed the political powers continued to forfeit any claim to national leadership by their failure of interest in Britain or the industrial and commercial classes. Britain would benefit, and it followed that the working classes would also benefit from protection and imperial preference. He chided that Seely's policy to alleviate unemployment was to do nothing. It was the goal of tariff reform, he told his working class listeners day after day, to provide employment. He recounted seeing twelve thousand unemployed marching in London chanting "curse your charity, we want work." What could Balfour do? Nothing, Croft answered, because "he had no weapon that he could use," other than a "speech of despair." Only by getting "to the root of the evil, which was foreign competition . . . they would be able to deal with the unemployed of this country."[79] In 1905 to many in Britain, Germany was the source of the foreign evil, and he reminded his factory audiences that German tariffs were to go into effect on 1 March 1906. Croft told his crowds to send a man to parliament who was not afraid of Germany, not afraid to raise tariffs on German goods. Equally important, they needed to look to the dominions and colonies. With a prophetic admonition, he called for the need to "bring Colonies closer together . . . so that in time of need, when we had to fight a great war, they should once more be able to come to our aid as they had done before."[80]

As the candidates approached the election on 15 January 1906, Croft was giving three and four speeches a day, many during the meal breaks at local factories. He asked, "why not a Trades Union to protect the whole British Empire against foreign sweated and dumped goods?"[81] Croft emotionally pleaded with the workers for their support of a policy "to keep the foreigner out, to think of their people, starving men in other parts of the country, to protect their own industry before it was too late. . . . Germany and America were beating them."[82] He pointed out that machine makers in Mannheim, Germany, employed more workmen than any Lincoln firm, and their wages were higher than their British counterparts. All this was the consequence of their products being protected by tariffs.[83]

Notwithstanding his emotional appeal, his reception was not always warm as working-class anxiety was highly charged. The cry of "dear food" issued by both Liberals and Liberal Unionists took root in the working classes of England and Lincoln. "On one occasion," Croft later recalled, "we had a real riot" when a rather hostile crowd began chanting "to the river with him." Only the determined resistance of his supporters, "some very energetic young Varsity friends" and "reinforcements of about fifty toughs" prevented the young candidate from taking an icy dip in the River Witham.[84]

A few days before the polling opened, there was a near riot as Seely supporters erupted with continued outbursts when Croft tried to address the Constitutional Club. Unshaken, Croft expressed his "hope there is no one in this room who is afraid to hear what I might say." Although narrowly, he secured the endorsement of the influential Constitutional Club.[85] On 12 January when Henry Chaplin came to Lincoln in support of Croft, he "was attacked by a small gang of young ruffians." Chaplin "had literally to fight his way into the building and in the scrimmage his cap was pulled from his head and his overcoat torn. The police came to the rescue and . . . managed to escort him into the Exchange."[86] As the campaign wound down, Croft urged workers "to stand up for their people, to stand up for their country, for the future of their homes, the future of their country, and above all, as wise men to look after the future of the British Empire."[87]

The landslide victory of the Liberal party swept across all parts of the kingdom and, notwithstanding Croft's herculean effort, Lincoln was no exception. In the seven borough constituencies of Lincoln, the Liberals won five seats. Even Balfour lost his seat at Manchester East, as did Gerald Balfour, Walter Long, Alfred Lyttelton, James Parker Smith, Henry Chaplin, and Andrew Bonar Law. Both Austen and Joseph Chamberlain retained their seats. Nationally, the Liberals won 400 seats and enjoyed the support from 30 Labour MPs and 83 Irish Nationalists, while Conservatives held on to only 157, of which 25 technically were Liberal Unionists.

As expected by Chamberlain, in Lincoln the Liberal candidate, C. H. Roberts, prevailed over the feuding tariff reformer and free trade Liberal Unionist. Even Croft conceded that he came in a weak third with only 11 percent of the vote.[88] With much credit to be extended to Croft and his energy and determination, the excitement of the campaign produced a record-setting 93 percent voter turnout for Lincoln. When Croft first met with the executive committee of the Lincoln and Bracebridge Conservative and Liberal Unionist Association in the spring of 1905, he was told by one of the members that "he did not stand a dog's chance."[89] He did not, however, become discouraged for the simple reason that he was totally committed to what he was preaching. In addition Croft unashamedly enjoyed the rough-and-tumble of electoral politics, the challenge, and fighting the odds. He was excited by the milieu in which a parliamentary candidate found himself, dining with city fathers one day and arguing politics with factory workers the next. He no longer would be content with the local politics of Ware and East Hertfordshire. He was genuinely moved when on 5 January 1906 Chamberlain wrote that "I shall be delighted if . . . I am able to welcome you as a colleague in the House of Commons."[90]

In his own analysis of the election results, Croft's conclusion was consistent with the contemporary judgments. Neither those close to Chamberlain nor Croft ever viewed the election as representing a defeat for their concept of tariff reform.[91] Croft recognized that the local situation in Lincoln, as well as the disheveled state of the Conservative party, presented serious obstructions to his candidacy and perhaps effectively reduced his possibility to "a dog's chance." The fact that Balfour resisted sending any letter of support until five days before the election, and only after Chamberlain's intervention, did not ease his reception in Lincoln.[92] He, as did most of the unsuccessful Conservative candidates, leveled a large degree of blame at Liberal party "lies" about Chinese labor in South Africa.

However, his most telling remarks came at a banquet given at Lincoln in his honor on 21 March. He urged Conservatives to reconstruct and reunify their party organization as well as to rethink their appeal to potential supporters and the electorate at large. They must "set to work thoroughly to reorganise the whole system in [Lincoln], and they should as far as possible, bring the working men into their confidence because he believed that by so doing they would influence a great many more than they had been able to do in the past."[93] Although introduced to the deficiencies of the Conservative party by his local experience in Lincoln, he soon would argue that the Conservative party itself needed to be purified, purged, and reconstructed to meet the challenges of the twentieth century.

As for its historical significance, the election purged from a large preserve of traditionally safe seats a mass of stale, aged, and irrelevant backbenchers. In so doing, the election of 1906 provided a future opportunity for a new generation of Conservatives to move into the party and eventually enter Parliament.[94] In Croft's case, Christchurch had been held by the Conservatives, with only two minor and limited exceptions, since 1832. However, the Liberals gained the seat in 1906, only to lose it to Croft in 1910. This new generation of Conservatives, which included Croft, was being forged under the fire of tariff reform struggles and tested by the 1906 election. It would be this generation that would press with dogged determination their claim to represent the true Conservative party as it approached the next general election in 1910; this political generation would produce the corps of activists to emerge as the party elite during the interwar years. In addition, having suffered defeat in 1906, Croft and this new generation would spend the succeeding years preparing for a revenge match. As a result, Croft and this new generation would bring a new political and ideological aggressiveness to the Conservative party. Much energy would be spent within the Conservative party trying to harness and even restrain the dynamics of this new political character. Out of 1906 came a cadre of radical Conservatives. This change may be reflected in the recognition that Croft expressed at the end of the campaign. What was his true political character? He gave a hint when he suggested that "he was a Conservative in that he did not want to destroy the cherished condition of this country." But he was, he fancied, a Radical more than any of the present Radicals, "because he demanded reform; he wanted to see progress in this country, that we should advance with the conditions of the day."[95]

3
From Lincoln to the Confederacy (1906–1907)

> If they found people on the Unionist side who tried to damp their ardour, Croft recommended them to put their foot on such people and squash them out like beetles.
> —*Hertfordshire Mercury*, 5 January 1907

Notwithstanding the crushing defeat suffered by the Conservatives in the 1906 general election, the advanced tariff reformers emerged with a sense of liberation. They were no longer muzzled by the existence of an ambiguous Conservative government and the attendant need for only a cautious promotion of tariff reform. Croft, in particular, emerged from his electoral experience with a sense of exhilaration for politics and a commitment to the empire. Due to the uncertainty of his geographical location, Croft was compelled to maintain a presence in Lincoln as well as in East Hertfordshire. There was no doubt in his mind that his future and the future of Britain rested with the success of the campaign in which he enlisted in 1903.

Croft spent the years immediately following the 1906 election giving expression to his political frustrations, frustrations that pivoted around his anxieties over Britain's future and about the inability of the country's leadership to protect it. Having no natural platform from which to promote his views—because he was not a journalist, an academic, or a scion of a landed and noble family who could command the nation's attention due to some historical greatness—a seat in the House of Commons remained the most conventional and rational method. With a demonstrably competitive spirit, he enjoyed the campaign. Croft's enthusiasm and enjoyment of the chase did not diminish the altruism that was the core of his belief in and commitment to the cause of tariff reform and the greater imperial idea. He believed that the future of the nation depended on the pursuit of the broad imperial idea.

At the same time, Croft's frustration with the incumbent political stalemate engendered new political approaches. Most significantly, his political frustration manifested itself in his relationship to the Conservative party.

Put simply, Croft believed that the broad economic, social, and strategic elements of his imperial idea could not successfully engage the country until the party enthusiastically embraced an expansive program of tariff reform. Croft and several other advanced tariff reformers soon gravitated to the same conclusion: the party must be reconstructed from top to bottom based on the view that an ambitious tariff reform program provided for the future of Britain with the foundation for a new imperialism. The party and state were merely requisite vehicles for change. Croft was only just beginning to appreciate aggressive alternatives should the party leadership resist the needed reform. When faced with that development, he was forced to consider promoting the imperial and tariff issue through a radical political organization that would be estranged from the Conservative party.

In the spring of 1906, Croft returned to the fundamentals of tariff reform propaganda, writing a series of articles in the *Lincolnshire Chronicle* and *Hertfordshire Mercury* under the title of "Free Trade or Tariff Reform."[1] Nevertheless, there was little doubt that Croft remained in an electoral campaign posture. He supplemented the personal contacts and relationships that he had initiated with various individuals in several of the important conservative bodies in the kingdom, such as the Primrose League, the National Unionist association, and the national Tariff Reform League; this brought him into contact with the earl of Malmesbury, with whom he was long to be associated in friendship and politics. He also expanded his own local organizational support in East Hertfordshire. Croft, with his father and brother, continued to maintain effective control over the Ware Conservative association.[2] Croft also maintained a prominence in Lincoln where he regularly harassed C. H. Roberts, the new MP, over the Education Bill and the question of Chinese labor in South Africa. In the process, he attempted to increase his influence among Lincoln Conservatives at a crucial juncture when the local Conservative and Liberal Unionist association needed to undergo a period of internal reconciliation and consolidation.[3] Events, however, soon conspired to dampen and eventually to extinguish his relationship with Lincoln.

When faced with the lack of an endorsement from the Lincoln Conservative and Liberal Unionist association during the 1906 election campaign, C. H. Seely and his supporters established a rival organization, the Imperial Unionists, with which to hoist his banner. It was the inevitable split within the Conservative and Liberal Unionist forces over tariff reform and free trade that facilitated the election of a Liberal. Croft feared that both he and Lincoln would be condemned to perpetual three-cornered contests unless some political accommodation could be achieved. This would effectively eliminate his electoral prospects at Lincoln. He took the initiative and threw out an overture in an effort to construct a political truce. In early 1907 he wrote to Seely's Imperial Unionist party to explore reconciliation. However, when rebuffed he realized that neither he nor Seely could hope to win at

3: From Lincoln to the Confederacy (1906–1907)

the next election. Croft was confronted by the fact that any further interest in Lincoln would be obstructed by the continued presence of C. H. Seely and the threat of local Conservatives being irreparably divided by Seely's unforgiving obstinacy. Many years later Croft recorded that "it was hardly likely that the hate which I had engendered in Lincoln would die down and I decided to seek pastures new."[4] Croft now decided to step away from the constituency with the understanding Seely would do so as well.[5]

Croft's diminished interest in Lincoln also accompanied his increased activities in East Hertfordshire. His developing voice and visibility on the national political stage corresponded with his developing influence over the East Hertfordshire Tariff Reform League, which by now boasted seventeen hundred members.[6] He was involved with other tariff-reform organizations at Hertford and St. Albans.[7] He was instrumental in the establishment of a tariff-reform branch in Hoddesdon where he was compared with "his great leader, Mr. Chamberlain, for his bull-dog perseverance." Demonstrating the continued tension within the Conservative party, Croft told the organizing assembly at Hoddesdon that "if they found people on the Unionist side who tried to damp their ardour, he recommended them to put their foot on such people and squash them out like beetles."[8]

Back in East Hertfordshire, Croft continued to pressure Abel Henry Smith but was not presently able to land any significant blows on the free-trader MP. Undaunted, the Ware tariff reformers continued to keep Smith under such scrutiny that he was unable to absent himself from a vote without promptly being condemned by Croft's rhetorical wrath. In unison with Croft's unrelenting criticism, the Ware Branch of the Tariff Reform League voted unanimously to condemn Smith's free trade and apathetic imperial position.[9]

Just as Croft scanned the political geography for hospitable constituencies, he was invited to Chatham. However, at the inauguration of the nearby Gillingham Branch of the Tariff Reform League, he was given an extremely rough reception, making it virtually impossible to give his speech. He was subjected to an equally frosty reception when he returned to Chatham a few days later. His public speech on behalf of the Chatham Branch of the Tariff Reform League was likewise attacked with rancorous interruptions.[10] Notwithstanding the hostile environment provided by the harassing, antiprotectionist crowds, Croft later suggested that he seriously considered standing for Chatham.[11] He was rescued from such a fate by the earl of Malmesbury who invited Croft to contest Christchurch. "Needless to say," as he reflected years later, "I jumped at the chance because, although a hard seat to win and hard to hold, it was a charming neighbourhood with very pleasant surroundings."[12] Croft soon hurried south to Hampshire where he spent the next month courting officials in Christchurch Conservative circles in anticipation of the constituency association's upcoming annual meeting. On 4

May, with the vigorous support of Lord Malmesbury, he was adopted by the Christchurch and Bournemouth Conservative Association.

In his initial speeches, Croft articulated a double-edged imperialism, that is, an economically aggressive imperialism combined with a strategic imperialism positioned to enhance Britain's military defense. He argued for a political and economic consolidation of the British empire through the application of colonial preferences in an effort to increase imperial trade and cement imperial relations. Britain must continue to defend itself economically and militarily from the dreaded foreigner.[13] He also blasted the Liberal government for "their misdeeds," which, he argued, were brought about by their attempt to "pen together the Socialist Lion and the Lamb of Liberalism and were now being devoured by the very men they sought to please by giving up their principles." In light of his diagnosis of the Liberal disaster, he "wonder[ed] how much longer the Liberal party were going to hold together."[14]

Although he now had a constituency, Croft still needed to translate it into a seat. However, his personal political objectives had to yield to what he considered superior, national obligations. He remained convinced that the party must first be converted to a full tariff reform program before the nation recognized its obligation to strengthen the empire. As the *Bournemouth Graphic* noted shortly after his adoption at Christchurch, "Mr. Croft is one of those who consider the cause of Tariff Reform can never be carried so long as the Unionist party allows members to represent it who attack that policy in the House of Commons."[15] Croft now operated on three political levels: he pursued his personal political fortunes at Christchurch; he embarked on an internal movement to construct a modern and aggressive Conservative party; and he conducted his own campaign of political reformation within the East Hertfordshire Conservative party, which was a virtual microcosm of the national movement. Although the levels clearly progressed concurrently, before we may resume any consideration of Croft's cultivation of the Christchurch constituency in the run up to the 1910 election, we must examine his developing role on the national political stage and the dynamics of the crisis developing within the Conservative party.

The general election of 1906 placed an indelible imprint on the Conservative party, the unity of which already had begun to unravel soon after Chamberlain's 15 May 1903 Birmingham speech. The election had cordoned off Conservatives into three factions: the tariff reformers, the free traders, and the Balfourites.[16] Of significance is an examination of the political objectives and determination of a core of aggressive tariff reformers, which soon developed into the party's radicalized right wing. It was this core of young Conservatives that, during the period between the 1906 and 1910 elections, moved to reform the party, define the party's ideology, and purge the party, if necessary, all in an effort to construct a new British imperialism.[17]

The historian Robert Blake once suggested that behind the success of the tariff reform movement was an "uneasiness at Britain's world role; fear of the rise of the great land-based continental powers, America and Germany."[18] To such external unease, one must add domestic challenges such as those found in developing popular politics, that is, the rise of the labor movement as well as the collectivist direction of the Liberal party. However, the success of tariff reform within the Conservative party also owed much to the generational change that had been ongoing for several years. A younger generation now viewed the party as being adrift, without leadership, principles, strategy, or will. Faced with such external challenges and the party's internal anemia, a youthfully energetic but frustrated sector soon surfaced. This youthful and radicalized right wing was prepared to step forward in an effort to define the party's ideological orthodoxy on a foundation of a new imperialism, even at the risk of removing important and establishment elements of the party. They sought to forge a dynamic, aggressive, and modern party, which would be capable of advancing a constructive program in defense of the empire and nation. There was a demand for a new style and tenor of political action. If the party and its reticent leaders refused to embrace the call from the ranks, Croft and others were prepared to purge the resisters and, if necessary, to abandon the leadership and even the party in favor of an entirely new political experiment.

The commitment of such young men as Croft and the views he shared should not be too difficult to appreciate when juxtaposed against the certain reasoning of Conservative free traders. As Hugh Cecil wrote at the beginning of the internal party struggle, "we are passionately afraid of Protection, we think that it will lead to corruption and class division, to a general Americanising of our politics."[19] With great irony Cecil and Croft both feared and were raising a determined defense against the same evil—class division, mass popularization, and political corruption, perhaps sequential phenomena. In their own peculiar way, the tariff reformers and free traders were resisting the development of modern mass politics, twentieth-century style. Yet they both resorted to it through the use of rigid party discipline and appeals for mass support in an effort to enhance their respective positions. Tariff reformers promoted their ideology not only as the requisite program for future national prosperity, security, and stability but also as defense against the appeal of popular, collectivist, and even revolutionary ideologies. Advanced tariff reformers and imperialists in the mold of Croft responded to these anxieties by gravitating to attractive and energetic ideas, such as empire, security, and defense, and calling for constructive political action. In this was found the seed of Croft's alternative political experiments. He initially considered it necessary to construct a movement within the Conservative party itself, one that could subsequently be used to define its ideology, reform the party, and purge it of wobblers.

The election, as well as the interpretations applied to it, led such aggressive tariff reformers to conclude "that it was manifestly impossible that we could continue to fight in the same party as Hugh Cecil and the Free Fooders."[20] The message was not so much in dispute as was the dilemma that now surfaced: With whom would leadership of the party now reside? Soon after the election, Chamberlain and Balfour were under pressure to act. Chamberlain was being urged to take the reins of leadership; others appealed for him to advance fiscal reform through an advantageous agreement with Balfour, but without appearing to pursue a determined and extreme course, which many feared would provoke a rebellion by certain Balfourites. Balfour was under equal expectations to construct a formula that he and Chamberlain could accept, and that would bring the party together.[21] Balfour was under equal pressure by Hugh Cecil, Robert Cecil, and the free traders not to sell the party's soul to the protectionists. Balfour somehow had to choreograph a difficult balancing act to keep both the Chamberlainites and the "Hughligans" within his house. The sense of anxiety may be found in a letter to Balfour, in which his cousin, Robert Cecil, despaired that "almost my only hope in the Party is yourself."[22] On the other hand, Lord Ridley, chairman of the Tariff Reform League, believed "that it is quite impossible for Balfour to continue as Leader. The present elections have in the main been a revolt against him and all that he stands for."[23]

The party intrigue as well as the political minuet in which Chamberlain and Balfour were engaged, culminating in the "Valentine compact," has been thoroughly traversed and warrants only limited attention here. The result was an exchange of letters between Balfour and Chamberlain on 14 February 1906, in which Balfour wrote "that Fiscal Reform is, and must remain, the first constructive work of the Unionist Party; that the objects of such reform are to secure more equal terms of competition for British trade and closer commercial union with the colonies."[24] Chamberlain responded, "I entirely agree with your description of the objects which we both have in view and gladly accept the policy which you indicate as the wise and desirable one for the Unionist party to adopt."[25] It appeared that the reconciliation of the two party leaders had been realized through the simple exchange of the letters.

However, the harmony was as superficial as the shallowness of the commitments contained in the Valentine letters. There had been no true reconciliation between the radical tariff reformers, the Balfourites, and free traders. Leo Maxse, in particular, had been waging a grueling war against Balfour the previous month, and he showed no signs of silencing his artillery. Immediately after the election, Maxse wrote that "Mr. Balfour failed to grasp the golden moment. . . . The Unionists went on the wobble and has been wobbling ever since, until finally it wobbled into the General Election. . . . We went to the country with little to show for."[26] It followed, he suggested, that Balfour should step down.[27] The advanced tariff reformers were not to be mollified by Balfour's ambiguous concessions. Revealing the depth of such discontent, J. L. Garvin, editor of *Outlook,* wrote to Maxse

3: From Lincoln to the Confederacy (1906–1907)

that he was "sick and tired of the mismanagement" of the party and its program. "My opinion of Balfour is the same as your own. . . . The man is ruinous . . . and while we are led by him we shall make no progress. . . . What are we to do? We have only to grit our teeth and wait, and work like pioneers, no longer crying for anything at all except that our faith is our faith."[28] The lack of confidence in Balfour was further expressed by Hugh Arnold-Forster, a former cabinet minister: "I honestly believe that, at this moment, he is thinking much more of how soon he can get Hugh Cecil back, of what Salisbury's view is, and, generally of a number of obscure personal matters, & individual preferences, than of the issues which really face the country."[29]

Yet there was very little they could do because Chamberlain did not and would not challenge Balfour for the leadership. This element of inaction was removed tragically when on 11 July 1906 Chamberlain was struck down by a paralyzing stroke. With the loss of their charismatic leader, who had long been the personification of the tariff reform movement, the radicalized right wing was now unleashed; and they promptly displayed an emerging determination as they fashioned a battle plan for the march of tariff reform. They were no longer restrained by the personal agreement between Chamberlain and Balfour but could now promote a full program of protectionism and imperial preference, with concomitant reform of the Conservative party.[30]

A shift in the movement's center of gravity away from Chamberlain enhanced the influence of the tariff reform press, particularly Maxse and the *National Review*.[31] Maxse lashed out at Balfour and "the obscurantism and apathy of our Front Bench, which is 'cumbered with the ancient and dreary wreckage of the late Administration,' and general discouragement of activity among the rank and file."[32] Maxse then warned that if the party leaders do not promote tariff reform at every chance, "there will be an explosion of opinion among the rank and file which will surprise all the mandarins, and will endanger those personal vested interests to which Party interests and national interests have so long been subordinated by Mr. Balfour and his colleagues."[33]

Maxse's anger was no more subdued when he wrote to Bonar Law condemning the "inactivity of Tariff Reformers, which . . . is largely due to the unfriendly, not to say treacherous, attitude of Balfour and Co., who are doing all they can to damp down and destroy our movement." Fearing the movement would forfeit its energy while waiting for Chamberlain's possible recovery, Maxse declared that "this won't do. We can't afford to waste the next few months . . . in the hope that Chamberlain may resume his position. . . . it seems to me disastrous to allow the Tariff Reform movement to hibernate."[34] By the end of the year, his assessment was shared by Garvin, who had become equally convinced "that Balfour means to let the [fiscal question] drop into oblivion."[35] Due to subsequent developments, it is most interesting that on 4 December Garvin wrote to Maxse, "the cause is lost, unless we can form at an early date a definite tariff group in Parliament." He feared that tariff reformers "shall be more effectively killed by the policy of silence than we could have been by a policy of repudiation. What is the good of talking to the country about the food tax while our own party are ignoring it or shirking it."[36] He, too, seemed to suggest direct action, first to purify the party and then to convert the country.

There were also stirrings among the radical tariff reformers, stirrings that ultimately gave birth to the Confederates. With Chamberlain incapacitated and the fiscal question having been divorced from Balfour's thoughts ever since the Valentine compact, direct action by the rank-and-file tariff reformers soon supplemented the press campaign. The crucial personalities and links between the press campaign and the direct action were Maxse and Croft, who were responsible for the first major direct action campaign under the auspices of the Confederacy. Croft had been introduced to several young and aggressive imperialists during his Lincoln campaign. In addition, he enjoyed the distinction of having had his name linked with Chamberlain during a caustic debate in the House of Commons. From the summer of 1904 to the election in January 1906, Croft also had become associated with a cadre of determined tariff reformers, including the earl of Malmesbury, Viscount Ridley, Henry Chaplin, Thomas Comyn Platt, Alan Burgoyne, Bernhard Wise, and Edward Goulding.

Suspecting Balfour's continued dalliance with the Conservative free traders, frustration finally boiled over in late autumn of 1906 when two "young and ardent politicians who determined to leave nothing to chance" met with Croft for dinner at Fanhams Hall.[37] Disenchanted with the party's "all-right-in-the-night policy" as it existed under Balfour, Croft, Thomas Comyn Platt, and Bernhard Wise felt "the time had come to strike and to strike hard."[38] It was here that the idea of creating an organization that could agitate outside the restraints of the Chamberlain-Balfour concordat was born.[39] Comyn Platt brought a "draft set of rules and plan of campaign. It was rough but after some hours' discussion, a workable scheme was evolved which it was decided to lay before a larger gathering of Tariff enthusiasts the following week."[40] The three rebels soon held a second meeting at which time another dozen members joined the movement, and by this time Maxse was probably included.

By December 1906 Croft and his associates expanded their circle. The movement, which Comyn Platt suggested be called the Strafford Club, took the name of the Confederates, noting the American experience.[41] A "private and confidential" letter, sent 12 December 1906, by Wise to Arthur Steel-Maitland, announced that Croft was summoning a meeting of advanced tariff reformers "to consider what steps should be taken to compel the selection of Tariff Reform candidates by the Central Office." The call proposed to establish a small cadre of Conservative MPs and candidates who "pledged to organize Tariff Reform meetings in the constituencies for which Free

3: From Lincoln to the Confederacy (1906–1907)

Trade Unionists have been selected as candidates, with a view to creating a sufficiently strong public opinion to compel the acceptance of Tariff Reform views." The letter set forth the Confederates' complaint that "the Tariff Reform League is hampered in this work by its loyal acceptance of the Chamberlain-Balfour concordat." They felt that the free traders had been given encouragement by both Balfour and the Central Office. Behind Croft's invitation was the anger that "Tariff Reform candidates [were] impeded by the influence of that small section of the Party which controls Headquarters." Accordingly, "a large number of Tariff Reform Members and candidates at the last election have expressed their readiness to support the movement in which others who (although they are not in active politics) have political influence—such as Mr. Leo Maxse—have already joined."[42]

A few days later, Wise informed Mrs. Chamberlain that a secret organization, composed of fifty MPs, candidates, and peers, had been formed as a political strike force for the purpose of challenging any free trade Conservative who stands for parliament. The Confederacy also sought to convert the party's Central Office and chief whip, Sir Alexander Acland Hood, to tariff reform. Wise described the Confederates as "extra-official—free lancers," who have money and determination. However, it was not intended to have their names disclosed, and the organization would be kept secret "in order not to embarrass Mr. Chamberlain."[43]

Croft suggested the Confederacy numbered about fifty at its peak and that its "principal success was due to the fact that nobody knew who we were."[44] As for the actual membership, it is not surprising that Maxse was often viewed as the father of the idea or at least the ringleader. An anonymous contributor to the *Contemporary Review* reflected the belief of many when he suggested that "the guiding spirit is that distinguished publicist who, when he is not fomenting war with Germany or intriguing against Balfour, finds the extermination of a few Unionist Free Traders a congenial relaxation."[45] On reading this suggestion, a chuckling Maxse wrote to Croft: "It must be as entertaining to you as it is to me to read in the first article of the February 'Contemporary Review' that I am the organiser of the Confederacy!"[46] Nevertheless, the membership has long been a source of mystery and curiosity, particularly as some of the well-known participants declined to identify their fellow confederates even decades later.[47] Croft recorded in 1947 that thirty Confederates entered parliament, nine secured office, and four became cabinet ministers.[48] Lord Winterton, writing in 1932, declined "to break faith by disclosing them now." He described the Confederacy as "a 'ginger' organisation of Peers, Members of the House of Commons, business men, lawyers and journalists. Many influential men were of our number."[49]

Very early on the *Daily Mail* reported a less-than-private meeting of Confederates held in February 1907 in one of the committee rooms at the House of Commons; it reported that seven peers and six MPs had joined, identifying lords Oranmore and Browne, Hardinge, and Harrowby, as well as Spenser Wilkinson and Maxse.[50] Shortly thereafter even Croft was being correctly identified as "the founder" of this new "mysterious political organisation styled 'The Confederacy.'"[51] Although Croft declined to reveal his colleagues, the press continued to report the membership as it became known, and occasionally Croft found it necessary to deny the membership of certain prominent figures, as was the case with Lord Milner, Lord Selborne, Henry Chaplin, and Joseph Chamberlain.[52] It took nearly a year before the *Daily Mail* was confident in its belief that the Confederacy was a "small band of some forty stalwarts," listing Lord Ridley, Earl Winterton, J. F. Remnant, Frederick Leverton Harris, Edward "Paddy" Goulding, and Croft as members.[53] The *Yorkshire Post,* which voiced the complaint of the Conservative free traders over "the veil of privacy which envelops" the Confederates, nevertheless identified Alan Burgoyne, Henry Lygon, Comyn Platt, and Croft as members.[54] The inclusion of Lygon was consistent with his vigorous support of the extreme tariff reform wing of the Conservative party and his attack on the cannibalistic politics first provoked by the duke of Devonshire's December 1903 letter during the Dulwich campaign.[55]

The most extensive public list was provided in early 1909 by the *Daily Graphic,* which included Andrew Bonar Law, Lord Duncannon, Sir Gilbert Parker, J. F. Remnant, Claude Hay, Harry Marks, W. F. Cabourne, Ratcliffe Cousins, Lord Ridley, Earl Winterton, J. W. Hills, Jesse Collings, Edward Goulding, Alan Burgoyne, and Croft.[56] The only inaccuracy was to include Bonar Law and Ridley. Young Winterton frequently socialized with Claude Hay, Harry Marks, George Courthope, Wilfrid Ashley, and Mitchell Thomson, and he may have been responsible for introducing them to Croft. Although Winterton may not have been one of the founders as was often believed, he soon became one of the most active members. His diaries give additional confirmation to the membership of Sir Charles Hunter, Capt. George Tryon, Lygon, Michael Temple, Vivian Stewart, Burgoyne, Malmesbury, George Churchill, Samuel Ridley, Arnold Ward, Sir Spencer Pocklington Maryon Maryon-Wilson, J. W. Hills, Arthur Steel-Maitland, Ronald McNeill, Sir George Armstrong, Col. Henry Bowles, and Geoffrey Skeffington Smyth.[57]

In late 1907 the principal core—or, in the words of Comyn Platt, "the greater brains"—of the Confederates began to explore the idea of issuing a publication that would address the major political, economic, social, moral, and defense issues facing the nation. In doing so, the Confederates believed they might make some ground in convincing the public they were not a "political mafia."[58] Regarding the project, Comyn Platt wrote to Arthur Steel-Maitland, that "the greater brains of the Confederates are contemplating a book which shall contain 12 essays on the most important political questions of the day. It is a mighty work & [Francis] Griffiths the publisher is very anxious to take it up. Will you join us?"[59] As with most of the

Confederates, Comyn Platt expressed frustration over the direction and commitment of the Conservative party. "Very few of us," he again wrote to Steel-Maitland, "know exactly *what* the National Union exists for. I am convinced that if our ignorance is to be relieved (to put it mildly) we must have a very cryptic explanation or we shall relapse into outer darkness again."[60] In spring 1908 under the editorship of Lord Malmesbury, the Confederates published *The New Order: Studies in Unionist Policy*, which contained fifteen essays written by Wilfred Ashley, Alan Burgoyne, Croft, E. G. Spencer-Churchill, G. L. Courthope, Ronald McNeill, Malmesbury, Lord Morpeth, Hugh O'Neill, Comyn Platt, Sir John Rolleston, Arthur Steel-Maitland, Michael H. Temple, Winterton, and Wise.[61] In addition James Fitzalan Hope, J. L. Garvin, W. Mitchell-Thomson, and W. A. S. Hewins originally appear on a draft list of contributors sent to Steel-Maitland.[62]

Determining the membership is not without dispute as evidenced by the case of Garvin, editor of *Outlook* and the *Observer*. Comyn Platt had approached Garvin early in the formation of the group, perhaps late 1906 but surely by early 1907. He was regularly invited to the meetings and kept informed of their progress. Although Garvin never attended the meetings in 1907 and 1908, usually pleading personal reasons, he was nevertheless listed in Comyn Platt's membership book.[63] Accordingly, when the Confederates began to recruit contributors for *The New Order*, Garvin was aggressively courted. It appears that he initially agreed to provide an essay on imperial federation but later withdrew due to his own workload.[64]

However, on 27 December 1908 Garvin wrote a harshly critical article about the Confederates in the *Observer*, which provoked Comyn Platt to send Garvin a protest.[65] "There is a huge mistake somewhere" as all along he considered Garvin a fellow traveler.[66] Garvin expressed amazement that his name was on the books. "Please take it off them at once," he demanded. He expressed disgust at the mischief that the Confederates had committed and demanded they "change that melodramatic name! Fling aside the claim to secrecy!" Garvin further warned that the English "will not stand for such methods, no matter by what party they are practised," and he suggested that Comyn Platt "lay a tight fist upon the coattails" of Croft and his Confederates. Interestingly, as will be discussed later, Garvin cautioned the Confederates to leave Robert Cecil alone.[67] Comyn Platt protested in a subsequent letter that the Confederates had done nothing but good for the party and cause, having converted the Central Office and fifteen MPs to tariff reform. He further reprimanded Garvin for his disingenuous criticism of the Confederacy's secrecy. "What is there secret in our movement? Simply this that we don't talk about one another. Our policy is known everywhere." He reminded that Garvin does not publish the identities of correspondents, reviewers, or leader writers.[68] On another occasion Comyn Platt again disputed Garvin's characterization. "What is their secret? Our policy is known; several papers published a list of members! A Confederate may proclaim his title to the whole world and very often does. I do, when asked. Is this a national crime?" In fact he suggested, "the secrecy of the Confederates is entirely a creation of the press." Defending the young radicals, Comyn Platt pointed out that in 1906 free traders infested the party, and "today there are four left. In another six months there will not be more than one. Then our work will begin. With over 50 of us in Parliament, the call of Imperialism shall be kept rolling until a greater Confederacy than the one I started . . . is set up for all time. This is our ideal. The goal of our labours."[69]

There were others interested in the identity of the Confederates besides the free trade press. Robert Cecil and his free trade associates were keenly interested in the membership and activities of the Confederates. In January 1908 the secretary of the Unionist Free Trade Club, E.G. Brunker,[70] promised "to find out something more about this precious 'Confederate Club,'" noting that "some time ago I heard of the formation of a Club of very advanced Tariff Reformers, the moving spirit being that little fire-eater Maxse, with the Duke of Sutherland (controlled by Mr. Chaplin!) behind."[71] Lords Ridley, Harrowby, Hardinge, as well as Goulding, Maxse, and Garvin, were charged as being Confederates by J. S. Sandars,[72] who served as Balfour's eyes and ears on the political world.[73]

Within a few days, Cecil had been given two lists identifying additional members. Brunker wrote that Comyn Platt was the secretary, which is correct based on Comyn Platt's own admission. He then named Winterton, Wise, Burgoyne, Maxse, Goulding, Remnant, and Herman as being members.[74] The second list agreed with the identification of Winterton, Maxse, and Remnant but also included Harry Marks.[75] Cecil immediately wrote to Balfour complaining about the Confederates and named Winterton, Comyn Platt, Maxse, Remnant, Herman, and Bonar Law as being the primary conspirators.[76] With respect to the duke of Sutherland and Lord Ridley, an intermediary had relayed to Cecil "that they had no connection or control over the Confederacy Club," but Cecil doubted these protestations.[77] It is more likely that neither were members but were well briefed on the Confederacy's activities.

Confirmation of Basil Peto and Ronald McNeill can be made by references in private correspondence.[78] Confirmation of J. W. Hills's membership is made in the Parliamentary debates. When asked by John Redmond if Hills was a Confederate, Hills responded: "Yes, I am a Confederate." The more revealing comment came when Hills continued to declare, "I have always said that between Protectionists and Free Traders there can be no truce. They are bound to oppose us and we are bound to oppose them. Five years ago the late Duke of Devonshire, Free Trader, gave an order that the Unionist Free Traders were to vote for the Liberal party, and they were quite ready to do so."[79] Amery also belonged to the Confederates but seems to have taken little action on their behalf as he later did not "remember it amounting to much more than a few of us getting together from time to time, usually

3: From Lincoln to the Confederacy (1906–1907)   65

over dinner, as particular constituency problems cropped up."[80] He was occupied with journalistic projects as well as trying to secure a parliamentary seat.

George Lloyd was most likely introduced to tariff reform and the Confederates early on, both as an extension of his university days' association with Croft and his introduction to Amery in December 1906. Not long after Chamberlain had engaged the battle for tariff reform with his 15 May 1903 speech, a young George Lloyd offered his assistance to the cause.[81] However, as with Amery, Lloyd was initially but only temporarily detoured by his own pursuits, which included work for the Board of Trade in the Middle East and a hunt for a parliamentary seat.[82] Lloyd and Croft were destined to become two of Britain's most adamant tariff reformers and uncompromising imperialists.

One also might be confident in suggesting that Leslie Scott, Harold Smith, W. A. S. Hewins, and Fabian Ware held peripheral links to the Confederacy, although they did not appear to take any significantly active roles. Given their intimate political and social associations with various Confederates as well as their strong fiscal reformist views during this period, one is inclined to include their membership.[83]

Because Austen Chamberlain and Bonar Law worked closely with Confederates in 1907 and 1908, there is a strong temptation to include them on the membership roster. However, it is more plausible to suggest that Chamberlain was not a member, but instead tried deliberately to maintain a distance from the meetings and dinners. Even Wise concedes a wish not to embarrass the elder Chamberlain. Through his close association with most of the members, he was kept fully informed of their plans yet still maintained a level of plausible deniability.[84] It is more problematic in locating Bonar Law. Although Robert Cecil and the free traders considered Bonar Law a Confederate, there does not appear to be other documentary support. However, where an inaccurate accusation of membership touched on a party leader, Croft usually issued a specific denial. None was ever issued for Bonar Law. The most persuasive evidence for his exclusion comes from Wise. In November 1911 shortly after Bonar Law succeeded Balfour as leader of the Conservative party, Wise wrote to his new leader, calling his attention to *The New Order*. "It was published in 1908," Wise recalled for Bonar Law's benefit, and it was "so badly handled that it got no circulation. It was a volume of essays by the members of 'The Confederacy' & might be of interest to you now."[85] Had Bonar Law been an active member, he undoubtedly would have been aware of the volume. As with Chamberlain, one is tempted to conclude that he was not only aware of the Confederacy's activities but often approved of them. Winterton's diaries also confirm that the Confederates had close associations with Ridley, Bonar Law, George Wyndham, Jesse Collings, and Henry Chaplin.[86] (For a complete membership list, see Appendix 1.)

Although there may have been as many as fifty members, as Croft suggests, most of the activities circulated around ten to twelve individuals. It must be remembered that the Confederates operated in a very clandestine and conspiratorial manner, although it seemed to be more for effect than of necessity. Of course their conspiracy was carried out as only English gentlemen can do it: "Each member of the Confederates had in turn to give the best dinner available in London to his fellow Confederates, but on no occasion were all the members to be brought together and only three of us knew who all the Confederates were."[87]

With the membership constructed, the question remains: Who were the Confederates? The Confederates clearly constituted a privileged group: 28 members or 55 percent were educated at "Oxbridge"; 15 Confederates or 29 percent came from the aristocracy; 14 members or 27 percent came from landed interests, several of which were substantial—including Lord Oranmore, 8,000 acres; Lord Malmesbury, 4,000 acres; Lord Winterton, 2,800 acres; and Maryon-Wilson, 1,200 acres. An equal number could be considered as having substantial business, industrial, or commercial interests; 12 members or 24 percent had been called to the bar; 8 or 16 percent were either journalists or held substantial positions among the nation's press; and 5 members or 9 percent were academics. A second feature was clearly their youth. Their average age was 37 years, with 26 members or 51 percent being 40 years of age or under. A further 13 members or 25 percent were 30 years of age or younger, including the core activists: Croft (25), Duncannon (26), Burgoyne (26), Winterton (23), Lygon (22), O'Neill (23), and Lloyd (27). The "fire-eater" Leo Maxse must have seemed utterly geriatric at 42.

As a result of their youth, their political experience had not yet matured. Only 12 Confederates or 23 percent had sat in Parliament in 1906 or before. In fact 15 of the radicals or 29 percent, such as Croft, unsuccessfully contested the 1906 general election, and only 8 were elected. However, the 1910 elections produced a significantly different result. Out of 26 Confederates who stood for Parliament in January 1910, 22 gained seats. Approximately 33 Confederates sat in the House of Commons at some point during their careers, and Croft's subsequent claim "that thirty of them entered Parliament" appears to be quite close.[88] Croft also notes that 9 held office and even 4 were in the cabinet.[89] However, 17 Confederates or 32 percent held significant government positions during the first half of the twentieth century, and an equal number held important positions of authority in local government.

Given their youth, it is not surprising that 17 Confederates or 33 percent saw active military service during the First World War; many of them, such as Croft (CMG), Spencer-Churchill (MC), Courthope (wounded, MC), Duncannon (CMG), Hills (wounded), Lee (dispatches), Lygon (wounded), Comyn Platt (wounded), Lloyd (dispatches, DSO), Skeffington Smyth (dis-

3: From Lincoln to the Confederacy (1906–1907)

patches), Ware (dispatches, CMG), Winterton (dispatches), and Burgoyne (decorations), served with seriousness and distinction. About 19 members had engaged in military service prior to 1914. Twenty-five or 49 percent of the Confederates received some form of civil honor during their careers, which included 20 privy councillorships, 10 knighthoods, 12 baronetcies, and a Companion of Honour. Fourteen members were subsequently elevated to a peerage or promoted in peerage in their own right.

Perhaps no better description can be given than that provided by an anonymous sympathizer:

> Here were dozens of young men of University training and culture, eager in the cause of Empire, amazed and pained at the calamities which had befallen their party and country, with no one to inspire or lead them but an ex-Cabinet largely consisting of mediocrities and party hacks without enthusiasm or purpose. . . . The Confederacy was a revolt of the intellect and youth of the party from the combined incompetence, impotence, and petty bickerings of the preceding three years, with its culminating disaster of the General Election. These men—and their ranks contain the flower of their party's talent—could not understand the chicaneries of Carlton Club politics, or why men should conspire, intrigue. . . . They knew, however, a deep game was being played by a clique. They knew and marked the men who are now playing it. . . . The popular cause wins; and with it the prospects of Social Reform, Tariff Reform and democratic methods inside the Unionist Party are looking brighter every day. . . . Their movement began in a burst of patriotism. . . . They are young men, many of them, of high character and noble aspirations, well-bred, capable, and of good address, and rare political intelligence. . . . They are men who are destined to make their mark in the political world.[90]

Within the Confederacy, which had been brought together for an overtly political program, there existed a fusing together of segments from the old aristocracy, business, commerce and industry, the officer ranks, parliamentarians, the bar, and the press. These primarily well-established, well-educated men of rank, status, comfort, and privilege were welded together by more than their youth, political ambition, and nationalist sentiment. They coalesced over their mutual anxieties. They feared a nation and empire facing an uncertain century and confronted by foreign and domestic dangers. They reflected a sophisticated, articulate, and rational discontent over the passivity of the nation's and the Conservative party's response to the spectre of a declining and endangered kingdom. What was it that they feared? In general terms they were excessively anxious about Germany's economic and military growth as well as her imperial ambitions. They felt similarly toward the American imperial and economic power and potential. The prospective domestic and strategic impact of the vicious competition of international trade also dominated their thoughts. The vision of the colonies spinning away from the British imperial orbit caused great consternation due to very serious economic, military, diplomatic, and strategic ramifications.

Equally nervous over the rise of socialism and grumbling by the trade unions, they feared the social discontent that would naturally follow the nation's general economic decline. Such social consequences could validate the inevitable appeal of socialism and subsequently ignite social revolution. Although they never said as much, for it was not necessary, they saw themselves as being more than just nationalists or imperialists but as the last line of defenders of Britain. In fact, they represented Britain, and her endangerment translated into their endangerment. They saw themselves as the first political generation for the twentieth century, the generation on whom the kingdom and empire would have to depend.

They were conservative in that they sought to preserve the existing social structure, social and political institutions. They sought to preserve the empire. For the most part, they fought for their program within the existing, legitimate, and constitutional framework. However, they were radical on two separate levels. They were prepared to alter aggressively the behavior and programs of the state to advance their nationalist vision of a future Britain, its empire, and society. The Confederacy could be considered the first British political force in the twentieth century to envision, accept, and promote an activist state, a state that was to be concomitantly conservative and radical. They also were conservative in that at this point in time they generally accepted the existing party system as being the vehicle for the promotion and advancement of their program. Although they generally feared the breakup of the Liberal-Conservative polarity as they knew it, they were radical in their acceptance of an substantial reconstruction of the Conservative party. They recognized that the success of their program and the future welfare and security of the kingdom depended on reconstructing the Conservative party "root and branch." As the protectors of the nation and empire, this they were prepared to undertake and accomplish. However, Croft's frustration was not without limits as we will find him being pushed further toward a rebellious course with an unorthodox political vehicle. The Confederacy also contained the seed of modern British conservatism in that their anxieties resulted in the affirmative construction of a policy and program of action. If the party and the remnants of its nineteenth-century leadership would not embrace their vision for the future of Britain and empire, many of the rebels were prepared either to cast aside their leadership or to find an alternative to the present reform of the party. Further, their view embraced a more radical role for the state, and accordingly their apprehensions were assuaged by a new and constructive program for the state. No longer was their view of the empire based solely on romanticism or tradition, but it now included a new and aggressive imperial idea, grounded in economics and strategic defense, as defining their approach promoting the empire and protecting the nation.

4
Croft, the Confederates, and the Balfour Question (1907)

> As one of those who have always taken up an advanced position upon the question of Tariff Reform, I was, with others who think with me, naturally delighted with Mr. Balfour's clear and decisive speech at Birmingham.
> —Henry Page Croft, 18 November 1907

By 1907 the acerbic rhetoric of such tariff reformers as Leo Maxse, now joined by the excommunication policy of Croft's Confederates, confirmed that the tariff reform question remained dangerously unresolved. Croft was determined that the country must be educated and brought around to an acceptance of protectionism and imperial preference. Yet he recognized that this objective could not be accomplished until such time as the party itself was unreservedly converted to tariff reform or, in the alternative, unless the party was purged of the remaining free-trade rump. This was an alternative that he and the other Confederates were prepared to pursue inasmuch as some considered purging to be as easy as pursuing conversions and perhaps more gratifying. Croft proceeded to carry out his objectives both within a national context and within the local setting of East Hertfordshire.

These goals were not the only political concerns of Croft in 1907. His overall ideological program traveled with equal importance alongside his own political need to secure a seat in Parliament. Accordingly, Croft expended his energy in a quest to achieve party purity and national conversion and to promote his future candidacy. Croft thought, as did many others with whom he circulated, that the Liberals soon would be forced to call a general election due to the controversial nature of the Liberals' program and, according to the view of Croft and others, popular dissatisfaction. There was, nevertheless, to be no compromising as each of Croft's objectives traded on the same currency, a determined dedication to tariff reform and imperial unity. However, he would be frustrated first by a core of free trade obstructionists within the Conservative party and second by a party leadership whose political ideas and strategies were still to be found in an earlier age.

In preparation for the eventual next election, the initial step was to convert and control the Conservative party and thus place it on a straightforward track toward tariff reform. This necessitated a settlement of the "Balfour question." The tariff reform wing, however, could not risk an outright coup at this early stage. Any attempt in 1907 to overthrow Balfour would seriously injure the party. With Joseph Chamberlain incapacitated, there was no heir apparent, and the party itself was caught in an awkward position of intergenerational transition. It therefore was more desirable to bring or push, if necessary, Balfour into the tariff reform camp. On the other hand, there existed the reality that Balfour needed the support of the tariff reform wing given its numerical dominance in both the ranks and the parliamentary party. This led Confederates such as Maxse to believe in "the absolute necessity of our not being mere 'hangers-on' of Balfour, as the more subservient we are the less we shall get out of him. The more independent and disagreeable we make ourselves, the more he will be inclined to follow us."[1] The Conservative party was merely the political instrument for tariff reform. He could not accept the assertion that the one-issue politics of tariff reform would be the destruction of the party. Along with Croft, Maxse considered "the conquest of the party was only the first battle for the cause; at heart he wanted to make it a non-party movement."[2] From the beginning Croft had embraced tariff reform as being so crucial to the defense of the kingdom and empire that it was above partisan politics.

In 1907 Balfour found himself under considerable pressure from the unresolved fiscal question. He had made no public pronouncements on the issue in any manner since the Valentine pact of February 1906. At the other end of the party, on 2 January 1907 Maxse—riding on the emotion and commitment of the Confederacy as well as his own intensity—wrote to Bonar Law about "the grievous plight of our Party, which fills me with dismay." He castigated Balfour and his entourage for their unresponsive residence on the front benches, waiting passively without any constructive program with which to appeal to the ranks and the electorate. "This seems to me to be perilous nonsense. The Balfour Government was smashed last January because it deserved to be smashed." Maxse warned that the party will not be returned to office until it offers a program, which will require it to stand for something. He then claimed that "Balfour is utterly discredited—this is the A.B.C. and the X.Y.Z. of the political situation. . . . How can we lift up our Party?" He suggested that until Conservatives decide not "to allow the Party to be permanently paralyzed for the sake of the few personal vested interests which are mainly responsible for the *débâcle* . . . the position must remain utterly hopeless."[3] Maxse reflected Confederate opinion and sentiment on the Balfour question when he wrote to Bonar Law that "a good many people feel as I do as regards the present situation. . . . What

4: Croft, the Confederates, and the Balfour Question (1907)

is required is the development of an Independent Opposition. The Front Bench may remain purely passive and negative—we must be constructive."[4]

In his "New Year Message," Austen Chamberlain proclaimed the need for the party to pursue a determined course toward fiscal reform.[5] In January 1907, still in the earliest stages of the Confederacy's development, J. S. Sandars had detected the serious discontent developing within the party ranks. He feared that in the face of Balfour's silence the constant pounding inflicted by the ardent tariff reformers would precipitate a hemorrhage of support from Balfour to the Tariff Reform League. Still uncertain as to what actually was emerging within the party, Sandars nevertheless sensed that "something has happened to give [the tariff reformers] a new lease of life." He warned Balfour that the party rank and file are demanding that a broad and determined policy be adopted.[6]

On 15 January 1907, the executive committee of the Tariff Reform League called for parliamentary action by the opposition front bench, urging Balfour to articulate an advanced fiscal policy for the Conservative party. Lord Ridley immediately wrote to Austen Chamberlain that "the feeling (of want of leadership) in the party is growing very fast indeed; & it is certainly one which will have to be reckoned with as it has now spread far beyond the Maxses and [Fabian] Wares"—a reference to Croft's Confederates.[7] Even Acland Hood, the chief whip, feared a serious revolt unless Balfour took some substantive action to rehabilitate the commitments contained in the Valentine compact.[8]

Balfour was under equal pressure from the Conservative free trade wing, consisting of his cousins, the Cecils. They too had sensed that the tariff reformers were out for political blood. Lord Robert Cecil complained that the radical tariff reformers were demanding that their view of the Valentine correspondence be a shibboleth of the party.[9] As the Confederates intensified the momentum toward protectionism, Cecil protested "that the tariff reformers have not abandoned their policy of proscription."[10] Notwithstanding such protestations, Balfour gave the free traders little comfort; of course they were stuck with Balfour and had little alternative but to sit by and watch.

With respect to the party's radicalized right wing, Balfour remained unconcerned. He casually refused to articulate or promote any specific fiscal policy while the party remained in opposition. He warned Sandars that "if the Party is to be destroyed—which can easily be done by either wing—the disloyal T.R.s have at least as much to lose as anybody else."[11] In his first public response in a year, Balfour warned that "if we become a party of one idea we shall fail to carry even that idea to any successful conclusion."[12] His use of the phrase "disloyal T.R.s" is most instructive of Balfour's view and temperament. Although one might nevertheless ask disloyal to whom and to what, the Confederates would counter that they could not be disloyal to an irrelevant leadership, an outdated philosophy, and an anemic political strategy.

The resolution of the Tariff Reform League's executive committee on 15 January unleashed the frustration of the more-determined tariff reformers. Croft was quick to attack Balfour's passivity arguing "that a so-called truce would finally extinguish the last spark of enthusiasm in the Unionist Party. . . . Whatever the leaders may say, this great reform has caught hold of the popular imagination as nothing has done since the Reform Bill." From his newly developed Confederacy, Croft warned the party leadership that if Balfour's proposed policy of inaction and neglect is adopted then "the flower of the . . . party will dissociate itself from those who have betrayed" the kingdom and empire. In melodramatic fashion he warned that the Confederates were "prepared to fight as long as we live."[13]

Maxse now rushed to the platforms, claiming to represent "the general discontent of the rank and file of the Unionist party." He blasted Balfour for his inactivity and his neglect of tariff reform.[14] On 5 February 1907 Croft and Maxse paired up at Hitchin in East Herts where the latter continued his assault: the Conservative party was in deplorable condition because of the estrangement between the parliamentary party leadership and the ranks. "The sycophants and satellites who surrounded Mr. Balfour were largely responsible for the Unionist disaster." Maxse exhorted tariff reformers to "insist upon a definite statement that Tariff Reform was or was not the accepted policy of the Unionist party, and was going to have the full party machinery to impel it." He exposed the Confederacy's forthcoming tactics when he demanded that tariff reformers "must insist on plain and specific answers, and no wobbling on that question from candidates, and if they got the candidates on their side, the leaders would follow suit."[15]

If Austen Chamberlain was not a member of the Confederacy, his close association with many of its members—Lee, Hills, Steel-Maitland, Cousins, Croft, Hewins, and Goulding—surely made him privy to their battle plans. They were then able to work in unison, with Chamberlain at times expertly playing off the more tenacious members of the tariff reform wing. Chamberlain coordinated a series of speeches in early 1907 in which he appeared to defend Balfour, claiming the party's leader was as dedicated a tariff reformer as any whole-hogger. He protested the treatment to which Balfour recently had been subjected, arguing that Balfour was committed to a policy of advancing tariff reform and colonial preference. Of course, Balfour was virtually checkmated and could do little in the way of protesting. Although he could not dispute the description and was forced to continue his ambiguous silence, his ambivalence was no longer acceptable to the radical tariff reformers.[16]

Balfour was not totally unaware of his situation. He now had significant discussions with Hewins who, as an advanced tariff reformer himself, was associated with the Confederates. In December 1906, not far removed from

4: Croft, the Confederates, and the Balfour Question (1907)   73

the organizational activities of the Confederates, Hewins was invited to discuss the situation with Austen Chamberlain, Goulding, and Bonar Law. This meeting was followed by a political dinner at which Arthur Lee, Alfred Lyttelton, and Balfour were also in attendance. Hewins subsequently expressed optimism over Balfour's conversion; the others did not, particularly Lyttelton who declared "that Balfour would never do anything against the Cecils."[17]

In January 1907 Hewins was summoned to Balfour's Scottish estate at Whittingehame where he briefed Balfour on the history and economics of the movement. Hewins also provided Balfour with a memorandum on the political ramifications within the Conservative party. Thereafter on 1 February 1907, Balfour made his first public comments on fiscal reform in nearly a year. At a meeting the next day, "Paddy" Goulding, Arthur Lee, Austen Chamberlain, Sir Joseph Lawrence, and Leo Amery did not display much satisfaction.[18]

The whole-hoggers wished to see the opposition front bench attack the king's speech with demands that tariffs and imperial preference be considered at the upcoming colonial conference. This would constitute an unambiguous declaration of party policy and would concurrently cast Balfour's position on protection and imperial preference. Hewins felt that Balfour was finally beginning to warm to the idea. The proposal still had to be vigorously pushed by Goulding, Ridley, Bonar Law, Sir Gilbert Parker, J. W. Hills, Arthur Lee, and J. L. Remnant, nearly all of whom had ties with the Confederacy.

While Hewins attempted to prepare Balfour for the confrontation, Chamberlain, Hills, and Bonar Law took responsibility for the Commons debate. On 19 February in response to the king's speech, Hills sought to have preferential trading relations with the colonies included in the agenda for the colonial conference. He was followed by the party leadership.[19] There was satisfaction with the showing by Chamberlain and Bonar Law, but Balfour was still considered to be a disappointment. Even the free trade press conceded that the tariff reformers must have been disappointed with Balfour's performance.[20] By the end of February, Sandars reported to Ridley and Hewins that Balfour decided to harass the government with questions, a strategy originating from the tariff reform meeting on 15 January 1907.[21] Although it has been implied that "the Confederates drifted into the more normal channels of tariff reform activism," it seems more accurate to conclude that the renewed tariff reform activism of the more mainstream political personalities was in fact ignited as much as anything by the energy and determination of the radical tariff reformers, which corresponded with the emergence of Croft's Confederacy.[22]

The Confederates—particularly Goulding, Remnant, Lee, Hills, Parker—were in the forefront of promoting a strategy consistent with the objectives held by the founders. Winterton was out of the country from November until late February;[23] neither Croft nor Comyn Platt were members of Commons, which was where the February performance had been conducted; and as mentioned earlier, Croft was involved in local political struggles of his own in both Lincoln and East Hertfordshire.[24]

Notwithstanding Croft's apparent distance from the parliamentary maneuvers of February, the press clearly viewed the Confederacy as being behind the attacks on Balfour. The Confederates were accused of being "a little knot of quite insignificant politicians—whose vanity excuses them from the charge of self-seeking—[who] have banded themselves together to oust Mr. Balfour." They were sharply criticized for having "phosphorescence which springs from vindictiveness"; from suffering "under the illusion that they are original"; and being so historically naive and politically immature as not to see the parallels to the "round-robins" of the 1850s and 1860s who tried to unseat Disraeli as leader of the party. "These Confederates . . . are simply reproducing the petty malevolence of small sections of partisans which have earned a passing notoriety on the morrow of all great political reverses."[25] The *Globe,* however, defended the Confederates. They have concluded that both the party and the program are "suffering from a deficiency of dynamic energy in the heads of the party." They only want Balfour "to make more fervent response to the national desires." However, the *Globe* warned, "the confederacy which forms the party van, is the nucleus of the great Tariff Reform majority that is coming. . . . Balfour has got out of touch with the young national party in London as well as with his old electorate. . . . His splendid intellectual powers and force of character are at present not 'pulling their weight.'"[26]

Croft was not inactive during this period, as he had launched an offensive in East Hertfordshire where he was attempting to isolate Abel Henry Smith. He sought to put Smith in a position whereby the radical tariff reformers could claim their loyal support for Balfour while concurrently discrediting the free trader. On 21 February 1907, Croft appealed to the Ware Working Men's Unionist Club to unite behind the Birmingham declaration and demand an affirmative party program to implement the tariff reform policy. Again, this strategy of pulling, or perhaps pushing, Balfour into their camp involved imprinting Balfour's speeches with their own protectionist interpretation. Balfour was being maneuvered into a position that he would eventually have to endorse or disavow. Croft could argue that this represented nothing short of the promotion of the Valentine policy pushed by the short steps contained in Balfour's subsequent speeches.[27] Croft then charged Smith with having a dismal attendance at Parliament and failing to support the party's protectionist and imperial program.[28]

A week later, on 28 February, Croft continued his campaign by reminding East Hertfordshire that in 1905 Smith had publicly professed his loyalty to Balfour and his support for an imperial conference. Further, it was agreed then that if Smith ever found himself unable to support Balfour's protectionist program, he had promised to inform the constituency. Notwithstanding this pledge, a pledge for which the local tariff reformers had agreed to extend their support in 1906, Croft accused Smith of failing to stand behind the Hills's amendment. This now licensed Croft to argue that Smith could no longer have any claim to be a supporter of Balfour. Further because Smith had violated his pledge to the East Hertfordshire tariff reformers, Croft suggested that "the time has come when the rank and file of the party must take the matter into their own hands."[29]

The Confederacy decided it was now time to advance beyond toying with the Balfour question. It was time to shift the attack from Smith and East Hertfordshire to the national stage. On 7 March 1907, at the annual meeting of the United Club, the Confederacy's strategy of purifying the party publicly erupted. As Croft had previously informed Garvin, it was his intention to move a "very important resolution with regard to the first constructive policy" of the Conservative party.[30] Following the tactic of pinning Confederate interpretations on Balfour's comments, Croft argued that Balfour had unequivocally established fiscal reform as being the first constructive policy and program of the Conservative party. Accordingly, the United Club should support only candidates who subscribed to the principles of an imperial, commercial union based on preference and a safeguarding tariff on foreign manufactured goods to protect domestic industries. Reflecting what he believed to be a very large section of the club, Croft expressed his frustration with the present arrangement, which made it possible for the club to assist candidates who opposed the party's fiscal policy.[31]

In an act of intentional provocation, Croft opened the Confederacy's second front when he claimed that "the younger members of the club object to their subscriptions being used to employ speakers to frustrate the policy of the party and to assist members of Parliament who refuse to vote in the Unionist lobby on fiscal divisions."[32] This was another direct shot fired at Smith who had abstained from voting on the protectionist and imperial amendments offered to the king's address by the Conservative front bench.[33] Croft's resolution, which was seconded by the industrialist, Sir Vincent Caillard, provoked intense debate and opposition. Sir Edward Carson, although a self-proclaimed protectionist, was more concerned about defending the Union than promoting tariff reform, and therefore opposed the motion. Ronald McNeill, having just returned from Aberdeen, declared that "Scotland was yearning to get rid of every Free Trader from the Tweed to the Shetlands." He was followed by "a member of the late Government, who declared himself a Tariff Reformer" and who further declared that he was in attendance "at the express wishes of Mr. Balfour."[34] The speaker let it be known that Balfour would resign from the Club should Croft's resolution succeed. Croft scoffed at "the idea of Mr. Balfour resigning on account of the members deciding to support his policy, described in his own words, is too absurd to consider even for one moment."[35] Opponents then proposed a six-month adjournment on the resolution, which passed seventy-nine to fifty.[36]

Another Confederate, Goulding, tried to put the developments in a positive light by pointing out that fifteen of the eighteen members elected to the committee of officers were now tariff reformers. Croft, however, was more concerned with the results. He dismissed those who claimed that "the time is not opportune to reform these gentlemen." Why, he demanded to know, should the party tolerate those members "who are determined to wreck the whole policy of Tariff Reform." To do so "will be cutting our own throats." Croft then issued a declaration of war against the free traders, warning that "it is high time that the . . . party whilst in Opposition rids itself of its open enemies." No longer can the party permit a "small section of the Party who are quite out of sympathy with the rank and file constantly voting against that policy with apparently the full sanction of the Whips."[37]

The import of Croft's declaration did not go unnoticed. As the *Morning Post* declared, it was further evidence of the developing discontent and frustration among the younger tariff reformers, who were now committed to purging the free trade obstructionists from the embrace of the Conservative party. However, the editorial charged, it was a frustration that really owed its existence to Balfour's tactical positions. It warned that Balfour remained the major obstacle to protection, and "Mr. Page Croft will find when he begins to round up the 'rebels' that his most resourceful opponent will be Mr. Balfour."[38] The battle between the free traders and the Confederates was now in the open. The objective, Croft later claimed, was to frighten the local constituency associations so they would not dare adopt or sponsor a candidate who had not fully subscribed to the Chamberlainite program.[39]

The Confederacy was not without a blueprint for their assault on free traders. In March 1906 an important section of the tariff reformers, led by Chamberlain ally and industrialist Sir Joseph Lawrence, launched an attack on Sir Edward Clarke, Q.C., a former solicitor-general under Lord Salisbury, for a speech in which he denigrated tariff reform and protectionism.[40] After intense pressure on his local association that was accompanied by veiled threats to vitiate any importance his presence in Parliament could provide his constituency, Clarke retired in May 1906. However, it was not before Robert Cecil, pained at the image of a free trader surrendering in the face of such outrageous attacks by the tariff reformers, pleaded with Sir Edward to hold on and resist. "If [the whole-hoggers] could say that they had driven so important a personality as yourself out of politics they would acquire fresh courage to attack the rest of us." Cecil decried that "this is always the result of civil war whether in party or country. . . . It is the leading spirits who are first attacked & destroyed."[41] Clarke held Balfour responsible because the party leader had remained silent during the siege by the whole-hoggers and particularly as it occurred in Balfour's own constituency. In addition, Lord Balfour of Burleigh, another free fooder, was expelled from

4: Croft, the Confederates, and the Balfour Question (1907)

the Constitutional Club after having endorsed a Liberal candidate in Chelsea.[42] In a third case, Robert Cecil held the radical tariff reformers responsible for blocking Sir Edgar Vincent's endorsement by the local Conservative association in Exeter.[43] With the advantage of these precedents and with an intelligent evaluation of Balfour's present dilemma, the Confederates were confident that in 1907 Balfour would neither have the political inclination nor be in a position to offer any effective assistance to a wounded free trader.

Within a few weeks after the United Club confrontation, Austen Chamberlain echoed the Confederacy's challenge and invited Conservatives of the ilk of the duke of Devonshire to leave the party.[44] There was a rational concern within the Balfour camp that Chamberlain's performance "is all part of a policy." Sandars had received complaints "that everywhere the Liberal Unionists—posing as Liberal Unionists but in reality being T.R. Leaguers—are, with the encouragement of Austen and Co., trying to squeeze out, or else to capture our local Conservative Associations."[45] In April 1907 Steel-Maitland advised Lord Ridley, "I rather think there is a method now for eliminating almost any wobblers from by-elections."[46] In early May, after Balfour's further acceptance of imperial preference, it was reported to the elder Chamberlain that "the sheep are hurrying into the fold."[47] Accordingly, Austen Chamberlain suggested to his father, "Robert Cecil will have to 'come on' if he means to keep the Marylebone seat."[48] Joseph Chamberlain now chided "the small knot of men who at first stood aside and boasted that they would smash Tariff Reform." The idea, he believed, was now recognized as being so vital that it cannot be dismissed.[49] In June, Lord Winterton recorded that it was decided to construct "a shibboleth to be put to all candidates about T.R. and preference." Steel-Maitland, Mitchell-Thomson, Temple, and Winterton were given the assignment.[50]

By June 1907 the Confederates were harassing George Stewart Bowles, MP for Norwood (Lambeth), who was an overly tempting target, a free trader, and long-time friend and political ally of Robert Cecil.[51] As a result, Cecil urged Balfour to provide Bowles with a letter of endorsement, believing that if he did that "it would really knock Bonar Law & Co. on the head." However, Cecil feared that Balfour, when faced with the Confederates, "will stand aside like a broken bow."[52] Cecil nevertheless renewed his complaint about the Confederacy, warning that Bowles's seat was at risk if the extremists were not halted. He demanded that the party and its members must support the candidate adopted by the local association.[53] Balfour eventually wrote to Bowles's Norwood association that each constituency should follow the guidance of their constituency association.[54]

The Confederates used their influence with the front bench to promote that a vote of censure be moved by Alfred Lyttelton on 15 July 1907. Inasmuch as the premise of the motion was to utilize preference to promote imperial unity, the most prominent free traders, Robert Cecil, Abel Henry

Smith, George Stewart Bowles, W. F. D. Smith, Colonel Robert Williams, Colonel Harrison-Broadley, and Sir Francis Powell, recognized their vulnerability. Accordingly, they voted for the motion, but, as Cecil conveyed to Bonar Law, they "desired it understood they are opposed to colonial preference based on the taxation of corn, meat or raw materials."[55] This humiliation of free traders provoked Hugh Cecil to admonish Balfour that any cooperation between the party's free traders and tariff reformers was out of the question. "I am fully resolved," Cecil claimed, "to destroy Tariff Reform and believe in my ability to do it."[56] Cecil tried to play the Confederacy's own game by calling Balfour a free trader, hoping to pull Balfour off the fence in their direction, but the attempt failed to move Balfour.[57]

During the summer recess, the Confederates again targeted Bowles for retribution. They persuaded the Norwood Conservative Council to summon Bowles to a meeting on 9 August 1907 for the purpose of explaining his free trade views. Remaining defiant, Bowles declared that he would never lend a hand to taxing the food of the people. The council resolved, with several abstentions, to continue its support for Bowles, but his support was weakening.[58]

In October 1907 Croft, having returned from his honeymoon with his new bride, Nancy Borwick, resumed active politics with an added message and task. The Conservative party must exterminate socialism from Britain. He likewise denounced the land reform proposals and admonished the Campbell-Bannerman ministry not to interfere with the Union, as the government had no mandate for such traitorous considerations.[59] The campaign for Christchurch seat had now begun, and one is reminded of the domestic anxieties that infected the party's radicalized right wing. To the electors he described himself as a big England imperialist and one who believed a crucial stage in history had been reached where Britain must act and reconstruct her empire. However, in his campaign he revealed the sense of anxiety over domestic challenges that were shared by the party's youthful and radicalized right wing. In response, Croft argued, Christchurch "must show that England [will] not tolerate men like Mr. Keir Hardie."[60]

When addressing the Liberal government's approach to home rule for Ireland and reform of the House of Lords, Croft suggested a political corruption emanated from the current arrangement of sectarian politics. He claimed the Liberals were afraid to address home rule head on, preferring the cowardly method of installments, and all for fear of losing the support of Irish Nationalists. Political corruption, he implied, was also found in the government's use of taxation policy to the benefit of wealthy mine owners, who supported the Liberal party. Speaking for the first time on women's suffrage, Croft denounced the aggressive and militant campaign that the women had employed.[61] He also indicted unemployment as an outrageous social, economic, and political disgrace. The reason flowed from the Liberal ministry's evisceration of the Alien Act of 1905 that "so mutilated it that

4: Croft, the Confederates, and the Balfour Question (1907)

swarms of aliens were coming in." The government had "welcomed these hordes of people, disease stricken, immoral, and without a penny in their pockets, and who by sweating undersold the British working man."[62] As an antisocialist chord sounded through the Confederacy and the tariff reform movement in general, there also appeared a distinct chorus of xenophobia or, more accurately, antialienism. In Bournemouth, with Bonar Law and Arthur Lee by his side, Croft noted that "although it was many years since the first foreigner landed at Hastings . . . they wanted no more of them."[63] He said the "A" in the A.B.C. of tariff reform stood "for Aliens who flock to our shores, bringing vice and diseases right up to our doors."[64] In a speech to the Mid Hertfordshire Conservatives, he charged that "there were welcomed into this country Anarchists, aliens of the criminal type, the diseased, scum of the earth. They came here and undermined the British constitution, and caused vast discontent among the working classes." He even suggested that because of the influx of this "scum . . . the flower of [the working class] were finding their way abroad."[65]

Many of the Confederates had expressed themselves on their determination to oppose socialism with a resolve equal to that being expended on behalf of tariff reform. The struggle for tariff reform was not merely a fight for unionism or empire. It was, Croft believed, the most singularly important bulwark against socialism. "There had recently been creeping into the back garden a worm of the worst kind which might grow into a serpent . . . Socialism. It had reared its head . . . , and because there was need and stress the hungry man would clutch at any straw, and they had to fight Socialism with something plausible."[66]

Socialism was not something to which the British working men and women would naturally turn, Croft claimed, due to socialists' hostility toward religion, marriage ties, and the monarch. Socialism had experienced a successful reception that, Croft concluded, emanated from the economic and moral malaise at present within the country. "Working men would turn to anything which they were told would improve their condition and give them comfort and work." It followed, Croft argued, that Socialism could not be fought with merely a negative retort. Such a response would not capture the imagination and vitalize the hopes of the working classes. It was free trade that had pushed Britain into the social and economic recesses within which she now found herself, and it would be tariff reform, protectionism, and imperial preference that would raise her up from such depths. "The time had now come," he argued, when Britain "must look after the employment of the people, when they must broaden the basis of taxation, and their first duty was to burst open that door which never ought to have been bolted against their loyal fellow countrymen."[67]

Throughout 1906 and 1907, Croft was unfailing in his criticism of the Campbell-Bannerman ministry, particularly attacking the government's Education Bill, army reform proposals, and its propensity to consider some species of an Irish appeasement policy. However, in 1908 with the ascendancy of Asquith as prime minister, the government adopted a Licensing Bill, which sought the elimination of thirty thousand public houses, as a sop to the temperance sentiment within the nonconformist forces. Although Conservatives quickly denounced the proposed legislation as confiscatory, for Croft the bill did more than just violence to his political philosophy; it had potential ramifications for his own economic status. It followed that early on he condemned the bill as "robbery," noting "that he was a large employer of labour in the malting industry employing 200 or 300 people" and that his "profits were narrowed so fine that this Bill meant closing down."[68] Nevertheless, the proposed legislation produced unintended political benefits for Croft as he entered into closer relations with certain industrial interests. As if holding a special brief for the trade, he urged them "to fight for their business lives."[69] He was able to motivate politically an otherwise benign business association when, claiming to speak for the industry, he admonished the government and country that there were over 1.5 million employed in the allied trades, with an unambiguous reference to their electoral strength.[70]

Speaking in Hertfordshire, he described the bill as "robbery, Socialistic, contrary to the teachings of the Christian religion, and contrary to every kind of British justice." Finally, he charged it "was a blow to the freedom of the working classes. A man who walked three miles on a Sunday had just as much right to have a glass of beer as the rich man who had only to walk three steps to his cellar to get a glass of wine."[71]

A few days later, Croft shifted the campaign to Bournemouth where he and fellow Confederate Edward Goulding addressed a massive demonstration and vigorously denounced the "grandmotherly legislation."[72] These several provincial rallies culminated on 27 September 1908 in a national demonstration of sixty thousand to seventy thousand in Hyde Park which was addressed by John Gretton, MP, Major Leslie Renton, H. C. Westgate, and Croft.[73] Invigorated by the victory of George Renwick, a tariff reform and antilicensing candidate at the Newcastle by-election on 25 September, Croft railed against the "deceitful, confiscating and iniquitous Bill." Although he expressed sympathy for the objectives of temperance, he argued that public houses were not responsible for drunkenness. Instead "the thing which drives men to excessive drink is misery, hunger, and lack of settled employment." Such conditions will not be ameliorated by increasing the number of unemployed, which he charged would be the consequences of the bill.[74] However, notwithstanding the king's support of the bill, on 27 November it was defeated in the House of Lords by a vote of 272 to 96.

The antilicensing campaign was not merely a distraction from the Confederacy's campaign of party purification. For Croft it added to the definition of his political and philosophical underpinnings. Although he seemed to be an anomaly with his advocacy of an aggressive state activism in reference to tariff reform, he represented orthodox conservatism with his defense of private property as manifested by his opposition to the Licensing Bill. However, the state activism to which Croft subscribed was an activism to define the overall economic system within which property operated; that is, the state possessed the right, authority, and responsibility to structure the playing field and set the rules. Through the construction of the economic system, Croft believed, the state was able to protect the kingdom and empire and concurrently provide an arrangement by which all classes would benefit. Although he never considered anything resembling a classless society, he did envision a state that designed, facilitated, and then refereed a cooperative arrangement and relationship between the classes. Croft merged twentieth-century expectations with a degree of nineteenth-century paternalism by arguing that the economic elite, be they the landed aristocracy or industrial captains, had the social responsibility as well as the moral and political authority to dominate the cooperative arrangement. The importance of his cooperativism was its envisioned ability to extinguish class tension and conflict. It followed that the state itself would then benefit not only from the economic and social stability provided by protectionism and imperial preference but would be given a significant degree of international security through an economic and strategic cohesion of the empire.

The bright lights of the tariff reform wing—particularly Remnant, Goulding, Winterton, Lee, and Bonar Law—began to show an interest in Hampshire politics as a result of Croft's activities. Although the antisocialist theme added new excitement and urgency, Bonar Law, for one, feared "that all this talk about Socialism might have the effect of making the weak kneed among our leaders use it as an excuse for shelving the fiscal question."[75]

In early September 1907, Lord Turnour's father, the eighth Earl Winterton died, and Turnour, who now succeeded to the Irish peerage as the ninth Earl Winterton, was occupied with overseeing settlement of the estate. When he returned to active politics, he echoed Croft's views. "We were in reality fighting on two fronts as we were attacking not only the Radical and Socialist Free Traders but also our weaker brethren in the Conservative Party who still considered Mr. Chamberlain to be their enemy and regarded with disapproval Mr. Balfour's advance toward his policy." He noted that the radicalized tariff reformers had become quite active in the autumn of 1907, and he concedes "that our methods of elimination in the constituencies of Conservative undesirables on the Tariff issue were often severe and even brutal." He also revealed that although "we younger ones did the work," the more senior members of the tariff reform wing were accomplices to the purge program of the Confederates.[76]

In October 1907, shortly after the return of Croft and Winterton, the Confederacy initiated a new campaign, this time targeting Lord Henry Bentinck, the Conservative candidate for South Nottingham. The Confederates sought to compel Bentinck to declare for tariff reform. Bentinck had been warned that his position in Nottingham "was to be threatened." He had been given copies of correspondence between the Confederates and the Nottingham Liberal Unionist Association in which the latter organization was encouraged to pressure Bentinck into accepting the tariff reform program.[77] Such audacious interference outraged Bentinck's brother, the premier landowner and peer in Nottinghamshire, the duke of Portland, who naturally enjoyed unobstructed access to the party leadership. His Grace protested to the duke of Sutherland, president of the Tariff Reform League, and to Goulding, the secretary, but afterward concluded that "it was all to no effect and the so called Confederates intend to continue their cause."[78]

Frustrated, Portland registered his complaints with Balfour. Thereafter, on 23 October, Balfour wrote to Austen Chamberlain, noting that Portland was an extremely important member of the party and that it was folly for the Confederacy to quarrel with him. Balfour then professed to have only a "very vague idea as to who the 'Confederates' are, but whoever they may be if they are acting in other constituencies, and towards other important members of the Party, as they are acting in Nottingham towards Portland, they seem to me to be doing a very ill service to the cause of Fiscal Reform as well as Unionism." Balfour conceded that "a great change has manifested itself within the past year" but argued that party unity was now the important goal. Without it the party will not gain office and tariff reform will not be carried through, and it is the Confederates who will be responsible.[79] Although Balfour clearly knew who the principal members of the Confederacy were, in anticipation of the upcoming Conservative party annual conference, he perhaps thought it wiser not to push the matter and risk a tariff reform rebellion at the conference.[80]

Chamberlain responded with an ingenious deception which he then advanced to trap Balfour. Chamberlain claimed that he did not know how much he could do, "for whatever the 'Confederates' are, they are not the Tariff Reform League. I have never been able to learn their names, nor can I find that they have any organisation or headquarters." He described them as a "small knot of men who are dissatisfied with the T.R.L. & with me & other of its leaders because we have not been willing to engage in or to countenance a general attack on Free Food Unionists." Although it did not constitute a major revelation, he conceded that "I learned that Leo Maxse is one of their leaders. Maxse is my personal friend as he is yours but I have so little political influence with him as you have, & can do nothing in that quarter." Chamberlain then promised to "communicate with Ridley and Goulding & do my best to prevent or to stop, if it has already begun, any action by the T.R. League at Nottingham which would be offensive to the Duke."[81]

Chamberlain exploited the opportunity innocently provided when Balfour appealed for unity. Chamberlain was now able to level charges against the free traders themselves for frustrating party unity, which he naturally claimed was his primary goal. He claimed the free traders had done nothing

4: Croft, the Confederates, and the Balfour Question (1907) 83

to promote the party. He attacked the duke of Devonshire, Lord George Hamilton, and particularly George Bowles who not only refused to support the party's policy on tariff reform but who had previously attacked the elder Chamberlain in the name of Balfour.[82] In an effective turnabout, Chamberlain cornered both Balfour and Bowles by suggesting that Balfour could not expect Chamberlain to use his influence among the radical tariff reformers to protect Bowles against the natural consequences of his own disloyalty. He further outmaneuvered Balfour by suggesting that the leader could do more to ensure that the party was unified around fiscal reform. Thus, when necessary it would be able to go successfully to the country and would then be able to implement tariff reform as soon as it regained office. Chamberlain concluded by articulating that the best policy to which the party should subscribe would be to prevent any free traders from being adopted by any constituency in the future, suggesting he was prepared to grant amnesty to the present free traders so long as they did not obstruct policy. Balfour was brilliantly checked.[83]

Lord Ridley responded with the same lack of candor exercised by both Balfour and Chamberlain.[84] "The League, of course, maintains its absolute right to do what it likes in the way of educating electors." And, he continued, "we cannot be responsible for what other people may do; and . . . I believe that there has been some interference in that constituency on the part of a body called the Confederates. I don't know who these people are: but have reason to believe they came into existence mainly because the T.R.L. was not militant enough. . . . It is obvious that we cannot control these people."[85] Balfour was without the instruments to take further action.[86]

Winterton records that on 14 November 1907 the Confederates and other advanced tariff reformers "assembled in force at the annual conference of the Conservative Party, held in Birmingham . . . prepared to take aggressive action if Mr. Balfour disappointed us. In fact we found nothing with which to quarrel in what he said."[87] Balfour was greatly influenced by the arguments for unity and fiscal reform—not to mention the political necessity—set forth in Chamberlain's 24 October 1907 letter. As a result he took another long step toward the Confederacy's vision of tariff reform and imperial unity by calling for the safeguarding of British trade and industries as well as calling for colonial preference. Balfour finally found himself incapable of doing anything but embracing Henry Chaplin's resolution that proclaimed tariff reform as the party's first constructive policy. Reform of the fiscal system was called for in an effort to broaden the basis of taxation, to safeguard industries from unfair competition, and to strengthen Britain's position in foreign markets. These three elements then provided the requisite foundation for the subsequent establishment of preferential commercial arrangements with the colonies.[88]

While politely applauding Balfour's conversion, Croft issued the Confederacy's response:

Mr. Balfour asked us at Birmingham not to "Court-martial" or "examine" those who are not prepared to follow his Fiscal lead, and our immediate answer is naturally forthcoming that the "Free Fooders" will be once more most welcome within our ranks if they will be prepared to sink their "minor" differences . . . and will pledge themselves in future to vote with their party on the Fiscal Question, in order to secure the success of the Unionist Party. . . . I am only asking of the little group who cannot now number more than a dozen members of the House of Commons to extend that loyalty to their party and their chief . . . and surely it is not too much to ask their support for one policy which, as Mr. Balfour has told us, really inspires enthusiasm within our ranks. If the Free Fooders are still blind to the feelings of the party and would still destroy their friends rather than establish the policy of Imperial Preference, then I would remind all Unionists that some eighteen or twenty of these gentlemen are seeking election or re-election and that twenty cross votes means forty in a division, or, in other words, the probable defeat of our party in the House of Commons.[89]

The *Morning Post* took its lead from Croft and on 20 November stated that although "there need be no excommunication," nevertheless "when elections come round we trust that every Free Trade Candidate . . . will be opposed by a Tariff Reformer. By this means alone can a certain Tariff Reform majority be secured."[90]

As 1907 drew to a close, the first stage of the Confederate program had been accomplished, because Balfour and the tariff reform movement appeared to be marching in unison. To assist in carrying out the second stage, the purge of the free traders, Balfour's Birmingham program became the test for Conservative orthodoxy. Croft now viewed the free traders as being on the run, and the Confederates were not far behind, "showing their teeth, in cases where Free Trade Unionists are being suggested as Parliamentary candidates."[91]

5
Croft, the Confederates, and Political Cannibalism (1908–1909)

> After six years of strenuous fighting and magnificent loyalty of East Hertfordshire Tariff Reformers to their cause, the path has been cleared to victory, and a square fight will be fought between Tariff Reform and Socialism.
> —Henry Page Croft, 18 October 1909

With the Balfour question seemingly satisfied during the last days of 1907, the rebels could now turn to the second stage of their campaign. The free traders were no longer able to appeal to Balfour for protection, and this allowed Croft and the Confederates to wage a devastating campaign against the exposed and vulnerable free traders. This new generation of radical Conservatives had embraced a new approach to political action. These rebels were no longer content to abide by the gentlemanly politics when, in their view, the future of the nation, empire, and party was at stake.

The new year began with the Confederacy intensifying the pressure on Lord Henry Bentinck. The Confederates let it be known that Conservative free traders would do the party the most good by stepping down, and the Confederates were bent on bringing it about if they did not step down voluntarily.[1] In late January 1908, Bentinck capitulated and accepted the Birmingham program to secure his local association's endorsement for Nottingham South.[2] The Confederates next suggested that they would persuade Captain J. A. Morrison, Conservative candidate for Nottingham East, to proclaim his support for Balfour and the Birmingham program.[3] The Confederates claimed that Morrison had never truly come to terms with tariff reform, and now he promptly did.[4] As the Confederates focused upon Morrison, Robert Cecil was again put on alert that they were preparing to put twenty tariff reformers up against the party's remaining free traders, and, in particular "they intend to use an extra effort to make sure that [Cecil] shall not be returned."[5]

In light of these new attacks, Cecil was quite anxious in his complaint to Walter Long,[6] claiming that "events are moving so fast that every day produces something new, the Confederacy movement is evidently developing fast." Cecil feared that the attack on Morrison "reveals a new danger—or one I had overlooked. It seems to be part of the policy of the Fiscal fanatics to refuse to allow any Unionist to stand who does not accept their fiscal policy." He denounced Croft's program to purify the party as suicidal.[7] Although a close friend who often regretted Confederate tactics, Long reminded Cecil that the constituencies were becoming more and more committed to tariff reform candidates.[8] Although he had consistently extended support and sympathy to Cecil, much to the annoyance of the tariff reformers, Long nevertheless dismissed Cecil's complaints. Long stressed that it was just not realistic to expect the party to proscribe the Confederacy from spreading its doctrines in a constituency occupied by a free trader.[9]

Another free trader, G. S. Bowles, could find little comfort when he approached the Central Office in December 1907 in an effort to avoid the difficulties he experienced the previous summer. To his dismay, Bowles was informed that he would enjoy official party support at Norwood only if he subscribed to the Birmingham program.[10] Pressure from the Confederates and other radical tariff reformers had succeeded in converting the Central Office as it was reflected in Acland Hood's position that he would not use the party's Central Office to support the free traders. He pointed out that the free traders would either fail to support or actively oppose the party's policy once the party regained office. In was quite simple, he told Sandars, "the laggards refuse to accept the official Party Policy as laid down by its recognized chief" and therefore cannot expect the party's support.[11]

At about the same time, the president of the Norwood branch of the Tariff Reform League was summoned to the Constitutional Club where a "number of wealthy persons who, calling themselves 'confederates,' have resolved, at whatever risk, to start and pay for Tariff Reform candidates in all seats whose candidate is not satisfactory on Tariff Reform." Because the Constitutional Club was known to be aggressively tariff reform, Bowles saw a Confederate behind every tariff reformer. In "accordance with the wishes of the Central Office," the local association then provocatively turned against Bowles.[12] Always defiant, Bowles declared that he would resist the interference by the Confederates.[13] A few days later, the Metropolitan Division of the National Union of Conservative and Constitutional Associations, under the influence of Confederacy persuasion, agreed to support no candidate who was not prepared to embrace the Birmingham program unconditionally.[14]

Notwithstanding Cecil's protests, even Long, who desperately wished to accommodate his friend, could not withstand Confederacy pressure. As a result he renewed his admonition to Cecil. "It is quite evident that the constituencies are becoming more and more determined to have Tariff Reform candidates. . . . This is," he continued, "the action of the constituencies themselves and is not in any way directed by the Central Office or the Leaders."[15] Cecil therefore took the step of warning Balfour that it was the intention of the Confederates, naming Remnant, Winterton, Goulding, Burgoyne, and Maxse specifically, "to run candidates against anyone they consider a free trader."[16] In a letter to Chamberlain, Goulding claimed to hold guarantees for £600 to assist any tariff reform candidate willing to contest the East Marylebone seat.[17]

The Confederates had succeeded in isolating the free traders and were now pushing them into an abyss. For the next several weeks, the prominent free traders, Salisbury, Robert and Hugh Cecil, Lord Cromer, John St. Loe Strachey, G. S. Bowles, and Arthur Elliot debated their dilemma. They vacillated between fighting or seeking a compromise that they hoped could be negotiated through Walter Long. The former option would include running candidates against tariff reformers. At times the free traders, revealing their personal anxiety and desperation, threatened "open war" if Balfour refused to repudiate the Confederates.[18] In January 1908 "feelers" were put out within the free trade camp in an effort to measure support for the creation of a "centre" party.[19] There existed considerable interest among some free traders to establish "a centre party of Free Traders to which all moderates can rally to fight Socialism and defend Free Trade."[20] In addition, they specifically considered the merits and ramifications of running William Ormsby-Gore against Edward Goulding in an upcoming by-election at Worcester.[21]

In mid-March 1908, Robert Cecil received reports that the Confederates intended to challenge him at East Marylebone, joining Bowles at Norwood and Abel Henry Smith at East Hertfordshire as the prominent targets of Confederacy attacks.[22] One report even suggested that twenty-three Conservative free traders were to be opposed. These reports provoked cries of "stab in the back" from Hugh Cecil.[23] Croft promptly responded to Hugh Cecil's accusation. He characterized Cecil's whining as an "appeal to moderate tariff reformers to save him from being stabbed in the back in order that he may cut the throats of all tariff reformers." Can the Confederates be blamed, Croft asked, for seeking to disarm the free-fooders while there is still time?[24] Even *The Times* was unsympathetic to Cecil's disingenuous complaints. If Conservative voters of East Marylebone and Norwood "desire upon the next opportunity to find candidates who represent their views more exactly, they are merely exercising an elementary constitutional right. . . . The voters in every case have the right to vote for whom they please." *The Times* defended the Confederates as merely trying "to stir up voters in various constituencies to choose tariff reform candidates. Such proselytizers are entirely within their right," which, it pointed out, was indistinguishable from Cecil's own efforts to push opinion in another direction.[25]

By early March, Robert Cecil was again feeling pressure from the Confederates.[26] Since early January, he had appealed vigorously for Balfour to intervene and put an end to the Confederacy's campaign of excommunication and purification. Balfour, recognizing his own vulnerability, nevertheless remained conspicuously silent while the Confederates' campaign gained intensity. Cecil even tried to appeal to Balfour through the earl of Selborne and his son, Viscount Wolmer.[27] Nevertheless, Balfour reminded Selborne, who was an unabashed imperialist, that the local constituency associations were absolutely free to adopt a candidate with whom they considered themselves to be in agreement. The responsibility of selecting or deselecting a candidate rested with the association.[28] Cecil complained specifically about Goulding's amendment, which he blasted as being "moved and seconded by Confederates"; it was an undisguised attempt to flush out and isolate the remaining Conservative free traders.[29] The free traders were now convinced that "the official leaders of the Party have joined the Confederacy."[30]

In what might best be described as desperation, Cecil constructed an arrangement, thereafter known as the "Marylebone pledge," whereby the East Marylebone Conservative association and the Central Office agreed to support him in the next general election. In consideration for their concession, he agreed that if the next Conservative government introduced a protectionist budget that he could not support, then he would resign and submit the issue for an electoral determination by his constituency. Cecil, however, was unable to persuade Balfour and the Central Office, who were under the keen gaze of the Confederates, to extend a comparable concordat to the other free traders, particularly Bowles and Smith.[31] Cecil again appealed to Balfour: "The Tariff Reformers are pressing home the attack in several constituencies as for instance, against Abel Henry Smith where I see Winterton has been down making a strong speech against him. It is quite plain," he told the party leader, that the Confederates "reason to make us either fight or fly." Cecil warned that "I have no doubt we shall choose to fight."[32] On 13 April 1908, the Norwood Conservative Council declared that they expected G. S. Bowles to vote with the Conservative party and Balfour even on fiscal questions and should he fail to do so the Council would withdraw their endorsement of him at the next election.[33] Notwithstanding this ultimatum, Bowles held tough and refused to recognize any obligation to comply with the resolution.[34] In the face of Balfour's silence, Cecil made one last appeal to Walter Long. "Is it impossible for you to intervene on their [Bowles and Abel Smith] behalf if they give the Marylebone pledge?"[35] It produced no response.

Croft scoffed at "all this talk about stabbing in the dark, and moonlighting," describing the Confederacy as an association of personal friends who are committed to promoting tariff reform and unity of the empire. He denied that they act unilaterally. The Confederacy took action at the request of the constituency, and it was understood that the constituency, although represented by a free trader, now wanted a tariff reformer. Because unionism

5: Croft, the Confederates, and Political Cannibalism (1908–1909) 89

implied unity of the empire and the Conservatives stood for defense of the empire, "how can an Imperial Party tolerate within its ranks men whose policy would destroy the Empire?"[36] Lord Winterton added to Croft's demand that the party must be purged of such apathetic imperialists by warning that "if the minority did not come round others might be found to take their places. . . . The time had gone when any man should remain in the party when he was clearly out of sympathy with the policy of his leader and with the first great constructive policy of its platform."[37]

In addition to London, Norwood, and East Marylebone, Croft's focus was on East Hertfordshire where he reminded Conservatives that the Birmingham pledge had made tariff reform the first constructive work of the party. Accordingly, it remained the obligation of the electors to ensure that their representative was a loyal supporter.[38] At a large tariff reform rally in Hertford, Croft noted that they had all been waiting to hear what Smith had to say about the Birmingham program and whether he would support the leader of the Conservative party. Under the influence of Croft, the Hertford tariff reformers pledged themselves to vote for no candidate who had not accepted the Balfour's Birmingham pledge.[39] This pledge was thereafter pressed by Croft and the Confederates throughout their campaign against the free traders.

The full political determination of the party's radicalized right wing can best be demonstrated by Croft's campaign against Abel Henry Smith, the Conservative MP for East Hertfordshire.[40] The "take no prisoners" approach suggests that segments within the party were shedding the nineteenth-century style, tenor, and approach to politics. The activities of Croft and the Confederacy demonstrate that a radicalized quarter of the party sought to make a determined bid to define a conservative ideology and to construct a more modern party. The radical Conservatives considered both actions critical in meeting the domestic and international challenges that the party, country, and empire now faced. This radicalized sector became focused on a set of intense political beliefs and suffered from no hesitation to sacrifice wobblers, no matter how senior, distinguished, or pedigreed. An examination of the struggle between Croft and Smith, which concurrently represented the conflict between the Confederacy and free trade Conservatives, provides a greater understanding of struggles within the party's constituency associations as well as the ongoing dynamics within Edwardian conservatism and the crisis from which the party suffered in the years before 1914.

Notwithstanding the struggle between Croft and Smith, which as noted concurrently represented the conflict between the Confederacy and free trade conservatism, historians have had more interest in the tariff reform fight involving Robert Cecil, primarily due to his famous name, ancestry, and even his subsequent positions of prominence in British politics.[41] It has been suggested by one historian that "since Cecil and Bowles were perhaps the two most articulate and obstinate of the free fooders, the pressure on Abel Smith, whom Maxse's *National Review* considered 'an insignificant and inarticulate member' is less understandable."[42] As a result of such dismissive treatment, Croft's relentless campaign against Smith has gone unexamined and disregarded. This neglect has caused one historian to suggest that the Confederates were ineffective and may even have degenerated into being "the protagonist of compromise and the opponent of proscription" and that the movement signaled no important development in Conservative party politics.[43] This neglect, however, does not diminish the significance of Croft's tariff reform activities and his campaign for ideological and party purity in East Hertfordshire.

Croft had promoted tariff reform both nationally and in East Hertfordshire since the summer of 1903. During the same period, Smith remained the principal obstruction to Croft's attempts to purify the East Hertfordshire Conservative party and convert the constituency to the idea of aggressive imperial reform. In his attempt to purge the local Conservative party of free traders, Croft faced an eminently popular politician who had long represented the constituency and whose father had represented it before him. His popularity was both personal and political as he was an effective representative for the constituency. Unlike Robert Cecil and Bowles, who were true carpetbaggers in their constituencies, Smith and his family had long enjoyed substantial ties to East Hertfordshire where he owned fourteen thousand acres. Further, Smith had an impressive array of national and local political allies, including the marquess of Salisbury and Walter Long.[44] He had extensive support and an organization within the district whereas the support and organization enjoyed by Cecil in East Marylebone and Bowles in Norwood were extremely tenuous and shifting. As distinguished from the East Marylebone and Norwood contests, where Cecil and Bowles merely packed up and sought refuge in Blackburn with its well-recognized free trade sympathies, the struggle between Croft and Smith was to be fought to an unambiguous conclusion. The determination of the founder of the Confederates represented the political resolve of a new generation of Conservative activists who were willing to sever questionable members to preserve the integrity of an idea and the purity of the party.

The first wound, initially slight but suggesting further problems, was inflicted on Smith on 4 April 1908 when the Bishop's Stortford Conservative and Liberal Unionist Association, with close tariff reform sympathies and ties to Croft, voted to support Smith only if he gave the Marylebone pledge and thus agreed to resign if he was unable or unprepared to support the Birmingham program.[45] At about this same time, the Bishop's Stortford branch of the Tariff Reform League sent Smith a set of interrogatories designed to clarify his views on fiscal reform; the tariff reformers then met on 11 April to consider his unsatisfactory replies. Led by Reginald Mortimer,

5: Croft, the Confederates, and Political Cannibalism (1908–1909) 91

a close ally of Croft, three hundred members resolved to support only an aggressive tariff reformer.[46]

Smith rallied his supporters for the annual meeting of the council of the East Hertfordshire Conservative and Unionist (EHCU) Association held on 14 April. Smith asserted that he believed the best policy to be one of "freedom of negotiation and the further discussion of financial relations with the colonies." However, he remained adamantly opposed to the taxation of food and raw materials.[47] According to reports fed to the press by Sir George Faudel-Phillips, his most important local supporter, it was announced that Smith retained the association's support.[48] R. B. Croft, supported by Croft and Mortimer, nevertheless moved a resolution that would require any Conservative candidate to give unqualified subscription to the party's Birmingham program.

Anticipating such a tactic, Smith's supporters responded with an amendment "that this Council recognizes that Mr. Abel Smith had adhered to the pledges he gave before the last election, and desires to express its confidence in him." Passage of the amendment constituted a tactical setback for Croft.[49] In light of Smith's position on the Birmingham program, reports quickly circulated that the Confederates intended to challenge Smith for the East Hertfordshire seat at the next election. It was further hinted in reports that at least four tariff reformers had stepped forward as candidates.[50]

By the summer of 1908, Croft returned to East Hertfordshire with unrestrained criticism of Smith. Croft took pains to point out the curious silence of their member.[51] In early November Robert Cecil recognized, with ominous resignation, that "the Tariff Reform season has begun." He received additional reports that he would be challenged for his East Marylebone seat, and he noted that "in Hertfordshire too A. H. Smith is in trouble and so is Bowles in Norwood."[52] Cecil wrote to his wife, "it seems incredible that I can remain in the . . . Party much longer."[53]

Faced with a new wave of attacks by the Confederates, Cecil warned the chief whip, Acland Hood, that such political tactics as those employed by the Confederates would have a devastating effect on public debate and British politics. "This method of potential warfare . . . will certainly be used by any other clique who may take a particularly strong view on any question of the day." Cecil even feared the adoption of "tariff reform methods to Women's Suffrage or even to Church questions." When this occurs, he admonished the chief whip, "you will have to look to a very different kind of men to fill the benches of the House of Commons," which is precisely what the Confederates hoped to accomplish by their campaign. Nevertheless, Cecil appealed to Acland Hood, "there can be no question that the Central authorities of the Party could put a stop to the whole system directly, if they chose." He strongly urged that "an intimidation" be conveyed "to the Confederates, if that be their name, that unless they abandon their methods all together the Leader of the Party would denounce them openly and by name would put an end to them directly." Otherwise, Cecil hinted, "it will be necessary for those who feel strongly the necessity of keeping politics as pure as possible to take action for themselves."[54]

Acland Hood, by now having lost his patience, responded that neither he nor Balfour would denounce these aggressive tariff reformers by name. "The situation is this. The Leader of the Party states his adherence to a certain policy in which he is clearly supported by the great majority of the Party." Rebuking Cecil he continued, "You and your friends do not agree with that policy—what you ask is that the Leader of the Party is to denounce by name in public those who accept his policy and are doing their utmost to support him in order to shield those who refuse to accept his policy. Surely this is '*reductio ad absurdum*.' "[55] Cecil brought the exchange to an end: "It is clear that we view the action of the Confederates from such different standpoints that it is I fear no use to continue the correspondence." He then chided the chief whip for holding that "the only thing of importance is to secure the unquestioning obedience of all members of the party to the policy of the leaders whatever it may be." Cecil warned that "if the Confederacy methods are to be a regular part of the machinery to secure party discipline . . . or even to secure the success of a particular policy it seems to me quite clear that no man of intelligence and independence will care to remain long in political life."[56]

As had Cecil, soon Smith began to feel the heat being turned up on the free traders. On 7 November 1908, he wrote to Sir George Faudel-Phillips, chairman of the East Hertfordshire Conservative association, concerned about the meetings being held in various parts of East Herts to discuss Smith's position on tariff reform. He proclaimed to be "most anxious to avoid a split" within the Conservative party and to be as conciliatory as he could toward his past supporters, who now "only differ from me on this one question." Accordingly, he sought to preempt any serious Confederacy challenge by unilaterally offering a Marylebone pledge. He announced his intention to support Balfour, but if a future Balfour government introduces a fiscal measure that he cannot support, then he will resign and submit the issue to a by-election. Of course he expected that in consideration the radical tariff reformers in East Herts will not sponsor or support a rival Conservative candidate.[57] His proposal was promptly conveyed to a hastily summoned executive committee of the E.H.C.U Association, and it was accepted by a vote of nineteen to two. The executive committee then distributed the letter to the party's several polling district associations for their endorsement.[58]

It was Smith's announcement, intended to be a preemptive move, that subsequently plunged the Conservative party of East Hertfordshire into a serious unity crisis and that gave Croft the long-awaited opportunity to wage an unrestrained campaign against Smith. With over fifteen branches and by now thirty-one hundred members, the East Hertfordshire Tariff Reform

5: Croft, the Confederates, and Political Cannibalism (1908–1909) 93

federation had considerable influence. With Croft as the engine of the tariff reform movement in the county, the tariff reformers held equally considerable command in the local politics. Croft and his troops were now in a position to purge the Conservative free trader from the local party.

For its part Smith's letter provoked a prompt response from the tariff reformers when on 9 November the Bishop's Stortford Conservative Club backed away from Smith, reminding him it would only support a fully committed tariff reformer.[59] At Ware, the Croft-dominated local Conservative association denounced the executive committee's support for Smith. Following Bishop's Stortford, the Ware members then voted to support a subscriber to the Birmingham program. The Hoddesdon and Broxbourne Unionist Association promptly followed the direction of Ware and Bishop's Stortford.[60] In the wake of Smith's letter, on 26 November the executive committee of the East Herts Tariff Reform League, followed promptly by the Ware branch, reaffirmed their intention to support only a committed tariff reformer at the next general election.[61]

Croft took the occasion to level a blast at Smith, claiming that the member for East Hertfordshire had never supported Balfour on the fiscal question and that as recently as April 1908, Smith failed to stand up for the Birmingham policy. Denouncing the Marylebone pledge, Croft argued that "it must occur to every intelligent political observer that no greater blow could be struck . . . than the simultaneous resignation" of a dozen free traders that would probably present itself at the time of the budget. Such a resulting "miniature general election . . . could result in nothing but disaster, and must inevitably mean the loss of the majority of these seats and possibly the defeat of the Government."[62] Croft's offensive produced a supportive letter from Joseph Chamberlain. Applauding Croft's letter in the *Morning Post,* the "chief" wrote that it was inappropriate for Smith to demand the right to represent the constituency on Smith's terms and that the Conservative electors should follow Croft's advice and reject Smith's proposed compromise.[63] Another Confederate, "Paddy" Goulding, concurred that Smith must be compelled to accept preference.[64]

Smith still remained vulnerable as East Hertfordshire Conservatives now squared off into two camps, with Smith's supporters concentrated at Hertford and Croft's tariff reformers controlling the remaining districts.[65] In early December the Chesthunt and Walthamcross Unionist Association followed Croft's lead and declared their support for only avowed tariff reformers.[66] On 14 December the executive committee of the Bishop's Stortford branch of the Tariff Reform League disassociated itself from Smith.[67] The Sawbridgeworth Conservative and Liberal Unionist Association followed suit a day later.[68] The next week the Hoddesdon, Broxbourne, and Wormley branch announced their rejection of Smith's proposition and urged the adoption of a tariff reform candidate as soon as possible.[69] On 21 December, Smith's faction responded at the meeting of the E.H.C.U. Association, which had been called under the presidency of one of his principal allies, Alfred Baker, to consider the member's offer of a Marylebone pledge. Representing the split within the East Hertfordshire Conservative association, the executive committee's original acceptance of Smith's terms was endorsed by the Hertford branch one hundred fifty to twenty.[70]

This meeting, which had been arranged by Smith's friends, provoked a strongly caustic response from Croft, revealing the seriousness of the schism in East Hertfordshire. Croft charged that, according to reports he had received, the association chairman, Alfred Baker, had reduced opposition figures from sixty to twenty and that nearly one half of those present abstained. If the chairman was an advanced tariff reformer as he claimed, Croft queried, then how could he support Smith? The tone of Croft's attack virtually guaranteed a response, as Baker suggested Croft's agitation originated from his intention to stand for East Hertfordshire as a tariff reform candidate, a claim that Croft, in a sequential retort, denied.[71]

On 12 January 1909, the executive committee of the E.H.C.U. Association met to consider the positions taken by the various polling districts. Although the meetings of the polling districts did not seem to be well attended, one report claimed the division of the eight hundred voters favored Smith by only twenty votes. The tariff reformers, on the other hand, promoted their claim that Smith had been rejected by an overwhelming majority of the voters. The results nevertheless suggested that the executive committee's original nineteen to two vote did not authentically represent the overall body of East Hertfordshire Conservatives. A week later the Hoddesdon Polling District Unionist Association, under Croft's influence, resolved to amend the East Hertfordshire executive committee's November report with a condemnation of Smith's position on the fiscal question. The vote, sixty-one to fifty-eight against the proposition, was immediately challenged. The meeting, however, broke up in utter chaos before the tariff reformers could effectively regroup. The executive committee was now faced with a disintegration of party unity, and naturally their greatest fear was that the present conditions would contribute to a Liberal victory at the next general election. Accordingly, on 19 January 1909, the executive committee met again, with thirty-six of its forty-eight delegates present, to consider the unity crisis. It was decided that a special committee should be appointed, and then confer with Smith in an effort to reconcile his position with official party policy. The special committee was instructed to report back to the executive committee on 2 February.[72]

To most outside observers, the precarious situation in which Smith now found himself was clearly the product of the Confederates.[73] The attacks on Cecil, Bowles, and now Smith were being attributed to the Confederates in light of the corresponding articles appearing in the *National Review* and *Morning Post*.[74] The *Daily Mail* denounced the Confederates as "jesuitry."[75] The *Spectator* of 23 January, with little surprise, denounced "the secrecy

5: Croft, the Confederates, and Political Cannibalism (1908–1909) 95

with which the Confederates carry on their operations. Why are they afraid of coming into the light? Why do they object to its being known who are their members, and why do they conceal the nature of their Confederacy? Is it because they are ashamed of the way it works, or of some of its members?"

Although the East Hertfordshire crisis had by now come under national scrutiny, Croft still continued to avoid personal criticism.[76] One local commentator sought to correct this omission and educate the public about Croft's "intentions in East Herts. . . . In the case of Mr. H. P. Croft and Mr. Abel Smith there need be no misunderstanding. So long ago as 1904 Mr. Croft has turned on to harass Mr. Abel Smith. I defy Mr. Croft to deny this."[77] In a state of utter frustration, the local free trade press also sought to flush out the local Confederates. "It may be useful to ask a question. . . . Who are the Confederacy? If they are not ashamed of their proceedings, as they may well be, let them give us their names, and we shall be able to judge their importance."[78] This adverse publicity melted some of the tariff reformers who were in difficult situations, particularly Lord Ridley, who vigorously denied any membership. However, more disingenuously he also denied knowing who they were and that no one on the executive committee of the Tariff Reform League knew their identity.[79]

There could be little doubt that the Confederates, particularly Croft, were using and were known to be using local tariff reform branches to carry out their purge of Conservative free traders.[80] In East Hertfordshire, for instance, the leadership of the tariff reform movement and the Confederacy were one and the same—Henry Page Croft. Somewhat encouraged by press support, the Conservative free traders proclaimed that they would not take Confederate attacks lying down. They promised to support anyone "who may be attacked by that organisation."[81] Hugh Cecil, revealing his utter frustration at not being able to block their offensive, called the Confederacy "a foolish and unimportant body of young men who greatly overestimated their importance in the affairs of the world."[82]

In a unique development, the leaders of the two local East Hertfordshire factions gave extensive newspaper interviews. Sir George Faudel-Phillips, who also served as chairman of the special committee, conceded that Smith's attitude had put the party "in a very difficult position." He even recognized that Smith must "go a little further" and support Balfour and the Birmingham pledge. He further conceded that by adopting any position approaching tariff reform, Smith could easily make East Hertfordshire the most secure seat in the country. R. B. Croft, speaking for the tariff reformers, reminded Sir George that the nearly two thousand members of the East Herts Tariff Reform League were unified in their opposition to Smith, and they will accept nothing less than unconditional subscription to the Birmingham program.[83]

The special committee was composed of two supporters of Smith, Sir George Faudel-Phillips and R. B. Cross, and two tariff reformers, Croft and his father. They met on 25 January 1909 for negotiations with Smith. The object was to gain a meaningful concession from Smith, which would permit the tariff reformers to support his candidature. However, Smith persisted in taking an uncompromising position. In a surprise move, the tariff reformers signaled a willingness to make concessions. R. B. Croft gave Sir George a statement that, if agreed to by Smith, would satisfy the tariff reformers. It provided that if returned at the next election, Smith will support imperial preference, so long as it does not involve the taxation of foreign corn by more than 2s a quarter, and that he will support a retaliatory tariff, providing that it does not exceed 10 percent and is not imposed on raw materials. R. B. Croft explained that the tariff reformers "were extremely anxious . . . to make one last effort to obtain a settlement. We tried to build a golden bridge over which Mr. Abel Smith might cross." Smith agreed to give the proposal his favorable consideration. The conference adjourned with everyone "believing," Croft suggested, "that a happy solution of the problem confronting us had been found."[84]

Immediately after the adjournment, a self-satisfied Croft wrote to Joseph Chamberlain that he had pushed Smith to the point where he was about to agree with the Confederacy's position. "Mr. Smith," he continued, "is taking two days to consider it and . . . may I put you to the great inconvenience of telegraphing whether you accept these terms?" Croft claimed that "this makes all Herts solid and safe."[85] Although he advised Croft to decide for himself, Chamberlain was "inclined to accept the concession and to let Mr. Abel Smith come in under the condition that you name." This, Chamberlain noted, would leave Croft and the Confederates free for other work.[86]

For his part Smith promptly wrote to his principal counsellor, Robert Cecil, with details of the Croft proposals, which he described as being "an extraordinary change of policy!" He informed Cecil that many of his local supporters were very eager for him to accept.[87] Although the local press was encouraged by the prospects of a political compromise in East Hertfordshire, it remained fearful that "if such men as Lord Robert Cecil and Mr. Abel Smith are not counted any longer as Conservatives because they cannot accept a fiscal doctrine which no more than half a dozen years ago had few believers and no defenders of any political weight in this country, what does Conservatism really mean?"[88] Perhaps it was the effect of such comments that pushed Cecil and Smith into an intractable position. Soon after meeting with Cecil, Smith advised the senior Croft that although "I appreciated very much the spirit in which your offer was made, then promised to give it favourable consideration, . . . I very much regret that I cannot see my way to give the pledge relating to Colonial Preference."[89]

The letter was read at a 30 January meeting of the executive committee of the East Herts Tariff Reform League that had been originally summoned to consider an anticipated settlement. With Henry Page Croft presiding, the committee expressed regret over Smith's inability "to accept the extremely

5: Croft, the Confederates, and Political Cannibalism (1908-1909) 97

moderate proposals" and then unequivocally stated "its determination to consider no further concessions." The committee resolved to request the E.H.C.U. Association to take prompt action toward securing a candidate who would unconditionally accept the party policy. In a move that signaled serious consequences, Croft announced that should the executive committee of the E.H.C.U. Association fail to adopt a tariff reform candidate, then the East Hertfordshire Tariff Reform League will sponsor their own candidate for the next election.[90] The executive committee of the E.H.C.U. Association met on 2 February 1909, at which time the special committee reported the results of the failed negotiations. Given Smith's rejection of the tariff reform compromise, R. B. Croft moved that the committee withdraw its support from his candidature. The resolution passed nineteen to sixteen.[91]

Smith responded with matter-of-fact realism. "It is, of course an open secret that I cannot see eye to eye with the Tariff Reformers, and the opposition of theirs is nothing new. I have met with very considerable antagonism from some of the members of this party for the last five years."[92] There was considerable pressure from friends to resign his seat immediately and stand as an Independent Unionist, believing that neither the Liberals nor the tariff reformers could respond to this approach with the timeliness or necessary effectiveness to win an election. He declined but announced that he was severing his connections with the association. He most likely had been briefed about Robert Cecil's communications with Asquith in which Cecil solicited the Liberal party's neutrality in such an election. Although sympathetic to the Conservative free traders, Asquith could not extend such a pledge.[93] Somewhat relieved now that the tension finally had been pierced, Smith asked Cecil to "keep my interests in view, if anything arises with the Liberal party." He then promptly departed for Cannes.[94]

On 24 February 1909 the executive committee of the E.H.C.U. Association met to consider what action should be taken with respect to the Smith controversy now that they had withdrawn their support. Demonstrating the seriousness of the situation, at the outset of the meeting Faudel-Phillips, E. S. Hanbury, treasurer, and Admiral Hastings, the association's secretary and Smith's election agent, announced their resignations. After accepting the resignations, the committee directed the constituency's polling district associations to hold their annual meetings. They were then to select their representatives to attend the annual meeting of the association council which was scheduled to be held on 6 April. The annual council meeting would then address the selection of a candidate.[95]

When word of the 2 February action by the executive committee reached Lord Salisbury, the honorary president of the association, who was in Egypt, responded with a terse protest and his own resignation.[96] With Salisbury's letter public, Croft had no hesitancy about rebuking the county's patriarch. He chastised Lord Salisbury for being "entirely misinformed as to the opinions which are held by Mr. Abel Smith." The loss of confidence experienced in East Herts was because Smith absolutely refused to support the Birmingham policy and that he opposed the safeguarding of industries against unfair competition and preferential imperial commercial arrangements. Further, Croft corrected Salisbury that the tariff reformers had sought to find a middle ground only to be given a negative reply once Smith had consulted with Robert Cecil. "Every effort has been made to conciliate Mr. Smith but it is quite clear that . . . he is going to oppose Mr. Balfour upon . . . the chief constructive policy of the party."[97]

The controversy ripped open a dangerous wound in the East Herts Conservative party as Smith charged that his overthrow was the work of the Confederates, naming Croft as the principal villain.[98] St. Loe Strachey, editor of the free trade *Spectator,* suggested sponsoring a dozen free traders to challenge the most determined tariff reformers, assuming they were all Confederates. This, he believed, should make the tariff reformers equally uncomfortable.[99] By March the free traders were eager to retaliate against Croft. In particular they considered putting up Sir Edward Brotherton, who was somewhat nervous about his own seat in Wakefield, to go to Christchurch and challenge Croft. A Conservative free trader, Percy Thornton, was sent to the constituency in an effort to stir up anti-Croft agitation. However, the free traders were forced to concede that they "have no members there, and it will be hard to move until we have some evidence of some anti-Croft feeling." In the end they were left to decry the fact that Croft's campaign against Smith in East Herts was not known even to the Conservative free traders in Christchurch.[100]

Both camps now prepared for the 6 April 1909 meeting of the E.H.C.U. Association. On 4 March the annual meeting of the Ware Unionist Association endorsed the executive committee's action of 2 February and then urged the council to adopt a fully committed tariff reform Conservative.[101] On 6 March 1909, seventy supporters of Smith held a private meeting to consider the most effective course of action. The initial overtures to the Liberals had now transformed into additional pressure on the free trade Conservative, particularly from E. B. Barnard, the prospective Liberal candidate. Behind the scenes discussions pivoted around the possibility of Smith standing in a by-election with open Liberal support.[102] However, Smith was trying desperately to evade the pressure for this course of action: "My feeling is that the by-election is quite uncalled for and ought to be avoided if possible—especially as I am not physically fit for it at present."[103] Although Smith treated with Joseph "Jack" Pease, Liberal MP, Hugh Cecil pressed for consultations with the prime minister over the possibility of Liberal support for Smith in a by-election. Many of his supporters were fearful of the political ramifications should their prospective alignment with the Liberals become prematurely public.[104]

Smith and his supporters needed to stall the Liberals, particularly Bar-

5: Croft, the Confederates, and Political Cannibalism (1908–1909)   99

nard, without trying their patience, which would provoke a challenge and mean a three-cornered contest. Smith held hope that the 6 April session would produce a reversal of fortunes.[105] The basis for his optimism was found in the fact that the association was to elect a new executive committee prior to the 6 April meeting. Smith optimistically informed Robert Cecil that "the annual meetings here have gone better than I expected and the council is so evenly balanced that no one can foretell the result. I fancy I have a small majority in the new executive committee!"[106] Supporting resolutions such as that issued by the Hertford Conservative association on 16 March also raised Smith's spirits.[107] Although the Hertford association represented the core of his support, he had never even attended one of their meetings until March 1909, after the unity crisis erupted and when his political future was in jeopardy. He addressed the Hertford Conservative with a strongly worded attack on Croft for his role in this episode.[108]

Within a few days, the East Hertfordshire Federation of the Tariff Reform League, representing over three thousand members, endorsed the executive committee's withdrawal of support from Smith. With Croft presiding, the assembly was presented with a letter from their president, Lord Ebury, who conceded the reality that a contest between Conservative free traders and tariff reformers would likely sacrifice the seat to the Liberals. Nevertheless, he continued, this alternative was preferable to the continued presence of a member who refused to sign on to party policy of fiscal and imperial reform.[109] Croft then defended the tariff reformers, explaining that they had gone to great lengths, made significant concessions, in an effort to reach an accord with Smith. No one was more pained than he, Croft submitted, at the failure of the negotiations and the consequential division among East Hertfordshire Conservatives. Revealing a willingness for further accommodation, Croft conceded that if Smith's opposition was limited to the question of food taxation, then it might be feasible to meet him halfway. However, Croft reminded critics, Smith had consistently opposed the party's policy of safeguarding British industries against unfair foreign competition. The tariff reformers, therefore, had been placed in a position of having to fight, and Croft promised that they would fight hard and clean. He held to the belief "that the great bulk of the working classes in East Herts were in favour of Tariff Reform [and] even if the whole house of Cecil threw its weight against them they would not budge from . . . their true course of duty."[110]

A major debate on tariff reform versus free trade was held under the lights of national interest at Caxton Hall, Westminster, on 2 April, and Croft had the responsibility of presenting and defending the tariff reform position.[111] Now under the gaze of the national press and with the concern of the party's leaders, the East Hertfordshire Conservatives reassembled on 6 April.[112] As Croft had feared, the situation became dangerously complicated as the result of the action taken on 6 April by the full council of the E.H.C.U.

Association. Smith's supporters opened with a resolution to set aside the executive committee's original 24 February resolution. Emotions flared during the subsequent discussions. Alfred Baker claimed that Smith was not answerable to the Tariff Reform League but was "responsible only to the association, his constituents, and his conscience." Baker challenged the assembly to point to any specific resolution that Smith had violated. Smith's spokesman was then greeted with derisive groans when he noted that "Abel Smith is a follower of Lord Robert Cecil," giving the assembly the distinct impression that he had dismissed Balfour as his leader. Immediately after the meeting, Smith was asked about this statement, but he refused to commit himself to any representations made at the meeting. He was nevertheless pleased with the results and by the fact that it apparently extinguished the prospects for a by-election.[113]

R. B. Croft sought to rally his forces with an amendment to the Smith resolution, which endorsed the council's earlier action in withdrawing support from Smith. The discussion became heated when Baker admonished the council that "if you do support the Tariff Reformers, you will be . . . promoting an alliance between the Liberal Free Traders and Unionist Free Fooders." The council then voted ninety-four to eighty-nine in favor of Baker's resolution.[114] The vote provoked immediate and angry protests from the tariff reformers. It was charged that five individuals representing Smith had been improperly placed on the council and permitted to vote. Further complicating and aggravating the division was the fact that the representatives from two thirds of the district associations had been issued strict instructions to support the Croft amendment. Regardless of these instructions, most of the delegates defied the directives by either abstaining or voting against the Croft amendment. What the tariff reformers considered as unacceptable and unprincipled conduct further inflamed their emotions.[115] It was also alleged that two votes against the Baker resolution had not been counted, which made the vote at least ninety-one to eighty-nine in favor of Croft's position.[116]

It was apparent that the East Hertfordshire Conservatives were divided over issues of personality as well as principle. Contrary to the circumstances of Cecil in East Marylebone and Bowles in Norwood, Smith and his family held a long association with Hertfordshire. He held substantial property interests in the vicinity; he was well liked personally and was considered to have represented the constituency's interests well. From all indications, the East Hertfordshire Conservatives, including those who locally led Smith's defense, were unabashed fiscal reformers. This high level of support fueled his tenacious struggle to retain the local association's endorsement; it also was the source of his conviction that he would prevail.

Under such circumstances there was little surprise that in the wake of the ninety-four to eighty-nine vote the local Conservative party quickly disintegrated. Almost immediately after the council meeting, the tariff reformers abandoned the existing association.[117] The schism spread down into the local associations. On 15 April the Ware Conservative association applauded their representatives for voting against the Smith resolution and then resolved to cooperate with the East Herts Tariff Reform League to adopt and elect a tariff reformer. One supporter of Smith, who was consistently outnumbered in the internal voting, suggested that the Ware association be dissolved. Croft, in an effort to maintain the tariff reform majority, proposed a requirement that new association members must be elected and not simply enrolled.[118]

On 17 April 1909, R. B. Croft convened a meeting of one hundred thirty delegates for the purpose of establishing a new Conservative organization "to be called the East Herts Constitutional and Unionist Association whose object shall be to secure the registration as voters of all persons holding Unionist and Tariff Reform principles." R. B. Croft was selected chairman of the new East Hertfordshire organization.[119] Henry Page Croft, who was partially occupied in Christchurch, declined leadership of the new body. Reginald Mortimer, a close associate of Croft, was selected as the organization's candidate to contest the East Hertfordshire seat.[120] Accompanied by Croft, Mortimer immediately launched his campaign, speaking to a demonstration of nine hundred supporters in Ware.

The seriousness of the breach among conservatives might be found in a rather callous act of retaliation. In June, Smith expelled the Ware Working Men's Conservative Club from a building he owned, having each member served with a legal notice to quit the premises.[121] Rumors soon spread that a free-trade candidate was being sent to Christchurch to challenge Croft in retaliation for his orchestration of the East Hertfordshire revolt, although the challenge never materialized.[122] Notwithstanding his general optimism over Mortimer's prospects in East Herts, Croft was both disappointed and angered by the Conservative loss at the Attercliffe-Sheffield by-election on 4 May. The official Conservative candidate, a tariff reformer, was challenged at the last moment by a free trade, independent Conservative. The free trader took enough votes away from the official party candidate to allow the Labour candidate to win. After the loss Croft wrote that "it is outrageous that any man . . . should, in opposition to the official association . . . foist himself on the party, for in nine out of ten cases it can only mean defeat of the cause he professes to support." His comments provoked a caustic exchange with Robert Cecil, which did more to reveal their mutual frustration with the present struggle in which conservatives found themselves than to convey anything resembling a reasoned argument.[123]

Although he was faced with increasing demands to commence a serious and full-scale campaign in Christchurch, Croft continued to play an important role in the new East Hertfordshire Constitutional and Unionist Association, particularly since he had invested so much time and energy in an effort to bring about Smith's political destruction. Croft often supported

Mortimer on the platform at important rallies and demonstrations.[124] For his part Smith began his own campaign, often supported on the platform by one of the Cecils.[125]

With two Conservative candidates as well as two purportedly Conservative associations in East Hertfordshire, it was evident that the position of the Conservative Central Office would be crucial. Smith took the initiative, writing to the chief whip in May, in an effort to secure the Central Office's recognition of Smith's candidature. Acland Hood declined, noting that Smith had refused to accept party policy. Smith, however, constructed false hope from the fact that Acland Hood's response did not come out and say bluntly that the Central Office recognized Mortimer and the Croft organization.

The free trade member for East Hertfordshire now called on Lord Salisbury to make inquiries. The situation nevertheless had been determined by the fact that the Central Office failed to notify Smith's association that a conference of association agents was to be held on 1 July 1909. The Central Office sent the necessary notice and invitation to Croft's Conservative association, thus providing it with de facto recognition.[126] Recognizing the political ramification, Salisbury complained bitterly to Acland Hood about this egregious treatment of Smith and the original association.[127] Acland Hood dismissed Salisbury's protests, explaining the old association had no officers because they had all resigned. Accordingly, the invitation was sent to the newly formed association that was represented by Colonel Henry Bowles, a Confederate. Further, "this association has," Acland Hood wrote, "been organised on the lines approved by the National Union and is on a thoroughly representative basis." But more importantly, "it supports the whole policy of the Party and of our Leader. Under these circumstances I do not see how it is possible for the Central Conservative Office or the National Union to decline to recognize it."[128]

Frustrated by the obstinacy of the chief whip, Salisbury now wrote to Balfour complaining that Acland Hood had extended recognition to Croft's new East Hertfordshire Conservative association by inviting it to a central party meeting. Although he also informed Balfour that Acland Hood recognized the new association primarily because it supports the entire party policy relating to fiscal reform, he unfairly diminished Smith's differences with the party policy. Nevertheless, he demanded to know: "Is the old established Unionist Association in East Herts to be recognised as the Unionist Association of East Herts or is it not?"[129]

Consulting with Acland Hood, Balfour was reminded that Smith supported neither the party policy nor the party leader. In addition, Balfour was told that Croft's new organization was "formed for the express purpose of securing the election of a candidate who has undertaken to give unhesitating support to the official policy of the Party and its Leader." The mandate of the Central Office is "to render aid to those Associations which support the official policy of the Party." Accordingly, the Central Office had no alternative but to recognize the new organization that had a modern constitution, was lawfully formed, subscribed to party orthodoxy, represented a substantial number of Conservatives, and was spreading throughout the constituency.[130]

Smith now mistakenly believed that Mortimer and his supporters could easily be persuaded to step aside. It would be necessary for party moderates to step forward, express their support for Smith, and publicly urge Mortimer to retire for the sake of the party and retention of the seat. Only such expressions of support for Smith would cause Balfour to announce publicly his own discontent with the Confederate challenge.[131] This, in turn, would then serve as a call to other moderates to surface and extend their support. Smith, having become rather nervous, decided to make an overture to Balfour and the moderates. He publicly claimed to be a more loyal supporter of Balfour than either Mortimer or the Confederates. He also urged "those who had withdrawn their support from his candidature to reconsider their decision and try at the eleventh hour to come to some understanding whereby they might go to the poll as a united party."[132]

Smith and Salisbury privately circulated a concession that should Smith be returned for East Hertfordshire he would agree not to cast a vote that would endanger Balfour's ministry. However, if he was unable to support a future Conservative budget, with its tariffs and preferences, then he would give Balfour his resignation. Of course, Smith pointed out, this "future action must . . . depend on the attitude of the more reasonable Tariff Reformers." He speculated that "they will come into line all right, if Mr. Balfour does what we hope he will—except the Crofts and a very few others whose support I do not care about."[133] He still thought he would be free not to vote; he would not be required to alter his views; the new association would be persuaded to withdraw Mortimer; and the Central Office would not recognize the new association.[134]

Unfortunately for Smith, Balfour remained aloof in his eventual response to Salisbury. "I understand," Balfour wrote, "that the question has been raised as to my friend Mr. Abel Smith's attitude towards myself as leader." Balfour nevertheless was confident that Smith was a strong Conservative, who will support any future Conservative government that comes into power. By that he clearly meant that Smith was "a supporter who will never permit himself, on account of differences on one particular point, to endanger its existence in a moment of difficulty." Balfour maneuvered around Smith's duplicity and effectively dashed his hopes.[135] The Confederates had been able to persuade the national officials to stiffen their resolve.[136]

Ironically, Britain's political landscape and the political future of the Conservative party were dramatically altered, not by the Conservatives, but by Lloyd George's "people's budget" of 1909. Its impact did not bypass the struggle in East Hertfordshire. Shortly after the introduction of the budget in April 1909, Hugh Cecil solemnly concluded that continued infighting would be disastrous for the party, as it would alienate the "'squire and parson' Tories who are our best friends against the Confederacy."[137] By late summer the tariff reformers at Ware suggested that the choice facing the country was straightforward and unambiguous—socialism or tariff reform.[138]

Faced with the need to confront Lloyd George's budget with a unified Conservative party, reports soon circulated that the warring factions had buried their differences.[139] Without more, the local East Hertfordshire free trade press concluded that pressure from the party leadership had forced the tariff reformers to withdraw and that Smith was now free to defend the seat against the Liberal challenger.[140] *The Times* reported on 16 September that the compact had the sanction of Bonar Law, Austen, and Joseph Chamberlain and was opposed only by Croft and the Confederates, whom *The Times* labeled as "the hot heads on the outskirts of the party who have little political instincts."[141] Both R. B. Croft and Acland Hood responded publicly and adamantly denied that any compromise had been arranged between the tariff reformers and Conservative free traders.[142] Joined by Henry Page Croft, Mortimer also denied that any compact had been or was being considered and that such a suggestion would "stiffen the backs of his most ardent supporters and give them fresh inspiration."[143]

Notwithstanding such protests, with the increasing expectation that an election was on the horizon, pressure now mounted on party officials to resolve the feuds in East Hertfordshire, Norwood, and East Marylebone. In late September 1909, R. B. Croft and the leaders of the new East Hertfordshire Constitutional and Unionist Association received a request to consider the possibility of a compromise with Smith and the local Conservative free traders. The senior Croft set out the minimum terms that must be met before the tariff reformers would accept. Smith must embrace Balfour's Birmingham program, and should he not be able to do so, he must agree to resign his seat. Additionally, he needed to agree not to contest the seat in a subsequent by-election. Smith agreed to all the elements, except that he refused the stipulation "not to come forward as a candidate were an election to follow his resignation."[144]

Compelled to find a resolution of the East Hertfordshire struggle, in early October Acland Hood intervened and summoned representatives from both Croft's new Conservative organization and Smith's faction to London. As speculation increased over a possible general election, the Central Office's anxiety heightened over the likely loss of the East Hertfordshire seat. Accordingly, on 2 October Acland Hood met with the three representatives of Smith and three representatives of Croft's new East Hertfordshire Constitutional and Unionist Association. Acland Hood took the initiative and suggested that if the two factions could not come to terms, then it would be in the best interest of the party for both men to withdraw. Smith still refused

5: Croft, the Confederates, and Political Cannibalism (1908-1909) 105

to entertain a compromise of his position on imperial preference so long as it involved a tax on food.[145]

At about the same time, a special meeting of eighty delegates from the council of the Crofts' East Herts Constitutional Association was held at Hoddesdon. The assembly reaffirmed their unqualified support for Mortimer.[146] On the morning of 7 October, R. B. Croft was summoned to London for an urgent meeting with Acland Hood. Henry Page Croft went in his father's stead and was informed that, at the suggestion of the chief whip, Smith had consented to withdraw, but only if Mortimer agreed to do the same. Smith had finally realized that, notwithstanding his personal popularity among a significant section of East Hertfordshire Conservatives, he would never be able to retain his seat in the face of Croft's determined opposition. On 12 October Acland Hood met with Mortimer, who also agreed to withdraw from the contest for the sake of the party. Acland Hood announced to the public that the only way to settle the conflict in East Herts was for both candidates to withdraw.[147]

The next day Mortimer announced to his associates that he was withdrawing from the East Hertfordshire contest. Smith followed suit within a few days.[148] On learning of the mutual withdrawals, Croft, who was campaigning in Christchurch, wrote triumphantly to the East Hertfordshire tariff reformers that "after six years of strenuous fighting and magnificent loyalty of East Herts Tariff Reformers to their cause, the path has been cleared to victory, and a square fight will be fought between Tariff Reform and Socialism."[149]

Although the original association remained in an irrelevant existence, the new, Croft-dominated East Hertfordshire Constitutional and Unionist Association became the recognized center of conservatism in the constituency, and invitations were soon issued to the other Conservative branches of the original association to join the Croft organization. However, the first task was to find an appropriate candidate to contest the East Hertfordshire seat at the next general election. R. B. Croft urged on Salisbury that Herbert Gibbs be put forward as a candidate satisfactory to both the Crofts and Smith. Smith, however, balked, claiming that Gibbs's nomination would provoke the opposition of Smith's supporters, a sentiment also conveyed directly to Salisbury. Instead it was suggested "that the associations . . . should appoint three representatives to confer together as to a candidate."[150] A selection committee was established that focused on Sir John Fowke Lancelot Rolleston, who had solid ties with the national tariff reform movement as well as to Croft personally. Both had stood on many tariff reform platforms together, and they both had contributed essays to the Confederate publication *New Order,* edited by Lord Malmesbury. Rolleston also had the benefit of having served with Smith in the House of Commons where they both worked on agricultural issues. Rolleston received the blessing of Smith and the Crofts, and on 31 October he was endorsed by a joint assembly of the delegates of both associations.[151]

The withdrawal of Smith from East Hertfordshire represented an unprecedented victory for Croft, the Confederacy, and the rebel right wing of the Conservative party. It provided a victory for the determined, "take no prisoners" politics that Croft and the Confederates practiced. It also exposed the dysfunction that infected the party as it seemed to struggle for a new and energetic program with which to meet the new economic, social, political, and international challenges. The rebels sought to define the ideological orthodoxy with which the party could more effectively meet these challenges. They sought to forge a dynamic and modern party, which would be more capable of advancing constructive programs in defense of the nation and empire. Rather than play the gentlemanly politics of the Cecils, Balfour, and Smith, Croft used the Confederacy to pursue a "scorched earth" strategy of politics with which to press forward his political ideas. Within this period heavily influenced by tariff reform politics, Croft merged a set of determined ideas and principles with an equally determined commitment to political action. To Croft ideas were worth little if they remained ideas. Although nationalism remained the defining feature of Croft's political ideas, he recognized that the sphere within which he must operate to promote his nationalism was changing. He recognized that politics was no longer a gentleman's avocation but was the method and mechanism by which political ideas can ensure the survival of a nation, a people, and an empire. Croft and the Confederates perhaps signaled a transition in British politics.

Croft's Confederate campaign against Smith further demonstrates the extent to which tariff reform and radical conservatism had taken hold in the constituencies and local associations. It also demonstrated the capacity with which the Confederates influenced national party officials and leaders. Arthur Elliot, therefore, was only partially correct when he wrote Lord Cromer in July 1909 that "the Confederates count for little. It is the countenance they get from the Leaders and officials of the Conservative Party that is important."[152]

Campaign literature for the General Election in 1910.

THE "CONFEDERACY."

Waiting For a Unionist Free Trader

The "Confederacy," the "Morning Post" tells us, is an association of Tariff Reform members of Parliament, candidates, and others whose business it is to see that no Unionist Free Trader shall ever be accepted as a Unionist candidate.—*Westminster Gazette,* **January 18, 1908**

ANOTHER INCIDENT OF THE REVOLUTION.

Masked "Confederate": *I arrest you, Lord Hugh in the name of Mr. Balfour.*
Mr. Balfour: *I don't know anything about it, but dare say its all right.*

["We are able to state that the Consevative Central Office will decline to give it's official support to any candidate who does not reservedly support the Leader of the Unionist Party in the policy laid down."—*Morning Post,* **January 19, 1909.**]—*Westminster Gazette,* **January 19, 1909**

6
Imperial Mission, Reveille, and the Call to Action (1910)

> I am an Imperialist first before all those other questions.
> —Henry Page Croft, 11 June 1910

> Croft, and the younger Unionists, feel the faith that is in them leaping up, and clamouring for expression.
> —*Hull Daily Mail,* 1 September 1910

The Conservatives in East Hertfordshire ended their civil war just as the national confrontation over the 1909 "people's budget" took center stage. While the struggle of the budget and its constitutional implications occupied the attention and energies of the Conservative leadership during 1910, Croft continued his effort to keep the focus on the empire. Accordingly, he furthered his political experimentation with two additional entities. Early in the year, he established the Imperial Mission, originally a propaganda enterprise for educating the British public on the imperial issues, but also to keep a steady pressure upon Balfour and the party's leadership. However, Balfour continued to disregard Croft's call for an empire first party program. As a result of his persistent rebuffs, Croft's frustrations over the condition of the Conservative party again pushed him to precipitate rebellious action against Balfour. On 30 August, Croft issued a call for a new Wellington and launched the Reveille movement. This political force initiated a campaign against Balfour that was soon joined by other elements and eventually contributed to Balfour's resignation in November 1911.

On 4 November 1909, the House of Commons passed Lloyd George's budget by a vote of 379 to 149, and at the end of the month, the House of Lords recorded their rejection, 350 to 75.[1] On 2 December 1909 their opposition was met by Asquith's resolution in which the peers were condemned for having breached the Constitution and having interfered with the rights of the House of Commons. The following day Parliament was dissolved, and the general election for which Croft had waited so long and campaigned so hard was now set for January 1910.

6: Imperial Mission, Reveille, and the Call to Action (1910)   111

Croft was sensitive to the particular constitutional issues subsumed in the controversy. He nevertheless postured the electoral confrontation in terms of the survival of the kingdom and empire for which the adoption of a tariff reform candidate, party, and program was essential. He was convinced that an aggressive program pivoting on tariff reform and empire would return a Conservative majority.[2] On the issue of the budget, Croft vigorously preached that the country should reject the budget because it represented socialism and that only tariff reform provided a defense against socialism.[3]

To prevail electorally with this position, it was imperative that Croft gain some support from the working class. Motivated by this necessity, he consistently incorporated appeals to working men into his campaign, arguing that if £8 million was taken from the wealthy it would, in effect, produce a concurrent decrease in the money circulated among the working classes. The proposed budget, he claimed, would hurt the working poor, not the rich. He further condemned the proposed tax on beer, whiskey, and tobacco. When challenged for evidence that the Conservative party had ever been truly concerned about the plight of the working classes, he was quick to cite the Truck Acts, Factory Acts, Workmen's Acts, Small Holdings Acts, County Council Act, and free education to working-class children.[4] He also countered that there was not any specific item in the budget that would ease unemployment.[5] Croft claimed to support old age pensions without the pauper disqualification, and land ownership rather than tenancy, and by the end of the campaign, he was occasionally introduced as "the working man's champion."[6] Similar to his experience at Lincoln in 1906, he was compelled to address the food question; and he eventually responded a few weeks before the polling with a short article in which he argued that the Liberals had failed to produce either the promised "big loaf" or "free breakfast table." Yet he blamed all governments that in the past had failed to keep domestic grainfields under cultivation and neglected to stimulate overseas wheat supplies. In an effort to secure cheap foodstuffs, Croft argued that Britain must bring it in from the dominions, sending, in return, manufactured goods.[7]

In addition, Croft aggressively campaigned on the issues of British supremacy at sea and keeping out foreigners and foreign goods; he also repeated the boilerplate opposition to home rule, socialism, and anarchy. His energetic campaign produced a 731–vote majority (5,538–4,807) over Arthur Acland Allen, the incumbent Liberal MP. In 1906 Acland Allen had gained a 567–vote majority, and although the constituency had been consistently Conservative since 1885, the majorities were never very secure. Until 1906 the largest majority ever gained was 371 in 1874 by Sir Henry Drummond Wolfe. Croft secured 54 percent of the vote, and, with what became a pattern, he produced a record turnout of 94 percent of the eligible voters. In his victory speech, he congratulated Christchurch: "Yours is a message to the Colonies that the door which was 'banged, barred and bolted' against them is going to be opened, and that we have struck one of the first blows on that door to burst it open." He continued, "we have given a message also to the workers of this country to tell them that the silly, sickly, sentimental, stupid policy of free trade is going to die very shortly, and that the foreigner will no longer flood our markets . . . which will give employment to our peoples."[8]

The national election results are well known. The Liberals, who won 400 seats in 1906, but had been reduced to 373 when Parliament was dissolved in 1909, were only able to retain 275 in 1910. The Conservatives, joined with the Liberal Unionists, possessed only 157 seats after the 1906 election and held 168 in December 1909. They now increased their seats to 273 in 1910. Labour retained 40 seats, which was down from 46 at the time of dissolution; the Irish Nationalists lost only one seat, retaining 82 in 1910. Tariff reformers were well rewarded for their energies. As Austen Chamberlain gleefully informed to Balfour, "tariff reform was our trump card. Where we won, we won on and by Tariff Reform."[9] The divisions of Hertfordshire went from a two-two split to giving Conservative tariff reformers all four seats with unprecedented majorities.[10] The Confederates in particular made impressive showings, winning 22 seats out of approximately 26 contests. On the other hand, the election devastated the remaining free traders, particularly those targeted by the Confederates. Both Cecil and Bowles were defeated in their Blackburn contests, and Lambton lost at Durham.[11] Croft's interpretation of the election results provided not only a vindication but an endorsement of his views and political strategies.

Croft had finally reached the first plateau for which he had tirelessly campaigned since 1903. If one element defined his political career from beginning to end, it was that he was a man of principle, and very seldom was he swayed by personal considerations. It was not the accomplishment at Christchurch that was important, other than to reinforce Croft's beliefs, but what was to be accomplished from there. "Our politics," he declared, "can no longer be chiefly of the village, town, city or even of our country. They have entered the wider field of Empire. Within the Empire are the unlimited possibilities of the future." His policies flowed from this fundamental vision and belief in the empire, which came to be an imperial idea. In the agricultural productiveness of the empire will be found the "exchange of commodities which will make for the financial solidity of the British race, and which will hasten the naval, military and commercial union of our people." It followed that "seapower can alone secure our future. Money can alone give us sea power. Man power can alone give us money power." His vision, both in and out of Parliament, was quickly revealed as an imperial mission. Everything, Croft argued, depended on the empire, as only "imperial unity can alone give us man power. . . . In this direction, namely imperial unity, lies our mission."[12]

When the new Parliament opened in February, his political accomplishments on behalf of tariff reform since 1903 as well as his political determination allowed Croft to claim a position in supporting Austen Chamberlain's tariff reform amendment to the king's speech. Speaking from below the gangway that was to become his home for the next thirty years, Croft charged that free trade had failed to provide unemployment or capital. Further, he asked "how . . . can we possibly stand unarmed and isolated against these wealth-producing forces of Germany and the United States? . . . I believe that the longer we delay the less chance there is of consummating the Imperial Union which I consider alone can secure the future."[13] Chamberlain recorded at the time that "the number and excellence of the maiden speeches—Steel-Maitland, Tryon, Mackinder, Page Croft and George Lloyd, all made their mark. We are enormously strengthened in debating power."[14] Even the *National Review* acknowledged the potential contribution as speakers to be made by Steel-Maitland, Tryon, George Lloyd, and Croft, all Confederates.[15]

Notwithstanding such generous comments, Croft was never truly suited for parliamentary debate. His great strength remained as a platform orator where he could fill the audience with the passion of his beliefs and the energy of his delivery. His ability on the stump did not go unnoticed. He gave hundreds of speeches on subjects relating to the empire during these early years, and he was in great demand as a supporting speaker in close campaigns. Garvin once wrote to Croft, "your speech . . . was a wonderful thing. I had no idea that you had a particle of that platform power."[16] Patrick Hannon conveyed similar compliments: "You were excellent last night and more power to you. . . . Ridley, Bonar and F. E. [Smith] were all full of praise and also Jim Garvin. Your ears ought to have flamed up last night and [Mrs. Croft] would have been proud had she heard the praises freely given on your speech."[17] The *Evening News* suggested that "of the younger men, Mr. Steel-Maitland and Mr. Page Croft stand in the very first rank."[18]

By the time Parliament stood down for summer recess at the end of July, Croft had made a distinct impression. The Parliamentary correspondent for the *Manchester Courier* wrote on 28 June that "he is always faultlessly dressed, wears his hair in a most approved fashion, is possessed of an open, pleasing countenance, and, in company with Lord Charles Beresford, keeps a watchful eye on the doings of Mr. McKenna at the Admiralty. . . . He is a Tariff Reform organizer of skill and experience." He was described elsewhere as being "big and serene, and deft at questioning."[19] Croft, wrote *The Standard,* "misses no opportunity of making a point for Tariff Reform."[20] On 6 August the *Morning Post* noted that "the mere thought of Tariff Reform conjures up visions of Mr. Page Croft . . . slick, immaculate, debonnaire." He preaches the "gospel in silken tones, and . . . listening to [him] is like taking the second liqueur after dinner—pleasant, although you know that it will not agree with you."[21]

Notwithstanding his impressive victory and a respectable maiden speech,

Croft's focus on tariff reform and imperial preference suffered from irrelevancy in the first few months after the general election. Westminster was whirling with a multitude of political issues that seemed to trivialize Croft's tariff reform agenda. The political whirlwind nevertheless demonstrated the paralysis from which the Conservatives continued to suffer. The Liberal, Labour, and Irish Nationalist parties had undergone a brief transformation to define their peculiar relationships, the consequence of which was to produce further constitutional confrontations—the vitiation of the Lords' veto power and the pursuit of Irish home rule. Having reached an accommodation with Labour and the Irish, the Liberals reintroduced the budget bill, which passed the House of Commons on 27 April; recognizing that the issue had been settled by the January election, the Lords promptly obliged by passing the bill one day later, taking only a matter of a few hours. In his maneuver against the House of Lords, in March 1910 Asquith introduced three resolutions: finance bills were to become law within one month after submission to the House of Lords; nonfinancial measures were to become law without approval by the House of Lords if they were passed in three successive sessions; and the length of Parliament was to be reduced from seven to five years. All three resolutions passed Commons by 14 April 1910.[22]

The Conservatives seemed paralyzed in the face of the political momentum that enveloped them.[23] Although the Liberals were operating with little resistance, the relative incompetency of the party's old guard was best demonstrated when several of the leaders gathered for dinner to consider informally "whether it was to our advantage to turn the Government out if we had an opportunity or whether it would be better to leave them to make the appeal to the country."[24] Although Conservatives made tremendous gains in the January polling, there was a degree of detachment by the leadership from any recognized need for immediate decisions and action.

For his part Croft clearly recognized that this was not the time to be content with the acquisition of 116 additional seats and debate the abstract advantage of forcing a dissolution, which everyone seemed to think was only a few months away, versus merely waiting for the government to self-destruct. Exercised by the continued inaction of the party leadership, Croft believed that Conservatives must seize all opportunities. The party was forfeiting opportunities to persuade the country to accept its imperial responsibility and rejoice in its imperial destiny, and it would be only through a vigorous education or propaganda process that the country would be unreservedly converted to tariff reform and preference. Croft nevertheless was in unfamiliar territory.

The subject that consumed his attention in and out of Parliament was the American-Canadian trade negotiations. Croft was quite determined that Britain should not sit idly by as its greatest imperial component was courted by its greatest economic rival. Instead, as he constantly argued, Britain must intervene in the Canadian trade talks.

6: Imperial Mission, Reveille, and the Call to Action (1910) 115

Although Croft managed to receive considerable attention for his parliamentary persistence, he clearly was more comfortable during his first session pursuing the extraparliamentary strategies that he had found so successful between 1903 and 1909. He borrowed heavily from the organizing and propagandizing experience gained from the tariff reform campaigns in East Hertfordshire, Lincoln, and Christchurch. Soon after arriving at Westminster, Croft began working with various colonials in an effort to construct an organization and movement with which to educate the public on the empire's viewpoint. Croft held to the position that imperial preference is of such urgent importance, any further delay will be fatal to its adoption. Those who shared Croft's sentiment had long believed it was necessary to educate the public with colonial viewpoints.[25] Accordingly, Croft inaugurated a movement to do just that. Dr. Levinge, from Christchurch, New Zealand, was in England at the time of the general election. He later recorded that it "seemed deplorable that the destinies of a great empire should be in the hands of those who were only concerned with parochial or their own comparatively petty interests." After communicating with Austen Chamberlain about a colonial organization, he was introduced to Croft who, he discovered, was "moving in practically the same direction by endeavouring to get colonials visiting England to address audiences throughout the country."[26]

During the spring of 1910, this loosely structured organization, occasionally referred to as the Pioneers of the Empire or Imperial Pioneers, operated as a speakers' bureau. Early participants included Daniel O'Connor, a former MP and postmaster general for New South Wales; Frank Fox of the *Sydney Bulletin,* who took an active part in the Australian federation movement; and W. F. Cockshutt, a former Canadian MP. Another member with whom Croft was to have a close political association and personal friendship for the next thirty-seven years was Patrick Hannon, an Irishman who as a young man sought adventure in South Africa. He now returned to pursue a political career at Westminster. However, the soul of the movement during its first few months was found in the speeches of J. B. Mulloy, a Canadian student who volunteered for service in South Africa in 1899. At Rietfontein he was shot in the face and blinded. Mulloy was a moving orator who spoke on the future of Canada and the empire. He shared Croft's desire to create an organization of men dedicated to placing the empire before either their own political careers or their party's fortunes.[27]

As part of their propaganda campaign, the pioneers appealed for men and women to go to Canada.[28] By June 1910 the movement included at least 130 colonials now resident in Britain.[29] Within a year by May 1911, the Imperial Mission addressed nearly five hundred thousand persons at four hundred meetings. During this same period, the pioneer movement was further organized with the establishment of a council. The duke of Argyll, former governor general of Canada, was named honorary president, and the earl of Dundonald, former commander of the armed forces in Canada, president.[30]

The council had several sections, each representing a colony. Croft served as chairman, and other officers included Sir Joseph Ward, the New Zealand prime minister, Sir William Russell, also of New Zealand, George Gould, G. A. M. Buckley, Arthur E. G. Rhodes, a young Canadian named Max Aitken,[31] and nominally Joseph Chamberlain.

This new organization, the Imperial Mission, was a creation of Croft, and it reflected his ideas and frustrations. With it he sought to launch a vigorous campaign to educate the country on questions of imperial preference and unity.[32] In mid-July 1910, the Imperial Mission held its first mass meeting at Regent's Park, and it claimed several hundred members.[33] With obvious tariff reformist tendencies, Croft often denied that the movement was an extension of the Tariff Reform League or that it had any connections with a particular party. Its participants, however, were overwhelmingly associated with the Conservative party. In fact, three party election agents once shared the Imperial Mission platform with Croft.[34] The Imperial Mission was often supported by Croft's long-time ally and patron, the earl of Malmesbury, who shared the same frustrations over the meager political commitment and fortitude displayed by both major parties, but particularly the Conservative leadership. At a rally in Bournemouth with Croft by his side, Lord Malmesbury warned that Britain needed imperial unity now, and it would be lost with any further delay. Croft declared that it was the time to construct an indivisible imperial union to be initiated with a major reciprocal trade treaty between Britain and the Dominion partners.[35]

During a visit to Lincoln, Croft warned that the upcoming trade negotiations between the United States and Canada provided grave concern for Britain's future. He feared that the creation of a reciprocal trade arrangement between the United States and Canada would produce a "community of interests between the two countries which no sentimental love of the Mother Country would ever be able to break down."[36] The Imperial Mission's position was accurately set out in Maxse's *National Review*. Britain must meet Canada halfway and put forward a constructive imperial trade policy.[37] Croft proceeded to take his Imperial Mission throughout the kingdom, from the North of Scotland to the South of England, in an effort to open the door to the Dominions, "which Mr. Churchill had banged, barred and bolted."[38]

Ever vigilant over the integrity of the defense and security of the kingdom and empire, Croft believed that "preference meant that they should, if possible, trade with those who built dreadnoughts for them rather than those who built dreadnoughts against them."[39] Croft again warned that the cost of defense was becoming precariously burdensome for Britain. However, with a population of four hundred million, Croft claimed that the entire empire could easily meet such an obligation to its common defense. He "wanted to see the fleets of the Empire lying together instead of having 2 or 3 tin pot fleets in various ports." How could they expect the colonies to

6: Imperial Mission, Reveille, and the Call to Action (1910) 117

join together, he asked, "if we were not prepared to help them" in terms of imperial preference?[40] Croft suffered from an acute fear of the economic and military development in Germany, Japan, and the United States. To ensure their future, Croft urged, Britain could delay no longer; it must act to hold the Dominions together. Given his anxiety over the potential dissolution of the empire and Britain being cast adrift, he suggested the Imperial Mission would not remain idle. He was convinced that if the movement for imperial unity "could only get a clear issue they were going to prevail, the flag was going to be run up to the masthead never to be lowered, and the strength of the Empire would never be so much increased."[41]

The problem remained that Croft had difficulty finding an opportunity to press imperial unity on to the front of the national political stage. Once Asquith's government had introduced the resolutions in March, as its first step to trim the House of Lords, the party's attention to imperial issues wandered. Conservative party strategy toward the House of Lords resolutions, on the other hand, seemed limited to mere contemplation accompanied by meager rhetoric. Eventually they were prevented from action by the death of King Edward VII on 6 May 1910. The king's unexpected passing forced the two main parties into a self-imposed truce in deference to the new king. The truce provided the two parties an opportunity to resolve the constitutional dispute over the House of Lords out of view and removed from the constant pressure caused by the ongoing debate. Soon an interparty conference was created, with four members from each of the two parties.[42] The conference met for twenty-two sessions from 16 June to 10 November 1910 without success.

The truce had the effect of silencing much of the political debate for several months. Croft, however, saw little value in any truce because it allowed the enemy to regroup its forces and strengthen its position. This could have provided an important initiative had the Conservative leadership directed its attention back to imperial issues. It was an opportunity that Croft believed was shamefully wasted. Then he sought to reengage the imperial debate and on 3 June 1910 urged Balfour to give a commitment that when the Conservatives returned to power he would reverse recent action on various taxes, particularly license and land duties. He implored Balfour "to give us some hope that the private attack on the Licensed trade may be least made more equitable."[43] Balfour responded with his ever-present equivocation, which Croft and other radical Conservatives found so frustrating: "I think it would hardly be wise for any Party Leader, in or out of office, to commit himself or those with whom he acts, as to the course which he would take in matters of detail should the revolutions of the political wheel of fortunes bring him into power. I am sure you will appreciate the wisdom of this course."[44] Under circumstances that Croft believed needed immediate amplification, he could not appreciate such hesitancy.

Similar to the days of 1906–7, Croft again became agitated over the future of the Conservative party with Balfour at the helm, and this feeling was only further exacerbated by the imposition of the political truce. Croft was not alone in his feelings, as similar sentiments were found in both wings of the party. Even Robert Cecil recorded his discontent with Balfour: "I think pretty soon I must write & tell AJB that I no longer regard him as my leader & then I can be quite friendly with him. At present I don't much like meeting him."[45] On the other end, Maxse, never known for his affection toward Balfour, declared that "our party has undoubtedly suffered from want of leadership, . . . nobody leads, and the followers are discouraged."[46]

Croft soon saw an opportunity with which to press forward the cause of imperial preference. It came in July amidst the debate on Lloyd George's budget statement that included a relatively minor resolution concerning the continuation of the custom duty on tea. The duty was presently five pence on the pound, and the resolution sought to extend it until July 1911.[47] James Fitzalan Hope, a fellow Confederate, offered an amendment providing for a four-pence duty on tea from within the empire. As Fitzalan Hope confessed, his "object is to establish the principle of Colonial preference."[48] Croft entered the debate by issuing a rejoinder to the comments of George Barnes, leader of the Labour party, and expressing dismay over the Labour party's refusal to support a reduction in the tea duty.[49]

The full significance of the proposal was exposed when Croft suggested that "there is a bigger question [than reducing food taxes]. . . . The other parts of the Empire would rejoice to see that we, for the first time, have really done something to show that we prefer to give better times to our people within the British Empire." He urged the government to "do something to bring closer together, by the only ties which can possibly be lasting—namely commercial ones—this great beast of the British Empire with its other members."[50] However, the great opportunity that Croft hoped would provide the first step in an aggressive procession toward imperial preference and defense quickly dissipated as the amendment was defeated 188 to 145.[51] Notwithstanding that the government had been reduced to a majority of forty-three, he was seriously disappointed but even more agitated over the feeble effort of the party's leadership to take advantage of the situation. Although several tariff reformers spoke in support of the Fitzalan Hope amendment, the activity of the Conservative leadership was limited to Bonar Law.

Shortly afterward, Parliament stood down for the summer, and Croft and other imperial missionaries feared that the recess would contribute to a further diminution of interest in imperial unity. He therefore took comfort in the news that Colonel Kyffin-Taylor, campaigning on tariff reform and imperial unity, won a by-election at the Kirkdale division of Liverpool. Kyffin-Taylor proclaimed that the election "showed also that the people were tired of a Government that did not look after the defense of the Empire

6: Imperial Mission, Reveille, and the Call to Action (1910) 119

and tired of seeing their own men unemployed when by Tariff Reform they could get employment."[52]

In an effort to grasp and retain the attention of the party and country on the issue, Croft and the Imperial Mission urged Balfour to give two or three speeches in the industrial centers. He wanted Balfour to provide clear direction for imperial preference and consequently sanction the Imperial Mission's campaign. The urgency of the request was intensified by being in the shadows of the forthcoming trade negotiations between Canada and the United States. Croft felt "confident that if such a campaign could be undertaken it will have the effect of entirely altering the trade policy of the Dominion which may otherwise be directed towards reciprocity with the United States to the permanent disadvantage of the Imperial connection."[53] He conveyed the Imperial Mission's resolution to Balfour, noting that it was brought forward by the Canadian section who believed that Canadians saw the British, and Conservatives in particular, as having ignored the Canadian trade developments. Accordingly, "the only chance of influencing Canadian opinion is to prove in this most critical time that the . . . party is in deadly earnest over its proposals." Croft also reminded Balfour that the Imperial Mission contained four hundred members, including thirty MPs, and they were beginning their campaign in Manchester in September. Further, he told Balfour, six members had gone to Canada "to carry to the people of the Dominion the true sentiments of our Party." Croft urged that it was critically important for Balfour and the party to focus the attention of Britain and the Dominions immediately on imperial preference, "otherwise we are advised by our friends in Canada that the fatal step will possibly be taken which will prevent 'preference' from ever being of any real value."[54]

Balfour departed for a holiday on the Continent without responding to the Imperial Mission's request, suggesting the lack of importance that he attached to Croft's plea and also revealing the distance between a leadership that had overstayed its welcome and the rebel activists. On 26 August, after returning to London but on the eve of departing for Scotland, he finally wrote to Croft. He timidly suggested that "I will try and make some further reference to the subject. . . . But, of course, there are many other subjects that have to be dealt with. . . . I hope and believe that other speakers of authority in the Party will press the matter further."[55] As background to the resolution, Croft had previously informed Balfour that "your speeches, and yours only, are taken to represent the views of our party, and . . . only garbled accounts of the sentiments of the Unionist Party ever reach the Canadian Press."[56]

Balfour's response to Croft's appeal for an imperial program was too little and definitely too late. In fact, Balfour was not scheduled to make any public statement until 17 November, which was two days after Parliament was to reconvene. This naturally aggravated Croft's disappointment and his ever-increasing frustration.[57] In an attempt to emulate the apparent success of the Confederacy as the strike force for the tariff reform movement, Croft, urged by his former Confederates, now conceived of and decided to launch a new campaign with which he hoped to reinvigorate Conservatives and commit the party to the empire. "Some of us," Croft wrote to R. D. Blumenfeld, the American-born editor of the *Daily Express,* "are not at all satisfied that the most is being made of the present political situation and that the great danger to Imperial Preference is being properly put before the people by our leaders." Croft invited Blumenfeld to join him and some forty peers and MPs for a dinner meeting on 6 October that was intended to inaugurate a new effort.[58] In the meantime, in the *Morning Post* of 30 August, Croft launched a political force, the Reveille. It was a new attempt to energize the Conservative party with a call for a new Wellington to step forward. It was not without risks. Given the insight it provides to his anxieties over domestic and international conditions, to his frustration with an anemic party leadership, and to his proposed determination to press forward and even challenge the leadership, its full quotation is warranted.

REVEILLE!
THE UNIONISTS' OPPORTUNITY
By Henry Page Croft, M.P.

Four weeks ago the House of Commons adjourned till November. The sleeping sickness brought on by the truce permeated all ranks, and especially the ranks of the Unionist Party. . . . No one need complain, . . . provided that Unionism wakes up in the next few weeks, or better still, days, but awakening is impossible unless there is a clear, united, and loud trumpet blast from the leaders of the Unionist Party, and that is why we want to hear the Reveille.

The past session brought together a party on the Unionist benches—enthusiastic, industrious, loyal, in sympathy with, and confident in, its leaders. That party is still a powerful engine, to be used with tremendous effect in Parliament and in the country, but the engine will not budge without steam. There never was such an opportunity as the present for putting forward a definite policy which will inspire the enthusiasm of the rank and file, and which can appeal to the higher and better instincts of the British electors.

Now, if ever, can statesmen get home to the hearts of the people and make a lasting impression on the political future. Is there a cause? Yes, and the greatest which the Unionist Party has ever set itself to win. Never was a cause more pressing. Sacrifice is demanded of everyone who cares for the Imperial Union.

Ten years ago the Empire consisted of the Mother Country and the children; to-day it consists of the United Kingdom and the "brother nations" of the Empire. Then the children were dependent, to-day they are strong and almost independent. For years the Colonies have held out the hand of partnership; to-day the whole world is rushing to grasp the hand of the Dominions which we have scoffed at and rejected. Our trade with British possessions means something like £60,000,000

6: Imperial Mission, Reveille, and the Call to Action (1910) 121

in wages annually to the British worker, and without it we should have had starvation, misery and despair the like of which we have never dreamed. Under Canadian Preference our trade has risen 196 percent., whilst with foreign countries it has only increased half as rapidly. Canadian Preference alone has meant £5,000,000 additional wages annually to the British workers. All things being equal with the tendency still British and flowing in the same direction, we stand to gain at least one hundred millions of trade with Canada alone before the century is out, or enough to end the misery of permanent unemployment, and sufficient to change entirely for the good the condition of the labour market.

But is this to be our lot? Not if the Unionist Party continues to slumber, not if apathy takes the place of duty. France, Germany, Italy, Belgium and the Netherlands have already concluded fiscal treaties with Canada, treaties which we have refused to Canada, treaties every one of which robs us of parts of the fruits of Preference, robs us of that which should be, ought to be, and can be ours, if we rouse the country to reap the priceless advantage of the harvest. During the coming autumn a Conference is to be held between the representatives of the Dominion of Canada and the representatives of the United States to discuss their trade relations. Can there be anyone so blind as to fail to see this hideous danger to our trade, our industry, and our Imperial existence which threatens us if reciprocal trade, with its attendant community of interest, between the United States and British North America is established? Granted then that these facts are appreciated, granted that the danger is imminent and pressing, what possible excuse can any Unionist find for his absence from the battlefield during the next few months? One thing and one thing only can avert the American danger and that is the voice of England and indeed the United Kingdom speaking in no uncertain terms, pledging the country to Imperial Preference and Imperial partnership, and pledging the country to a decisive victory in this cause at the polls. The Guards are ready to "up and at 'em"; we wait only for a Wellington to give the word.[59]

Underlying Croft's call for a Wellington was a publicly proclaimed disappointment with the leadership of Balfour and particular dissatisfaction over the failure of the Conservative leadership to pursue vigorously imperial unity. Croft complained to Acland Hood, "at present there is no heart in platform work because we simply don't know where we are."[60] Another element aggravating Croft's frustration was the utter failure of the party's leadership to embrace either the imperial idea or to recognize the need for a new and aggressive political strategy to correspond with a new political era. Balfour, still submerged within the nineteenth-century political culture, failed to see the new view of the state and that it could construct an aggressive program for the advancement of the empire and nation.

Croft's sentiments were in close alignment with those held by Leo Maxse. On the day after the appearance of the Croft's Reveille call, Maxse confessed to Garvin, "what worries me . . . is the feeling which amounts to a conviction that under Balfour there is a very small prospect of the Unionist Party securing a mandate to carry out what they believe to be his policy, though what his policy may really be Heaven only knows."[61] After all, Maxse wrote to Bonar Law, "we are led by a tactician without convictions or enthusiasm, who can only be got to espouse any cause under pressure."[62] In a letter to Edward Goulding, Maxse declared that he found "the present situation . . . thoroughly disquieting." It followed that Maxse was to be invited to Croft's dinner, which was to inaugurate the Reveille movement.[63]

Croft now resorted to the strategy of the complementary but alternating alliance he used with the tariff reform branches and the Confederates but this time under the banners of the Imperial Mission and Reveille. The party ranks and then the country as a whole could be rallied by the Imperial Mission, and pressure could then be applied by the Reveille to reinvigorate the leadership to abandon its humdrum toryism. With an infusion of commitment and energy provided by the Reveille, it was expected that the leadership and party ranks would be able to promote the party and imperial idea successfully to the nation. Once in office they would have the determination and capability to put the program into operation. However, Croft first had to struggle against an aged party structure that allowed the leadership to become estranged from its foot soldiers. He was also up against a leader who held no democratic or popular inclinations. Balfour was generally more comfortable the greater distance he maintained himself from the party ranks.

Croft's Reveille call prompted a wave of response from the press. The *Morning Post* called for Conservatives "to wake up. . . . The rank and file are ready and eager for the forward move and the constructive policy; they merely wait the summons of the trumpet in the form of a big autumn campaign to charge home."[64] The *Morning Advertiser* amplified Croft's critique, claiming the party has made "little progress since the House met, because, the engine will not budge. . . . Steps should be taken now, . . . to display greater activity and to inaugurate a political campaign throughout the country." The newspaper endorsed Croft's assessment that the party and nation are "sacrificing the chance of securing Imperial Unity. With almost every day that passes the colonies are becoming more independent." The young rebel was "right when he insists that . . . apathy should be thrown off, and a vigorous campaign commenced."[65]

The Liberal press, as illustrated by the *Lancashire Daily Post,* expressed anxiety over Croft's demand for "Balfour to head a great agitation in favour of Tariff Reform and Preference prior to the Colonial Conference."[66] The most accurate characterization of Croft's pronouncement is found in the *Hull Daily Mail.* "Mr. Page Croft, and the younger Unionists, feel the faith that is in them leaping up, and clamouring for expression. They see the Party coming to its own again, but fear those periodical attacks of 'sleeping sickness.'" Croft's view of Balfour was painfully extracted with the recognition that "they resent the careful tread, the halting manoeuvres of an Army which doubts whether it is 'out to win or not.'" Under such frustrating circumstances, the editorial reasoned, Croft was compelled to "sound a Reveille to a dozing camp. . . . Mr. Croft is confident that a decisive victory at the polls would follow the digestion by the voters of a Popular Party

6: Imperial Mission, Reveille, and the Call to Action (1910)   123

Programme."[67] Not very deeply submerged within Reveille's fervor was an indigenous distrust of both Balfour's commitment to the cause as well as his leadership capabilities. The inherent warning to the leader was clearly evident in the rhetoric that Croft's Reveille unleashed.

Croft was not alone in his concerns over the fate of the party, country, and empire. Although there was substantial work to be undertaken in promoting preference and imperial unity, observers found nothing being done by the party's leadership: "There is to be no great outburst of Unionist oratory by men of the front rank between now and November. . . . No meetings have been arranged." It was feared that "sleeping sickness appears to be affecting all ranks in the party." However, critics refused to lay a "charge of slackness" against the party organization when "the leaders are not able to offer guidance." Borrowing a military analogy, a "campaign by non-commissioned officers is always difficult with the commissioned ranks holding aloof and the rank and file indifferent." The warning that the Reveille provoked was clear: "that unless vigorous action is taken soon a dry rot is likely to set in which will have fatal effect in the future."[68]

Croft did not remain idle. He set out immediately, taking his Reveille first to the provinces where he repeated his charges against the government while concomitantly increasing the pressure on the conservatives.[69] He was soon joined by Lord Willougby de Broke as they took the Reveille movement on a two-man campaign to the North of England.[70]

Although the *Morning Post* extended its support to Croft's proposed campaign for an invigorated Conservative party, it was also important to bring Maxse's *National Review* on board, as it would further press the Reveille into the ranks of the party and consequently extinguish the latent sentiment of helplessness that Croft believed was creeping over the party. As both Croft and Willoughby de Broke were close friends with the fiery editor, his recruitment presented little difficulty. On 20 August Willoughby de Broke offered Maxse an article on the call for a new Conservative campaign, to be characterized by "enthusiasm, keenness, courage, something of the Dervish." Although Willoughby de Broke predicted they had the subscription of the party's heart and soul, he warned that "if our present leaders do not take care, a middle party of Tories who mean business will smash them. No more tactics."[71]

Enlisted by Croft and Willoughby de Broke for the Reveille movement, Maxse came out swinging in the September *National Review*. Elaborating on the Reveille themes, he claimed that the party was in desperate need of someone with "explosive energy and forceful personality, who knows no fear and refuses to be hocussed by mandarins, mugwumps, and 'rotters.' . . . Candour compels us," he continued, "to recognize that an atmosphere of weariness and boredom pervades the powers that be in our party." Suggesting that the party has neither, Maxse argued that "a political party dependent for its power upon the democracy, demands competent management and inspiring leadership. Otherwise it cannot get a mandate for its policy."[72]

Although he condemned both front benches for treating politics and government as a trivial game of ins and outs, he betrayed a sense of hope when he noted that "a new and more serious spirit is spreading among the Unionist rank and file, especially those who have not yet had the heart taken out of them by the enervating atmosphere of the House of Commons." Saluting the energy and commitment of Croft and Willoughby de Broke, Maxse was encouraged that "there is a healthy spirit of unrest in the Unionist Party outside of the small coterie who imagine that the party exists for their benefit. Men feel that things cannot go on as they are, and that drastic changes are needed in our methods and our personnel." Echoing Croft's often-expressed criticisms, Maxse further suggested that "there is too much tactics and too little strategy." Charging that it was apparent to all observers that the present party leadership does not wish to destroy the present government, Maxse called for such men to step aside and make way for those who were not infected with such reluctance.[73]

Lord Willoughby de Broke came forward with an elaborate denunciation of the corruption represented by the constitutional conference. Although he posited that the long-term remedy was to install a determined Conservative ministry, the "first thing to do is to infuse into all ranks a proper fighting spirit." He warned that if it appears that the party leadership is treating with the Liberal, or pulling its punches, even for tactical purposes "then a dry rot may set in that might relegate us to the shades of Opposition for another decade. The country," he declared, "is sick of tactics and meaningless debates." Echoing Croft and continuing the Reveille theme, he urged that the party must wage an aggressive campaign against the Liberal government, which would also serve to rally the party ranks and the kingdom as a whole.[74] With the silence broken by Croft's Reveille call, the press now commenced a discussion of the discontent and discord within the Conservative party and specifically focused on the estrangement between the leadership and the rank and file.[75]

Croft and Willoughby de Broke put substance to their discontent by transforming their Reveille call into an organization, bringing together "about 100 wealthy members of both Houses." The movement sought to push the party leadership into action, demanding that they take a sustained role in the campaign for the empire. They called on Balfour and his lieutenants to exchange "the 'present merely defensive policy' for a definite programme, clearly and precisely indicating the questions on which Unionists, if returned to power, would legislate."[76] Croft sought to demonstrate that "the reserve of activity and force within the party is so great that no fears need be entertained as to the future." In distinct Croft style, "the call is for a plain and definite 'lead' and the new body claim as their motto, 'Fight, fight, and go on fighting.'"[77]

6: Imperial Mission, Reveille, and the Call to Action (1910) 125

In early October 1910, Maxse returned to the Reveille campaign, where he berated the Conservative front bench for its paralysis and summarized the political situation from the vantage point of the press. Although the *Morning Post* had revealed rank and file frustrations with the leadership, it was "by no means alone in demanding activity where apathy now reigns." The call for action was strongly supported by the *Standard,* the *Globe,* the *Pall Mall Gazette,* the *Saturday Review,* the *Observer* and the *Outlook,* as well as several powerful provincial papers. The criticism focused on the ineptitude of the Central Office, the indifference of Balfour, and the party's failure to determine and articulate for the country "a concrete and constructive policy of tariff, land and social reform." The problem with the Central Office, which had been pointed out by various quarters, was its centralization in the Whips' room of the House of Commons. Acland Hood, it was suggested, was attempting the unachievable, trying to "whip" the parliamentary party and run the constituencies. The reality was that the Conservative party was "ill-organised" for running political campaigns and educating the public in a modern fashion. It needed to establish "a serious and properly equipped electioneering department."[78]

The Reveille produced a liberating experience for critics, as it provided political cover. Maxse's *National Review* leveled the most serious and politically challenging charge at Balfour. It claimed that he "takes no interest in party management and seems indisposed to delegate this distasteful task to any of his colleagues." In addition he is "reluctant to appoint a deputy leader during his absence from the House of Commons, . . . is probably more ignorant of his party than any of his predecessors. This is the crux of the problem for which no one suggests any solution." Although not a pleasant task, Maxse declared that "we have reached a stage in the fortunes of our party, when the only service that can be rendered by those who have its interests at heart is to speak the truth, however unpalatable."[79]

Croft's motto to "go on fighting" was soon followed by a call for a "militant unionist policy." As one Conservative observer posited, "the people want a lead. Where is the man? Do we realize what is at issue?" He built upon much of Croft's complaint: if the party does not awake and act, the great hope for the preferential agreements with the Colonies "will be relegated to oblivion, and the desire of all true lovers of the Empire will be frustrated." He resounded the Reveille's call for immediate action.[80]

In Balfour's absence the Central Office was forced to react to the party's troubling developments. In an effort to imitate the energy of the Confederacy's campaign against the free fooders, on 19 September Acland Hood, the chief whip, and Percival Hughes, party agent, announced that the party would commence a massive campaign that in the next three months would produce ten thousand meetings in all of the counties and over four hundred constituencies.[81] Further, the chief whip now claimed that as soon as Parliament returned in November the party would spare no effort to turn out

Asquith's government—an early Reveille demand.[82] Ironically, others close to Balfour tried to deflect criticism from the leader by indicting the Central Office, claiming "its want of modern precision and its type of staff are responsible for directing the fire on to our Front Bench leading men."[83] However, such hollow distractions were not sufficient to extinguish the rank and file discontent. Another way of framing Croft's grievance was that he failed to see that Balfour and the party's leadership were setting forth any specific program that could be taken to the voters as the party's promised legislative and governmental agenda. The Central Office's tactical announcement was merely a display of motion, not energy, and wishful thinking, not concrete programs. Therefore it did little to diminish Croft's frustration.

Croft also saw a further opportunity forfeited when on 22 September Austen Chamberlain gave a major speech in Birmingham to the consultative committee of the Liberal Unionist association. It was squandered when Chamberlain did little to promote the overall strategy of imperial unity. Instead, his speech was an insignificant reaction to the Labour party's call for reversal of the Osborne judgment and payment of members.[84] Again the rank and file witnessed the leadership's obsession with tactics prevail at the expense of strategy, which Croft found particularly disheartening when faced with the fast approaching American-Canadian trade talks.

In the absence of a coherent and articulated program set forth by the party leadership, various individuals had begun to consider other options.[85] With Balfour in seclusion at Whittinghame, the debate raged within the party over its position on the payment of members. *The Times,* H. A. Gwynne at the *Morning Post,*[86] Maxse, Arthur Lee, and Bonar Law were vigorously opposed to such a proposal.[87] In his speech, Chamberlain joined in with perhaps an overly aggressive denunciation of the proposal as well as what he called trade union tyranny. Nevertheless, the *Morning Post* dismissed his speech and position as irrelevant. "Generalities have ceased to be of the slightest use. What is needed," the paper demanded, "is a concrete and alternative constructive programme. . . . What is wanted is not a declaration . . . but for a scheme which will carry those principles into practice, . . . not vague professions of belief in a Tory social policy, [but] the production of that policy."[88]

Although Balfour was not scheduled to make a public speech until mid-November, the chaos that raged within the party ranks and particularly the pressure from the Reveille persuaded him to accept an invitation to speak at the Scottish Conservative Club on 5 October.[89] Hostile to trade unions, Austen Chamberlain hoped "that AJB won't give way about payment of members—a subject on which many of our men are coming to a hasty conclusion." It was conceded to be risky to address Labour's demand for payment of members.[90]

It was ironically on the morning of Balfour's scheduled speech that the announcement of Croft's organization was issued throughout the nation's

6: Imperial Mission, Reveille, and the Call to Action (1910) 127

press, although a copy had been sent to Balfour a few days earlier.[91] In announcing his new organization, it was complained that "despite the reorganization of the party, no candidate or member of Parliament outside the circle of ex-ministers or special private secretaries ever really meets or sees the leaders of the party, a state of things which tends to create an atmosphere of aloofness among the leaders and a sense of stagnation and slackness of the party."[92] As one newspaper sarcastically, but with keen precision, noted, "Croft and his friends have fallen back on the desperate hope that Mr. Balfour will read in the newspapers what could not be conveyed to him privately."[93] The "committee of 100" nevertheless waited for a "lead" to come out of Balfour's Edinburgh speech.[94] The Liberal *Daily Chronicle* suggested that the insurgents had sent the leadership into a panic as "shown by the feverish activity which they are now exhibiting." Percival Hughes, the party's chief agent, hurriedly met with Acland Hood and on 4 October rushed to Scotland to confer with Balfour. On his return Hughes and Acland Hood managed to coax invitations to the Reveille's inaugural dinner scheduled for 6 October.[95]

Meanwhile, in his Edinburgh speech Balfour dashed the proposals floated by F. E. Smith and Edward Goulding on the payment of members, spending most of his lengthy address denouncing the evils of trade union tyranny, the perversion of trade unions and party politics, and the corruption that would follow the payment of members. Whereas Smith and Goulding realistically viewed the political dilemma as accepting either reversal of the Osborne judgment or payment of members, Balfour, on the other hand, refused to concede to either. Under the challenge being mounted by the Reveille, Balfour was enjoined to remark on the more urgent issue of imperial unity. However, he was equally unimaginative, if not actually self-indicting. "Every month that goes on in which we do nothing imperils the prospect of our being able to do anything. . . . I look forward with increasing hope to the prospect of reform in our fiscal system."[96] Croft must have been seriously disappointed on reading Balfour's unassuming comments. The *Morning Post,* with its Reveille tendencies, chided the leader for a speech that "resembles far more the impartial summaries of . . . the *Annual Register,* than a fighting proclamation." Balfour refused to take the nation or party into his confidence and reveal what he stands for or what will be the driving policies of the next Conservative government. Accordingly, as long as he proceeded along this tactic, "the divergences in the ranks of Unionism will grow more numerous every day." The more significant consequence, however, was that a nonexistent party program would compel the rebels on the right to define the party's ideology and programs with "their own constructive policy."[97] The Liberal press also was not impressed by Balfour's performance, evaluating it as did Croft. The *Westminster Gazette* wrote, "truly, it cannot be pretended that this is the speech of a fighting leader about to enter on an aggressive campaign."[98]

Lord Balcarres recorded that "Balfour's soliloquy at Edinburgh is a curious example of his strength and weakness. His criticism of the existing situation in Labour politics is penetrating and suggestive, and must command attention." However, "the serenity with which he disregarded the urgent demands for a 'fighting lead' will disconcert many, and perhaps disappoint others." Reflecting his own and perhaps even Balfour's own contemptuous self-denial of the emerging rebellion, Lord Balcarres nevertheless dismissed the Reveille, doubting that "serious or influential people desire Balfour to commit the party at this stage."[99]

On reading the *Morning Post*'s attack and aware of Croft's dinner with the insurgents scheduled for the evening of 6 October, a panicky Garvin begged Maxse, "for heaven's sake don't revive at present the movement against him." The problem with overthrowing Balfour, according to Garvin's assessment, is that "there is nobody else. Austen is *more* nor *less* Conservative and never can hold the leadership successfully unless he comes to it in a regular way with Balfour's blessing, and it seems to be that to attack Balfour in the *Morning Post* manner . . . does more injury to tariff reform that other efforts can make good."[100]

It has since been revealed that this occurred on the eve of Lloyd George's overture to the Conservative leaders and his proposal for the construction of a coalition or "national government," and Garvin was one of the few outsiders to be privy to the chancellor's scheme. Accordingly, it might be suggested that Garvin was fearful about what an aggressive and hostile back-bench movement would do to Balfour's resolve.[101] After the Reveille meeting, Maxse answered, "I only wish I knew the true answer to the problem which harasses me. I feel in my bones that so long as Arthur Balfour leads the Unionist Party there is no hope of majority or mandate." Although instinct told him "to close your ranks in the face of the enemy," Maxse nevertheless believed that the party's only chance of victory would come "if by one explosive effort we could secure a change of leadership."[102]

Croft's Reveille dinner was held as scheduled, with Lord Malmesbury presiding, and attended by nearly fifty MPs and peers.[103] In a step toward a new and aggressive program for the party, Willoughby de Broke set out essentially a national program. The party must maintain the supremacy of the Navy, completing the Naval program, and improve the quality and strength of the Army. They must go forward and design a scientific tariff to safeguard industries against unfair foreign competition. This led to the party's priority of establishing a commercial partnership throughout the empire, built on imperial preference. The Reveille not only called for a scheme of industrial insurance to complement safeguarding of industries but also low-interest government loans to assist the working classes to purchase land. Last, the party must reform the poor law to reflect the needs and problems caused by new economic and social realities.

Croft encouraged the right wing of the Conservative party to believe that

6: Imperial Mission, Reveille, and the Call to Action (1910) 129

they represented a "forward movement," adding that "our policy in the country has been too indefinite. Let us be definite from a hundred platforms; let us go forth and preach our policy with all the faith that is in us. This is not the time for recrimination; this is the time for loyalty, unity, work, and a fighting policy." The chief whip extended his approval of their efforts and promised his support and cooperation.[104]

However, Malmesbury tried to soothe the panic that he had probably been led to believe was infecting the leadership circles over the emergence of the Reveille and that they believed would damage the party's fortunes. He declared that the statement which had circulated in the press on 5 October "to the effect that a new organization had been formed within the party in opposition to the authorities was entirely unauthorized and did not represent the views of the committee, which had promoted the movement. The object of the dinner," he suggested, "was to give the fullest support to the leaders of the Unionist party in promoting a fighting policy."[105] Because Malmesbury was very soon to distance himself greatly from the character of these remarks, it may be suggested that he made the moderating comments to mollify an anxious chief whip who sat before him.

The Reveille's announcements did not occur without a resulting irritation among other party factions. Although F. E. Smith was not in attendance, he issued an anticipatory defense of Balfour on 6 October.[106] He "protest[ed] against the tendency in very few quarters indeed to make complaints against the attitude of the leaders of their party and their policy." The insurgents "must remember that Mr. Balfour and the leaders of the Conservative party agreed some months ago to enter into a Conference . . . and it seemed the height of unreasonableness for some few members of the Conservative party to criticize Mr. Balfour because . . . he did not make aggressive and provocative political speeches."[107]

Believing his Confederacy to have been responsible for pressuring a recalcitrant leader and ambivalent party to embrace tariff reform fully, Croft had now publicly ignited the debate for a new Conservative program and campaign; he put into place a new rebel organization to promote that debate, and effectively brought about the party's conversion to a new imperial departure. However, the contributions made by Croft's movement and the debate within the party that it initiated would not be realized until 8 November 1911 when Balfour announced his resignation as party leader, but the process had now commenced in earnest, and there could be only one unambiguous resolution.

* * *

Although there may have been as many as one hundred members of the Reveille, the general work and activities of the Reveille movement seemed to be limited to about three dozen individuals. (For the Reveille membership list, see Appendix 2.) Their character and background were not greatly different from the Confederates, and in fact seven were former members of Croft's earlier movement. Accordingly, it is no surprise that the Reveille were a privileged group of men. Forty percent were "Oxbridge." Twenty-two percent succeeded to a peerage, and 11 percent were granted peerages after 1910. Although 34 percent of the Confederates came from landed interests, this figure declined to 19 percent with the Reveille. However, 43 percent of the Reveille were men of substance originating from business, finance, manufacturing, or commercial activities; and 30 percent were from the legal profession.

As was expected, the Reveille was a little older than the Confederates with the average age in the Reveille being forty-two; 35 percent were under forty years of age, and over 80 percent were under the age of 50. Only 27 percent of the Reveille had sat in Parliament prior to 1910; 24 percent of the Reveille unsuccessfully contested seats in the 1906 election; 46 percent were elected to Commons for the first time in 1910; only 13 percent of the Reveille were never to sit in Commons; and in 1910, 16 percent of the Reveille sat in the House of Lords.

Thirty-five percent of the Reveille had significant military service prior to 1914, and 43 percent were to serve in the First World War, including Major Kirkwood (DSO), Lt. Col. Alan Burgoyne (decorations), Lt. Col. J. W. Hills (severely wounded), Lt. Col. John Norton-Griffiths (DSO), Cmdr. Oliver Locker-Lampson (DSO, CMG), Brig.-Gen. Croft (dispatches, CMG), Maj. Martin Archer Shee (severely wounded and dispatches), Capt. Leslie Wilson (severely wounded, CMG), and Lt. Gerald Arbuthnot (killed in action). Over 60 percent of the Reveille received some form of civil honors during their political careers, which included thirteen knighthoods, eight baronetcies, eight privy councillorships, and four peerages. As with the Confederacy, the Reveille represented the energetic, ambitious, but anxious youth of the Conservative party.

7
Croft, the Reveille, and the Fight against Humdrum Toryism (1910)

> The time has come for placing before the electors . . . a detailed and constructive policy, as a denial to the oft-repeated charge that when the party holds the reins of office nothing is ever done, and "things go on" just as in the days of the old humdrum Toryism. . . . The Reveille . . . realise only too bitterly the dangers which must arise if any real attempt should be made to keep the Unionist Party on the old lines.
> —Lord Malmesbury, 2 November 1910

Discontent within the Edwardian Conservative party, which emanated from the internal debate and struggle over adoption of tariff reform in 1904–6, diminished somewhat after Balfour's apparent embrace of the Birmingham program in November 1907. Although centers of disenchantment remained, its expression was generally found behind drawing-room doors or in private correspondence. However, with the extensive public coverage of Croft's Reveille movement, it was as if public remonstrance of Conservative disillusionment had now been sanctioned, and it soon became the subject of discussion in the nation's press and by major political figures. Croft, Willoughby de Broke, and other Reveille members held over forty meetings between 13 October and 7 December, and it was difficult to ignore either the movement or its argument.

A few days after the inaugural dinner in October Croft launched the Reveille's autumn campaign with a series of interviews and speeches.[1] At nearly twenty Reveille rallies, Croft argued that the most immediate and consequential issue was the need for the Conservative party to send an unmistakable message to the Canadians affirming the party's commitment to the immediate establishment of imperial preference once they returned to office. In an effort to wake up a drowsy party, Croft was not hesitant to take the battle into the party's soft underbelly, demanding the attention and action of all Conservatives. He castigated "those thousands of property owners who will forcibly denounce Mr. Lloyd George and his socialistic measures while reclining in their clubs." He complained that "their opposition usually ends in smoke . . . it passes away as rapidly as the smoke of their cigars." With equal energy he turned on those "countless country squires who are badly hit and who yet have never taken their share in political work. . . . The Reveille calls upon the country gentlemen, among others to do something. . . . We want Unionists to wake up."[2]

On 19 October, H. J. Mackinder, the geographer, sent a Reveille manifesto to the press for publication, resulting in some aggravation for Croft. In his letter to the newspapers, Mackinder implied that the manifesto enjoyed sanction by the chief whip.[3] Maxse wasted little time in expressing his outrage to Croft. He was incensed by the apparent suggestion that the committee was "acting under the patronage of Acland Hood." Reminding Croft that "the value of the Reveille depends entirely on its independence of all officialdom," he threatened to withdraw from further participation on the Reveille steering committee.[4] Croft was forced to respond immediately to assuage Maxse's indignation. He explained that Mackinder's comments to the press were merely unintentional enthusiasm and that he, Croft, had not approved or even seen the correspondence. After having calmed himself, Maxse responded, "I am delighted to hear that you had no responsibility for the inopportune dragging in of Hood's name before our Manifesto." Maxse stated that he was most eager to work for and support the Reveille "which is one of the more hopeful signs in politics." In fact, he added, "independence should be the key note of our movement, as it was of the Fourth Party, which so far from taking its marching orders from Front Benchers ultimately forced Front Benchers to take their marching orders from it." Maxse's comments reinforced Croft's developing idea of an independent national party that would reject the paralysis and corruption he believed was so evident in the parliamentary parties. Notwithstanding his temporary anger, Maxse applauded Croft. "It was a great stroke getting out our Manifesto on the morning of Balfour's Naval speech, as everybody thinks the Reveille prompted that speech. Had we come 24 hours later we might have been in the cart."[5]

The manifesto continued to push toward an overall constructive program and an activist party.[6] It was the distillation and articulation of those strongly held beliefs that Croft had tirelessly promoted over the past six years. It argued that tariff reform, colonial preference, imperial unity, the navy and national defense, and social reform (as represented in this instance by small ownership of land and reform of the poor laws) were integrally connected and that their mutual and coherent promotion would produce synergistic benefit and security for all sections of the British and imperial community. For Croft it was the essence of the imperial idea. In a betrayal of his anxiety, but consistent with Croft's arguments over the past several years, the manifesto conceded that it was no longer adequate merely "to find the joints in the Radical armour" and peddle it as conservatism's alternative policy and program. Croft and Reveille stood for "a coherent and united plan of action," for a "national policy," and for the "constructive side of Unionism."[7] (For the text of the manifesto, see Appendix 3.)

The manifesto revealed the depth of anxiety and height of urgency held by the Reveille. Defending their act of rebellion, it was argued that these were not ordinary times. "Real and bitter discontent is sweeping through the popular mind" both in Britain and Europe. Fearful that the revolutionary movement will "unsettle opinions . . . for some years to come," constructive unionism must intervene and balance the popular forces. Accordingly, the Reveille sought to remind both the Conservative party and the kingdom that it is a great democratic party. It is a democratic movement that can stand for a practical and real hope, but it must be founded on a complete and constructive program and promoted by a dynamic and visionary leadership. It was tariff reform, as a national policy, that provided the core of a coherent and united program; it will produce national security and prosperity.[8] The concept of a common foreign policy for the empire was an effective method of countering the international balance of power handicap suffered by the individual imperial partners. Founded on interlocking commercial interests of the partners, the common foreign policy idea was a specific strike against Liberal free trade dogma and their recently touted concept of imperial federation. The Reveille denounced this as being nothing more "than the rebaptism of a policy of disintegration" behind which Liberals sought to hide Irish home rule.[9] As digested by the *Morning Post,* the Reveille argued "that it is the business of the State to conserve and foster the dynamic energies of the people." In promoting this principle, the young Conservatives advocated an "interrelated scheme which embraces the whole field of national life, from foreign policy to the Navy and Army, from military forces to the defensive development of national industries, . . . and from the industrial security behind the tariff to social advance and prosperity within the area the tariff protects."[10]

With a speech on naval policy at Glasgow on 19 October, Balfour sought to mute the criticism from the rebel MP and the "wild peer," the latter appellation having been attached to Willoughby de Broke. Notwithstanding the subject, which was near and dear to their hearts, Balfour's comments were uninspiring and did not give the Reveille much encouragement. "I have been appealed to," he confessed, "to express in precise formulae and in exact numbers what I should do and what I should recommend. I do not think that is the duty of those who are responsible for the policy of an Opposition." Instead, he adhered to his tactic of repeating his general attacks against the government, describing "the naval position of the country under the present Administration as perilous."[11] It was just such timidity that Croft and the Reveille now sought to extirpate from the party.

The emergence of the Reveille did not occur without controversy. The schism within the Conservative party had a generational characteristic as well as being philosophical and ideological. It was best illustrated by the reaction of Lord Londonderry, who criticized Croft and Willoughby de Broke as "the Prince Ruperts" of the party. Although he conceded that they may be effective "skirmishers," his comments documented the unbridgeable distance that existed between the party's ranks and its leaders. He admonished them to leave the campaign strategy "to the judgment and experience of the general at the head of their affairs." He further asserted that it rested with Balfour "to decide when and how the decisive and final blow should be struck." The opposition, he reminded the rebellious Conservatives, was "to oppose—to oppose, not to propose." He recalled that at Hull in 1907 Balfour declared that "to go into details was to place themselves in the position of the criticized instead being critics."[12] Of course it was just this attitude and sedentary position taken by the opposition front bench that gave rise to the Reveille movement in the first place.

As Croft explained, "it was no good for Conservatives . . . to be political passive resisters. They had got to take off their coats and go out with him into the open in that greatest of political fights in history for honest political administration."[13] Croft's experience in the tariff reform campaign convinced him that Balfour would not act unless pushed or pulled, as demonstrated by Balfour's reluctant subscription to tariff reform at Birmingham in November 1907. It was for this reason that the Reveille movement "laid down in concrete, in concise, form what were the main objects of the Unionist party."[14] Croft had consistently and vigorously argued that Conservatives could not parry the appeal of socialism and thus gain the working-class vote by remaining merely passive critics. Conservatives must confront socialism with an aggressive and affirmative program.

Lord Londonderry's criticism neither discouraged nor deterred Croft who, without hesitation, personally carried the Reveille program into the political fray of two by-elections. At Walthamstow, which had voted Liberal in 1906 and 1910, Stanley Johnston, a Conservative and Tariff Reform candidate, was repeating his challenge against Sir John Simon, the newly designated solicitor general. At South Shields, which had consistently voted Liberal since 1868, R. Vaughn Williams was challenging the Liberal candidate, Russell Rea. Croft's efforts, however, failed to bear fruit as both the Conservatives lost. This only deepened his resentment as he saw the party's leadership sit passively on the sidelines during these contests. He was disgusted by the failure of the leadership to use these opportunities to promote the program of tariff reform and imperial unity.

Witnessing the stagnation of the opposition front bench, Croft embarked on a campaign that took him to Hull, Derby, Bradford, Halifax, Luton, Scarborough, St. Helens, Reading, and several rallies in Bournemouth. Joined by Willoughby de Broke, he launched a campaign at Hull where they revealed their vulnerability with the working-class electorate. In response, they claimed that the Conservative party legitimately appealed to the best instincts of their fellow countrymen, because the Conservative party is a true *"National Party"* that represented all sections of the kingdom.[15] Croft was vigorously opposed to reversal of the Osborne judgment as well as to payment of members. He believed that such practices would surely contribute further to the corruption of politics. The Reveille campaign itself was conducted at a time when Britain was engulfed in serious industrial conflict with major lockouts and strikes at the dockyards and in the coalfields.

At Derby, Croft gave an exceedingly militaristic oration, putting "naval supremacy first in the programme" and urging Britain to "build, build now before it was too late." He scoffed at the charge that he was advocating an arms race, suggesting instead that the only way to stop it was to demonstrate a resolved determination to maintain supremacy of the seas. He was, however, equally appreciative of the domestic significance found in the consequential employment of British workmen. Again, reflecting his view of a modern, activist state, he urged reform of the poor laws, which would remove children from the system, and place them in the country. There they "might learn to do something on the land." In addition to enforcing the Alien Act, he suggested that "the time had come when [the British] should cease to put their hands in their pockets for professional tramps. . . . These men should be put into labour colonies and then repay the State for their keep."[16]

Croft and Willoughby de Broke were not alone in their frustration. On 3 November 1910, Lord Malmesbury declared that although the Reveille leadership is supportive of Balfour, he warned that the party could not continue to cling to outmoded tactics, anemic programs, or stand by cautious and tepid leaders. Accordingly, the Reveille promoted the cause of security, progress, and imperial unity, founded on three great principles: national defense, reform of the fiscal system, and a wide scheme of social and land reform. Exposing an intellectual transition within conservatism, Malmesbury also argued that "evolution is a theory which to-day is accepted as a dominating factor in the affairs of men. Change is the essence of life, and this incontrovertible dictum is nowhere more true than in the sphere of politics."[17]

Malmesbury viewed the Reveille as being "the outward expression of a growing and important consensus of opinion among the rank and file" of the Conservative party. These young and anxious Conservatives, as represented by the Reveille, are sensitive to the "charge that when the party holds the reins of office nothing is ever done, and the 'things go on' just as in the days of the old humdrum Toryism." He believed "that the time has come for placing before the electors of this country a definite and constructive policy." This opinion, which was held by the general rank and file as well as the new generation of Conservative MPs, "fully recognised that there is no longer time for delay." They demanded that "the camp must be struck, and another sweeping, decisive move made against the enemy's position."[18] In a scathing indictment of Balfour, Malmesbury charged that the Reveille leadership pivots on the realization that there was substantial danger from a continuing apathy and passivity of the Conservative leadership, more so than from Lloyd George himself. Employing romantic imagery, he suggested that the British people, like the Reveille, were "like young trees seeking the light, each generation of electors yearns for the warming sun and the life-giving air of leadership, freed and untrammeled from the overgrowth of time-expired, worn-out platitudes."[19]

The frustration within the party's rank and file was well represented by the Reveille, and it was eloquently set forth in an anonymous MP's letter to the *Morning Post*. The unknown MP first warned that although the Conservative party needed reform as well as organization, the present momentum for reform was coming from the ranks and not from the leadership. He lamented that the party did not know how to appeal to the electorate. He complained that candidates could not explain to electors what a Conservative government was prepared to do. For instance, he illustrated that "we do not really know whether Colonial foodstuffs are going to be taxed or not. This is a question on which the party has spoken two voices." With respect to the question of land taxes, something had to be decided by the leadership or even a party council. Instead, "as it is I am a wandering sheep." In conclusion, the article issued a plea to Balfour that Conservatives "are urgently in need of a more definite programme. If it only deals with general principles it will be sufficient. At present we are left too much in the dark on the matters of the highest interest. . . . Party reform must come from the head." He again warned that "if those now at the head are not ready to recognise the grave weaknesses of the Party, and if they do not act soon and firmly, both the Party and Tariff Reform are doomed to failure."[20]

The Reveille movement was not the only ongoing political development. In the secretive inner circles of politics, strange maneuverings were underway. By mid-August, Lloyd George had come to the conclusion that the problems facing the kingdom were so extraordinary and the times in which Britain found herself so precarious that they could only be tackled and resolved by a "national government."[21] In his proposed "non-Party solution" to the great national problems, the chancellor envisioned settlement of the major social issues and reforms, including improved housing, restrained drinking, effective insurance, reduced unemployment, and poor law reform; settlement of educational policy in light of denominational struggle and resistance; determination of trade issues, including fiscal reform and preference; the institution of efficient land reform; and a consistent and determined resolution of imperial and foreign policy issues, meaning the Irish question.

In early October, Lloyd George began discussions with a very select coterie of Liberals and Conservatives as to the possibility of creating a "ministry of all the talents" to resolve the nation's paralyzing problems.[22] Two of the

7: Croft, the Reveille, and the Fight against Humdrum Toryism 137

proposal's strongest supporters were F. E. Smith and J. L. Garvin, which goes a long way to explain their severe criticism of the Reveille movement during this time period. Garvin feared the collapse of the constitutional conference, and on 9 October he issued a stinging rebuke of the Reveille movement and their "malcontent manifestoes." Expressing more than mere pessimism over the future of the conference, Garvin argued that the Conservative party's prospects at a forthcoming election were hopeless as long as certain annoying and rebellious sections of the party continued to attack Balfour's leadership.[23]

F. E. Smith reminded Bonar Law that the success of Lloyd George's maneuvering would mean a "national party & well directed power for ten years."[24] On 11 October the chancellor approached Balfour, who in turn consulted Lord Cawdor, Lord Lansdowne, Austen Chamberlain, Lord Curzon, and Bonar Law.[25] Although negotiations continued throughout October, Lloyd George was nevertheless given to believe that they were all in favor of establishing a coalition. Smith sent an assessment to Balfour that revealed the level of frustration within Conservative ranks. He believed that, apart from the Ulster faction, the party hungered for a settlement. His assessment concluded that Churchill and Lloyd George cannot return to their party without ruin, and by remaining in such a national government, "they will be more influenced by the Tory party than it by them." Expressing concerns similar to Croft's, Smith wrote that "there is a widespread weariness & distrust of party combined with general apprehension of the national dangers into which party extremists are leading us."[26] Notwithstanding the inherent desire for an all-inclusive resolution as that being pursued by Lloyd George, the negotiations continued to be frustrated by the issue of Irish home rule, an issue on which Balfour ultimately demonstrated some determination.

Beyond the conference and coalition negotiations, two important propagandists were urging modification of the party's home rule position. Garvin, editor of the *Observer,* and F. S. Oliver,[27] who wrote as "Pacificus" for *The Times,* had converted to the concept of an "Imperial Federation."[28] On 6 October, Garvin suggested that it was imperative for the party to undertake "some fundamental alteration of . . . attitude on the Irish question."[29] With a hint of some knowledge of the secret affairs, a few days later he wrote that "to save the Unionist party this time will require a . . . rather a bolder effort—effort of a different kind."[30] By 16 October, Garvin, who by now had learned of the secret proposals, was using the *Observer* to call for the Irish question to be considered within the context of a larger settlement. Garvin wrote to Balfour that the Conservative party had reached a "turning point, and cannot attempt to fight the battle of the Union on the old terms in utterly changed circumstances, without the gravest risk of disaster to all its causes." He feared a continuation of present policies would "work a long series of other mischiefs by crippling us in parliament and the constituencies perhaps for years, and damaging us—the Imperial Party—almost fatally in the sight of the self-governing Dominions." He continued to think some form of devolution inevitable and therefore urged Balfour "that if we are to fight another General Election soon, we shall fight for a strong Second Chamber as the 'only bulwark' against Socialism . . . but that we shall not close the door to a reconsideration of the Irish question whether we win or nominally lose at the polls."[31]

The campaign by Garvin and Oliver had not gone unnoticed by Croft and the Reveille movement. In early November 1910, the Reveille movement responded with their "Manifesto on Home Rule," written by Croft. With a return strike at Garvin and Oliver, the Reveille declared its "desire to enter an early and emphatic protest against the absurd attempts of various armchair politicians, who have no right whatsoever to speak in the name of Unionism, and yet are endeavouring to pilot the party towards the dangerous abyss of Home Rule, via one of its many aliases." Inasmuch as the Reveille movement stood for the reconstruction of the British empire as being essential for both international security and domestic prosperity, Croft could not conceive "how the disruption of the United Kingdom can possibly promote the consolidation of the Empire."[32]

Many felt the Reveille had become too intransigent, as evidenced by R. D. Blumenfeld's resignation from the executive committee when Croft refused to repudiate the manifesto. Blumenfeld believed that the Reveille's extremist position would jeopardize support from even the Tory press. Croft answered that he had fully informed the committee to anticipate no help from the press. Further, he parried, the Reveille committee "quite appreciated the situation and went into battle with their eyes open, and we are quite prepared for the consequence, and even hostile opposition." In response to Blumenfeld's general protest over the Reveille, Croft reminded him "that it was our decision to unite the Party on a constructive program, but at the same time, we are determined to maintain the tradition, and fight for the principles of Conservatism and Unionism." Therefore, he suggested, the proposals that are being floated in the Conservative press clearly violated those principles. Reinforcing the manifesto, Croft held firm. "It would be madness to hope to establish a closer union of the Empire if you begin breaking up the central union at home." In addition, he feared the present financial conditions rendered it impossible to maintain several separate governments within the British Isles. He asked if Ireland was to have financial independence. If so, she would have a separate tariff system contrary to Chamberlain's imperial policy. On the other hand, Englishmen would not permit an arrangement whereby Britain financed an Irish government run as she sees fit. Lastly, he admonished Blumenfeld that "there is nothing so disastrous for a great Party than that it should sell every single tradition in order to win votes from those who will betray it whenever the hour suits."[33]

J. S. Sandars, who was sympathetic and supportive of Garvin's efforts to moderate Conservative opinion, complained correctly that the Reveille

7: Croft, the Reveille, and the Fight against Humdrum Toryism

"wanted to break the crockery—or at least to damage it so much that a new service may be wanted."[34] Garvin, for his part, renewed his public criticism of Reveille in the 6 November *Observer* where he denounced them for being dangerously shortsighted: "we are not sure whether they still put first, as we do, Imperial union, tariff defence, and the maintenance by national consent of an effective Second Chamber, or whether with the celebrated light heart, they mean not so much to march as to waltz to war under the saving device of 'Death or Dublin Castle.'" Garvin, now exceedingly frustrated over the collapse of the coalition talks, complained to Maxse that the Reveille were "devoid of vision."[35] Maxse responded, chiding the editor of the *Observer* for criticizing the Reveille as "wreckers" and for refusing to publish the Reveille statements. Their only offense was to demand a modern and aggressive party that would resolutely defend the nation and promote the empire.[36]

Although Croft's early public pronouncements demonstrated a rigid determination to maintain the Union, Ireland, which he viewed as part of greater Britain, remained separated from his imperial idea. His public dialogue over imperial preference and unity, by its lack of any constructive reference to Ireland, seemed to suggest that nothing was specifically required from Ireland. As a consequence of the Reveille's manifesto, Croft now entered into communications with Walter Long over the Irish question. It appears that Croft's consistent hard line over Ireland and union was capable of formulaic moderation. During these communications Croft had proposed that parliamentary consideration of Irish legislation should be physically carried out in Dublin. This altered view was the product of conversations with several Irishmen who enjoined Croft to see "whether there was not a way of meeting a legitimate grievance. We have got to face the fact," he conceded, "that Irishmen are not in touch with England and conversely there is no real understanding in England of Ireland. . . . They feel they are divorced and are outvoted by England from governing." Accordingly, Croft suggested, Parliament should sit for one month a year in Dublin, where British politicians could then "breathe the atmosphere of Ireland and study their wants first hand." Witnessing the Imperial Parliament opened by the king in Dublin would win Irish confidence and trust. He confessed to Long, "you may think I have travelled far since we met the other night but no man is right." Although Croft proposed a strategy to raise this proposal, it went no further than to being the subject of perfunctory discussion with Long.[37]

Notwithstanding a temporary moderation by such hard-liners as Croft, Garvin's appeal for compromise did not take root among the Conservative leadership. Given the strong rank-and-file opposition to the home rule elements, Lloyd George's coalition talks collapsed when Balfour withdrew his support. This came shortly after the party leader consulted his former chief whip, Aretas Akers-Douglas,[38] who informed Balfour that the rank and file, who had worked up such personal enmity toward those advocating compromise, would erupt at even the prospect of a rapprochement.[39]

On 8 November, Lord Esher found Balfour "in low spirits. He is most anxious," Esher recorded. Balfour "sees no immediate hope of party advantage in a general election, and believes that for the country's sake a compromise on the lines almost agreed to is the right thing." Esher concluded that Balfour fears the opposition of the stalwarts but primarily "the young wreckers," a reference to the right-wing rebels in the Reveille. Balfour, Esher recorded, "does not fancy the role of Sir Robert Peel." Accordingly, "he is inclined—if he finds persuasion hopeless—to resign the leadership of the Party."[40] It was clear that pressure from the Reveille movement had now been felt at the highest level of the party's leadership.

The negotiations over Lloyd George's proposal to establish a national government irrevocably broke down on 3 November. This development was followed seven days later by the final collapse of the constitutional conference. As early as 8 November, the cabinet had been advised that no further compromise was realistically possible, and, as the king's biographer noted, "the period of reprieve had come to an end."[41]

Asquith and the cabinet were resolved upon an immediate dissolution and an election before Christmas. Croft had consistently demanded that in preparation for going to the country, the party needed to set forth a definite, coherent, and determined program for both the party ranks and the electorate. Although few British elections had been anticipated more, this admonition was regularly ignored by Balfour and the leadership. Instead, the Conservative party was utterly unprepared and coerced into a "hurried announcement of policies they had hoped to avoid."[42]

While the Reveille movement was in full campaign gallop, the identity of their prey appeared more often to be Balfour than Asquith. Although Balfour pleased the Reveille and the other hard-liners by holding fast on the Ireland, his support for tariff reform and imperial preference was unraveling. By early November 1910, he had been put under considerable pressure from Garvin, Sandars, and even John Norton-Griffiths to abandon food duties, which for the latter was ironic inasmuch as he originally was a member of the Reveille movement. Balfour had been softened up on the issue so much that by 11 November he wanted to see Austen Chamberlain immediately. Meanwhile, Sandars wrote to Acland Hood "with an outline of the new policy, so that he may reflect upon it, & meet us, prepared to discuss it." Clearly, an antitariff reform conspiracy, for pure electoral tactical purposes, was under way: "So let us," Sandars wrote Garvin, "propagate the idea, carefully, judiciously & semi-confidentially until, as I hope, the public deliverance comes and falls upon a willing party. . . . But Austen will be the difficulty."[43]

Chamberlain saw Balfour on 12 November 1910 and realized that G. E. Buckle, editor of *The Times,* Garvin, John Norton-Griffiths, and others had all been in to frighten Balfour and persuade him not to accept tariffs without a subsequent appeal to the electors. Chamberlain now spent an hour and a half trying to prop up Balfour. He warned that if Balfour "took Preference off his flag he could never put it back again." He feared that by abandoning the corn duty, then "all the Colonies would say (with truth) that the game was up." He admonished Balfour that the party policy that the wobblers were urging on him "would be a mere repetition of the mistake of 1906. We should still have the odium of the Corn Duty attaching to us. The only difference would be that we should not defend ourselves." He argued that any abandonment of food tariffs would cost the party the artisan vote because industrial tariffs remained, and the agricultural vote because the tariff had been lifted.[44] In the end, writing to his father, Chamberlain was confident that "Balfour stands firm and will nail the flag to the mast tomorrow."[45]

However, appreciating the extensive pressure being applied on Balfour by Lord Derby and Sandars, Lord Balcarres recorded the greater apprehensions of other opinions. "Yesterday Harry Chaplin told us in consternation that Balfour was meditating the announcement that he will drop the food taxes." Recognizing that food taxes are unpopular, Balcarres nevertheless believed nothing would be gained by dropping them. Instead, "it would split the party." Austen Chamberlain, Bonar Law, and other determined tariff reformers would be unable to join a resulting Balfour government, which would then face enemies from Liberals and rebel Conservatives.[46]

Both Chamberlain and Balcarres were concerned about Balfour's speech to the annual party conference in Nottingham, scheduled for 17 November. The dilemma in which Balfour found himself was fully revealed at Nottingham where he needed to appease the whole-hog tariff reformers such as Chamberlain and Croft's Reveille as well as to convey encouragement to the wobblers. This dilemma resulted from Balfour's inability to resolve the internal party debate over tactics versus strategy, a consistent demand by Croft. Further, the party leader failed to define future governmental programs. Accordingly, at the Nottingham party conference, Balfour declared that he had nothing new to say on the substance of tariff reform other than it remains the party's first constructive policy. However, he satisfied both wings of the party by pledging "that no increase . . . in the cost of living due to any change in the taxes on consumption in consequence of Tariff Reform shall fall on the working-man's Budget."[47]

On behalf of the Reveille, Croft responded with "A Call to the British People" in which he applauded Balfour's "magnificent speech." Croft's document was in fact an electoral manifesto in which the Reveille denounced destruction of the House of Lords as well as dissolution of the Union. He further called for a resolute naval program to ensure the national security. Domestically, the Reveille called for social reform founded on tariffs and the safeguarding of British industries.[48]

The wobblers continued their pressure on Balfour, and their success sent shock waves through the Reveille. The internal party crisis over food duties took an unexpected turn when the idea of a referendum was publicly injected into Balfour's deliberations. It was aggressively promoted by Garvin in the *Observer* and by Sandars behind the scenes. They hoped to convert Balfour before his speech at the Albert Hall which was scheduled for 29 November 1910.[49] They were soon joined in their effort by lords St. Aldwyn, Salisbury, Cromer, Derby, and Archibald Savidge.[50] On 27 November Garvin received a telegram from the editor of the *Textile Mercury,* a Lancashire cotton trade journal, warning that Lancashire could only be gained if Balfour consented to a referendum. The *Observer* responded immediately with a call for referenda on both home rule and tariff reform. Soon the idea of submitting tariff reform to a referendum was endorsed by the *Daily Mail, Evening News, Daily Graphic, The Times, Standard, Globe,* and *Daily Express*. The unknown factor was Andrew Bonar Law, who had been persuaded to abandon his safe seat at Dulwich to contest a seat at Manchester and hopefully to spearhead Conservative gains in Lancashire. The moderating forces of Lancashire, which had never embraced tariff reform with any enthusiasm, finally began to soften Bonar Law's edge. On 28 November he wrote Balfour that he did not perceive much objection to submitting the issue to a referendum, but if this was to be the decision, it must be done promptly to be of any electoral value.[51] The chief forwarded Bonar Law's letter to Austen Chamberlain, with an accompanying endorsement for the proposition.[52] Without much surprise Chamberlain's response was to ridicule and condemn the idea.[53] With the whole-hogger leadership now split and apparently being convinced that rigid adherence to tariff reform and food duties would cost the Conservatives another election, Balfour made his decision. Although Bonar Law soon had second thoughts,[54] on 29 November in a speech at Albert Hall, Balfour charged forward, declaring that he had no objection to submitting tariff reform to a referendum. Inasmuch as it constituted a major national and imperial policy, he announced that he was "perfectly ready to submit it to the judgment of my countrymen."[55]

Although the referendum announcement appears to have done little to encourage or energize Conservative candidates, MPs, or workers, it unrealistically inflated the hopes of the party's free traders. St. Loe Strachey now claimed that he felt like a Conservative once again, and he renewed his membership in his constituency association.[56] Chamberlain, however, confessed to Lord Lansdowne that Balfour's declaration "was a great blow to me—the worst disappointment I have suffered for a long time in politics."[57] After the heat of the election had subsided, Walter Long severely chastised Balfour for making the declaration without consulting members of the shadow cabinet.[58] However, during the election, the tariff reformers, moderates, and radicals buried their hurt and anger in favor of public displays of party loyalty. Croft was no exception.

Given the very brief time within which the contest at Christchurch was

7: Croft, the Reveille, and the Fight against Humdrum Toryism 143

conducted, Croft did not have the luxury of dwelling on his disappointment. During a campaign rally held the day before Balfour's Albert Hall address, Croft was asked if he would be prepared to submit tariff reform to a referendum. Without any hesitation, he answered, "undoubtedly I would for . . . I have not one doubt but that the ayes would have it, and would vote from Tariff Reform. . . . I say 'Trust the People.'"[59] Although he never unilaterally addressed himself to the issue, when subsequently questioned he responded that "he would be quite prepared to see the question referred to a straight vote of the people, and if his party were returned to power, and his leader on behalf of the party decided to put the matter to the Referendum, he stood by his leader."[60]

The campaign revealed the stamina and energy for which Croft was well known. On 16 November, even before Asquith had announced the dissolution, Croft returned to Bournemouth after a three-week Reveille campaign in Yorkshire and the north of England where he addressed fifteen separate rallies and over thirty thousand people. He returned south knowing another campaign loomed on the horizon, this time to defend his seat, which was not considered tremendously safe. He was opposed by Frederick W. Verney who retired from his seat at North Buckinghamshire with the hope of recapturing Christchurch for the Liberals.[61] Verney was much more aggressive than Acland Allen had been in January, and as a result Croft was kept on the defensive over such issues as the House of Lords, religion, old-age pensions, food duties, licensing and temperance issues. Croft responded with fifty-four rallies in twenty days, including eight separate meetings on 2 December, and his Christchurch campaign came on the heels of a Reveille campaign in the north of England.[62] Further, in the midst of his own campaign, Croft returned north for major Reveille rallies at Scarborough and then proceeded to stump for four Reveille associates. While in Scarborough he campaigned for G. V. A. Monckton-Arundel and then headed south to Reading where he campaigned for Captain Leslie Wilson. He also provided time and energy to go to Poole where he tried to bolster the candidacy of Maurice Glyn in his contest at East Dorset. After his Christchurch election had finished, he responded to requests for assistance from Basil Peto at the Devizes division of Wiltshire, from the Conservative candidates in Hertfordshire, and from his brother-in-law, George Borwick, who was standing for the Eye division of Suffolk.

In addition to the constructive program that was elaborately set out during the Reveille campaign—strong navy, scientific tariff, imperial unity, and social reform—Croft continued to defend the House of Lords generally, and specifically with respect to its treatment of the 1909 budget. Yet very early on, he was compelled to agree to the theoretical need to reform the second chamber, not unlike the step finally taken by Balfour and the leadership.[63] He often chastised Lloyd George for resorting to the politics of "envy, hatred, malice, and uncharitableness."[64] The issue of trade unions appears to have arisen only once, and he confessed not to understand or accept the arrangement whereby Radical, Liberal, or Conservative trade unionists were required to subsidize the election of Socialist candidates. He also remained unalterably opposed to any reversal of the Osborne judgment.[65]

With respect to the Irish question, Croft declared that "this loathsome corpse of Home Rule which was buried by the people of this country so many years ago, is apparently going to be dug up and paraded in all its ugliness before the people of the land."[66] He considered the recently circulating notions of federalism to be nonsense and impossible to implement. In the heat of the election, he provocatively suggested that the kingdom was faced with either union or separation; there was no middle ground. England would not continue to pay for Irish old-age pensions or finance Irish land purchases. Similarly, Ulster would not tolerate its money flowing to Dublin to finance the governance of Ireland by Dublin. Thus, he suggested, it meant the establishment of a parliament in Dublin and one in Belfast, and in his view Dublin would not be able to exist without Ulster's money.

Although the national polling extended from 2 to 19 December, it concluded at Christchurch on 5 December, and Croft now had his second victory in twelve months. This time it was by a slightly reduced majority of 656 (5,275–4,619). The national results followed the pattern illustrated by the polling at Christchurch and provided little change. The Liberal and Conservative parties each won 272 seats while Labour secured 42, a gain of 2, and the Irish Nationalists gained 84, also an increase of 2. The Conservatives failed to make any significant improvement on their holdings in Lancashire, increasing from 9 to 13 out of well over 40 possible seats. Even Bonar Law was defeated at Manchester. Balfour's rash declaration at Albert Hall on 29 November produced no demonstrable advantage. Instead, it compromised the party and reopened the internal wounds over tariff reform. His leadership, which had been openly questioned by the Reveille movement, was now exposed to serious and determined challenge.

As the results came in, Maxse, in a letter to Goulding, framed the struggle within which the party would soon find itself. Balfour, he wrote, "has done more harm to Tariff Reform during the last two months than he did good in the previous five years" and that the referendum speech "cost us 40 or 50 seats. It is unpardonable. Balfour must go, or Tariff Reform will go—that is the alternative."[67] Similar anger and frustration surfaced when Maxse wrote to Bonar Law. He denounced Balfour's Albert Hall speech as being "nothing less than a crime." Conservatives, he predicted, will no longer choose Balfour over tariff reform "as the discontent is too present and widespread."[68]

When the polling finally ended and the results were known, Maxse claimed that "we should have won this General Election if it had not been for Arthur Balfour side-tracking Tariff Reform."[69] In the exercise of considering historical "what ifs," one may flirt with a view of the consequences of a Conservative victory in the December 1910 election under Balfour's tactics. Most

7: Croft, the Reveille, and the Fight against Humdrum Toryism 145

likely both the tariff reform movement and the rebel factions would have been rendered irrelevant and quickly disintegrated. As it was, tariff reformers continued to point to Balfour and his tepid support as being the primary reason why the party remained out of office.

The message that the election results conveyed to Croft was that the empire could not depend upon the present Conservative leadership. Accordingly, two alternatives presented themselves to Croft. If Balfour would not advance the empire, he must go. Failing that, a new political entity must be established that will fight all foes on behalf of imperial unity regardless of where they are found, in or out of the party. In fact, should opponents be found to be within the party, they must be destroyed first before the imperial reformers can legitimately call on the country to embrace a new imperialism.

8
Croft, Conservative Party Politics, and the Balfour Question (1911)

> Unionism must arouse itself. Unionism must be militant.
> —Henry Page Croft, 3 February 1911

> If there is a further move on let me know as I am now an "Independent" and all for war with the mugwumps.
> —Henry Page Croft, 13 August 1911

The twelve months that followed the December 1910 general election constituted a crucial period for Conservative and national politics. Croft had resolutely concluded that the leadership was incapable of leading and that the party organization was incapable of winning elections, obvious prerequisites for the implementation of any imperial reform. He also concluded that he was witnessing the destruction of the British constitution and the disintegration of the British empire. However, he refused to suffer such conditions passively. His assessment of the political situation pushed him further into the area of rebel and militant politics, where he sometimes considered himself an independent and where he took steps toward the creation of a national and imperial party. In 1911 Croft believed the imperial question required a settlement of the Balfour question, and if it did not occur, he was prepared to act unilaterally. Although Britain and the Conservative party suffered a significant weakening of the House of Lords in 1911, for Croft the year ended with another optimistic swing as the Balfour question was resolved. He became convinced that the party would commit itself to fiscal reform and imperial unity, but it was a precarious political journey to the resolution of the Balfour question.

Within forty-eight hours after polling in the second general election in twelve months had concluded, an agitated but determined Croft issued another Reveille manifesto. Expressing his frustration and rage as well as apprehension, Croft announced that with half the electorate opposed to the government's demolition of the second chamber, the Reveille movement would "refuse to take this lying down. [We] will fight. Our efforts at compro-

8: Croft, Conservative Party Politics, and the Balfour Question

mise have been taken for weakness, and our attempts at conciliation for fear . . . and proposals put forward as a solution for Parliamentary deadlock have been scorned as death-bed repentance." Accordingly, he warned, the Parliament bill will bring "Home Rule for Ireland with all its damning results in the shape of bankruptcy and civil war." Truly alarmed by this prospect, he feared that "tariff reform, which offers the only serious solution of our social evils, will be delayed. . . . Imperial Preference, and the closer commercial union of the Empire, will be dead for all time." It was the position of Croft and the Reveille that "Ulster can never be betrayed, and the Constitution shall never be surrendered. The Parliament Bill must be fought with no quarter all along the line . . . and must be rejected."[1]

With significant implications for internal party dynamics, Croft knew that the election would be subjected to a scrutinizing inquest. While both the party ranks and lieutenants waited for someone to fire the first shot, Croft provoked public discussion with his own examination and detailed prescription for the party. In January 1911 he arranged with Fabian Ware, editor of the *Morning Post,* to publish a four-part series on the Conservative party under the title "How Unionism Can Win" that sequentially addressed the problems and prescriptions under the categories of organization, men, tactics, and strategy.[2]

Although he had never been an apologist for the Central Office, Croft believed that the failings of the party rested on the overall condition of its organization. His prescriptions pivoted on the conclusion that improvement required local associations to come into a general system wherein they will "be put under a disciplinary government from headquarters." This meant that "every ward or polling district association will be responsible to the Parliamentary Divisional, and that association shall be responsible to the Chief Agent of the party."[3] Revealing his own philosophical view of political democracy, in which were found conflicting tenets of populism and the efficiency of authoritarian submission, Croft argued that the strength of local associations needed to be harnessed to and by the Central Office. To carry out this reform, Croft set forth a multipoint program.

First, local constituency organizations must accept a scheme to include all classes, especially working men. Second, local associations must accept periodic inspections that would review and evaluate local operations. This would not only give the national party further control, but more importantly, it would provide the mechanism and opportunity for practical and political assistance from the Central Office. Third, if the local association cannot or fails to implement the inspection's remedial recommendations, then the matter shall be reported to the Central Office. Fourth, continued resistance to remedial actions by a local association or an inability to implement the suggested improvements would bring a visit by someone of front bench who would meet the executive and "ask them to accept the reorganization of the association by a Central Office inspector." The next step would be to require the local constituency to elect new officers, who will put the scheme into operation. Fifth, each constituency should establish a women's political association, either Primrose League, Conservative, or Tariff Reform. Sixth, Conservative Club Defence Leagues should be formed in each constituency to form parties of stewards to secure a fair hearing for speakers. Seventh, in order to integrate the participant of young men and women, junior Conservative associations should be formed in all constituencies. Eighth, the national and local party organizations must implement a systematic and quarterly distribution of literature in every constituency. Croft went on to argue the obvious: the Conservative organization, cause, and policies still require the right men. Beginning at the bottom, with the canvassers or "private soldiers of the party," the future of British politics required the inclusion of the working class. Accordingly, "intelligent political enthusiasts" should be recruited into the party associations and given important assignments. It was also obvious that the ward secretaries be "extremely energetic and popular" and that ward chairmen must hold "some position in the neighborhood." The executive committee, a popularly elected body, should distribute its responsibilities among subcommittees for finance, literature, registration, and meetings. The president of the executive committee may be a figurehead who has paid for the honor, but the chairman must be able to devote himself to politics—a businessman, for instance. The chairman must be able to maintain a constant procession of party meetings and functions and be able to raise funds. It was also imperative that the party agent be a full-time professional; no longer will a local solicitor, who was unwilling to make more than a token contribution of time, be acceptable.[4]

Croft next charged that constituency associations must no longer rely on the unilateral appearance of wealthy candidates. This assumption and consequential passivity on the part of local associations have allowed situations to develop whereby no candidates were selected in many constituencies until very late November or early December 1910. By then it was too late to mount a credible campaign. This situation was tolerated even though all but the politically illiterate had been anticipating a subsequent election since the spring of 1910. "No self-respecting candidate," Croft admonished, "will offer himself for a constituency when no attempt has been made to organise and when no money is subscribed." Where these inexcusable conditions were permitted, the chairman must be held accountable and removed.

He also condemned the existing situation where enthusiastic, eloquent, and hard-working individuals were rejected as candidates because they were not independently wealthy, while local "rich men sit around dinner-tables sipping their champagne and complaining that there is no Croesus who will come and save them from Lloyd George!" Accordingly, Croft demanded to know, "when will the local captains of industry, squires, professional men and tradesmen pay for their own defence?" A constituency must put its money down and be vigilant in the anticipation of and preparation for an election. Those deriving their wealth from industry should choose one of their own who understands their industries and who can fight their battle. "Let businessmen come out for business centres" and let "university men take the field in the small boroughs and agricultural experts in the counties." He sharply criticized the men of wealth who demanded to be saved from socialist ruin and argued that they must prove they deserve it by doing their share.[5]

In his third essay, Croft returned to the issue that long had been gnawing at him, and with his usual display of emotion and energy, he leveled a volley at the party leadership. In doing so he again raised the question of tactics. The party "has suffered more from its tactics than anything else in the last few years." Specifically, his charge traveled from the 1904–5 period when the leadership held on to office without any aim or policy, when instead it could have energized the party and country with the program of tariff reform. In 1906 and twice in 1910, the leadership did nothing when Conservative candidates were accused of being food taxers. In fact, Croft alleged, the leadership actually intrigued with the party's free traders. Leveling his aim at Balfour and the leadership in general, Croft claimed that the party fought the 1906 election "with no single good man to champion the cause." During the budget fight, the leadership rested its hopes on rallying public opinion against the land taxes. As a consequence, the party was tainted as the defender of the landlords, while the party's response to increased burdens on the working classes, to the income tax increases on the middle classes, and to attack on the licensed industries was apathetic and wide of the mark. Croft further ridiculed the Anti-Budget League for being "a miserable failure," consuming funds and wasting energy. Instead, the party leadership should have responded with an alternative budget based on the principles of tariff reform and promoted it with a vigorous and articulate national campaign.[6]

Croft also condemned the party's deathbed conversion to second-chamber reform as being a public admission that it "was unfit and wrongly constituted. . . . If the House of Lords desired to change its composition it should merely have reduced its members so that only the ablest of the Peers should sit in the Upper House." Similarly, he argued, the party leadership had forfeited their credibility by failing to provide any strategy and program with respect to questions of defense, the budget, agricultural policy, political reform, and imperial unity. He pointed out that in November 1910, when the backs of the party's ranks were turned and without consulting leaders of the tariff reform movement, Balfour suddenly pledged that tariff reform would not be passed without a referendum. "Here was a present to the enemy, without anything in return. The stupidity of these tactics," Croft continued, expressing what members of the radicalized right wing of the party surely felt, "is clearly reflected in the mirror of the election, for not a single net gain can be recorded." It appeared to be "an election dodge, . . . an eleventh hour betrayal amongst Tariff Reform working men."[7]

Croft threw down a challenge. The leadership must lead and cease its endless tactical minuets that were performed to the tune played by Asquith and Lloyd George. The party must adopt, articulate, and adhere to a bold, aggressive, and constructive program based on tariff reform, empire union, a strong navy and defense, no home rule without a referendum, no aliens, and poor law reform.[8] The party's constructive policy must be a British policy advancing the kingdom and empire by providing British workers with a defense of their industries. This can only be accomplished by tariff reform, imperial preference and unity, a strong regular army supported by universal military service, and an unrivaled navy, all subsidiary components of Croft's imperial idea.[9]

Believing that "alien hordes are overrunning our labour markets, cramming our workhouses and filling our prisons," Croft feared that "the flower of our race is being driven away from our shores to hostile countries." It is imperative that "the diseased, the destitute, and the criminal must be barred out and no longer infest our slums." Further, if emigration must take place, it is the duty of an imperial party to see that people go to "lands under the British flag." The party must also defend the constitution, "even to the last ditch in defence of the Loyalists of Ireland." Ironically, he demanded that such major constitutional issues must be decided by the people and the people alone. With the House of Lords strangled by the veto proposal, he warned that the entire constitution was in jeopardy, including the hereditary monarch. The gates were open for a wave of destructive measures from the Radicals and Socialists. He alerted conservatives to be prepared for the government to make another run at home rule that he feared would destroy any idea of imperial union; for an attempt to disestablish the church in Wales, and perhaps even in England; for an attempt to destroy manhood suffrage; and for the nationalization of property. The Conservative party, Croft declared, "must arouse itself. Unionism must be militant."[10]

Notwithstanding the more general criticism leveled by the Reveille, there remained the temptation by many inside the party to make the party machinery the scapegoat for the third electoral defeat. Lord Selborne refused to believe that the confusion provoked by the last-minute call for a referendum for tariff reform contributed to the Conservative party's defeat. He tried to insulate Balfour from criticism, suggesting "that everywhere I heard dissatisfaction expressed with the Central Office, sometimes very strongly. It is my profound conviction that it has become humanly impossible for one man to manage the party organisation, finances, etc., and to act as Whip in the House of Commons."[11] Also taking aim at Acland Hood, Leo Amery expressed concern that although it remained out of office, the party would continue to be frustrated until the chief whip had been either "poisoned or pensioned."[12]

Although he may have often appeared alone in the public expression of his discontent, Croft's sentiment represented only the tip of the iceberg as the private expressions of aggravation increased. Sir Joseph Lawrence, who was equally close with Croft's Confederacy and the party leadership, questioned whether, in the face of his tactical misjudgments and lack of any constructive strategy, "A.J.B.'s prestige will ever recover from this third defeat. I meet no one who forgives him his bad tactics."[13] Walter Long took his concerns, which reflected much of the Reveille opinion, privately to Balfour and suggested that the party's weakness went beyond the Central Office or the chief whip. Long complained that unlike the procedure in the 1890s, Balfour no longer took counsel or advice from the party leadership or his parliamentary colleagues. Instead, Acland Hood and Sandars had come to control the business in the House of Commons, including topics for debates. "Is it quite fair," Long inquired of Balfour, "to ask men who have held high office under you and who have served in several Cabinets, to subordinate their judgment and views—not to yours, but to those of men who have never been in Cabinets, and who have no claim of any kind to the position in which by some strange accident they have found themselves?" As a result, Long suggested, "the system has worked disastrously, has produced great friction among some of your Front Bench colleagues and profound dissatisfaction among many of your followers in the Back Benches and in the country." He urged Balfour to return to a practice of taking regular and weekly counsel to decide upon and formulate party policy. Long also pointed out that no Conservative MP had been assigned the responsibility of overseeing the actions of several important government departments—Foreign Office, India Office, Local Government Board, or the Board of Agriculture. The Conservative's front bench could not keep the Liberal government in check under these circumstances.[14] Notwithstanding such criticism and pressure, Lord Esher recorded, "I have seen A.J.B [and] A.J.B. doesn't care a damn for his critics and will see them at the devil."[15]

It has been suggested that perhaps Balfour was persuaded to take some reforming action on receiving an expression of concern from Lord Lansdowne and, further, after lords Salisbury, Derby, Curzon, and Hugh Cecil gave an ultimatum "for a high-powered committee to investigate and reform the whole organization."[16] Balfour nevertheless was forced to face certain facts. "I think," he wrote to Akers-Douglas on 17 January, "we must get on with the organization business." He believed criticism of the Central Office was warrantless. However, the system that remained unaltered for nearly twenty-five years needed updating, particularly with respect to the National Union. Yet he considered the remedies circulated by his critics—including Croft—to be "absurd and impracticable" and to prevent their subscription Balfour recognized the necessity of conducting a thorough examination of the party organization. Such a process needed to be executed by a committee in which the young rebels would have confidence. He accepted that there must be a major reformation of the position of chief whip as he found "it hard to believe that any single person can do the work demanded of a modern head whip." It was impossible to coddle the parliamentary party, maintain an influence within the constituencies, preserve his own seat, and carry out the massive volume of correspondence that was required.[17]

On 1 February 1911, the composition of the Unionist Organization Committee (U.O.C.), to be chaired by Akers-Douglas, was announced, and it included significant representation from the rebel elements: Edward Goulding, Tariff Reform League, Confederacy, and the Reveille; Lord Willoughby de Broke, Imperial Mission and the Reveille; Arthur Steel-Maitland, Tariff Reform League and Confederacy; Ralph Glyn, the Reveille; and Walter Long, Budget Protest League, who was developing a close association with the Reveille and whose brother, Richard Chaloner, was a member of the Reveille movement. The committee of inquiry also included Sutton Nelthorpe, National Union Lincolnshire area chairman; George Younger, Scottish whip; and Lord Selborne, a former Liberal Unionist chief whip who became closely associated with Croft's Imperial Mission in 1911.[18]

In response to the announcement of the committee, Croft, who opened the Reveille's 1911 campaign at a rally in Bristol with Walter Long, called for democratization of the organization throughout the party. Naturally, Croft's call for such reform of the Conservative party was not for its own inherent value but with the intent to use such populism as a means of purging the remaining resisters to an aggressive party and advanced imperial program. These obstructionists could be found, Croft hinted, at the top as well as in the constituencies. He was convinced that only by unleashing an internal populism on the party would it finally be purged of the obstructionists and others who were out of step with the needs of the new age and who failed to recognize the type of political party and strategy required to survive in this new age.

Croft believed the party would unite around an ambitious program of imperial reconstruction, to be pursued by policies for tariff reform and imperial preference. This new cohesion of dedicated party and ambitious program would promptly translate into electoral success. The last layers of insulation between the popular message and humdrum toryism needed to be removed through party reform and reorganization. He argued "that in the constituencies [the party organization] should not be a government of the few; but should select their officers and carry the standard of their party forward. . . . If their organisation was to be successful they must have fundamental alteration from top to bottom."[19] In a supporting response from the *National Review,* Maxse charged that "three defeats in five years should satisfy any man . . . where responsibility lies, namely, upon the leader." However, he claimed, the party's front bench and the conservative press refused to accept this reality and, instead, "denounce as traitors those of us who insist on fixing responsibility." They hunt for scapegoats, attaching blame "upon underlings, subordinates and systems for which the leader is wholly and solely responsible."[20]

The condition that protected Balfour from a party revolt was best described by Lord Balcarres: "When somebody complains of Arthur Balfour's attitude a simple query as to his possible successor brings the conversation to an abrupt close. There is no available heir to the throne . . . and to talk of a change of leadership is futile when no potential substitute can be named." Chamberlain declined to challenge Balfour; Bonar Law had lost his seat. "Long is not of the necessary calibre, Wyndham distrusted by the Ulster Unionists and the rest are mostly lawyers."[21] Without an available and agreed-on successor, deposing a leader was always rather difficult. Thus the rebels pinned their hopes on the populism of party reorganization.

The U.O.C. eventually produced a set of recommendations that were implemented by November 1911:

1. Two new posts should be created so that the direction of the party organization would be tripartite. The Chief Whip would continue to look after the House of Commons; a "Party Treasurer" would raise money; a "Chairman of the Party" would take over Central Office and the party outside parliament. This last would need to be "of Cabinet rank" so that he could deal with National Union leaders on equal terms.
2. Central Office and the National Union office should be merged and the close relations of the two organizations, interrupted in 1906, should be resumed. Central Office should use the National Union as a sounding board, but only Central Office would have executive authority.
3. The accommodation of Central Office should be improved, and the new Chairman should have a free hand as to its staffing.
4. There should be coordination between the Whips and Central Office. Each Whip should supervise an area corresponding to a Central Office Area and a National Union Provincial Division. Scotland should remain separate, with a Scottish Whip occupying a position much like that of the Party Chairman.
5. There would need to be a wholesale improvement of the methods of the local parties, a transition to permanent organization, and a more active concern with propaganda. Agents should be trained and should be encouraged to regard themselves as a profession.[22]

In June 1911 Acland Hood was given a peerage, as Baron St. Audries, and Lord Balcarres was then appointed chief whip, a decision that was greeted with general approval from the back benches.[23] In a surprise move, Arthur Steel-Maitland was named as the first chairman of the Conservative party, and Lord Farquhar made treasurer. By the end of the year, the reforms had shifted most of internal authority away from the National Union and constituencies to the Central Office.[24] The reforms of 1911 provided a retransfer of authority over finance, organization, and propaganda back to the Central Office.[25] While Steel-Maitland and Balcarres were quietly engaged in reforming the party organization, the rebels, as well as the whole kingdom, were transfixed on more consuming public controversies. At the end of

January 1911, it was announced that Canada and the United States had reached an agreement for a reciprocal trade pact. Second with the opening of Parliament, the Asquith government promptly reintroduced the Parliament Bill, and on 22 February it passed its first reading by a vote of 351 to 227.[26]

Croft's interest in reforming the party organization soon fell by the wayside as he became more and more obsessed with saving both the constitution and the British empire. During the crises of 1911, Croft had steadily shifted to a position that any reform of the party under the present leader was irrelevant to the promotion of imperial unity. If, as continually demonstrated, the leadership failed to promote ideas and programs that would make the party an imperial party, then Croft was prepared to embark on the creation of an independent national and imperial party for such a purpose. The campaign waged by Croft and his Imperial Mission to preserve and unify the empire will be discussed in the next chapter, although in many instances Croft embraced the two issues concurrently.

In his first response to the newly introduced Parliament Bill, Croft accused the government of trying to use its rather flaccid majority to force a bill on nearly 50 percent of the electorate. He quickly penetrated the government's disingenuousness, pointing out that during the December 1910 election the Liberals based their case on the condemnation of hereditary peers, but still all the anomalies of a hereditary chamber remained under Asquith's legislation. The government's veto bill was not the reform peddled and promised during the campaign. Instead, the bill would establish single-chamber government against which Conservatives had warned. Croft asked, "What is the crime which the House of Lords has committed? Is it that it is hereditary? If so, why does not the Government reform it immediately? Is it because of the backwoodsmen? Then why not accept the scheme of the House of Lords for reform? Is it that the House of Lords lacks ability?" Croft invited a comparison between "the 300 best men in the Lords with a similar 300 in the Commons. In oratory, in experience, in service to the State, and in ability they are immeasurably superior to the Commons." He suggested, "what then is the crime of the Lords? Simply this, that there happens to be a Conservative majority." However, the government rejected the peers' own offer of reform. Issuing a virtual call to battle, Croft declared, "there is one course, and one course only," for Conservatives, and that is "to fight to the bitter end to save the country from this great Government betrayal. . . . Too long have we dallied; the reveille must sound to-morrow, and the battalion must move into the firing line."[27]

The Parliament Bill passed its second reading 368 to 243 on 2 March and then its third reading by a vote of 362 to 241 on 15 May 1911.[28] In Croft's personal campaign against the Parliament Bill, he routinely charged that the government was not opposed to the hereditary principle but only to the Conservative majority. Otherwise the government would have considered the reform proposals of Lord Lansdowne.[29] He also claimed that there was no comparison between the qualifications of the peers and the government's front bench. After pointing out that two hundred peers had served in the army and navy and one hundred of them had been under fire, he sarcastically added, "it is only right that I should remember that the Home Secretary [Churchill] served his country, although by the end he deteriorated into a war correspondent; . . . and one other occupant of the Front Bench opposite had, I think, the honour for nearly one hour of wearing the uniform of the King on the occasion of a meeting in Birmingham." When challenged by a Liberal backbencher that "there are other ways of serving your country than fighting," Croft protested. "I was only mentioning that the Chancellor of the Exchequer [Lloyd George] did wear a policeman's uniform for a short time during the South African War, and I want to give credit for it."[30] The Bill was quickly sent to the House of Lords, where on 29 May it received a second reading without a division. By the end of June, the House of Lords went into committee where they began amending the Bill.

With the matter resting in the upper chamber and as it steadily progressed toward its final consideration, the Conservative party now began to struggle over where it should draw its defensive position. Walter Long wrote to Maxse, "of course for the present our attitude must be one of determined opposition . . . but I am very anxious about the future."[31] For his part Maxse sought to intensify the pressure on Balfour, suggesting that the leader's silence implied some "collusion between the front benches."[32] Maxse, now joined by Garvin and *The Observer,* sought to incite a party rebellion against Balfour, Lansdowne, Long, and the others who were prepared to surrender.[33] Lord Balcarres, the newly installed chief whip, believed that the aloofness of Balfour, Long, and Chamberlain had infected the ranks with anxiety. After extensive interviews, he concluded, "the bulk of our men are frankly opposed to any action on our part which might involve a further appeal to the electors."[34]

On 6 July 1911 Balfour learned that in November 1910 the king had provided Asquith with a guarantee to create a sufficient number of peers to pass the Parliament Bill. The next day, Balfour, who abhorred party meetings, presided over a caucus of the shadow cabinet. Lord Balcarres noted that "the room was half filled with the Ashbournes, Londonderrys, Chaplins, Salisburys and Derbys—excellent though discredited politicians whose inclusion in a future Conservative Government would create dismay, and perhaps revolt among the rank and file." When Selborne, Salisbury, and Halsbury announced their own hard-line position, Steel-Maitland warned that a substantial majority of the MPs wanted a course of action that would not provoke another general election.[35] Croft and the party's rebel right wing had no such qualms because principles must always prevail over personal political considerations. While Balfour and the leaders agonized over the party's position on the Parliament Bill, Croft, Peto, Burgoyne, and Viscount

Wolmer summoned sympathetic MPs who were interested in "commencing an agitation in the country in support" of the House of Lords. Nearly forty MPs of the party's right wing met under the chairmanship of Sir Frederick Banbury.[36] They called for the party leadership "to abandon the conciliation programme and start an agitation in the country in favour of the Lords' amendments." A resolution that urged a policy of "fight, fight, fight" was forwarded to Balfour and Lord Lansdowne.[37]

With little fanfare, on 20 July the Parliament Bill with Lansdowne's amendments was read a third time in the upper chamber and sent back to the House of Commons. Balfour was informed that Asquith would request that the king exercise his prerogative and create the requisite number of peers to secure the passage of the bill in substantially the same form in which it left the House of Commons and that the king had agreed to comply.[38]

The following day Balfour met again with twenty-two members of the shadow cabinet. Fourteen members were prepared to acquiesce and avoid the creation of new peers, and eight members, whom George Wyndham[39] now labeled "ditchers," wanted to fight to the bitter end.[40] Later that same afternoon, approximately two hundred peers convened at Lansdowne House, where the political situation was examined. Lord Lansdowne suggested that "the more prudent course might be to allow the Bill to pass, the peers of course making it clear that they accepted no responsibility for it, and would, whenever the opportunity presented itself, take steps to restore the balance of the constitution." Although lords Halsbury, Salisbury, Selborne, Willoughby de Broke, and the duke of Bedford opposed any form of surrender, it appeared that the "ditchers" possessed only fifty votes among those present.[41] It was agreed to await the statement of the prime minister that was scheduled for 24 July when the Lords' amendments would be addressed. Detecting Balfour's reluctance for a fight, Maxse wrote to Sandars, "it is quite impossible for things to go on as they are, with a total want of confidence between the Leaders and followers."[42]

In the meantime an agitated Croft, who was included among the die hards,[43] sent an address to his constituents warning that "the constitution of this country, which is so gloriously associated with its history, which is responsible for its greatness, and which is the envy of the world, is to be smashed and pulverised." As he had often done, he denounced the so-called "Will of the People!" rationale for the Parliament Bill. As was appropriate to his imperial concerns, Croft complained that a miniscule Liberal majority sought to alter the constitution radically without any consideration of the four hundred million citizens of the empire, who had in interest in the institution. Further, he continued, electors were promised that the House of Lords would be reformed, and they had been deceived. The second chamber, as well as the people, have the right to have the question referred to the people. Although somewhat melodramatic, Croft decried the fact that the people are ignored, and "the Second Chamber, the last barrier between the Monarchy and a tyrannical Cabinet, is to be broken down." For Croft the situation provided little room for maneuver. The Conservative party was asked if "it will fight and there can be but one answer for patriots and men of honour." He argued that Conservatives must not compromise; "surrender of any description is impossible, and never must we lay down our weapons, . . . never can we rest till we have hounded from office the Government which would coerce the Sovereign and muzzle the electors."[44]

On 24 July the Commons assembled to hear Asquith make the formal response to the peers' amendments. However, when the prime minister rose to speak, he was greeted with an extraordinary scene as the Tory rebels shouted him down with cries of "Traitor, Traitor, Traitor." The speaker's call for order only excited the opposition to continue. After forty-five minutes of continued interruption, Asquith finally sat down in utter frustration.[45] What occasionally has been called the "Cecil scene," due to the prominent role of Hugh Cecil in the affair, had been planned in advance by Cecil, F. E. Smith, and Goulding. However, Lord Balcarres identified the supporting conspirators to be Harold Smith, J. L. Remnant, Richard Cooper, Harry Samuel, Rowland Hunt, George Sandys, J. R. Kebtey-Fletcher, George Haddock, Clement Kinloch-Cooke, William Peel, Sir Frederick Banbury, Major Archer-Shee, Charles Dixon, Arnold Ward, Capt. James Craig, Charles Craig, Basil Peto, and Henry Page Croft.[46] One account noted that "the front opposition bench below the gangway was especially vociferous. Mr. Page Croft, Major Archer-Shee, and Mr. Peto practised undergraduate acts of interruption with a vigour."[47]

Whereas many recoiled in disgust at the recent events in the Commons, the unaffected die hards remained determined and defiant. On 26 July they held a dinner in honor of Lord Halsbury that was attended by fifty peers and six hundred guests, including Croft. The event was to be a public protest against Balfour and Lansdowne. Balfour had been forced to cancel an address to his constituents inasmuch as he would not issue a cry of "no surrender." Instead, Balfour issued a letter to Lord Newton, published on 26 July, in which he expressed support for Lansdowne's position and counseled acceptance of the unamended Bill.[48] Although the letter could be read as a party manifesto, it had been drafted without any advance consultation with other party grandees or even the shadow cabinet. As a countermove against the impact of the letter, Balfour was urged by Long, Chaplin, and Lord Curzon to summon a party meeting, but Balfour, who loathed such political activities, refused.[49] Those attending the festivities for Lord Halsbury, however, were not disappointed as they were treated to defiant speeches from lords Milner, Salisbury, and Halsbury that unequivocally denounced Balfour's policy of acquiescence.[50]

The attitude and determination to fight expressed at the Halsbury dinner provided an emotional lift for Croft and the other rebels. He was moved to suggest that "the spirit of battle has returned to Unionism, and the National

Party has arisen in the hour of the country's needs."[51] In the wake of the Halsbury dinner, many of the diehards commenced their own campaigns against the Parliament Bill.[52] Although an auxiliary in the die hard opposition to the Parliament Bill and to Balfour's policy of acquiescence, Croft did not reflect the thinking of a Halsbury or a Salisbury. Croft represented a peculiar bridge between the prejudice of the Victorian aristocracy and the needs of a rising political generation. Fundamental to this activist faction within the party, which Croft personified, was a constructive program founded on a new populism as well as on a strong and vigorous state. He was convinced that the pillars of populism and statism were prerequisites for the implementation of a constructive and modern program. The populism would be used to pressure the political structure and the elite to commit themselves to the empire, while the state would implement and enforce the programmatic transformation. The question that gnawed at Croft, and to which he still had not answered even to his own satisfaction, was whether the Conservative party, as it now existed, was essential to carry forth his national and imperial program with its resulting political, social, and economic reforms. He questioned whether either major political party was relevant to Britain's social, political, and economic future inasmuch as they both failed to pursue truly national and imperial issues.

Croft scorned Balfour's fear "that if the Peers hold out, the House of Lords may be weaker even than at present." Croft's argument seemed more considerate of broader and longer-termed principles that were more a part of the twentieth century than either Lansdowne's surrender or Halsbury's opposition. He chided Balfour for being one of those conservatives who merely want "to get the Constitutional Question off their backs." Croft had long been haunted by the dilemma that the party faced in regard to the options presented by the Parliament Bill.[53] He finally reached a rather novel approach to support his own position of resistance. It was an approach that sought to maintain the strength and function of the second chamber. Croft argued that the present weakness of the House of Lords stemmed from the fact that the Liberal party publicly proclaimed that the second chamber was a "Tory House." This campaign in effect challenged the credibility of the House of Lords as an integral component of the British constitution. Croft thus asked how it was to be strengthened if it continues to count only forty or fifty Liberal peers among its six hundred members?[54] He argued that "if Peers are created . . . at once you will have a Chamber which the electors consider fair. Therefore . . . the creation of Peers would strengthen rather than weaken the second Chamber." Further, he recognized that in the next two or three years the House of Lords must be reformed. This acceptance nullified the traditional Conservative contention that the creation of additional peers would degrade or dilute the peerage. The eventual reform or reconstitution of the second chamber would transform but not diminish the

8: Croft, Conservative Party Politics, and the Balfour Question 159

status, prestige, and power of the peerage by a system of gradation and representation.

Croft suggested that the peers should participate by not assisting in the passage of the Bill, because it would then be intellectually and politically impossible for the House of Lords to reverse the legislation. "If the Peers become assenting parties to the passage of a Bill, . . . it is impossible to conceive that they can ever undo that which they have joined in accomplishing." In conclusion, Croft proclaimed, Conservatives "can only continue to fight for the final Veto of the People (either by election or referendum) if it refuses to be a party to the passage of this iniquitous Bill." However, in response to the suggested tactic of abstaining, he answered, "why should the . . . Party go to winter quarters" when there is "no snow?" The electors would never understand nor support a political party or movement that "advances to the rear." If the party voluntarily consents to this political tragedy, "then, indeed, there is no question of 'winter quarters,' for Unionism will have entered its grave."[55] When asked if the Conservative peers should follow Lansdowne in his acceptance of the Parliament Bill, Croft responded, "ten thousand times No, for to give in now would tie our hands for all time. The Bill has got to go and we will start by refusing to pass it until forced to . . . [and] then . . . never rest until the Parliament Bill is reversed."[56]

With the Parliament Bill having been sent back to the House of Lords without their amendments, Balfour made one last vain and futile effort to salvage his leadership role by introducing a censure motion founded on the government's alleged unconstitutional abuse of the royal prerogative.[57] On 7 August the motion, not unexpectedly, was defeated by a vote of 365 to 246.[58] Notwithstanding the campaign of the die hards, when the Parliament Bill came for its final reading in the House of Lords on 10 August, it passed by a vote of 131 to 114, carried by the support from 13 bishops and 37 Conservative peers. The overwhelming majority of the 644 peers abstained.[59]

On the morning of the peers' vote, Balfour departed for the Continent, creating a "very bad impression" in the party.[60] He remained abroad at Gastein until 2 September when he returned to London. However, on his return, he promptly left for his Scottish estate, Whittinghame, and did not return to the capital until 3 November. Balfour had hardly departed Dover when pressure was renewed for his removal. William Bridgeman[61] suggested to Balcarres that "the only salvation for Balfour or the party was for him to resign quickly on medical advice from Gastein . . . because . . . there was so much dissatisfaction in our ranks that it would break out within the next two months, and then the party would be split hopelessly and helplessly." Bridgeman argued that so long as Balfour remained leader the party would be paralyzed by an inability to select a successor. An early retirement would save both Balfour and the party. The chief whip seemed to concur.[62] Although Bridgeman was convinced that if Balfour did not retire the leader eventually would be "hounded out of the party," Bridgeman held the private concern that "if the extremists like the Maxses, Page-Crofts & F. E. Smiths make a row now, they will ruin their cause, because they will drive back all the moderate men into Balfour's arms; and it is the more moderate men (who all want a change) who will turn the scales."[63]

Shortly after the monumental vote in the Lords, Croft wrote to Willoughby de Broke, a fellow Reveille member with whom he had been working closely on several issues over the past year: "Just a line to thank you for your magnificent fight. Whatever people may say today about the 'traitor peers' you at least are clear and have earned the respect and gratitude of all decent citizens." Recognizing that further action was likely to be taken by one or another of the various rebel factions, Croft prophetically added, "if there is a further move on let me know as I am now an 'Independent' and all for war with the mugwumps."[64]

It has been suggested, at least in the view of Willoughby de Broke, that "from the night of the 10th August 1911, when a great principle was sacrificed to expediency; when the right course was departed from for fear of the consequences, the Conservative Party received a shock from which it has never really recovered. Faith in all leadership has been shaken." He further feared that "the thought has gained ground whether, after all, the Constitution can be so vital to the welfare of the State, when a majority of those in high places, who should know best, were unwilling to take any risks in its defence."[65] The day before hearing from Croft, Willoughby de Broke wrote to Lord Selborne that the die-hard movement must be continued into a general campaign reminiscent of the Reveille campaign in the autumn of 1910. "We have now got all the men on our side both in and out of Parliament that are worth having. We must keep them going and occupy the whole of the autumn platform."[66]

On 17 August Amery dined with Lord Milner and discussed the future policy for the party. With his characteristic directness, Milner urged "that the only thing was that a small group of younger and independent men should get together, agree on a common policy and advocate it in the House and outside without bothering one way or another about Balfour and the authorities. . . . The only thing was to let events take their course and to go ahead with our own policy."[67] Henry Chaplin, whose view of Balfour was often difficult to ascertain, decried that no major party leader stood out as a leader of tariff reform.[68]

At about the same time, F. E. Smith complained to Austen Chamberlain about Balfour's "nerveless leadership" and warned that "things cannot again be as they were . . . let us meet when we can with Carson and Wyndham."[69] George Wyndham agreed on the need for "prompt and definite action."[70] Such private sentiment was made public by both Garvin in *The Observer* and Maxse in the *National Review*. Maxse declared that "any attempt . . .

8: Croft, Conservative Party Politics, and the Balfour Question   161

made to replace our heads under the Balfourian yoke is doomed to failure. B. M. G." Maxse now routinely included in his articles the initials B. M. G.— "Balfour Must Go."[71] The long campaign against Balfour reached its zenith with the October *National Review* in which the leader was blamed outright for the destruction of the constitution.[72] Although R. D. Blumenfeld and the *Daily Express* did not attack Balfour so viciously or call for his prompt replacement, they had clearly abandoned him as suggested by their positive view of Willoughby de Broke's activities to energize the party.[73]

It was evident from very early on that pressure was mounting for some action.[74] Lord Selborne dismissed the suggestions that called "for the formation of a New Party." Instead he urged his allies to force their view within the party that he claimed would amount to "the same thing as capturing the Party and the Party machine."[75] Ever since the emergence of the crisis over the Canadian reciprocity agreement, Croft had suggested consistently and regularly that there was a need for a national and imperial party.[76] Such proposals for some new organization provoked serious concerns for the new party chairman, Arthur Steel-Maitland, who was in close contact with Balfour during this period. He thus wrote to Lord Halsbury, "it is really of the very first importance that care should be taken and that any new organisation of a general character not rashly be established."[77] Lord Selborne soon called for a meeting of the most capable die hards for the purpose of determining "how the Constitution should be reconstructed." Those attending the 2 October meeting included Selborne; Salisbury; Willoughby de Broke; Mayo; Lovat; Sir Edward Carson, MP; E. G. Pretyman, MP; Hugh Cecil; and Robert Cecil.[78] Inasmuch as they had more than just a program of constitutional reconstruction on their plates, it was decided to summon a wider assembly for 12 October 1911. The die hards were facing up to the problem of the party's leadership and sought wider counsel as well as cover.

The discontent was no longer restricted to a collection of agitated peers or Croft and his Reveille rebels, but it was now being expressed by local constituency associations.[79] The Dartford and Dorsetshire associations had "passed a veiled vote of censure against Balfour," and the rank-and-file workers at Ealing were demanding that a party meeting be held by MPs and peers.[80] Even Steel-Maitland was convinced that local associations would refuse to extend Balfour a vote of confidence.[81] Croft's close political associate, Lord Malmesbury, warned that "from every direction and from every sort of constituency comes the same complaint, the same unhappy story of people resigning their posts on local committees or canceling their subscriptions to the party funds (local or central or both) due to the apathy and discontent out of the present situation."[82]

On 12 October 1911, in a move that suggested an open rebellion against Balfour was underway, fifty peers and MPs met and established the Halsbury Club as a "forward Unionist movement."[83] The Halsbury Club also represented a current from Croft's Reveille inasmuch as the latter sought to organize the opposition Conservative party around the advocacy of a defined and constructive program.[84] However, due to the apparent anti-Balfour feature of the new organization, Halsbury felt compelled to disclaim "any disloyalty towards the Leaders of the Party."[85] It was observed that "during the recess the most marked thing was the strong feeling against Balfour among many of the rank and file both inside and outside the House. The foundation of the Halsbury Club was an outward and visible sign of that feeling, though the promoters of the club denied it."[86]

In the wake of the Halsbury Club's announcement, there were increasing anxieties that the internal discontent would provoke an irreparable breach.[87] As will be examined in detail in the succeeding chapter, the Halsbury Club was not the only organization with political ambitions in action. Although a member of the Halsbury group, Croft concentrated on expanding the Imperial Mission, which now claimed six hundred new members during October, to include a parliamentary group. The parliamentary group held forth the possibility of being the seed of an imperial party.

A great explosion was anticipated from Maxse, who in September 1911 filed a proposed resolution that was to be debated and considered at the annual Conservative party conference at Leeds on 16-17 November. It was his intention to maneuver the party conference into endorsing the "No Surrender" peers who were led by Lord Halsbury, while concomitantly condemning the approach taken by Balfour.[88] After filing his proposed resolution with the conference organizers, Maxse wrote to Croft complaining that Balfour's Central Office was trying to block his motion. Rather than deal with his motion, Maxse predicted that the rank and file were "to be electrified by a Rule Britannia speech pumped into Arthur Balfour and pumped out by him," and then we "will be asked the following morning, when most people have gone away, to pass a vote of unabated confidence in our great and glorious leader."[89] Maxse nevertheless remained confident that "there should be a sufficient body of stalwarts at the Conference to stop all this rot, and to insist that the resolution shall come on the first day, and if on a show of hands we could manage to carry it." Although Maxse claimed that he did not want to impose on his parliamentary friends for assistance, he was properly concerned that the Central Office and some local associations would pack the delegates with Balfourites. Accordingly, given their long political association, Maxse suggested that "anyone who can exercise any influence either in the selection of delegates to attend the National Union Conference, or on the delegates themselves, should do whatever they can in order that this resolution may have a good show."[90]

Maxse, however, was denied his moment. On 4 November 1911, Balfour informed his closest colleagues that he intended to resign. The Conservative parliamentary party was then informed on 8 November, only a few hours before the leader publicized his decision in a speech to a hastily assembled constituency association in the City. The press found the announcement coincidentally interesting. The announcement was made the same day that Chamberlain spoke to the Tariff Reform League and repudiated Balfour's tariff referendum pledge. It was made on the same day that Maxse was scheduled to initiate a discussion of "the continued subordination and sacrifice of tariff reform to party tactics" at a Tariff Reform League meeting, but that was canceled after a hint from a party whip. It was made at the same time that the question of party leadership was to be discussed by Selborne, Halsbury, Milner, Willoughby de Broke, Carson, Chamberlain, and Wyndham at the first public meeting of the Halsbury Club. Finally, the announcement preempted Maxse's resolution in support of Halsbury's "no surrender" policy, which had been laid down before the annual party conference.

Notwithstanding the interesting timing, the evidence establishes that the decision to retire had been made in late September and that only the precise timing of the announcement remained to be determined.[91] In a meeting at Whittinghame with Balcarres and Steel-Maitland, Balfour confessed that "I am coming to the conclusion that it would not be at all a bad thing for the party if I were to resign my leadership." As he rationalized the decision, he had led the party in the House of Commons for twenty years; he was sixty-three and probably too old to survive a ministry should the party win the next election; "his health from time to time causes anxiety"; and it would be fair to give his successor a few months of relative calm before being forced to confront home rule and the other great political struggles that loomed on the horizon. When asked by Balcarres about the cause of his decision, Balfour responded, "there were many symptoms of disquiet. The diehard agitation was one, but that in itself was symptomatic of previous discontent."[92] Until August, Croft's Reveille provided the most public and serious attack on Balfour.

On 2 October Balfour again met with Balcarres and remained convinced that a change would be "good for the party" and that "he is tired—felt the Ditcher movement more than anything else in his whole political career—resented it more." He found "that those who called loudly for a lead were prominent in disregarding his last lead. Hence a fresh leader is imperative who can begin by securing closer discipline."[93] Accordingly, Balfour was giving recognition to the long period of opposition that he had suffered from certain quarters of the Conservative party, both inside and outside Westminster. Such opposition had manifested itself in the Confederacy movement, the Reveille, the Imperial Mission, and most recently in the "ditcher" or die hard movement, although the latter had not been given any formal substance until the creation of the Halsbury Club on 12 October. This was long after he had made his decision to retire. On 4 November 1911, Balfour began privately to advise his shadow cabinet colleagues. He then informed the king and on 8 November announced to his constituent association that he was retiring.

The selection of a successor commenced as a three-way race between

Walter Long, Austen Chamberlain, and Andrew Bonar Law. Although Bonar Law originally could only muster some forty supporters among the nearly two hundred eighty MPs, his candidacy prevented either Long or Chamberlain from winning outright. On 13 November 1911, after two days of discussions and negotiations, Long and Chamberlain withdrew their candidacies, and Andrew Bonar Law was chosen leader of the Conservative party in the House of Commons.

Goulding recorded that Croft, F. E. Smith, Carson, and Pollock supported Chamberlain.[94] This is not surprising. Croft's association with Long was limited and fairly recent, whereas he had long been associated with the Chamberlains and the tariff reform organizations, and he viewed Austen's policies as an extension of his father's whole-hog program. In addition, throughout his life and political career Croft carried the burden of a political indebtedness to Joseph Chamberlain. This sentiment was later even to restrain Croft's action during the crisis in May 1940 over Neville Chamberlain's loss of confidence.

Although his association with Bonar Law extended back several years, Bonar Law appeared to waffle and hesitate over food taxes and a referendum for tariff reform during the most recent general election. Further, Bonar Law was relatively silent during the recently concluded struggle over the Parliament Bill. Nevertheless, Croft promptly extended his congratulations to Bonar Law to "say how proud I am to be a soldier in your army." The significance of Bonar Law's ascendancy to the leadership was found in the fact that it restored in Croft a crucial level of confidence in the party. He felt obliged to advise Bonar Law that "it may interest you to know that the 'Reveille' that came into being last year have unanimously decided to bank fires and funds and to cease any independent action in the country, and that we agreed to do this as a mark of our esteem and confidence in yourself."[95] As will be discussed further, Croft's interest in and efforts on behalf of a national and imperial party appeared to dissipate with the retirement of Balfour.

9
Militant Unionism or a National and Imperial Party (1911)

> I ask are we such puny creatures that we cannot put aside our petty, party passions in regard to this question and raise our senses of the grander and wider problem which confront us at the present moment?
>
> —Henry Page Croft, 31 May 1911

Alongside the struggle over the Parliament Bill, a second political crisis consumed Croft's attention and energy in 1911. It erupted in late January when reports of a possible American-Canadian reciprocal trade agreement began to appear. The agreement was viewed by the tariff reform and imperial preference forces as a devastating development. The terms were to provide for free trade between Canada and the United States in farm products, a negligible duty on agricultural implements, machinery and building materials, and virtually no duty on processed lumber, wood pulp, and paper products. The agreement would have the effect of negating the Canadian preference policy unilaterally extended to Britain in 1896. According to Professor W. A. S. Hewins, one of the intellectual dynamics behind fiscal reform and imperial preference, the proposed free trade pact meant that "one State of the Empire would become party to an agreement under which it received preferential treatment in a foreign country which was not to be shared by the United Kingdom or other parts of the British Empire."[1]

Although the response of the party leadership seemed somewhat muted in the wake of the announcement, an alarmed Croft held the same appreciation for the agreement's potential economic consequences as Hewins. He feared that the agreement, combined with other most-favored-nation treaties, placed future Canadian-British commercial intercourse in jeopardy. The economic pull of the United States would be too great for Canada to fight. He also feared for the future of the British empire and British security, which was likely aggravated by a statement of the speaker of the U.S. House of Representatives: "I hope to see the day when the American flag will float over every square inch of British North American possessions clear to the north pole."[2] Croft was specifically concerned by President Taft's comment on making Canada an "adjunct" of the United States.[3]

Croft had just embarked on the 1911 Reveille campaign, which generally focused on domestic and internal party politics, and he now incorporated the Canadian issue into his Reveille agenda. He suggested that the announcement of the reciprocity agreement should cause tariff reformers to "clench their teeth and go into the fight more vigorously and with greater faith than ever before." He hoped the recent Canadian announcement "would quicken the interest of all Englishmen on the question of Empire. . . . They would see that the American was taking that which ought to be ours."[4] Croft was never one to give up. He pointed out that Canadian export of wheat was only 35 percent of its total exports to Britain. Thus the 65 percent of Canadian exports to Britain that was beyond the U.S. reciprocity agreement could be used to hold Canada as part of the empire. He optimistically believed that preference could still be applied to Australia and the other Dominions.[5]

The announcement of the reciprocity pact also provoked a breach within the tariff reform forces with Bonar Law, Max Aitken,[6] and Lord Northcliffe[7] leading a charge to abandon food taxes, and Austen Chamberlain, Goulding, Garvin, and Croft holding fast to the entire Chamberlain program.[8] Bonar Law was moved to suggest, probably for electoral prospects, "that the time had arrived when Preference should be abandoned." Hewins admonished Bonar Law against such precipitous decisions.[9] Fearing an irrational rush to abandon crucial parts of the dual tariff reform and imperial preference program, H. J. Mackinder also urged a "delay in judgment," noting that the agreement still required ratification by the United States and Canada. Failure to ratify the agreement would, in the absence of an internal revolt, leave the substance of the Conservative party's position on tariff reform and imperial preference intact.[10] As a result of these well-founded concerns, Croft took the initiative and called a meeting on 7 February of the prominent members of the Imperial Mission, together with several distinguished Canadians associated with finance, commerce, and industry, who resided in London. The objective was to construct a plan of campaign against the Canadian reciprocity agreement.[11]

The first charge was led by Croft and a handful of MPs. On 8 February, during the debate on the address from the throne, Croft made another appeal to rise above partisan politics. He urged Parliament to set aside its blinding partisanship, which had accomplished nothing for the progress and security of the kingdom, and address the issue for "Imperialist rather than party grounds." The reciprocity agreement was disastrous from both imperial and national standpoints. Croft conceded that the Conservatives were not free of complicity in neglecting the Dominions. They "hesitated far too long before they realised the difficulty." However, he leveled a more serious condemnation at the present Liberal government "for the stupendous folly

9: Militant Unionism or a National and Imperial Party (1911) 167

which has led to the present situation of allowing the treasures of the future to slip from the hands of the nation."[12] In the new Parliament, Croft wasted little time in pressing the government with uncomfortable questions and speeches on the Canadian question.[13] He was joined in his attack on the treaty by long-time advanced tariff reformers, Rowland Hunt, James Fitzalan Hope, Charles S. Goldman, Alan Burgoyne, Basil Peto, and Sir Gilbert Parker.[14]

Croft soon carried the issues of the Canadian reciprocity pact, trade, security, and imperial dissolution into the midst of the West Wiltshire (Westbury) by-election. Speaking in support of the Conservative candidate, Croft warned that if Britain did not reengage its Dominions, they would drift away as Canada now had begun to do. This would cause irreparable damage as substantial trade would flow away from Britain and into the United States.[15] In March 1911 Croft, chairman of the Imperial Mission, announced a series of meetings to be held throughout the kingdom as a campaign for imperial preference. He also announced that his organization would supply organizations with speakers from Canada, Australia, and New Zealand.[16] Also in March 1911, as a result of the pressure from Croft and Lord Willoughby de Broke, the Tariff Reform League joined the efforts of the Imperial Mission and launched its own imperial preference campaign. Willoughby de Broke pledged "that so long as she [Canada] remains one of His Majesty's dominions, so long would the Conservative Party keep open to her Imperial preference."[17]

In a more practical appeal, Croft tried to educate the public on the trade issues, pointing out that Canada purchased per capita £8 from Britain while non-Dominion states spent "shillings and pence." Eight million Canadians purchased £19 million worth of goods.[18] Australia and New Zealand, with a population of 6 million, imported as much from Britain as did 60 million Germans; Canada and New Zealand, with a population of 9 million, imported as much as 90 million Americans; and Canadian, Australian, and New Zealand imports from Britain accounted for £26 million in British wages.[19]

Notwithstanding such efforts by Croft and several others, the difficulty in waging the campaign against the Canadian reciprocity agreement, as well as an affirmative campaign for imperial unity, stemmed from the distraction over the Parliament Bill crisis. In effect, after the reintroduction of the Parliament Bill, the energies of Croft and the Conservative party as a whole were weakened by the emergence of a two-front political war. Once Asquith reintroduced the Parliament Bill, Croft was forced to wage two political campaigns throughout 1911.

In addition, submerged beneath the public struggle over imperial preference and the House of Lords remained the embers of the anti-Balfour movement that had been fueled by Croft's Reveille movement during the latter part of 1910. It was now being aggressively tended to by Leo Maxse. In the February *National Review,* Maxse was convinced more than ever that Balfour was incapable of leading the Conservative party into the upcoming battles. He urged that "Mr. Balfour's friends, if they be real friends, should exhaust their persuasiveness in trying to induce him to relinquish the tremendous task of leading the Opposition in revolutionary times, for which he has neither the physique, the health, nor temperament."[20]

To further the campaign against Balfour, Maxse approached his friend, the founder of the Reveille. He sought to enlist Croft in a new and aggressive campaign against Balfour which Maxse intended to inaugurate on 14 February 1911 with a major speech at Chelsea. Although not usually so apprehensive, Croft demurred, claiming that "I do not think that as a nominal supporter in the H. of C. of A. J. B. that I can take that way of clearing him out.... Platform speeches from a few of us will only stiffen his back and give much to the enemy." Croft declined the invitation to join Maxse at Chelsea.[21] Perhaps it was the fear of a hostile right wing, represented primarily by the Reveille, with the scent of blood that contributed to Balfour taking a hardened position on the constitutional confrontation during the early months of 1911.[22] Notwithstanding Croft's usual unrestrained criticism of Balfour's leadership style, it must be noted that it was during this period that he considered a political alternative. He contemplated the possibility that his newly energized Imperial Mission could be transformed into an imperial party, which would be founded on the principle of the imperial idea and would rise above the other political parties. Both the position of Balfour and Maxse's attack on Balfour lacked relevance to addressing the important political, social, and economic problems.

As the imperial pioneers took to platforms and propaganda writing, Croft merged his campaign against the Canadian reciprocity agreement with the growing struggle against the Parliament Bill. The campaign of the Imperial Mission intended to pressure the party leadership to state unequivocally that the door remained open for imperial preference and imperial unity. He concurrently sought to persuade the government to renounce any support for the Canadian-American reciprocity agreement that may have been implied by the government's silence. Through public rallies by the Imperial Mission, Croft sought to place imperial preference and unity before the imperial conference scheduled for May.[23] Croft and his colleagues wasted little time in mounting the platforms. At a major Imperial Mission rally at Shoreditch on 8 March, Croft and Major Archer-Shee assailed the government's neglect of Canada and the empire. Mackinder and Croft took the same message to Battersea on 10 March.[24] They were followed by a large demonstration at Deptford which was addressed by William Peel and Croft. Their objective was to strengthen the hands of the colonial premiers who supported imperial preference. Croft next used the annual meeting of the Hertfordshire Tariff Reform League as an opportunity to reinvigorate his home territory with imperial enthusiasm.[25]

Croft's activities in the spring of 1911 culminated in a mass meeting of

9: Militant Unionism or a National and Imperial Party (1911)

the imperial preference campaign at St. Pancras where he was joined by Felix Cassel and William Ormsby-Gore. Croft saw the need to approach imperial unity through the question of social reform. He claimed to be "a sincere social reformer" who was convinced that only by examining the questions of housing, the poor law, and the general social conditions from "the bigger point of view . . . could [they] have a permanent solution." As he had done so often since 1903, Croft called for a national policy as an effort to avoid the paralyzing passions and prejudices engendered by party politics. "Only by a National Policy could they strengthen the State as a whole and that only by that policy could they benefit permanently the individual in the community."[26] Fundamental to his envisioned national policy was the requirement that the nation and state recognize the value and engage the resources of the British empire. Accordingly, he consistently condemned appeals to class, sectional, and egotistical feelings and interests, and instead he urged a return to "the national spirit which had made this country great." It was only through the creation of an imperial union that the national spirit would reemerge and provide the key to national economic prosperity. It followed that such economic prosperity, flowing as benefits of imperial unity, would improve the nation's economic, social, and moral conditions. The anticipated economic prosperity would consequentially ameliorate the divisiveness of class and sectional politics and nullify their appeal. However, it was the state's responsibility to organize the empire, and this cannot be accomplished if Britain, whether under a Liberal or Conservative Government, turns its back on Canada. This would drive the Dominion into the arms of foreigners. Croft maintained that "the door can yet be opened. . . . If we chose to change our policy they [Canadians] are still ready to extend the existing preference in return."[27]

He concluded by urging that when the imperial premiers arrive in May the nation must rise above party for the sake of the empire. Croft's audience responded with a resolution "affirm[ing] its adherence to the policy of the Imperial Preferential Trade within the Empire, believing it to be calculated to increase employment in this country, foster the development of the Dominions, and strengthen the bonds of sentiment and interest which unite the Empire." Accordingly, the rally urged the colonial premiers to adopt the policy when they meet at the imperial conference.[28]

As he sought to force Parliament's attention to the Canadian reciprocity agreement whenever possible, Croft could not ignore the parliamentary component of his Imperial Mission's campaign. He insisted that Britain must act immediately, and he provocatively charged that the government was engaged in treasonable conduct by not intervening to maintain commercial ties with Canada. Without commercial ties the imperial and strategic bonds will be dangerously loosened.[29] The June coronation of King George V, with representatives of all the colonies assembled in London, gave Croft cause for reflection and anticipation. He saw the occasion as an opportunity for imperialists to bring His Majesty's subjects together into a newly organized empire. By developing a new imperialism from this nationalist revival, the king's subjects "will understand each other's troubles and aspirations, and will mutually assist each other." This will provide for a "common defence amongst British nations, and the greatest weapon for peace and justice will be forged." Further, a community of people, supported by understanding and sympathy, will bar the growth of class hatred.[30]

As Croft carried on the Imperial Mission's campaign throughout the summer and autumn, the Canadian aspect was an immediate but yet merely a tactical component of the overall program of imperial unity. He soon began to incorporate overtly political considerations into the mission's development, program, and activities.[31] He was often obsessed with structural symmetry, organizational hierarchy, and responsibility in his political activities. Thus, in the Imperial Mission, he wanted an imperialist organization with which he would unite imperialists throughout the empire with imperialists in the United Kingdom.

Of course, the present political arrangement compelled Croft to function in the arena of traditional parliamentary and partisan politics. He nevertheless often expressed disdain for such conditions that he considered contributing to an infection of political corruption. By this he meant that the struggle for office was fought through shameful appeals to sectional interests and class prejudices and that personal political interests superseded the needs of the nation. He further suggested that this behavior concomitantly failed to appreciate and protect the nation's true interests. There was, however, a paradox in Croft's own thinking. In his view of the way government should be conducted, he continued to accept traditional methods, that is, popular appeals to the electorate. He differed in that he believed the populace would cast aside the shallow promises of sectional parties if countered with appeals to protect the nation and empire.

From his earliest embrace of tariff reform, Croft consistently presented the movement as being a national and popular movement. That is, he argued the tariff and imperial program provided a national policy with subsidiary elements of economic and social reform, which would synergistically promote and strengthen the British empire, nation, race, and state. Croft sought to transform the tariff and imperial reform movement into a movement that would rise and operate above partisan politics. His view of the tariff and imperial reform program was his first image of a national party. Croft originally joined the Conservative party for more reasons than merely the influence of his social and economic environment. The Conservative party, although not perfect, held forth the potential for promoting more of the fundamentals of a national party than did the rival Liberal party. Perhaps because Croft had to plant one foot firmly within partisan politics, he ended up supplementing his idealism with a ruthlessly political and partisan creature. This may explain the underlying basis for the Confederacy and its relationship to the national tariff reform movement.

His approach to the Imperial Mission, the Reveille, and their mutual relationship is equally fascinating. During the last five months of 1910, the Reveille resembled the Confederacy. They were both aggressive and politically puritanical in that they sought to push the Conservative party in a direction more in line with Croft's perception of the national problems and solutions. The Imperial Mission, on the other hand, originally represented his desire to construct a national propaganda movement and a nonpartisan organization based on the imperial idea. But he soon sought to transform the Imperial Mission into an "imperial organization . . . which can be called an active fighting political organisation." He wanted an organization of empire-first politicians who would operate within the existing parliamentary configuration but "without being in any way connected with the fortunes of any party division."[32]

Thus, Croft sought to establish "a small body of Imperialists in the House of Commons who shall make it their business to give expression to views of the Imperial Mission, and, . . . devote themselves above all to the Imperial aims which the mission seeks." Such a parliamentary group would rise above partisan politics, and "vote even against their own party at any time . . . when the other party was putting forward a more practical Imperial proposal. . . . We put empire before party." Croft hoped "to draw members from all sections of the House of Commons into a compact body, which will put national and Imperial questions first."[33] In effect, Croft preferred to rearrange and simplify the existing political spectrum by pushing individuals into either an imperial party, the seed of which was the Imperial Mission, or into a nonimperial party that would be composed of anyone else remaining. It followed that the imperial party would in effect be a national party, as it would represent his defined and identified national interests.

In September 1911 Croft announced that twelve MPs had agreed "to work together under our organisation." By October the MPs, who now constituted a parliamentary group or committee, were holding weekly meetings to consider and decide on the Imperial Mission's "parliamentary plan of campaign." With the appearance of the parliamentary committee, the Imperial Mission had expanded well beyond the modest role of providing colonial speakers for English audiences. Now "for the first time imperialists in different countries of the Empire will be able to get their views expressed in the home Parliament."[34] However, the madness of the politics in 1911 made it difficult to maintain the regularity or focus of the parliamentary committee's activities. Although the Imperial Mission listed a respectable number of MPs on its membership rolls, the parliamentary group initially consisted of L. S. Amery, Ion Hamilton Benn,[35] Major Martin Archer-Shee, John Norton-Griffiths, Alan Burgoyne, Basil Peto, George Sandys,[36] Arthur Shirley Benn,[37] Ronald McNeill, and Croft.[38]

During this period Croft completed the operational and organizational structure of the Imperial Mission. (For a membership list of the Imperial Mission, see Appendix 4.) Inasmuch as "the whole of the Imperial Mission is to take Imperialists into a practical brotherhood," Croft recruited its officers from former governor-generals or lieutenant-governors, former Colonial Office officials, and men whose personal or business interests associated them prominently with the colonies and Dominions. The duke of Argyll became the honorary president of the Imperial Mission, and Joseph Chamberlain consented to be the vice president, although his physical incapacity prevented him from doing anything other than attaching his name to the organization. He was joined by the duke of Marlborough, the earl of Selborne, and Viscount Milner as vice presidents.[39]

The executive branch of the organization was located in the Central Council with Earl of Dundonald, Lord Tennyson;[40] Lord Northcote;[41] Lord Leith of Fyvie,[42] Lord Wolverton,[43] Major Martin Archer-Shee, M.P., Basil Peto, MP; Dr. Alfred Hillier, MP;[44] Almeric Paget, MP;[45] J. G. Jenkins, from Australia; Sir William Russell, who was a former postmaster general, colonial secretary, and justice minister for New Zealand; George Gould, also from New Zealand; G. A. M. Buckley; and Arthur E. G. Rhodes. The day-to-day operations were centered in an executive committee, of which Croft served as chairman.[46]

Croft occasionally overstated his expectation of the appeal of the empire and imperial sentiment, as when he announced in September 1911 that the immediate goal of the Imperial Mission was "to enlist a million members and to raise £100,000 throughout the Empire within six months."[47] Branches were established in Canada, where George Tate Blackstock, K.C., formed a branch after the visit of William Ormsby-Gore;[48] in South Africa; in Australia at Sydney, Melbourne, Victoria, and Perth, which were established through the work of Sir John Quick, Lewis Cohen, mayor of Adelaide, and Sir John Forrest; and in New Zealand, at Dunedin, Auckland, Wellington, and Christchurch, primarily through the efforts of Sir Joseph Ward, prime minister, and Sir J. G. Findlay, minister of justice and attorney general.

To supplement the various colonial branches, Croft constructed an additional level or component, referred to as the Permanent Council, which, in turn, consisted of six sections or committees located in London: United Kingdom,[49] Australia,[50] New Zealand,[51] Canada,[52] South Africa,[53] and India.[54] As imagined by Croft, when one of the constituent branches in the Dominions identified a particular situation, development, or issue involving imperial policy, the Dominion branch would transmit "instructions" to the corresponding section within the greater council. The latter would then provide input based on its own expertise. The issue would then be forwarded to the Central Council where it would be discussed and the appropriate position and course of action determined. In certain cases the matter would then be transferred to the Parliamentary Committee "who are pledged to

9: Militant Unionism or a National and Imperial Party (1911) 173

watch the imperial interests, . . . [and] will use ordinary parliamentary action for bringing before the Imperial Parliament the views and suggestions of the Overseas States."[55]

Croft and Willoughby de Broke initially took the campaign to the North reminiscent of the 1910 Reveille campaign.[56] As he had done a year earlier with the Reveille, Croft arranged a massive autumn campaign to be marked by a mass meeting at the Queen's Hall, London, on 31 October, and with an address by the earl of Selborne. As the Imperial Mission prepared for its campaign, the imperial movement was handed a tremendous victory. On 21 September 1911 the Canadian electorate overwhelmingly rejected the reciprocity agreement with the United States. Sir Wilfrid Laurier's Liberal ministry, which had held a 133 to 88 seat majority in the Canadian House of Commons since the 1908 election, was routed. Canada's Conservative party, which had campaigned against the reciprocity agreement, was now handed a 129 to 86 seat majority. Even eight of Laurier's cabinet, including the finance and customs ministers who negotiated the agreement, were defeated. For Croft the results provided a definitive rejection of the agreement. In his postelection victory statement, the Conservative party leader, Sir Robert Borden, declared that "the people have given their answer to those who desired to drive the reciprocity compact through Parliament." Canada "will continue in the old path of Canadian unity, Canadian nationhood, and the British connection. She has emphasised the strength of the ties that bind her to the Empire." The reciprocity agreement with the United States was effectively dead.[57]

Croft was elated with the results as he suggested that "Canada has de clared for permanent Union of the Empire, and . . . shown that there is only one way for her, and that is the path of British Empire Union."[58] Interestingly, Earl Grey cautioned Croft not to place too much faith in the results.[59] Croft stressed, however, that the greater lesson is for Britain to reject the present partisanship that he believed infects the political system and that subsequently fails to address the nation's needs. He accused politicians of "wasting their time declaring for certain principles and then running away from them, . . . fostering class strife and class warfare." Standing equally condemned, he accused both the government and opposition parties of neglecting "the great Imperial questions which could have solved half the economic evils from which we suffer."[60]

Still disheartened by the humdrum toryism of the party under Balfour's leadership, Croft returned to his idea of an imperial party that would extinguish the present political groupings. He now considered that "the time for words is past and the time for action is with us. There is an organisation now forming throughout the Empire which will unite British Imperialists all over the world—the Imperial Mission." He believed that the imperial fight in Canada proved what the Imperial Mission can do for Imperialism in the United Kingdom. He "appeal[ed] to the people of Great Britain and Ireland to join the Mission and help the consummation of the Union of the British Empire. The movement has won already the support of most of the great living British Empire builders, and now it claims the support of all true Imperialists from the highest to the lowest in the land."[61]

Building on what he considered to be the movement's success—Canadian rejection of the United States trade agreement—the immediate political objective of the Imperial Mission was as straightforward as it was unattainable. "We want," he proclaimed, "sufficient members to turn out any Government in any part of the Empire which is false to the policy of Imperial Union, and for this reason we appeal confidently to every man or woman who puts Empire first to join our ranks and share the victory which we are determined to win. We want a million members now."[62] Even Lord Roberts, the field marshal, echoed Croft's dissatisfaction with the leadership of the Conservative party. Roberts charged that the party had no definite policy for social reform, national defense, or Imperial unity. Further, the party leaders only halfheartedly supported tariff reform, and some of the party's more prominent names actually opposed the policy.[63]

The domestic significance of the Imperial Mission campaign found expression at a massive demonstration held at the Chelsea Town Hall on 17 October "to celebrate the victory of Imperialism in the Canadian elections." The speakers included the earl of Stanhope; Lord Willoughby de Broke; Samuel Hoare, MP; J. S. Fletcher, MP; Sir William Porter; Maxse; and Croft. Lord Stanhope suggested the significance of the Canadian election, which he considered to be an embrace of empire, was found in the fact that they were guided by ideals and practical politics rather than from sectional appeals and partisan gamesmanship. They threw themselves unequivocally into the struggle against an attempt to destroy the British empire. The Canadian election now made the question of imperial reform a national policy that demanded Britain's immediate attention. Only by entering into the struggle for empire would Britain make the policy of preference and imperial unity a national policy. "Now was the time to plunge into the struggle" and construct an alternative to the present parties. He was certain "that the tide had turned."[64]

Lord Willoughby de Broke advanced the discussion. Although he disclaimed representing any political position, he shared Croft's vision of a great national imperial party, which he suggested "may not exist in the parliamentary sense, but which does exist and always will exist in the minds and hearts of the people." The emergence of an imperial party, which existed in some form of collective consciousness or spirit, would nevertheless be the instrument of a "great national and Imperial revival." Its presence and energy would compel Britain to decide whether it intended to "remain inside the orbit of the British Empire" as demonstrated by the Canadians. "If the British Empire is going to keep its place as a decisive force in determining the world's peace and the world's commerce, then," he suggested, "we shall

9: Militant Unionism or a National and Imperial Party (1911)   175

have to set our house in order without any delay." Both the major parties demonstrated that over the last decade they lacked the commitment and capability to pursue imperial unity with any degree of seriousness as to method or purpose. Therefore, he argued, "we have got in this country to organise the resources and the spirit of the National and Imperial party."[65]

Croft noted that since Joseph Chamberlain's preeminence there had been no minister or party leader who had given anything more than just superficial support for an imperial policy, although, as Croft claimed, imperial sentiment was extremely vibrant throughout the kingdom. If only they could find "men to raise the torch and sound the tocsin the people of England would rise to their duty like the people of Canada." Although he suggested "he had not come there to speak against any individual in their party," his target was undisguised as the crowd responded with shouts of "shift Balfour." His disclaimers merely provoked loud and unrebuked demands from the crowd for a "new leader." Croft again argued that in these times of unprecedented industrial unrest, high prices, and static wages, only the empire held the promise of "ending nearly all the social evils from which the workers of the country were suffering." In the wake of the Canadian example, he charged that they, as British imperialists, had not carried their burden on behalf of the British empire and that their leaders were not fighting the imperial question as it deserved and needed to be fought.[66]

Croft suggested that they must ignore the present partisan incoherency and collectively rise above the long-standing parliamentary neglect of the empire. They may then set out and "conduct a national policy instead of setting one class of the community against another, a policy which would not fan class hatred, but which would lift up the whole community to a higher level, thereby doing something which was going to make our country stronger in the future than it had been in the past."[67] The following day Maxse wrote to Croft, "I did not have the opportunity of thanking you for your really splendid speech . . . everybody feels, that it was most eloquent, convincing and impressive." Maxse recalled how several years earlier Croft had once expressed trepidation "about tackling London audiences; those hesitations must have vanished long ago and I am sure no London audience ever enjoyed a speech more. . . . It was a wonderful demonstration." Croft was exhorted to maintain the imperial momentum because "the spirit of the rank and file is unabated. It will devolve on people like yourself to keep it up."[68]

Maxse, for his part, dispensed with any hesitation over offending particular politicians. While he accused the Asquith ministry of conspiring with President Taft "to build a Chinese wall around North America to keep out British goods," he charged that the Conservative leadership has been sitting idly by as the empire disintegrated. Balfour had occupied his exalted position for many years, yet the party was "drifting without guidance or leadership." The result was great unrest within the party. "A great many people are uncertain as to what our policy really is. . . . We have been dallying with Tariff Reform now for eight years, and I say it is time for us to get forward." He called for the rank and file to seize back their party, as he ripped into Balfour's capitulation on the Parliament Bill. He warned that it "will not be forgotten."[69] Also in October, Croft's parliamentary committee resolved to maintain focus and pressure on imperial issues by harassing the ministers with empire related questions.[70]

The campaign continued at a rally on 31 October at Queen's Hall chaired by the duke of Marlborough and addressed by both Lord Selborne and Croft.[71] Croft sought to include Aitken in the program and boasted that "the Imperial Mission is going to be the greatest movement ever started for Empire unity." Aitken was leaving for Canada on 4 October and was unable to participate at the demonstration.[72] Lord Selborne argued that the question of imperial unity should never rest "only on a material basis" and that a moral responsibility existed within the imperial partnership. The empire was an expression of the Anglo-Saxon ideal "that the State was made for the man, opposed to which was the Continental ideal that the man was made for the State." Accordingly, self-government for the Dominions provided the "great instrument to the happiness of the individual man." The empire, which the present generation held in trust, represented "the heritage of existence, but also the heritage of responsibility, the heritage of duty, which was the making of the soul of a nation." Selborne had long been concerned with imperial defense and the respective role of the Dominions. It followed, therefore, that in time of war the imperial partners may determine the extent of cooperation as in the provision of men and ships, but they may not remain neutral.[73]

Building on Lord Selborne's suggestions, Croft cast aside the moral and sentimental motives and set forth the rational basis for a constructive policy for imperial union. In the time of an escalating arms race, with its negative impact on economy and society, it was imperative to harness the empire's resources, people, and cooperation. World peace depended on a strong Britain, which, in turn, depended not only on a strong empire but an imperial union. Further, he argued, in the face of nearly one thousand emigrants leaving the United Kingdom each day, such emigration must be directed to the Dominions where they may continue "to build up the strength of the Empire's trade, the Empire's Fleet, and the Empire's throne."[74]

As signified by the negotiated Canadian-American reciprocity agreement, there was considerable international pressure to gain access to the resources and markets of the Dominions that would have the consequence of dangerously isolating Britain from her associates and thus dismantling the remains of the empire. Finally, the economic component of a constructive imperial union would ignite a prosperity capable of eradicating unemployment and all its consequential social evils. Croft later boasted to Aitken that the

9: Militant Unionism or a National and Imperial Party (1911)

Queen's Hall rally produced an additional four hundred members and a total of one thousand for November.[75]

As planned, Croft and Willoughby de Broke took the Imperial Mission campaign to the north for rallies at Bishop Auckland, Durham, Jarrow, Newcastle, and Hartlepool.[76] Croft also managed to carry the campaign to a number of large rallies in Reading and Hampshire.[77] Great encouragement came when Croft took the Imperial Mission's program to the electorate in two by-elections. At Oldham he and the Imperial Mission supported E. R. Bartley-Denniss, who on 13 November regained a seat held by the Liberals since 1899. At South Somerset, Croft pushed the Imperial message in support of Aubrey Herbert, son of the earl of Carnarvon, who on 21 November successfully captured a seat held by the Liberals for nearly four decades. In fact the Imperial Mission held forty meetings in support of the Conservative candidates.[78]

The Imperial Mission also arranged for several "discussion" meetings to be held at Caxton Hall. The first, on 21 November, was conducted by Leo Amery on the establishment of a council of empire. On 12 December, Croft addressed the issue of "trade relations of the Empire."[79] He urged the Imperial Mission to lead a movement based on the "true gospel of Imperial Union." When conducting a self-interrogation as to why he had not progressed further with the program of imperial union, Croft responded that "there are enormous areas in this country where Unionist candidates and Unionist members, who have paid lip service to this Imperial policy have hidden their heads, like great big ostriches, in the sand, and have allowed everyone to accuse them of being food taxers." These individuals have con sistently failed to rise to their own defense or a defense of the policy with even the minimal argument that the empire can meet all the nation's food requirements. Thus, it was the role of the Imperial Mission to provide the ammunition not only to defend the policy but to bring the nation, which he was convinced held pro-empire sentiments, to a full subscription to Imperial union.[80]

The significance of the event rested in the implication that Croft slightly adjusted his tactical views on an imperial party. The shift in his position with respect to an imperial party reflected a new political optimism that arose from the retirement of Balfour. Only a few days earlier, Croft informed Bonar Law that "the 'Reveille' . . . have unanimously decided to bank fire and funds and to cease any independent action in the country."[81] It was an issue that Croft needed to explain intellectually and politically, and he seemed to anticipate the dilemma in his address on 12 December by engaging in self-interrogation. He asked why he should continue to go on in this fashion. "Why don't you raise these questions above party politics altogether?" He explained that it is clear his activities and public comments lent credence to such an interpretation. But, Croft said, although he belonged to the Conservative party, he was always prepared to vote against his party "if

I thought the Government was going to do something better for the Empire as a whole on that particular question." In addition, he promised, as well as warned, that if the party begins to dilute its position on the empire, "then I believe the country will take to a new movement and will have a truly Imperial movement divorced from party." In response to his own query, Croft suggested that presently they might find "10, 12, 15, 20 people to stand for Parliament outside party politics but they would go under except where the man had a very great personality," because, he explained, "they would go against the machine." Instead, he suggested that a core of imperialists MPs "may be able to become such a force in the country that we may find men of all parties joining their ranks." Croft suggested that if this occurs, then "they will be the people who will in the end dominate their own parties just the same as is happily the case in some of the Dominions." Notwithstanding what appeared to be a modification of his political tactics, he was content in the belief "that the people who do stand up for a real definite policy, and an Imperial policy appeals more than anything else, are the people who are going to get home."[82]

It therefore appears that the discontent within the party had now been eased by the Canadian elections and the resignation of Balfour and that the frustrated imperialists no longer felt they were being pushed over the cliff and out of the party. The option of forming a new party could be sidelined, although Croft continued to believe that an imperial supraparty would eventually emerge from the present conditions not only because its economic, social, national, and sentimental arguments held merit but because they would also translate into electoral advantages. This was the ultimate paradox in the political venture for an imperial party.

During 1911 Croft had been engaged in two separate but interlocking struggles. The first was an internal campaign in which he was forced to question his own association with the Conservative party while confronting his superior loyalties to the empire. As examined in this and the previous chapter, the increasing political irrelevancy of Balfour and the party's neglect of both Canada and the empire pushed Croft further toward a serious breach with his party. Having now accepted this direction, Croft then continued to labor throughout 1911 in an effort to construct an organizational and political alternative for such nationalists and imperialists. This took the form of his Imperial Mission. However, just as he approached a possible point of no return with regard to his political departure and direction, Balfour's resignation appeared to make a nationalist and imperialist revolt unnecessary.

As Croft entered the new year, he felt assured that he was entering a new era for both the Conservative party and for national and imperial politics. However, as will be seen below, Croft's hopes for the empire were dashed by an overly pragmatic Bonar Law, who wobbled when faced by his first internal party challenge and chose improved electoral chances over party

9: Militant Unionism or a National and Imperial Party (1911)

principles. Then, when faced with what certainly must have been considered a devastating betrayal of imperial politics by Bonar Law, Croft's options were checked as the party, including its rebellious right, became obsessed with preservation of the Union, even at the possible risk of both civil war and loss of the empire.

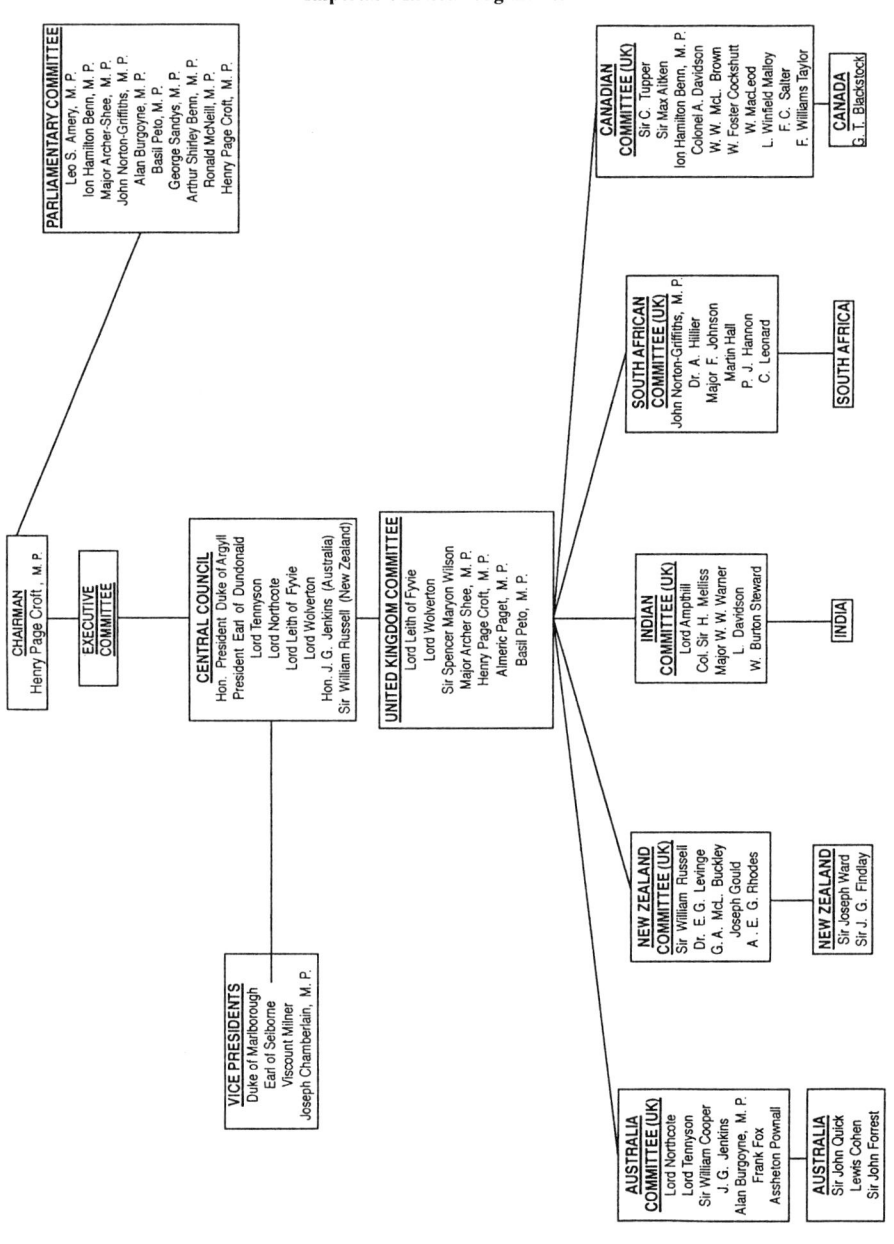

10
Croft, Bonar Law, and the Betrayal of the Imperial Idea (1912–1913)

> The Imperial Mission is not concerned with the Unionist Party. . . . It is necessary to make clear that this is to be no party question. . . . All Governments, to whatever party they belong, must heed or give place to another.
> —Henry Page Croft, 3 February 1913

> We have had years of incessant party warfare in this country. . . . We have all been thinking too much of party and too little of the State.
> —Henry Page Croft, 3 April 1913

With the retirement of Balfour, Croft was given hope that an energetic and aggressive party would rise from the leadership of Bonar Law. Such optimism emerged even though Bonar Law had previously suffered from political nervousness when faced with the electoral consequences of the party's promotion of food taxes. As evidenced by Croft's congratulatory letter of 30 November 1911, he was willing to overlook the referendum incident in November 1910. He was further encouraged when in early December he was nominated by Bonar Law for membership on the governing body of the Tariff Reform League.[1]

With a positive rapport seemingly to have developed between the determined rebel and the new leader, Croft approached Bonar Law for another endorsement. On 22 September 1911, inspired by news of the Canadian elections, Croft began writing a political tract entitled *The Path of Empire*. Excited by the possibility of the party leadership now dedicated to the imperial idea, on 14 December 1911 Croft sent Bonar Law a copy of the book, asking if the new leader would write a preface. "I need hardly say," Croft suggested, "that if you can, the book, if worth anything to our cause will receive much wider attention than could possibly be the case otherwise."[2] Without comment Bonar Law declined the invitation.[3] The dismissal of Croft's solicitation may have been symbolic of their future relationship, polite but distant and cool.[4]

Croft and the others associated with the Confederacy or the Reveille may have concluded that with Balfour's retirement the party's position on fiscal reform was now solid and secure. In a speech at Albert Hall on 26 January 1912, Bonar Law seemed to remove any lagging doubt by reminding the party's remaining free traders they faced only two options, "Tariff Reform, which they dislike, and Lloyd Georgism, which they detest."[5]

Energized by this new optimism, Croft and Captain George Tryon teamed up with a fiscal amendment to the address from the throne. Croft gave a strongly worded speech linking prospects for higher employment and higher wage rates to protectionism and imperial preference. With Britain in the throes of serious industrial unrest, he compared the increased wage levels in protectionist Germany with the stagnant levels in Britain. He feared that the fruit of free trade would be an unprecedented level of labor discontent.[6] In the euphoria of a new level of party unity and determination, Croft, supported by the other members of the Imperial Mission's parliamentary committee, now felt at liberty to reengage the campaign. He therefore continued to attack the government for its failure to establish any organization or mechanism with which to facilitate imperial relationships. This was not only requested by the colonial premiers but was demanded by the present international and economic circumstances. He asserted that the industrial strife sweeping the kingdom required the government to reconsider its neglect of the empire. Rather than turning to riches that a reconstructed empire would provide British workers, he chided that "we have had six years of incessant party warfare in this country over questions of the greatest magnitude, none of which will cure the diseases from which the nation is suffering. . . . We have all been thinking too much of party and too little of the State, with the results that we have not dealt with these problems."[7]

However, the party's unity was soon threatened as a renewed struggle over food taxes erupted. The controversy reflected an unconscious coalition between the veteran free traders and an amorphous collection of opportunistic wobblers who had witnessed their party lose three successive elections. Notwithstanding Bonar Law's Albert Hall speech, during the early part of 1912, the party's leadership councils still seemed to be paralyzed by an internal debate over food taxes.[8] Finally, in April 1912, Bonar Law informed the shadow cabinet that the party's tariff reform program must include food taxes and that the referendum pledge unilaterally made by Balfour in November 1910 must unequivocally be abandoned.[9] This naturally provoked expected protests from Lord Salisbury and Lord Derby, neither of whom had ever accepted tariff reform.[10] Feeling the ever-present pressure from the party's advanced tariff reform faction, Bonar Law informed Salisbury that food taxes "are part of our [imperial preference] policy and to change it now would in my opinion increase our difficulty of winning the election rather than diminish it."[11] Perhaps due to the incessant complaints from the Lancashire and Cecil factions, Bonar Law moved to assuage the party's free

10: Croft, Bonar Law, and the Betrayal of the Imperial Idea

traders by postponing any public announcement of the party's position on food taxes and the referendum. He agreed to wait until the Canadian prime minister, Sir Robert Borden, had concluded his visit in August. This meant that the announcement was to be held in abeyance until the autumn of 1912. Croft and the advanced tariff reformers surely detected or had been alerted to the ongoing campaign by Salisbury, Derby, and some backbench wobblers. Although engaged on several political fronts during the spring of 1912, Croft and others nevertheless worked with H. A. Gwynne of the *Morning Post* and R. D. Blumenfeld of the *Daily Express* to keep the entire tariff reform and imperial programs intact.[12] The possibility of the party backsliding pushed the remnants of the Confederacy to reappear with a warning.

Croft, supported by Basil Peto, Ronald McNeill, and Thomas Comyn Platt, announced on 15 June that "the Confederacy, an organisation about which little has lately been heard, has been carefully considering the tendency shown by several Unionist candidates at recent by-elections to place Tariff Reform in the background of their programme, or even to repudiate Imperial Preference altogether." Reminiscent of the position taken in 1908–9, the announcement went to state that "the Confederates, who have ample means at their disposal, have decided that in the event of any Unionist candidate adopting a similar policy at any further election the Confederates are fully determined to put forward a candidate who will subscribe to the full policy of the Unionist party."[13]

Word soon drifted back to Croft that Bonar Law was quite displeased with the Confederates and with what he took to be a challenge to his leadership. On 20 June, Croft sent an explanatory letter, cosigned by Peto and McNeill, in which they disclaimed any disloyalty. To ensure that the leader appreciated their concerns and had no misunderstanding as to their position, Croft requested an interview. "We feel sure we can convince you that any action we have taken was designed to assist the unity of the party and the last thing we would have dreamt of was to do anything which could have been interpreted as conveying the slightest reflection on your leadership; for you have no more devoted and loyal supporters than our members."[14] Comyn Platt, who was desperately trying to secure a seat in Parliament, wrote separately, also claiming that "you have no more loyal supporter than myself." However, he continued, "all I hope and pray is that you may see your way to stand by us who have done our best to fight the cause you have championed so splendidly. If you cannot, then the only thing left to us, is to fight alone, and depend upon it, we shall win, in the end."[15] Acknowledging the campaign by Croft and Peto for fiscal and imperial reform, Sir Joseph Lawrence publicly warned the party against thoughts of surrender to the wobblers in a *National Review* article.[16]

During the first six months of 1912, there were fourteen by-elections, and the Conservatives managed to hold on to their six seats as well as to take a seventh from the Liberals. Croft and the Confederates were convinced that the party would have fared better had the candidates not backed away from the fiscal question. The situation was further aggravated when the party lost the Crewe by-election in late July. The tactic of dodging the fiscal issue was continued by Sir John Randles in the Manchester North West by-election in August.[17] After Randles's victory, *The Times,* which now reflected Lord Northcliffe's antifood tax position, declared that "the inference is clear. The Free Trade Unionists . . . have accepted Sir John Randles' invitation to sink the fiscal issue for the time in order to join with Unionists in other parts of the country in condemning the policy of the present Government."[18] Lord Derby recorded, "I am coming out against Food Taxes. I can't stand them any longer. If Tariff Reformers had had their way we should have lost North West Manchester. Tariff Reform hasn't gained the least ground in Lancashire."[19]

With the pressure and discontent increasing in both wings of the party, Bonar Law could no longer allow the ambiguity to continue. On 14 November 1912 at the annual Conservative party conference at Albert Hall, Lord Lansdowne announced the party's repudiation of the referendum. He proclaimed that "the soundest foundation for such a closer union of the Empire is to be found in the establishment of closer commercial relations between the different parts of the Empire. And that is why we give Tariff Reform a foremost place in our policy; that is why we desire that it should keep that place." He announced that the next Conservative ministry "must come in free" to institute a protectionist program for the purposes of raising necessary taxation as well as defending British markets against unfair competition and providing imperial preferences.[20]

This announcement was met with another wave of protests. As Lord Derby's biographer describes, "Bonar Law was snowed under by indignant letters from the Free Trade wing of the Party."[21] Although Croft was delighted by Lansdowne's positive declaration against the referendum, the young MP recognized the sound of the free trade attack and the electoral nervousness of many of the backbenchers.[22] He responded with a vigorous campaign—in the press, in Bournemouth, and in several other constituencies—to explain that food taxes would not produce any significant increase in food prices.[23] His ever-present concern was that the public still failed to see the importance of imperial preference and unity, which were, of course, underpinned by the need for food taxes. He recently had been elected chairman of the Tariff Reform League's organization committee, perhaps one of the league's two most important bodies, and he promptly embarked on a whirlwind campaign to the north to keep this issue alive.[24]

Bonar Law continued to set out party policy with a speech in Lord Derby's own backyard, Ashton-under-Lyne, the heart of free trade territory, which was also Max Aitken's constituency. Here the new Conservative leader declared that "first I want to tell you exactly what it is that we propose in regard to food taxes. . . . If our countrymen entrust us with power we do not intend to impose food taxes." Rather, he proposed a colonial conference "to consider the whole question of preferential trade and the question of whether or not food duties will be imposed will not arise until those negotiations are completed."[25] The speech was viewed by Croft and other advanced tariff reformers as a retreat from the full tariff and imperial program set forth on 14 November at Albert Hall and was to have been provoked by pressure from Derby and the Cecil clan. Bonar Law confessed to Henry Chaplin that "the strongest Tariff Reformers are all coming to me saying it is impossible to fight with food taxes. The position is a very difficult one, and I really have no idea how it will end." He further conceded that in the end the party would have to modify its position on food taxes, but he "doubted whether this modification will be possible under my leadership."[26]

With inexplicable speed the advanced tariff reform wing, which had held control of the backbench since 1906, now found itself under siege from within the party. William Bridgeman, a Conservative party whip, estimated that antifood taxers outnumbered the hardline tariff reformers by a margin of four to one.[27] Chamberlain thought Bonar Law had "no stomach for such a fight" in support of the full tariff reform program.[28] On the evening that Bonar Law was at Ashton, Chamberlain spoke at Carlisle, where he announced his disagreement with Conservatives who thought tariff reform should be delayed. He warned that any postponement would be unwise and disastrous to the party. It "would split the party from top to bottom and shake the confidence of their countrymen in their honesty, good faith, and courage if they postpone consideration of this great subject."[29] At the same time, Goulding suggested to Garvin that Bonar Law, when faced with his first party crisis, had lost his nerve.[30]

The Lancashire free-trade faction was quickly building to a state of rebellion as they threatened to pass several hostile resolutions at a local party meeting scheduled 21 December 1912. Derby was able to delay such action until 11 January, apparently after a direct appeal from Balfour. Immense dissatisfaction was conveyed to Bonar Law when he met with the Lancashire Conservatives on 2 January 1913.[31] Discontent and anxiety now infected both the protectionists and antifood taxers. Both wings suggested that internal party relations were worse off than at any time during the three previous election campaigns. Critics pointed out that if a candidate was asked whether the Conservatives would tax food if elected, he would be compelled to respond with only "perhaps," which was condemned as being more damaging than either the "no" or "yes" given on earlier occasions. Further shifting responsibility to the dominions for the determination of British food taxation could only raise tempers at home and overseas.[32]

With the reopening of the fiscal controversy tearing any fabric of unity from top to bottom, the policies and leadership of Bonar Law and Lansdowne now appeared to be in disarray. As a result both leaders decided to resign. A depressed Chamberlain recorded, "Law's decision is to call a Party meeting . . . and to resign on the ground that his policy is impossible." It was his assessment that although 50 or 60 members would readily back Bonar Law "if he determined to stick to his guns, not more than twenty-five wished him to do so. . . . Page Croft confirms this estimate."[33] The news of Bonar Law's intention to step down sent Sir Edward Carson and others, who were more obsessed with Ulster than the empire, into a panic.

In the wake of the Ashton speech, Croft's spirits plunged as he confessed that the party was in another one of those "moments of difficulty."[34] As the new year began, he became more "perturbed about the political situation."[35] He returned to the press columns as "Plain Tory" and urged that those who pursued tactics not be so short sighted as to sacrifice the empire in their effort to save the Union. "It is advisable that those who are appealed to to drop Imperial Preference in order to save the Union should consider whether Preference can be dropped and, secondly, whether dropping Preference will in fact save the Union." He warned that "if we throw over the certainty of great worth, if we betray the Empire at the moment of the Empire's great gifts, shall we so save the Union?" In an emotional conclusion, Croft reminded the party that

> for nine years we have fought for Empire Union, and for nine years we have won support for this great ideal. Thousands upon thousands have joined us because of the greatness of our cause. Shall we win votes by disgusting all believers in our Imperial Policy? Shall we gain favour by permitting every Radical to ascend the platform and accuse us of fleeing from what we have preached as essential? To-day we are advised to play the opportunist game because our opponents use an unscrupulous electioneering lie which no educated man believes. To-morrow if we run we gain far worse opprobrium, for every Imperialist will leave us as a party accursed, every man who looks for consistency and honour in public life will cry shame upon us, every child will know we put a greater price on votes than on principles. We shall lose the Union and we shall lose the Empire as well. Surely now is the time to play a man's part, to go out and meet the enemy, to expose his falsehoods, to appeal to the greater, nobler side of our countrymen. Unionism is on trial, our leaders have spoken, and if we would save our cause and our party we will cease listening to those who attack us through the Press, and will fix bayonets and charge the enemy behind our leaders with that only war cry which we will win: "Union and Empire."[36]

Over this particular view of the political situation, Croft split with former Confederate Ronald McNeill, who now was singularly obsessed with preserving the Union.[37] The struggle over the party's fiscal policy further jaundiced Croft to the political corruption that he believed was becoming ingrained in modern partisan politics. Becoming further disenchanted with the present conditions, he charged that "party politics have tended in the direction of doing what is popular, and the counting of noses has been the decisive factor determining policy." It was his belief that "the country is utterly sick of the policy of bribes for the individual . . . and I am certain

10: Croft, Bonar Law, and the Betrayal of the Imperial Idea 187

the country is looking for men who will do that which they believe to be right." Therefore, Croft warned, "remove Imperial Preference from the Unionist policy, and you take from it the only great ideal we possess."[38] Jesse Collings, Joseph Chamberlain's long-time lieutenant, agreed that what was needed was not timidity, wavering, and postponements but a vigorous campaign to educate the public. He echoed Croft's constant refrain that food taxes were only unpopular because they were misunderstood.[39]

Lord Northcliffe and *The Times* tried to frighten the tariff reformers by claiming that the "food taxers" could only claim seventeen members.[40] On 5 and 6 January, Liberal and antifood tax Tory papers began publishing the names of the remaining "food taxers," presumably in an effort to isolate, if not intimidate, them. By now the holdouts included Austen Chamberlain, Amery, Archer-Shee, Chaplin, Collings, Croft, Goulding, Hewins, Hills, Gilbert Parker, Rowland Hunt, Steel-Maitland, Wyndham, Sir George Doughty, Ebenezer Parker, and Oliver Locker-Lampson.[41]

On 6 January, Croft invited thirty-five MPs to consider the situation over dinner at the Constitutional Club. There, Amery, Hewins, and Goulding took the position that the party's character and not its policy was the obstacle. At least five members in attendance had privately informed Bonar Law they would prefer to abandon food taxes.[42] The next day Croft learned of Bonar Law's intention to resign. On the same day, Carson began circulating a "memorial" urging Bonar Law and Lansdowne not to resign but instead to modify the party's fiscal policy to provide that food taxes would be subjected to a referendum. Carson's proposed draft urged that if given the choice of submitting a tariff and imperial preference program to Parliament or the electorate, the memorialists believe that "no abandonment of principles is involved. It would invoke a modification in procedure, but one which could be accepted for the sake of closing our ranks."[43] Contrary to everything Croft had stood for in his political life, Carson and his supporters were proposing to cast aside Conservative principles in favor of "closing ranks."

F. E. Smith approached Chamberlain about the party's difficulty, but the latter refused to sign the memorial. Although he also refused to approve or disapprove such a proceeding, Chamberlain recommended that Smith and his coconspirators "had better take the letter first to men like Hewins, Amery, Page Croft and George Lloyd and see if they would sign, or sign after alteration." Chamberlain later reported that "they refused to sign the letter as it stood."[44] When confronted by Smith and Carson, Hewins, Croft, and Goulding brought in Amery to assist in revising the petition. After reading the original draft, Amery warned that they "could not possibly agree to such a thing," because it actually implied a postponement of imperial preference. Goulding, Amery, Carson, Hewins, Smith, and Croft were now joined by Waldorf Astor, as they spent several hours in an effort to redraft the document and construct a much stronger position from protectionist and preference standpoints. Amery recorded that "Croft and the others were more and more succumbing to the idea that all would be well if the principle of Preference were asserted sufficiently vigorously in words, regardless of the real meaning and effect of the document."[45]

It was then subjected to additional revising by Hugh Cecil and McNeill, who joined Carson in viewing Ulster as the priority. Eventually all but a handful of party backbenchers signed the memorial.[46] Although Amery's observation of Croft during the drafting and negotiation of the memorial may have caught sight of the latter's desire to preserve unity if at all possible, Croft would never do so at the sacrifice of principles. Apparently Croft had been brought over to sign the memorial, believing it had been moderated enough to preserve his imperial objectives and the Chamberlain program. Goulding, who also signed, nevertheless expressed the right wing's disgust, "we are a rotten Party with no faith."[47]

On 13 January 1913, Bonar Law and Lansdowne accepted the memorial that strongly implied a new direction for Conservative party policy on fiscal reform and imperial preference.[48] On 24 January Bonar Law announced the party's new fiscal policy in a speech at Edinburgh. It has been suggested that the compromised "policy was, to all intents and purposes, that devised by Derby."[49] Bonar Law explained, "Lord Lansdowne and I realized at that time that the majority of our party were reluctant to have what are called food duties and that if that was the feeling of the members of Parliament, and of the candidates who had to fight our battle, then the course of action of the party ought to be changed." When returned to office, Bonar Law continued, the party intends to "impose a tariff, a moderate tariff, lower than exists in any industrial country, on foreign manufactured goods," to give preference to the dominions without the imposition of new duties upon food, and to pursue cooperation with the empire on trade and defense issues.[50]

The situation as it then existed, that is, the state of party policy, which Croft refused to accept, was that tariff reform had been effectively postponed. It was subordinated to other issues, and its resurrection depended on the intervening disposition of those crises. With the advantage of historical hindsight, we now know it would have to wait nearly ten years before the issue was resurrected. Although not a true divorce, the party had now separated itself from the one constructive program that Croft was convinced would arguably compete with the appeal of the new liberalism and socialism for the hearts and minds of the British working classes.

The Tariff Reform League claimed to be undaunted by the change in Conservative party policy. Others marked the cause as now lost.[51] Croft, however, did not for a moment abandon his campaign for a full and immediate program of tariff reform and imperial preference. Croft seemed to receive a cue from Austen Chamberlain who provided an extensive examination of the episode in the February *National Review*. He castigated the mischievous miscreants who had shamefully provoked the stampede of timid politicians. He wrote, "I am afraid that this change may be a calamity for the party with which all my public life has been associated. I am afraid it may prove a misfortune for the Empire which it has been my earnest desire to serve." Although "it may be that in present circumstances the full fruition of our hopes must be postponed," he held hope in that "the spirit of the Empire is with us, the force of events is fighting on our side. The movement has made progress." For his part, Chamberlain asserted, "I abandon no part of the convictions that I have expressed to you; I retract nothing." He promised that "wherever and whenever I see an opportunity I will do my utmost to promote that common organisation of Imperial trade . . . with the common organisation of Imperial defence as the twin pillars which for the future must carry the arch of Empire."[52]

Notwithstanding the Edinburgh compromise, Croft shared Chamberlain's view as he tirelessly campaigned throughout the kingdom in 1913 on the full program of fiscal reform and imperial preference. Recognition of the extent and quality of Croft's commitment was reflected in his increased stature within the tariff reform movement. He was elected to the most important committees of the Tariff Reform League, including the executive committee, the general purposes committee, and the organization committee, for the last of which he served as chairman. He also was selected as chairman of the Lancashire, Cheshire, and North West Counties Federation of the Tariff Reform League, which claimed fifty thousand members and oversaw Lancashire, Cheshire, Westmorland, Cumberland, the North and East Ridings of Yorkshire, and parts of Derbyshire and Staffordshire.[53] Lord Duncannon as chairman of the league and Croft as chairman of the organization committee were now the two most powerful figures within the Tariff Reform League and the enveloping movement. In June 1913 Croft was also elected chairman of the United Empire Club, and of course he continued to govern the Imperial Mission as its chairman. Under the leadership of Duncannon and Croft, the Tariff Reform League held or sponsored 9,900 meetings in 1913, greater than any year save 1910 with its ten thousand meetings and two general elections.[54]

Croft's advantage in not accepting either the result or the message of the Edinburgh compromise was the liberty with which he could continue to campaign for a full tariff reform program, inclusive of food taxes, while also pleading deference to the leader's policy declarations. On those occasions when Croft wished to attack Lloyd George's government policies, he would conveniently do so as a Conservative MP.[55] At other times he was able to shed his association with the Conservative party and campaign throughout the kingdom as either the chairman of the Imperial Mission, chairman of the United Empire Club, chairman of the organization committee of the Tariff Reform League, chairman of the Lancashire and North West Counties Federation of the Tariff Reform League, or merely as a prominent official of the tariff reform movement. As he once told Bonar Law, Croft received two invitations daily to speak somewhere in the kingdom on tariff reform and imperial unity. Accordingly, Croft, a highly regarded and popular platform speaker, was not without ample opportunity and standing to continue his campaign for a full tariff and imperial reform program. His ability to blur the lines between the party and the extraparty organizations was most aggravating to Liberals and Conservatives alike.[56]

Croft now pushed himself further outside of the restraints of the Conservative party. Although the party had pledged itself not to impose duties on agricultural products, Croft nevertheless was free to claim that "the Imperial Mission is not concerned with the Unionist Party. . . . This is to be no party question." The imperial idea was "an undying faith" for which they were prepared to sacrifice "and to which all Governments, to whatever party they belong, must heed or give place to another." He expressed regret that the party felt compelled to abandon protectionist and preference programs "owing to the fear of misrepresentations."[57] He often maneuvered the debate skillfully toward the arena of national security, noting that "the military position of the nations of the world in the last 50 years, has completely changed to the disadvantage of the British race." It followed that Britain's physical security depended on an imperial unity that would then be able "to resist on land and sea the attack of any powers or combination of powers." The imperial amalgamation that was essential for such military and defensive collaboration could only be achieved through the establishment of an imperial community of interest in trade. Preference was the requisite cornerstone of that community of interest.[58]

In a campaign through the north of England and Scotland, Croft confessed that "he was not what was called a party man; he was an Imperialist. He fought the last election as an Imperialist."[59] At Glasgow he explained eloquently that he was a tireless advocate of tariff reform "because he desired to see a return to a more robust faith, to a policy of nationalism and imperialism, not the stirring of class against class, which might weaken the whole body of the state, the whole strength of the nation." He urged them to recommit themselves to the principles of Lord Beaconsfield, who "taught the country of making us first concerned with our own affairs, doing everything possible to consider our people." With respect to food taxes, Croft claimed he was not looking forward to the next election, but as he said he was looking with anticipation to the establishment of the United British Empire.[60]

A few days later in Manchester, the center of free trade sentiment, he stated the Tariff Reform League's position without qualification: "We as a League do not intend to go back. We have a great army, and we intend to go forward, marching irresistibly to our final triumph of imperial union, and the brotherhood of the British races." Croft chastised the party for running away from the "unworthy falsehoods of our opponents." He suffered from little hesitation in declaring that his friends in the party's leadership ranks

10: Croft, Bonar Law, and the Betrayal of the Imperial Idea 191

"have made a great mistake." In a thinly veiled but critical message to the Central Office and the Carlton Club, Croft wanted it understood "that Tariff Reformers have not abandoned one jot or one tittle of their full policy, and we intend to preach it, not because it is necessarily popular, not because we are out to catch votes, but because the policy is right, because our sole concern is for the ultimate good of our people, and the preservation of the British Empire."[61] He carried this similar manifesto into his old territory in Hertfordshire.[62] Here Croft made his position provocatively clear. Although he openly professed courteous support for Bonar Law's Edinburgh compromise because it went at least halfway, it was his intention to support and press for the full tariff reform program, which meant food taxes and preference.[63]

For six months he had been attempting almost single-handedly to push Bonar Law off his Edinburgh compromise and into a protariff reform declaration. Ever since late 1912, Croft had been vigorously trying to save Lancashire for tariff reform, but inside he feared that the Lancashire man "is a simple protectionist and knows nothing of the Imperial position."[64] At Bolton in early October, Croft still refused to accept the notion that Lancashire could not be converted to tariff reform. He suggested that a "great number of capitalists were fighting tariff reform tooth and nail," but he "believed Lancashire working classes particularly would be amongst the first to adopt such a National Policy."[65]

From Bolton, Croft traveled to York where he declared that notwithstanding the Conservative party's decision "to take the policy of Tariff Reform in two steps, there was no abandonment of the agricultural Tariff policy." It seemed evident to him that there existed some misconception as to the party's true position with respect to food taxes, and because no member of the leadership was concerned enough to defend the party's integrity, Croft was compelled to venture forward to make the clarification. He noted that "it had been decided that the party should appeal at the next election on the whole policy of Tariff Reform with the exception of . . . wheat and meat. In other words," he argued, "a tariff would immediately be imposed on all foreign manufactured goods, thus enormously increasing home production and putting millions of pounds [£] in wages and profits into the pockets of the home consumers, who were the people on whom agriculturalists entirely depended." There would follow an increased demand for British agricultural products as had been the case in all tariff countries. In an effort to provoke a response from the leadership, he declared that "there were never any suggestions made that duties should not be imposed upon all imported agricultural products other than essential food products, thus we still could place a duty on foreign barley, foreign oats, and foreign flour."[66]

He recounted how legislation had been proposed for a minimum wage. But, he asked, how could the farmer pay higher wages unless he himself gained greater profits? It followed, Croft provocatively urged, that "as business men . . . they must organise and press for . . . the time had come when they must show determinedly that they must have Tariff Reform, and once the tariff was established it was impossible to deny the same boon to agriculturalists that we granted to other industries." Notwithstanding the timidity demonstrated by the party leadership, "the [Tariff Reform] League had abandoned not one jot or one tittle of its policy, and it asked their help to win a cause which was so good it could not fail."[67]

Shortly after his York speech, Croft was able to pursuade a body of the Tariff Reform League to increase the pressure on Bonar Law. By the end of 1913, the other hard-line tariff reformers on the general purposes committee also had become disenchanted with the party's disaffection. Accordingly, on 5 November 1913, the committee—consisting of Duncannon, Goulding, Hewins, Remnant, Sir Joseph Lawrence, Sir Alexander Henderson, and Croft, five former Confederates—issued a resolution. Because of the ambiguous and anemic pronouncements the party's rank and file feared that the party's leadership no longer subscribed to tariff reform as the party's first constructive program. Accordingly, to "allay this misapprehension," the committee demanded "an authoritative declaration by Mr. Bonar Law at Norwich next Thursday."[68] In the face of his general divorce from the movement since his Edinburgh compromise speech in January, Bonar Law recognized the need to mollify slightly the elements of the party's right wing. Thus, he let it be known that he would address tariff reform in upcoming speeches at Norwich and Birmingham.[69]

In addition to leading the general purposes committee into pressing Bonar Law to defend tariff reform, Croft made a last attempt to salvage the imperial idea for which he had selflessly worked for the past ten years. He wrote to Bonar Law and advised that "the feeling amongst the farmers with regard to Tariff Reform is growing more intense and there is no doubt that thousands of farmers are greatly exercised about that part of the Unionist Party." After confessing that his York speech before three thousand farmers was an intended "kite," he admonished the leader. "Unless we are going to give the farmers an assurance that they will receive Tariff consideration on non-essential foodstuffs, such as barley, oats & hops, we shall lose far more votes amongst farmers than we shall ever gain from the postponement of that party of our policy which has already taken place." He further argued that "the only answer to industrial unrest and the drop in real wages is Tariff Reform and that therefore that policy even in its emasculated form should be pressed with all the vigour we possess."[70]

Although Croft always embraced principles over politics, he often found himself forced to appeal to the raw political or electoral considerations of his colleagues. He claimed that being the opponents of home rule and Welsh disestablishment would not give Conservatives one single seat. Always sensitive to the inherent contradictions contained in political positions and tactical maneuvering, he posed the uncomfortable questions to Bonar Law.

10: Croft, Bonar Law, and the Betrayal of the Imperial Idea 193

Should there be a settlement of the Irish issue based on the exclusion of Ulster "then where will the Unionist be as regards policy since our leaders and candidates have talked about nothing but Home Rule in the last years? . . . Unless we answer Lloyd George with the Tariff we are doomed to remain in opposition for another five years." Croft recognized that a failure to salvage the Conservative party's one constructive program would submerge the program and hamper the party indefinitely.[71] He refused to apologize for being "a fanatic upon this question." Strained by the last ten months during which he almost single-handedly kept the movement and debate alive, he emotionally warned that "we are making the same grave mistake that we made prior to the 1906 election, we are out of touch with the working classes." Croft claimed the working classes "are concerned with one question & one question only which is the wage question & unless we grapple with it fearlessly & unless our leaders can inspire all candidates to place the Tariff in the forefront . . . our working class supporters will go over to the Labour party."[72]

Croft's kite clearly had upset Bonar Law, particularly because they had discussed the issue immediately prior to Croft's trip to York. Bonar Law wrote, "I am sorry to say that it was with much regret that I read your speech." They had talked previously, at which time the leader pointed out that "if there was any proposal to put new duties on any food stuffs as the result of the coming election we should have had all the disadvantages of having changed our policy and no advantage." Bonar Law claimed that Croft had agreed with him. Revealing his political anxieties and perhaps his lack of convictions, Bonar Law declared, "I am absolutely committed to the policy that we shall not, as the result of the next election, put any new duties on any kind of food stuffs. We are by no means rid of the difficulties connected with the tariff, for every day I receive letters urging me to drop it altogether." Cautioning the rebellious MP, he warned, "in my opinion the only chance of a successful issue is that the compromise should be strictly and literally adhered to on both sides."[73]

Notwithstanding Bonar Law's appeal, Croft could not permit such assertions to stand unchallenged, and he immediately shot back. "I well remember our conversation when I urged you to limit the change to meat & wheat which would have killed the dear food cry & yet left a substantial advantage to home agriculturalists." Countering, Croft reminded that "I also remember that you stated that your pledge must include all food stuffs, but this I understood to mean meat, wheat, bacon, poultry, eggs, vegetables etc." Seeking any elasticity with which to protect if not actually to advance the imperial idea, Croft somewhat disingenuously suggested that he "had no idea whatever that it meant to include barley, hops or oats or such other agricultural products which cannot be described as food stuffs." He pressed further by warning that "the position amongst agriculturalists is so grave that I hope you would be able to calm the fears by showing that agriculture was not to be excluded from a National tariff policy since with regard to those products which are the staple food of the people, & I still hope that you will not close your mind to this possibility." If the agriculturalists sensed their abandonment, Croft suggested, "the resentment will be far more widespread than imagined."[74]

Trying to soften his attack, he condemned those around Bonar Law "who behaved so disgracefully to you at the time of the stampede [and] are now urging you to drop Tariff Reform altogether." Croft again requested an interview with which he hoped to counter their case and dilute their influence. "I am quite confident," he added, "that such people are out of touch with the masses, enormous numbers of whom are only attracted to our Party by the belief that we intend to go on with Tariff Reform." Croft concluded with a most fascinating and prophetic statement: "I should very much like to have a talk with you sometime about the whole situation & meanwhile you can rely upon me *whilst I remain a member of the Unionist party* to do my best not to embarrass the arrangements of the compromise."[75] Croft seemed to be coming closer and closer to a point of leaving Bonar Law's Conservative party.

On the same day, the executive committee of the Tariff Reform League wrote to Bonar Law asking to present him with a deputation.[76] Bonar Law had been privately alerted by Herbert Pike Pease, one of the executive committee members, that the committee was "very exercised about the position of Tariff Reform." In an effort to prevent further intraparty divisions, he suggested the leader merely include a general but noncommittal reference in his upcoming speech at Norwich that "Colonial Preference and Tariff Reform are still the first constructive policy of the Unionist Party."[77] Accordingly, on 13 November 1913 during his speech in Norwich on the Irish crisis, Bonar Law announced, almost in terms of an afterthought, that he wished to add a word about tariff reform. As a sop to the Tariff Reform League and Croft, he stated that, while they would not impose any food taxes, there would be moderate tariffs on foreign manufactured goods. A Conservative ministry would also immediately establish imperial preference, combined with readjustments of local taxation for British farmers.[78]

Bonar Law felt his comments at Norwich should have put to rest the entire discussion over tariff reform within the Conservative party. He therefore became somewhat annoyed as Lord Duncannon sought to continue the debate with a request for a deputation in an effort "to demonstrate . . . the strength of the Tariff reform movement throughout the country, and to submit to you reasons which they consider vital why the leaders, members and candidates should give a prominent place from now on to the advocacy of the constructive policy of the party." Bonar Law was adamant that he did not want to receive a deputation from the Tariff Reform League, so Duncannon suggested an alternative deputation of trade unionists, businessmen, manufacturers, and agriculturalists. The leader then insisted that it be abso-

10: Croft, Bonar Law, and the Betrayal of the Imperial Idea

lutely private with no notice or acknowledgment to the press, a condition Duncannon would not accept.[79]

Croft and Duncannon now witnessed the door being slammed shut on any further dialogue on fiscal reform and imperial unity within the party. A few days later, Bonar Law, speaking in, of all places, Birmingham, the capital of tariff reform and fiefdom of Chamberlain, declared that "at present my mind is so filled with the dangers in front of us in connexion with Home Rule that, till that question is settled, I have hardly interest enough to argue any other."[80] Now the empire must await the Union. The party leader's comments surely persuaded Croft that the betrayal was complete. Croft saw Bonar Law, the businessman, as a simple-minded, wobbling protectionist for whom the imperial idea was mere romanticism, if not just so much rhetoric. Accordingly, he supposed that Bonar Law viewed protectionism as providing no electoral advantage particularly when faced with an attack on the Union. Bonar Law's hostility even to discuss the question further barred any deputation from ever being held. Accordingly, as 1913 fell to a close, so did the Conservative party's "first constructive policy," and it was to remain dormant until resurrected by Stanley Baldwin in equally controversial circumstances in the autumn of 1923.

As 1914 opened Croft was now no further advanced in pushing a recalcitrant party leadership toward his imperial idea than he was in the summer of 1911. Instead, at this time the leadership's intentional distance from the advanced programs of tariff reform and imperial preference was reinforced by an obstreperous core of party backbenchers. With this serious setback to the imperial idea, the question that followed was whether Croft would be able to return successfully to his course toward an independent national and imperial party or at least to pursue alternative political action as represented by the Confederacy, the Reveille, and the Imperial Mission. More fundamental was the question, would Croft be able to redirect the party's attention away from the Ulster crisis and back to the empire?

11
All for Naught
(1912–1914)

> And then suddenly Ireland was forgotten, tariffs were forgotten, all was forgotten, for a cloud hung over the world and the greatest storm of all history was about to break.
> —Henry Page Croft, *My Life of Strife*

Croft entered 1912 "full of hope and yet full of anxiety; for never before have the prospects of Empire Organisation looked brighter; and at the same time never yet has the Empire had to face such difficulties as now confront it."[1] However, the serious divisions over tariffs and preferences quickly reappeared within the Conservative party, and Croft's attempts to maintain the imperial idea as the party's first constructive program ran headlong into the crisis over Ireland. In addition, Asquith's Liberal ministry did not cooperate, as it produced a significant corpus of legislation that Croft and other radical Conservatives found quite disturbing. Nevertheless, in the years immediately following Bonar Law's ascendancy it remained Croft's principal concern to promote British nationalism by advancing the empire.

With the substantial volume of controversial legislative proposals coming from the Asquith government, it was expected that Conservative party energy would be diverted from any constructive program and instead would be engaged in more traditional opposition. Such was the case with the Disestablishment of the Church in Wales Act that Croft obediently condemned but in which he saw truly little to threaten either the nation or the empire. In addition, he routinely expressed his opposition to the Payment of Members Act (1912) and the Trades Disputes Act (1913) that collectively had reversed the Osborne judgment.[2] He also took exception to the National Insurance Act (1911), which, being an instrument of social reform, he approached in his usually abstract fashion. He argued that the amelioration of social conditions would be accomplished more effectively through an overhaul of the state's fiscal and imperial programs. The great industrial and working-class unrest, as evidenced by the number of days lost to work stoppages, was on the rise and a serious concern to Croft. He regularly argued

11: All for Naught (1912–1914)

that "the whole trouble is due to the low standard of wages existing in the country and the increasing of the necessaries of life," which was not an inaccurate assessment. The cause of this condition was indisputable in his eyes. "The wages of this country were kept at their present low level by the national policy which admits products of labour from any competitive source."[3]

The issue of women's suffrage also plagued Croft as it did many politicians at that time. Ironically, Croft had vigorously supported the formation of women's' branches both in the Conservative party and the Tariff Reform League; he supported the British Women's Emigration Association and advocated women's emigration to the dominions.[4] In March 1912 Croft received a deputation of representatives from the Bournemouth area suffrage organizations who urged him to promote the suffrage bill. The women wanted a voice in choosing representatives who raised and spent the kingdom's money. As a general principle, Croft responded, "there ought to be no extension of the franchise in any direction . . . without a specific mandate of the existing electorate." More directly, however, he suggested there were three points to consider before supporting an extension of the franchise. He must be confident that it benefited the country, that it benefited the women themselves, and that the majority of the country supported extension of the franchise.[5]

With respect to the first criterion, he expressed concern that women would concentrate their attention on one issue. He noted that women have previously focused their concerns on temperance, divorce reform, labor, and social questions. Such single-mindedness, he feared, might "possibly to lead to an unsettlement and instability of Government." As a way of further illustration, he suggested that if women "felt strongly upon an international wrong, or say upon some massacre of Christians, they might, if they held the balance of power in the constituencies, be able to force the country into war."[6]

Furthermore, he did not see what women would gain by an extension of the suffrage. When one of those in attendance shouted "justice," Croft responded that he saw no justice resulting from women voting in local and municipal elections. It was his contention, left unchallenged, that while 70 percent of the men voted in local elections, women voted at a much lower rate, and therefore the "justice" argument did not hold together.[7] Croft generally believed that extending the franchise to women ratepayers would merely encourage the Liberal government to pursue universal woman suffrage. If granted to ratepayers, how, he asked, could it then be denied to married women? He explained that Britain's "national character was dependent on the womanliness of the nation," that women were responsible for the nurturing of the nation, and for imbuing children with religion. He feared that women would soon demand a role in government, which he believed would be a "depart[ure] from that sphere where their real influence lies, and their influence in the nation will be weakened."[8] Of course Croft was mocked for his views, which were not altogether out of mainstream conservative thought. He subsequently extended his support to a resolution of the National League for Opposing Women Suffrage that argued suffrage "would be detrimental to the best interests of the Empire, and, in view of recent events and the actions of the militant section of the Women's Suffrage Societies, no such Bill should be passed without a direct appeal to the electorate."[9]

The Liberal programs did not deter Croft from promoting his ideas. In addition to the empire, he vigorously urged that the military be upgraded, particularly to include national service. Very soon after the end of the war in South Africa, Croft had concluded that the military needed to be restructured. He not only believed that the present land forces were inadequately trained and ill-prepared for the call to action, he was equally disturbed by the fact that during the war Britain had been denuded of troops, officers, and transport, leaving the nation exposed to other dangers, both domestic and foreign. In his 1908 article on the "Citizen Army," Croft promoted what he believed to be minimum standards for the national defense. He argued that boys should militarily and physically train at school each day; that during their last two years of schooling, boys should be "certificated" in musketry; that a cadet corps should be established at secondary schools; and that rifle clubs or boys brigades should be actively encouraged at the end of formal schooling.[10] Croft also set forth detailed proposals to improve both the militia and yeomanry for service abroad. However, underlying his view of military reform was the requisite national service component. Except for those members of the regular armed forces of the Crown—such as the Royal Navy, Regular Army, and even the militia or yeomanry—all young men should be required at age eighteen to undergo two years' military training and service as part of the Territorial Army. This would provide for adequate home defense, thus unencumbering trained forces of the militia and yeomanry for overseas service. With a minimum Territorial Army of two hundred fifty thousand troops and a reserve of 1.8 million, additional trained troops would be available "to fill gaps caused by the wastage of war."[11]

Five years later Croft remained convinced of the inadequacy of the military manpower situation, and he continued to advocate national service and an expanded and better trained Territorial Army.[12] He complained that Bulgaria, with a population equal to Glasgow and Birmingham, "could put more men in the field in one week than the British Empire could do in six months."[13] As with his position on imperial issues, he was vexed over the fact that national defense could be dragged into partisan politics.[14] "It is evident," Croft asserted, "if we are to remain an Empire and to be included among the first class powers, that we must be able to defend every country in the Empire from attack and at the same time possess such an Expeditionary Force as will give us a strategic influence in Europe." Accordingly, he suggested that the Expeditionary Force be maintained with a minimum of two hundred fifty thousand troops, and the Territorial Army, which would have the burden of home defense, be increased to a minimum of eight hundred thousand troops through the institution of universal national service. He also continued to advocate the establishment of compulsory military education for school-aged boys.[15]

However, Croft's energy and determination remained targeted on the empire, and while he continued to press forward with his advocacy of the imperial idea, the bulk of the Conservative party confined themselves to arranging relatively futile obstacles to the Liberal government's legislative proposals. Shortly after Bonar Law's installation as party leader, Croft ventured into South Wales with his imperial idea and blasted the socialist strategy of "pulling down to raise the community." In this area that had been hard hit by industrial strife in recent years, Croft proposed to harness "the forces of the state to defend the health and mental and physical powers of the workers and to raise the wages of the workers."[16] With the assistance of the Imperial Mission's parliamentary group, Croft vigorously supported a proposal for an imperial cable system that again implied an active state role in constructing imperial unity.[17]

In a series of articles entitled "The Future of the British Race" and published in *Outlook,* Croft exhorted the kingdom to awake to the dangers of the world. In somewhat ominous tones, he warned that "rival empires of the world are consolidating and holding their man-power," yet Britain is "shedding the best of her sons to the extent of a quarter of a million a year." Although Britain is being "challenged as a naval Power," her land forces has been reduced to second-class status. In sum Britain "has been left behind in man-power." He still remained hopeful that a united British race will be "supreme and unassailable." But, he cautioned, "we are not united." Therefore it was imperative that the British race "shall act together, think together, trade together, and if necessary fight together."[18]

As a supporting institution, Croft proposed the establishment of a permanent imperial council to address and coordinate issues of defense, commerce, trade and shipping, treaties, communications, and emigration. "Britain was staggering under an unequal burden of defence," and Croft urged, if not demanded, Dominion contribution to imperial defense. The imperial council theoretically would satisfy the principle of concurrent Dominion participation and cooperation. He did not wish a body that would be associated purely with party or faction and would therefore fail to enjoy the requisite level of prestige and respect. Instead he envisioned an organization that would set forth the collective view of the empire. It was necessary that the proposed forty-seven council members should be appointed by both the respective government and opposition parties:[19]

	Government Appointments	Opposition Appointments	Total
United Kingdom	15	7	22
Canada	4	2	6
Australia	4	2	6
South Africa	4	2	6
New Zealand	3	1	4
Newfoundland	2	1	3
Total			47

The imperial council would not be an executive body but a deliberative and advisory group that would vote recommendations to the constituent governments. The secretaries of state for War and Foreign Affairs as well as the first lord of the Admiralty would be permitted to attend council sessions, but they would have no voting rights. Obviously frustrated by the British government's long neglect of imperial matters, Croft's council represented a method by which public pressure for imperial attention and action could be applied to the government. The permanent council "should have the power to vote on resolutions which will carry only the power of recommendations. The authority of this body will be so great that its decisions will naturally receive the weightiest consideration from every Parliament in the Empire, and it will be in the interests of all parties to send some of their best men to represent them." It had been Croft's goal to prevent imperial issues from being suffocated by parliamentary wrangling and political corruption. He returned to the often overworked theme of trade. "If the Mother Country and the Dominions," he explained, "are to pay for a Fleet common to all citizens of the Empire, it is reasonable to expect that each must strive to help the others by assisting their growth and financial strength." It followed that patriotism demanded the promotion of mutually beneficial trade policies, while concurrently the resulting commercial intercourse between members of the imperial family would itself engender and cement the public feeling of British patriotism. This translated into nothing more complex than preference as being the cornerstone of an economic community of interest among the Dominions.[20]

Croft took the imperial idea on a vigorous campaign throughout the north of England during the summer of 1912.[21] However, when Parliament stood down for its recess, he and his wife departed on 17 August for an eight-week trip to Canada, a journey that also corresponded to the return of the Canadian premier, Sir Robert Borden. Croft met with imperialists from Quebec to Alberta, and for the first time he came to appreciate the truly expansive character of Canada and the empire as a whole. As they traveled west, Croft reported, "we suddenly found ourselves in the great prairie country, and for 24 hours we sped through wheatland. There was wheat as far as the eye could see, to the right, to the left, in front, and behind—nothing but a continuous sea of golden corn. Imagine yourself," he wrote

11: All for Naught (1912–1914)

home, "traveling by an express from Bournemouth to the North of Scotland and back again through wheat, and you can partly grasp the extent of the prairie of Canada. . . . When one realises that only a fraction of the possible wheatland is yet under cultivation, we then see that there is practically no limit to the wheat production of Canada."[22] Croft returned to Britain in October possessed of renewed enthusiasm which he again tried to translate into agitation for his imperial idea,[23] and with which he sought to cement a political and emotional relationship with Canada.[24]

Such enthusiasm was to be dashed by the troubles that rocked both the Conservative party and Britain in 1913 and 1914. The anxieties over the prospects for the empire, which Croft revealed ever so slightly in January 1912, had by the beginning of 1914 proved themselves as having substance. By 1914 party leadership effectively abandoned the tariff reform program he so faithfully embraced. Faced with Bonar Law's abandonment of any constructive imperial idea and capitulation to the wobblers, Croft now sought to raise the Reveille and merge it with his Imperial Mission. However, when Croft tired to initiate a campaign against Bonar Law, he was effectively stymied by external forces beyond his control and developments from which the Conservative party could not walk away. For all practical purposes, Croft's campaign for empire would be cast aside while the party sought to save the union with Ireland. He was now faced with few options as he found it impossible to resurrect either the Confederacy or the Reveille because other developments consumed the party's attention. On 11 April 1912, Asquith introduced the third Home Rule Bill.[25] Accordingly, from early 1912 to the summer of 1914, the organizational and propaganda activities of the Conservative party were obsessed with one particular issue. As a result Croft's imperial idea was displaced by the Irish crisis.

Circumstances had not changed by 1914 but clearly had intensified. No Conservative politician was insulated from the pressure of the crisis. Croft's political activities in 1913 and 1914 pivoted between his dogged campaign for imperial unity in general and his opposition to the government's home rule bill. By the summer of 1912 it was evident that the party suffered from a significant schism over the approach to home rule.[26] Croft, as well as the Conservative party in general, would have opted to block home rule if at all possible. However, the legacy of the Parliament Act of 1911 made this preferred outcome very remote at best. The Conservatives were forced to construct a strategy in response to Asquith's Home Rule Bill and the likelihood of its passing. The cornerstone of the strategy became Ulster, and the only issue or question was the length to which the party was prepared to go in using the Ulster card.

Notwithstanding speeches in support of physical resistance, Bonar Law's biographer suggests that the leader "was ready to recognize that in the last resort it was impossible to use the position of Ulster as a means of checking Home Rule for the South. If an offer of exclusion were made by Asquith, an offer acceptable to Carson and the Ulster Unionists, he realized that the Conservatives could not and should not reject it."[27] On the other hand, there existed a substantial block of backbenchers led by Walter Long who "cared little for Ulster save as a means of stopping Home Rule entirely." Long told Bonar Law on 4 June 1912, "as an Englishman I cannot assent to H.R. in any form."[28]

Croft did not play a highly visible role in this drama over Ireland and Ulster, but as a Conservative MP and the most determined imperialist in the party, he was forced to traverse his way through the emotional, intellectual, and political arguments that flowed through Conservative and Unionist camps. Before the introduction of the Bill, Croft counseled that "it would be indeed foolish for Unionists to make a general demonstration against Home Rule until the Bill has come before them, almost as foolish as it was for the Government to say that the electors gave them a mandate for Home Rule."[29] He could not resist warning the government that there were most assuredly certain conditions that he would never accept. In particular, neither he nor the Conservative party would ever agree to a taxpayer grant to finance or underwrite the dissolution of the Union. Although very few seriously considered the option at this point in time, Croft came out very early to declare that if the Asquith ministry attempted to press forward with home rule, "then we must be prepared for a separate Parliament in Belfast." However, the principal bogey associated with this development, which Croft continued to raise, was that any separation of Ulster from Ireland could only mean economic ruin for Nationalist Ireland.[30]

The party's strategy was somehow to force a dissolution before the Home Rule Bill became law. It followed that throughout the entire crisis Croft and virtually every other Conservative politician used every available public and parliamentary opportunity to condemn the government for dissolving the Union without a popular mandate. As with the party in general, he recognized that the Parliament Act of 1911 gave the government a clear legislative road. Consequently, his strategy was to appeal to public opinion in hopes of pressuring the government into either a general election or a special referendum.[31] In these early stages, Croft attempted to make gain from the government's inconsistencies. He claimed that if Britain was to grant Ireland home rule "they must trust Ireland," and that was not evidenced by the provisions for dual control of Irish government and legislation contained in the Bill. Such a relationship would only perpetuate friction and discontentment.[32] At the same time, Croft revealed his own inconsistencies as he occasionally argued that the safeguard provisions were ineffective.

To pressure the Liberals toward an election, it was necessary to make the electorate nervous with suggestions that the government's policy implied a forced home rule for Wales, Scotland, and England. As most of the parliamentary party in the forefront were doing, Croft tried to alarm the public with fears of a civil war. He claimed that "the Government are well aware

11: All for Naught (1912-1914)

that this policy can only be carried out by force, and therefore they, and they alone, are responsible if civil war follows." He further warned, "be it said on the heads of Mr. Churchill and his colleagues rests all responsibility, and no amount of whining on their part will save them from the ignominy which awaits them."[33]

Only two options could save the country from such an apocalypse—drop the Home Rule Bill or submit to an election.[34] Speaking at fifty-four demonstrations, he continued this plan into 1913 when in January the bill passed the House of Commons for the first time under the provisions of the Parliament Act.[35] Croft stressed that while Ireland would not contribute to the empire, she would collect huge subsidies from the British taxpayers. Rather than see civil war, he was prepared to support "a Referendum measure so that the people of the United Kingdom should have an opportunity of saying whether they desire the United Kingdom to be dismembered or not." He thought "that a very large number, if not the great majority, would say the same as we do." He argued that the bill will "not only go to divorce one part of Ireland or one part of the community but the whole of the Irish people from British citizenship." Accordingly, "Ireland is not going to contribute to Imperial Defence. . . . She is not going to take any part in any Imperial function whatever, and it is almost impossible to conceive that Irishmen can really take an *interest in Imperial affairs.*"[36] He added that "Ireland would not contribute a brass farthing towards army, navy, the consular service, or anything else of an Imperial Nature, but she was to have 42 members to decide the fate of ministries of this country."[37] Yet the British taxpayer would be called on to pay £2 million for the divorce even though he was the innocent party. The British Isles, he argued, must be one unit within the federal imperial system represented by one Parliament at Westminster.[38]

In 1913 the intensity increased. On 27 March 1913, Croft's close political friend and associate, Lord Willoughby de Broke, announced the formation of the British League for the Support of Ulster and the Union. If an appeal to the electorate "is denied us," so stated the league's mission, "then we must fall back on the only other means at our disposal."[39] Willoughby de Broke advised Lord Milner that "the object of this League is to . . . arm all Unionists on this side of the water who wish to fight with the Ulstermen."[40] The central committee included the duke of Bedford, Lord Willoughby de Broke, Viscount Castlereagh, Viscount Lewisham, Lord Charles Beresford, Col. T. E. Hickman, Basil Peto, Ronald McNeill, Arnold Ward, and Charles C. Clarke.[41] Thomas Comyn Platt, another close political associate of Croft, became the league's secretary. It was reported that over one hundred peers and 120 MPs signed a letter of support for the league. In late May, Willoughby de Broke wrote that British Conservatives must "convince both Parliament and the Executive that we are as much in earnest as the Ulstermen and intend to stand by them until at least we have the opportunity of voting against the repeal of the Union. For this purpose the [BLSUU] has been formed."[42]

As the league took shape, on 7 July 1913 the House of Commons passed the Home Rule Bill for the second time; of course on 15 July 1913, it was defeated by the House of Lords.[43] In August, Parliament was prorogued for the rest of the year. The closer Parliament came to confronting the final vote, the greater the concerns that plagued Croft. Naturally, he feared that the present Home Rule Bill "would make it almost impossible for a federal and federation scheme of the Empire in the future." By the end of 1913, the extremist wing, led by Walter Long in Commons and Willoughby de Broke in the Lords, was pushing for a complete abandonment of any consideration of a compromise.[44] Croft, however, responded with a proposal for four provincial legislatures—Ulster, Munster, Leinster, and Connaught—which would address local functions such as local education and transportation. Because they did not rise to the status of a national parliament, there would be no destruction of imperial unity. The appeasement of local concerns would consequently extricate Westminster from the congestion caused by purely parochial and administrative issues.[45] However, neither party seemed willing to consider compromises at this stage.[46]

In November 1913, Robert Sanders, a Conservative whip, recorded that most MPs were convinced there would be no compromise, "but a great many expect a January election." By February he was anticipating a spring election.[47] The principal component of the party's strategy was to pressure Asquith to dissolve Parliament in favor of a general election or, in the alternative, to maneuver the government into submitting the question to a referendum. This was to be pursued by creating within the general public the image of imminent civil war, which was not at all a difficult assignment. By the end of the 1913, even Croft warned that ninety thousand men were training in Ulster to resist their subjection to Dublin rule. He described the prospect of Ulstermen waving the Union Jack being fired on for the crime of defending king and country. He urged that "it was the duty of every single individual to prevent the Government from taking hasty action, to call upon them to pause, to remind them that they could not do that thing unless they desired to remain for ever beyond the confidence of the people of this Country."[48] Rather prophetically, he warned that if those on the government benches "pursued the present course never again would a Liberal Party be sent back to Westminster. They would be absolutely kicked out in such a manner that it would be impossible for the party to ever recover, and there would have to be another party in its place."[49]

By 1914, there was a feeling of anxiety present in his comments and his view of the crisis. Croft was becoming distinctly nervous as the direction of the crisis was becoming more evident. "Has any Government any right," he asked, "to order 25,000 troops and eight battleships, with all the instruments of war, against their fellow men, without the consent of the King or

11: All for Naught (1912–1914)

Parliament? It was tyranny of a Cabinet which no longer represented the will of the people."[50] Notwithstanding such rhetoric, he continued to press for an election. If the government was not willing to test their mandate at a general election, then he was perfectly willing to submit the proposed legislation to a referendum.[51] There was only one way to peace. The government must submit themselves to the electorate. In March he proffered an amendment nearly identical to a Liberal backbench amendment that provided "for the exclusion of clearly defined areas of Ulster pending the establishment of a complete federal system for the United Kingdom during the next six years." It followed that a statutory commission would devise the establishment of the system.[52] Utterly frustrated, Croft claimed that for the past month he had been working round-the-clock promoting a federalist solution, which, he believed, would permit management of local affairs while concurrently strengthening the Union. More important, however, it not only would save the honor of the government and both sides, but it would prevent a civil war.[53]

He continued to press for an election or a referendum. Yet he began to express his own fear that such a course would not extricate the nation from its dilemma. Although he was confident that a Conservative victory at the polls was a certainty, he acknowledged that a small majority would not settle the Irish question as eighty Irish Nationalists would obstruct any program of a Conservative ministry. Under such a settlement, the Liberal party, dependent on the Irish Nationalists, would soon return to office complete with a new but identical Home Rule Bill. Notwithstanding an intervening appeal to the voters, Croft still feared that "we shall have every evil of civil war, and at the same time Nationalist Ireland will have the separatist Home Rule Bill, thousands of lives will be lost, financial ruin will visit the City of London, commercial ruin the cities of Ireland, the Army and Navy will break over such hell-work." Perhaps of greater import, he held additional fears that "whilst the fratricidal war is raging at home every rebel throughout the Empire will believe his opportunity has come." He counseled that "the gamble is too great and Unionists ought also to be too great to play with fate. . . . There is one road to peace with honour, and that is what is known, for want of a better word, as the Federal Solution." He proposed a three-part scheme, which included the establishment of statutory Commission to devise a federal plan for the entire United Kingdom. The present Bill will be passed after the exclusion of customs, excise, the post office, and the judiciary. Lastly, Ulster will be excluded from the present bill until the federal scheme is completed. Ulster would then have the option of inclusion at anytime, if and when it decided so by referendum.[54]

This scheme, Croft argued, would provide Ireland with a Parliament and a responsible executive, thus devolving to the Irish power and responsibility for Irish affairs. By so agreeing, the Ulster Unionists would be assenting to the policy of devolution, albeit limited to local or parochial affairs but which, he suggested, "is overdue." The Unionists in Southern Ireland would not be forced into a separate nation but would retain their loyal position within a separate province of the imperial union. It provided an escape from a civil war, and it provided a settlement with which everyone's honor remained intact. Lastly, Croft believed that the scheme would strengthen the sovereign powers of the state as well as the empire.[55]

Although the Conservative party's attention and energies were being exhausted by Ulster, the demand that the Irish crisis also placed upon Croft's thoughts and activities ensured that advancement of fiscal reform and imperial preference would be abandoned until such time as the party could find calmer waters on which to resolve its ideological struggle over tariff reform and the empire. Of course the intervention of Sarajevo postponed the party's internal reconciliation for nearly a decade. Croft simply was unable to force either an intraparty or a national debate on the imperial idea during the continuing crisis. Croft was also blocked from taking a rebellious political course of action in an effort to push imperial politics to the forefront of the party's agenda, as might have been pursued by the Confederacy or Reveille. He was equally foreclosed from pursuing an imperial program through the establishment of an independent national and imperial party. Instead, pending resolution of the Ulster crisis, Croft was forced to set aside all that he thought crucial to the future of the kingdom and the empire and to make futile overtures toward a compromise in Ireland.

His anxieties were heightened further when, during Parliament's Whitsuntide recess in May 1914, he visited Ulster as the guest of the Londonderrys at Mount Stewart. Accompanying Sir Edward Carson, Croft toured many areas of the province where he observed nearly 7,000 men in arms, including a parade of 1,800 men from the West Belfast Regiment before an audience of 30,000 to 40,000. He was convinced more than ever that civil war was inevitable. With an ulterior desire to see support for his compromise proposals, Croft warned that England would lose 50,000 men and Ulster 70,000 men in such a violent confrontation.[56] He found the positions too entrenched, and consequently in July 1914, he was compelled to return to his plea for an electoral determination. "It would seem advisable," he wrote, "even now at this late hour, to call the attention of the country to the fact that this great constitutional change is being made without any reference whatever to the people of the United Kingdom."[57]

As he wrote this last plea for the preservation of the imperial idea and the British empire, Croft learned that Joseph Chamberlain had died at age seventy-eight. To the thirty-three-year-old MP, Chamberlain had represented the excitement and strength of the British empire; and his ideas, to which Croft unreservedly subscribed, had been the source of Croft's hope for the nation's future. Chamberlain's passing at this juncture was quite sad for Croft, and perhaps it even conveyed an ominous image to Croft of the future for Britain and its empire.[58]

11: All for Naught (1912–1914)

The international events ignited by the assassination in Sarajevo on 28 June 1914, which rapidly consumed all of Europe in the great conflagration of the First World War, are well known. Four weeks after Chamberlain's passing and Croft's appeal for imperial unity, Britain, her empire, and all of Europe were engulfed in war. For all of his faults and excesses, Croft stood unashamedly as a defender of his king, his country, and their empire. He was the ultimate patriot in a time inundated with political patriots whose only validation of such sentiment remain in their rhetoric.

In August 1914 on the day of his own mobilization, Croft wrote to his constituency, "for my part I support the Government. I have no party until Europe has been saved from the piracy of the German nations. Mr. Asquith, Mr. Grey, so long as they do their duty, are my leaders and my parting word to my legion of friends in the Christchurch constituency is to urge them to husband their resources, carefully to eschew luxuries, and above all to provide for the families of the men who go to save England."[59] In August 1914 Croft departed for France where he served the cause of Britain and the empire for "twenty-two months under fire."[60]

When Croft departed for the military battlefieds, he left a Conservative party no stronger, with no more defined ideology, and with no more ability to compete in the popular politics of the twentieth century than when he joined in 1903. Only the condition of the Liberal party and liberalism hid the true condition of the British conservatism. As did Croft, the various factions and sections of the party did not feel any overwhelming confidence in the leadership of Bonar Law. Perhaps Bonar Law was only just beginning to feel confident with his own leadership by 1914. Further, the party had failed to articulate an ideology with which it could meet the wide range of domestic and international challenges. It followed that the party had no universal intellectual foundation on which it could construct policies and programs and with which it could politically challenge the Liberals and Socialists. The party's intellectual foundation and programs were perhaps narrower in 1914 than in 1903. The party's strategy, with which to gain office and protect the kingdom, was no more evident under Bonar Law in 1914 than it was under Balfour in 1906 or in 1910.

Although Croft recognized the domestic and international challenges which Britain faced at the beginning of the twentieth century, he was unable to bring the party around to his views. He nevertheless had labored for eleven years warning the party and nation of the dangers threatening Britain. He sought to articulate and advance an ideology on which the party was to have constructed its affirmative programs, and he worked tirelessly in an effort to energize both the party's ranks and leadership. In the end Sarajevo intervened, and the crisis of British conservatism was put on the back bench.

Conclusion

> There was something fine and buoyant—something very English, almost Elizabethan—about him and I always admired him very much.
> —Wilfrid Miles to Lady Croft, 9 December 1947

In 1903 as a brash young man of twenty-two, Henry Page Croft picked up the baton of tariff reform and imperial preference passed by Joseph Chamberlain, advanced it into an imperial idea, and carried it faithfully and with determination until his own death in December 1947. What he had begun in 1903 and what he continued to do in developing and promoting the imperial idea during the succeeding decade did not represent an ambitious young man with political aspirations. What was represented by this commitment was the conviction of a nationalist who believed that the objectives carried within the imperial idea would not only provide a defense for, but would also advance the British race, nation, and state.

Croft was more than the sentimental or romantic imperialist; he was more than merely a cultural nationalist. He firmly believed that by setting in place the elements of the imperial idea Britain would be able to harvest the benefits of international security, economic prosperity, and social stability. The components were simple—fiscal reform accompanied by protectionism and imperial preference to promote unity. In addition, throughout his life, no matter what the character of international threat and danger, Croft was unalterably convinced that Britain would receive all the necessary security from the political, military, strategic, and diplomatic integration of the empire and dominions. The prerequisite for such advanced levels of cohesion remained strong economic integration and unity.

Contained within Croft's nationalism and his companion imperial idea was found a new ideological departure for British conservatism. The state of international politics, the popular discontent bred by precarious economic conditions and inequitable social arrangements, the desperate economic rivalry, and the struggle for national survival placed new pressures on the British state. The state could no longer be viewed in nineteenth-century terms as a passive institution. The state possessed both the moral authority and responsibility to define and implement constructive national and imperial programs. However, Croft's political activities and development during this period revealed a paradox and ambiguity within the Conservative party caused by the process of this ideological transition. The party, with its representation of the privileged and the elite, had long stood for a deference to tradition and standing. Yet much of the new political generation in which Croft was located had come to believe that only through the construction of a determined party and an activist state would the nation and empire be protected. As a result the active, state-promoted nationalism of the rising generation clashed with the deference and traditionalism of nineteenth-century conservatism that remained orthodox in the salons of the party's leadership.

A second tension was found in Croft's political development. He believed that consideration and promotion of national and imperial issues, by their very nature, must be above partisan politics because of the corruption engendered by popular appeals to sectional and class interests for a base personal political gain. However, to commit the party and state to national and imperial programs, it was necessary to resort to a vigorous campaign of popular politics. He consistently used the "constructive policy" as the litmus test for Conservative party candidates and MPs. His strategy was to purify the party based on a new imperial and national ideology; it was based on the belief that the masses embraced the same superior view of the nation and empire as Croft and the other radical Conservatives. Yet this strategy often presented tariff reform and imperial unity as a tactical alternative to the popular appeal of socialism and the new liberalism. His own activities and development demonstrated a new style, tenor, and approach to political action and debate. Croft exposed the transition toward a more modern Conservative party through his popular and demagogic appeals on behalf of British nationalism. He saw no inconsistency or competition in the pursuit of British nationalism and popular support concurrently within the same policy. The party's developing appetite for popular support created an additional tension within the party. The party was caught between the competing demands of establishing and rigidly adhering to the party's pillar principles versus the need to secure election, office, and power. It perhaps was this inherent contradiction that Baldwin had in mind when in 1935 he counseled R. A. Butler on the need to steer a course between Croft on the right and Macmillan on the left.

Croft was not the only young man who was full of excitement, energy, and ideas on the nature of the British nation and its relationship with the British empire. He stood out because he believed that ideas were worthless so long as they remained ideas. For all of his controversies and flaws, he remained a man of action, a man who sought to accomplish something for the nation. He recognized the need and accepted the challenge to translate ideas into action, programs, and results. He also stood out, as Viscountess Milner reminds us, because he refused to sacrifice or even dilute his convictions to the tactical needs of the system within which he was required to pursue his ideas. "Although he was a strong Conservative, he cared more for the defence of the nation and the Empire than for Conservative Party allegiance."[1] The import of an examination of the public life and career of Henry Page Croft does not rest solely on the fact that he was an uncompromising nationalist and an ardent imperialist. There were many others imbued with similar sentiment. This study has attempted to set forth a detailed examination of the course that Croft pursued to convert his nationalism into action. Quite naturally he turned to the Conservative party, believing it to be the most appropriate mechanism and most formidable instrument with which to translate his nationalist ideology and imperial demands into policy and action. Croft once said he joined the party because he considered it the closest approximation of a national and imperial party. The significance of his activities is demonstrated by Croft's routine frustration with his own efforts and that he was reluctantly forced to clash with and challenge an ambivalent and, at times, dysfunctional party. As a result he found himself compelled to explore and eventually to adopt unorthodox and rebellious political alternatives, as demonstrated by his tariff reform organizations, the Confederacy, the Reveille, and the Imperial Mission.

After his 1903 embrace of tariff reform and imperial preference, Croft pursued a rather acceptable and conventional course of action. He organized his local community with tariff reform. Notwithstanding his impressive success with planting local branches of the tariff reform league all across the East Hertfordshire political landscape, he nevertheless had to concede that little could be accomplished from the backwaters of Ware in East Hertfordshire. Croft had no natural platform; and although he had the benefit of a comfortable life, he did not represent a great landed or noble family; he was neither an intellectual nor a journalist. A seat in the House of Commons remained the most conventional and rational course with which to promote his national and imperial ideas.

Croft, however, soon became frustrated as he found most Conservatives hesitant and doubtful and others outright hostile to the policies with which he sought the reconstruction of the British empire. As early as 1904, Croft recognized the prerequisite need to convert the party to preliminary steps of tariff reform and imperial preference. This conversion was needed before further progress could be made throughout the country. In simple terms the broad economic and imperial elements would not engage the country unless they were unreservedly embraced by Conservatives and promoted as party policy. His initial response was to try to pressure the free trade Conservative MP for East Hertfordshire, Abel Henry Smith, to accept tariff reform. Frustrated in this early effort, Croft turned elsewhere and resolved to mount a personal challenge against his party's free trade MP for Lincoln. The consequence of his 1905 campaign and the subsequent 1906 election was to remove a free trader from the party and a Conservative from Parliament.

With Joseph Chamberlain effectively removed from the political scene

Conclusion 211

after July 1906, Croft and other radical tariff reformers were unleashed to pursue more determined and aggressive actions in their effort to convert the party. The Tariff Reform League was no longer sufficient to accomplish this task. Croft's frustration with the party's dubious commitment intensified until late 1906 when this rebel on the right established the Confederacy. As self-proclaimed protectors of the nation and empire, the Confederates resolved to purge the wobblers and purify the party. However, their principal disappointment rested in the continued aloofness of the party's leader. Balfour failed to appreciate the ideological and generational transition ongoing within the party, and he remained ambivalent about tariff reform. Accordingly, the Confederates first needed either to pull Balfour toward tariff reform or to push him out of his leadership position. Finally, in November 1907, under relentless pressure from the advanced tariff reformers led by the Confederacy, Balfour accepted tariff reform as the first constructive policy of the Conservative party.

Having removed this last source of protection for free trade within the party, the Confederates were now able to press an unrestrained attack on the remaining Conservative free traders. From late 1907 until late 1909, Croft and the Confederacy moved to purify the party even further. The battle in East Hertfordshire between Croft and Abel Henry Smith best demonstrated the Confederacy's determination to root out free trade from the party, even at the risk of sacrificing the parliamentary seat to the Liberal party. It also served to demonstrate to the national figures that tariff reform was strongly rooted in many constituencies. This was further evidenced by the unqualified success of Confederates in the general election of January 1910.

With the return of a Liberal government in January 1910, Croft's satisfaction with the Conservative leadership was short-lived. Balfour remained personally, politically, and ideologically indifferent to the ranks; he failed to appreciate the discontent and the demand for an aggressive party with a constructive program. Croft was frustrated by an apathetic leadership, as well as with passive strategies to promote nonexistent programs. This heightened frustration pushed Croft to issue his "call to action" and to establish the Reveille. This represented not only an effort to energize the party, but it also signaled the beginning of a direct and open challenge to Balfour's leadership. In 1910 Croft went further than merely trying to energize the party with the Reveille. He also established the Imperial Mission that provided organizational substance to the promotion of his imperial ideas.

Even more significantly, the Imperial Mission represented Croft's further consideration and exploration of an alternative political movement. The conditions within the Conservative party pushed Croft to consider an independent imperial and national party. Building on the image of the Imperial Mission's constructive programs, combined with the determination found within the Reveille's discontent, Croft was now close to accepting an independent national and imperial party as having a role in his political future and the future of imperial politics in Britain. The infrastructure, momentum, and even personnel for such an alternative political movement were all present in 1911.

The pressure on Croft to take such unconventional action dissipated considerably as Balfour succumbed to the opposition from the party's right wing and stepped down as leader of the party in November 1911. His successor, Andrew Bonar Law, was viewed as a determined tariff reformer and strong imperialist, which allowed an optimistic Croft voluntarily to scale back the activities of the Reveille and to forgo resurrecting the Confederacy. However, under pressure from backbenchers nervous over electoral prospects, by early 1913 Bonar Law betrayed the imperial idea by abandoning duties on food, a component necessary for the implementation of imperial preference. In 1913 the country and the Conservative party were engulfed by the crisis over Ireland, and Croft found it impossible to resurrect the dormant Confederacy or even to reignite a flickering Reveille to campaign for imperial reform. Energies and emotions were fixed on other issues. Frustrated, disenchanted, and even betrayed, Croft nevertheless refused to abandon "one jot or one tittle" of the imperial idea. He did not compromise its essence, and he did not accommodate what he considered to be the tactical and electoral maneuverings of the party's wobblers and apathetic leaders. Croft cared more for the nation and the empire than for the party. As a radical he believed that the existing conditions could only be countered by a national party of action.

This examination is more than just a study of a young Henry Page Croft; it tears away the layers of assumptions and traditions to reveal a political party in crisis. It exposes the dysfunction that engulfed the party as it experienced a series of transitions—generational, ideological, and political—while at the same time, it was being confronted with new economic, social, political, and international challenges. Under the stress of such conditions and changes, a youthfully energetic but frustrated sector surfaced within the party. This radicalized right wing was prepared to step into the vacuum that emerged during this transitional period in the development of the party. This radicalized sector sought to define the ideological orthodoxy with which the party could meet these new challenges of the twentieth century. They then sought to forge a new and modern party founded on this dynamic ideology that they viewed as being more appropriate for the new century.

However, the process occurred with little intellectual intercourse or dialogue between the party's youth and the incumbent political elite, and soon serious tensions developed. These tensions rose to distrust and then to estrangement as the radicalized right wing saw a failure of intellectual creativity, political will, and determined leadership. Croft, for his part, feared that continued impotence under such conditions would not only sacrifice the party but would eventually forfeit Britain's future. Burdened by such apocalyptic visions, Croft and his associates within the Confederacy, Reveille, and Imperial Mission were pushed to excommunicate and exterminate wobblers and even to seek the overthrow of their leader. They abandoned the gentlemanly politics of the nineteenth-century style, the gentlemanly politics of Balfour, the Cecils, and Smith, and turned to a radical conservatism. However, for Henry Page Croft, his discontent with the humdrum toryism of a nineteenth-century Conservative party and the corruption of popular partisan politics were never truly exorcised, and in 1917 he found himself compelled to leave the Conservative party. In the manifesto of the National party, Croft wrote that "after earnest consideration we have come to the conclusion that we can best assist our country in the present grave situation by severing our connection with the [Conservative] Party and by taking independent action, in which National considerations will be our sole concern."[2] Nevertheless, his lifetime struggle for the British race, nation, and empire, which began during the crisis of British conservatism, was summed up by Viscountess Milner: "Among his many excellencies he was a good soldier and his character fitted him well for the harsh discipline and the good comradeship of war."[3]

Appendix 1
Confederate Membership

LEOPOLD S. AMERY (1873–1955); born in India; Harrow, and Balliol, Oxford; journalist, *Manchester Guardian* and *The Times;* unsuccessful contests (1906, 1908, 1910); MP (C), South Birmingham (1911–45); intelligence officer, 1914–15; deputy secretary for the War Cabinet (1917–19), parliamentary undersecretary for the Colonies (1919–21), parliamentary and financial secretary of the Admiralty (1921–22), first lord of the Admiralty (1922–24), secretary of state for the Dominions (1925–29), and secretary of state for India (1940–45); PC, CH.

SIR GEORGE ELLIOT ARMSTRONG (1866–1940), 2d Bt; lieutenant, Royal Navy; former editor, *Globe.*

VERE BRABAZON PONSONBY (1880–1956), 9th Earl of BESSBOROUGH (I), styled Viscount Duncannon until succeeded father to the Irish earldom (1920); Harrow, and Trinity, Cambridge; called to the Bar (1903); unsuccessful contest (1906); MP (C), Cheltenham (1910), Dover (1913–20); served in Gallipoli (1915) and France on the staff of Gen. Sir Henry Wilson (1916–18); governor-general of Canada (1931–35); raised to U. K. earldom in 1937; CMG, GCMG, PC.

COL. SIR HENRY FERRYMAN BOWLES (1858–1943), Bt (1926); Eton, and Jesus College, Cambridge; called to the Bar; MP (C), Enfield (1889–1906, 1918–22).

LT.-COL. SIR ALAN BURGOYNE (1880–1929); Queen's College, Oxford; unsuccessful contest (1906); MP (C), Kensington North (1910–22); rank of major (1917) and lieutenant-colonel (1918); King's (Liverpool) Regiment and Middlesex Regiment in France, Italy, Palestine, and NW Territories of India (1914–18); personal assistant to Brig.-Gen. Lord Montagu of Beaulieu (with several decorations); controller of the Priority Department, ministry of Munitions (1918–19); founded and edited *The Navy League Annual;* officer of the Navy League, the 1900 Club, Parliamentary Air Committee; Kt, CMG.

CMDR. WARREN FREDERICK CABORNE (1849–1924); Royal Naval Reserve; served in Burma and Egypt; assessor, formal investigations into shipping casualties; inspector, board of Trade for marine inquiries; nautical assessor, Court of Appeal, Supreme Court of Judicature; nautical assessor, HM Privy Council.

CHARLES HOWARD (1867–1912), 10th Earl of CARLISLE, styled Viscount Morpeth until he succeeded his father (1911); grandson of 2d Lord Stanley of Adderley; Rugby and Balliol College, Oxford; extension lecturer at Oxford; progressive candidate on

Appendix 1: Confederate Membership 215

London School Board (1894–1902); Militia Battalion of the Borders Regiment, South African war; unsuccessful contests (1895, 1900, 1904); MP (C), South Birmingham (1904).

GEORGE COURTHOPE (1877–1955), 1st Baron COURTHOPE (cr. 1945); Eton, and Christ Church, Oxford; called to the Bar; MP (C), Rye division of Sussex (1906–45); BEF, Flanders (dispatches, wounded, M.C.); commanded the 5th Battalion Royal Sussex Regiment (1920–26); cofounder of the Imperial Federation League; PC.

JOHN RATCLIFFE COUSINS (1863–1928); University College, London, and St. John's, Cambridge; called to the Bar; London County Council (1898–1903); organizer and secretary, Tariff Reform League (1903–1906).

HENRY PAGE CROFT (1881–1947), 1st Baron CROFT (cr. 1940), Bt (1924); Shrewsbury and Trinity Hall, Cambridge; married daughter of Baron Borwick; businessman and industrialist; 1st Battalion, Herts Regiment, 1914–16 (hon. brigadier-general); unsuccessful contest (1906); MP (C), Christchurch (1910–18), (National party), Bournemouth (formerly Christchurch, 1918–22), (C), Bournemouth (1922–40); CMG.

RONALD MCNEILL (1861–1936) 1st Baron CUSHENDEN (cr. 1927); born Co. Antrim; Harrow, and Christ Church, Oxford; called to the Bar; editor, *St. James' Gazette;* unsuccessful contests (1906, 1907, twice in 1910); MP (C), Kent (1911–18), Canterbury (1918–27); parliamentary undersecretary of state for Foreign Affairs; financial secretary to the Treasury; chancellor of the Duchy of Lancaster; acting secretary of state for Foreign Affairs; PC.

HENRY HARDINGE, 3rd Viscount HARDINGE (1857–1924); succeeded father 1894; grandson of 3d Earl of Lucan; married niece of the 1st Marquess of Abergavenny; Harrow; served as ADC to Lord Roberts in Nile Expedition (1885).

FREDERICK LEVERTON HARRIS (1864–1926); Winchester, and Gonville and Caius College, Cambridge; shipowning firm; hon. captain in the RNVR; parliamentary secretary, ministry of Blockade (1916–18); MP (C), Tynemouth (1900–4), Stepney (1907–10), Worcestershire (1914–18); Tariff Commission; PC.

JOHN RYDER, 5th Earl of HARROWBY (1864–1956); succeeded father (1900); married the daughter of W. H. Smith, MP, and 1st Viscountess Hambleden; Trinity College, Cambridge; Staffordshire Yeomanry; financier; MP (C), Gravesend (1898–1900).

CLAUDE HAY (1862–1920); son of 11th Earl of Kinnoull; businessman and financier; first secretary, Primrose League; unsuccessful contests (1892, 1895); MP (C), Shoreditch (1900–1910).

MR. HERMAN. Nothing is known of Herman, other than he was active for Confederacy in South Nottinghamshire.

WILLIAM A. S. HEWINS (1865–1931); son of iron merchant; Pembroke College, Oxford; political economist; director, London School of Economics (1895–1903); professor of economics, King's College, London; secretary, Tariff Reform Commission (1904–17), chairman (1920–22); three unsuccessful contests (1910, 1911); MP (C), Hereford City (1912–18); undersecretary for the Colonies (1917–19).

JOHN W. HILLS (1867–1938), Bt (1939); Eton and Balliol College, Oxford; solicitor; captain, acting lieutenant-colonel, Durham Light Infantry, France, 1914–18 (wounded); MP (C), Durham City (1906–18), Co. Durham (1918–22), West Riding of Yorkshire (1925–39); financial secretary to the Treasury (1922–23); PC.

SIR CHARLES RODERICK HUNTER (1858–1924), 3d Bt; Eton; Imperial Yeomanry; MP (C), Bath (1910–18).

SIR ARTHUR H. LEE (1868–1947), 1st Viscount LEE of FAREHAM (cr. Baron 1918, Viscount 1922); Royal Artillery; professor of strategy and tactics, Canadian Royal Artillery College; military attaché, U.S. Army, Spanish-American War; military attaché, Washington; served, BEF 1914–1918 (dispatches); chairman, parliamentary Aerial Defence Committee; civil lord of the Admiralty; parliamentary military secretary to the secretary of state for War; director-general of Food Production; minister of Fisheries; 1st Lord of Admiralty; MP (C), Hampshire (1900–1918); gave Chequers estate to the nation in 1921 for the official residence of the prime minister; KCB, GBE, GCSI, GCB, PC.

GEORGE AMBROSE LLOYD (1879–1941), 1st Baron LLOYD of DOLOBRAN (cr. 1925); Eton and Trinity College, Cambridge; served, Warwickshire Yeomanry, Dardanelles, Egypt, and Mesopotamia, 1914–18 (dispatches); attaché, Constantinople; special British trade commissioner, Turkey and the Middle East; high commissioner in Egypt; governor of Bombay and secretary of state for the Colonies; MP (C), West Straffordshire (1910–18), Eastbourne division of Sussex (1924–25); DSO, CIE, GCIE, GCSI, PC.

MAJ. HENRY LYGON (1884–1936); fourth son of 6th Earl Beauchamp; Eton and Magdalen College, Oxford; London County Council (1907–19); Suffolk Yeomanry (1907); served 1914–18 with the Eastern Mounted Brigade, Flying Corps (wounded) and Intelligence (decoration); four unsuccessful contests.

JAMES EDWARD HARRIS, 5th Earl of MALMESBURY (1872–1950); succeeded father (1899); married daughter of 6th Lord Calthorpe; Christ Church, Oxford; captain, Hampshire Regiment (1899–1902); major, 1914–18; assistant private secretary to the undersecretary of state for Colonies; Primrose League; president, Anti-Socialist Union.

HARRY MARKS (1855–1916); University College, London; journalist, proprietor, and editor, *Financial Times;* London County Council; MP (C), Tower Hamlets (1895–1900), Isle of Thanet (1904–10); East Kent Regiment; author, *The Case for Tariff Reform* (1905).

LEOPOLD MAXSE (1864–1932); son of Admiral F. A. Maxse, grandson of Earl of Berkeley; Harrow and King's College, Cambridge; journalist; editor of *National Review;* sister married Lord Edward Cecil (d. 1918), fourth son of the 3d Marquess of Salisbury; after Lord Edward's death, she married Viscount Milner; Maxse's brother, Sir (Frederick) Ivor Maxse (1862–1958) married the eldest daughter of the 2nd Baron Leconfield.

WILFRED W. ASHLEY (1867–1939), 1st Baron MOUNT TEMPLE (cr. 1932); grandson of 7th Earl of Shaftesbury; great grandson of Lady Palmerston; Harrow and Magdalen College, Oxford; Ayrshire Militia, Grenadier Guards, Hampshire Militia, and commanded the battalion of King's Liverpool Regiment (1914–15); MP (C), Blackpool (1906–18), Fylde division of Lancashire (1918–22), New Forest (1922–32); parliamentary secretary for Ministry of Transportation; undersecretary of state War; minister of Transport; chairman, Anti-Socialist Union; president, Anglo-German Fellowship; chairman, Navy League; chairman, Comrades of the Great War; father-in-law of Adm. Lord Louis Mountbatten; PC.

GEOFFREY BROWNE (1861–1927), 3rd Baron ORANMORE and BROWNE (I); Baron Mereworth (cr. 1926); succeeded father to Irish peerage (1900); sat in the House of Lords as representative Irish peer (1900–1926); married daughter of 8th Earl of Bessborough; Trinity College, Cambridge.

SIR HORATIO GILBERT PARKER (1862–1932), 1st Bt (1915); born in Canada; author and playwright; MP (C), Gravesend (1900–1918); organized the first conference of the Universities of the Empire in 1903; chairman of the Imperial South African Association; Kt, PC.

SIR BASIL PETO (1862–1945), Bt (1927); Harrow; businessman and industrialist; MP (C), Devizes division of Wiltshire (1910–1918), Barnstaple division of Devon (1922–23, 1924–35); associated with Croft and Empire Industries Association (1924–45).

SIR THOMAS COMYN PLATT (1875–1961); served in embassy, Constantinople (1904), Foreign Office (1906–7, 1909–11), British Legation, Athens, and commissioner in Uganda; served in 1914–18 (wounded); unsuccessful contests (1891, 1923, 1929); closely associated with Croft, the National party, and Empire Industries Association; Kt.

JAMES FITZALAN HOPE (1870–1949), 1st Baron RANKEILLOUR (cr. 1932); great grandson of Sir Walter Scott; grandson of the 14th Duke of Norfolk; raised as a Roman Catholic by his grandmother, Dowager Duchess; second marriage to daughter of 9th Earl of Drogheda; Christ Church, Oxford; MP (C), Brightside division of Sheffield (1900–1906), Central Sheffield (1908–29); treasurer, HM Household; lord of the Treasury; financial secretary to the Ministry of Munitions; chairman of committees and deputy speaker of the House; author, *History of the 1900 Parliament;* served on the joint select committee on India; PC.

SIR HUGH O'NEILL (1883–1982), 1st Baron RATHCAVAN (cr. 1953), Bt (1929); born in Co. Antrim; Eton, and New College, Oxford; called to Bar; captain and major, Ireland Yeomanry and Royal Irish Rifles (1915–17), Palestine (1918); first speaker of the Northern Ireland Parliament (1921–29); unsuccessful contest (Ulster Unionist) (1906); MP (Unionst), Antrim (1915–18, 1922–52); father of the House (1951–52);

chairman, 1922 Committee (1935-39); parliamentary undersecretary for India and Burma (1939-40); PC (I), PC (GB).

SIR JAMES REMNANT (1863-1933), 1st Baron REMANT (cr. 1928), Bt (1917); Harrow, and Magdalen College, Oxford; called to the bar; MP (C), Holborn (1900-1928); London County Council.

SAMUEL FFORDE RIDLEY (1864-1944); MP (C), SW Bethnal Green (1900-1906), Rochester (1910).

SIR JOHN F. L. ROLLESTON (1848-1919); King's College, London; businessman; chairman, Leicester Conservative Association; unsuccessfully contested Leicester (1894, 1895); unsuccessful contests (twice 1906); MP (C), Leicester (1900-1906); Hertfordshire East (1910-18); Kt.

SIR LESLIE SCOTT (1869-1950); Rugby, and New College, Oxford; called to the Bar; solicitor general (1922); Lord Justice of Appeal (1935-48); MP (C), Liverpool Exchange (1910-29); international and maritime issues; represented HMG at international conferences (1909-10, 1922, 1926); chairman, Agricultural Organisation Society; founding member, Council for the Preservation of Rural England; Kt, PC.

SIR WILLIAM MITCHELL-THOMSON, (1877-1938), 1st Baron SELSDON (cr. 1932); 2d Bt; Winchester and Balliol College, Oxford, and Edinburgh (LL.B.); advocate, Scotland (1902); extensive business activities in the West Indies; MP (Cons and Tariff Reformer), NW Lanark (1906-10), North Down (1910-18), and (C), Glasgow (1918-22) South Croydon (1922-32); hon. lieutenant, RNVR; director of restriction of enemy supplies (1916-18); British representative on the Supreme Economic Council, Paris (1919); parliamentary secretary for the ministry of Food; secretary to the board of Trade; postmaster-general and chief commissioner; KBE, PC.

LT. COL. GEOFFREY SKEFFINGTON SMYTH (1873-1939); Eton; married daughter of 7th Viscount Galway; served South Africa (1899-1900, dispatches, wounded, DSO, Queens' medal with six clasps), Lt. Col., 1914-18 (dispatches); assumed name of Fitzpatrick (1938).

SIR HAROLD SMITH (1876-1924); called to the Bar; MP (C), Warrington (1910-22), Wavetree division of Liverpool (1922); Kt.

CAPT. EDWARD GEORGE SPENCER-CHURCHILL (1876-1964); son of Lord Edward Spencer-Churchill; married to daughter of Lady Northwick; Eton and Magdalen, Oxford; unsuccessful contests (1906, 1910); Grenadier Guards, South African war (two medals and seven clasps), in 1914-18 (MC, Croix de Guerre with palm).

SIR ARTHUR STEEL-MAITLAND (1876-1935), Bt (1917); Rugby and Balliol College, Oxford; unsuccessful contest (1906); MP (C), East Birmingham (1910-18), Erdington (1918-29); chairman, Conservative party (1911); private secretary to Austen Chamberlain, chancellor of the Exchequer (1904-5); undersecretary for the Colonies (1915-17); joint parliamentary undersecretary of state for the Foreign Office and

Appendix 1: Confederate Membership 219

parliamentary secretary to the Board of Trade; head of the Department of Overseas Trade-Development and Intelligence (1917–19); minister of Labour (1924–29); PC.

VIVIAN STEWART. Nothing is known of Stewart.

MICHAEL TEMPLE. Nothing is known of Temple, other than he was associated with *The Globe*.

MAJ. GEORGE CLEMENT TRYON (1871–1940), 1st Baron TRYON (cr. 1940); son of Vice-Admiral Sir G. Tryon; nephew of 1st Earl of Ancaster; Eton and Sandhurst; married daughter of 1st Lord Swansea; Grenadier Guards, South Africa (1899–1900, medal with two clasps); MP (C), Brighton (1910–40); undersecretary state for Air (1919), parliamentary undersecretary, ministry of Pensions (1920–22), minister of Pensions (1922–24, 1924–29, 1931–40); author, *A Short History of Imperial Preference* (1921); PC.

ARNOLD WARD (1876–1950); Eton, and Balliol, Oxford; called to the Bar; correspondent for *Times* in Egypt, India, and Sudan (1899–1902); unsuccessful contest (1906); MP (C), West Herts (1910–18); Herts Yeomanry, Egypt (1914–15).

SIR FABIAN WARE (1868–1949); secondary school master; director of education in the Transvaal and Orange River Colony; member of the Transvaal Legislative Council; commander of mobile British Red Cross units detached to French military (1914–18, decorated); KCVO, KBE, CB, CMG.

EDWARD GOULDING (1862–1936), 1st Baron WARGRAVE (cr. 1936), Bt (1915); son of an MP; St. John's College, Cambridge; called to the Bar; businessman; chairman, Central London Electricity Distribution and Rolls Royce; London County Council; MP (C), Devizes (1895–1906), Worcester (1908–22); member of the Empire Industries Association; PC.

HENRY SPENSER WILKINSON (1853–1937); Merton College, Oxford; called to the Bar; staff of the *Manchester Guardian* (1882–92), *Morning Post* (1895–1914); professor of military history, All Souls' College, Oxford; wrote on military issues and affairs; cofounder, Navy League (1894); writings influenced Croft's article in *The New Order*.

SIR SPENCER POCKLINGTON MARYON MARYON-WILSON (1853–1937), 11th Bt; businessman; captain, West Kent Yeomanry.

EDWARD TURNOUR (1883–1962), 6th Earl of WINTERTON (I), Baron Winterton (I), Viscount Turnour (I), Baron Turnour of Shillinglee (cr. 1952, UK); styled Viscount Turnour until succeeded his father (1907) to Irish earldom; grandson of 1st Duke of Abercorn; declined a UK peerage (1935) to remain in the House of Commons; New College, Oxford; married daughter of 2d Baron Nunburnholme; proprietor and editor of the weekly *The World;* served 1914–18 in Gallipoli, Palestine, and Arabia (with T. E. Lawrence, mentioned in dispatches); MP (C) Horsham (1904–51); Father of the House (1945–51); financial secretary to the Admiralty (1904–5); undersecretary for India (1922–24); chancellor for the duchy of Lancaster (1937–39); deputy to the secretary of state for Air and vice president of the Air Council (1938); assistant to the Home secretary (1939); paymaster general (1939); cabinet member (1938–39); PC.

BERNHARD WISE (1858–1916); born in Australia, son of judge; Rugby, and Queen's College, Oxford; called to the Bar; attorney-general of NSW (1899–1904); agent-general for NSW in London (1915–16); granted retention of the title of Honourable by the King (1907); supported Croft's National party.

Appendix 2: Membership of Reveille

GERALD ARBUTHNOT (1884–1916); served, HMS Britannia; private secretary to Walter Long, board of Agriculture, Local Government Board and Irish Office; MP (C), Burnley (1910); vice chairman, Budget Protest League; chairman, Lancashire and Cheshire Federation of Junior Unionist Associations; killed in France (1916).

LT.-COL. SIR MARTIN ARCHER-SHEE (1873–1935); Sandhurst; Royal Navy (1886–90) and Army; rank of Adjutant and Brevet-Major, South Africa (1899–1902, dispatches, wounded, Queen's and King's medals with six clasps, DSO); 12th Batt. of the Gloucester Regiment, 1914–18 (dispatches, wounded); MP (C), Central Finsbury (1910–18) and Finsbury (1918–23); associated with the Empire Industries Association; CMG, Kt.

A. E. BECK. Candidate at Derby (1910).

SIR ALFRED FREDERICK BIRD (1849–1922); Birmingham manufacturer; MP (C), Wolverhampton (1910–22); Kt.

RALPH DAVID BLUMENFELD (1864–1948); born in the United States; editor, New York *Evening Telegraph*, London *Daily Mail* (1900–1902), *Daily Express* (1902–32); cofounder, Anti-Socialist Union.

WILLIAM ORDE-POWLETT, 5th Baron BOLTON (1869–1944); succeeded father (1922); grandson of 9th Earl of Scarborough; married daughter of 1st Baron Ashbourne; lieutenant in the Yorkshire Hussars Yeomanry; MP (C), Richmond division of Yorkshire (1910–18).

CAPT. HENRY BRACKENBURY (1868–1920); Corpus Christi College, Oxford; called to the Bar; captain, 3rd Lincoln Regiment; MP (C), Louth division of Lincolnshire (January-December 1910, 1918–20).

SIR WILLIAM BULL (1863–1929); solicitor; businessman; MP (C), Hammersmith (1900–1918), South Hammersmith (1918–29); chairman of the London MPs; parliamentary private secretary to Walter Long; several municipal government positions; KB, PC.

SIR ALAN BURGOYNE. See Appendix 1.

HENRY PAGE CROFT. See Appendix 1.

RUDOLPH ROBERT BASIL ALOYSIUS AUGUSTINE FEILDING, 9th Earl of DENBIGH (1859–1939); succeeded his father (1892); married daughter of 8th Baron Clifford of Chudleigh; served in Egypt and India; ADC to Marquess of Londonderry in Ireland; MP (C), Rugby division of Warwickshire (1889–92); substantial business interests.

CAPT. EDWARD ALGERNON FITZROY (1869–1943); son of 3d Baron Southampton; Eton, Sandhurst, and Cambridge (DCL); served in France (1914–18); MP (C), Northamptonshire South (1900–1906, 1910–18), Daventry division (1918–43); speaker of the House of Commons (1928–43); his widow was raised to the peerage as Viscountess Daventry (1943); a supporter of Croft's National party; PC.

PHILIP STAVELEY FOSTER (1865–1933); Eton and Magdalen College, Oxford; hon. major in Staffordshire Yeomanry; unsuccessful contest (1899); MP (C), for Stratford-upon-Avon (1901–6, 1909–18).

JAMES GALBRAITH (1872–1945); Oriel College, Oxford, called to the Bar, KC; unsuccessful contests (January and December 1910); MP (C), East Surrey (1922–35).

RICHARD CHALONER (1855–1938), 1st Baron GISBOROUGH (cr. 1917); brother of Walter Long but took the name of Chaloner under will of Admiral Chaloner by Royal License; served in the army in India and Afghanistan (1888–93); commanded the 1st Batt. Imperial Yeomany; served as lieutenant colonel with 1st Wiltshire Volunteers in South Africa (1900–1903); served as major in 4th Reserve Cavalry in 1914–18; MP (C), Westbury division of Wilts (1895–1900), Abercromby division of Liverpool (1910–17).

RALPH GLYN (1884–1960), 1st Baron GLYN (cr. 1953), Bt (1934); grandson of 8th Duke of Argyll; married daughter of 2d Baron Derwent; Harrow and Sandhurst; Rifle Brigade, France, Gallipoli, Balkans, and Russia (1914–18); businessman and industrialist; secretary, Unionist Reorganization Committee (1911); member, Whitley Council; parliamentary private secretary to the prime minister (1931–35); three unsuccessful contests (1910); MP (C), East Stirling and Clackmannan (1918–22), Abingdon division of Berkshire (1922–53).

CHARLES SYDNEY GOLDMAN (1868–1953); born in Cape Colony; married daughter of 1st Viscount Peel; significant business interests in East African and South African mining operations; correspondent, South African war (1899); cavalry (1899–1902); major in Cornwall Royal Garrison Artillery; official, National Service League; member, African Society and South African Union; MP (C), Penryn and Falmouth (1910–18); author, *With General French and the Cavalry in South Africa, The Empire and the Century, Cavalry in Future Wars;* proprietor, *The Outlook,* a tariff reform weekly associated with Chamberlain.

SIR PATRICK JOSEPH HANNON (1871–1963); born in Ireland; University College, Dublin, Royal College of Science, and Royal University of Ireland; served in several Irish agricultural organizations; director, Agricultural Organization to the government of Cape Colony (1904–5); positions in the Imperial Mission, Tariff Reform League, National Service League, and Navy League; director, British Commonwealth Union (1918–25); founder, Comrades of the Great War; secretary, Industrial Group in House of Commons; unsuccessful contest (1910); MP (C), Moseley division of Birmingham (1921–50); associated with Empire Industries Association; Kt.

HENRY HARDINGE, 3d Viscount HARDINGE. See Appendix 1.

WILLIAM ORMSBY-GORE (1885–1964), 4th Baron HARLECH; succeeded father (1938); married daughter of 4th Marquess of Salisbury; Eton and New College, Oxford; served in Shropshire Yeomanry, Egypt (1914–17); assistant secretary, War Cabinet (1917–18); parliamentary private secretary to Lord Milner (1917); member, British delegation to Paris peace conference; member, Permanent Mandates Commission; parliamentary undersecretary of state for the Colonies (1922–24); secretary of state for the Colonies (1936–38); MP (C), Denbigh (1910–18), Stafford division of Staffordshire (1918–38); GCMG, KG, PC,

MAJ. JOHN W. HILLS. See Appendix 1.

MAJ. ROWLAND HUNT (1858–1943); Eton and Magdalene College, Cambridge; served in South African war with Lord Lovat's scouts; MP (C), Ludlow division of Shropshire (1903–18); associated with the National party.

SIR LOUIS STANLEY JOHNSON (1869–1937); solicitor; mayor of Hackney (1914–19); unsuccessful contest (January and December 1910); MP (C), East Walthamstow (1918–24); Kt.

SIR HENRY SEYMOUR KING (1852–1933); Charterhouse and Balliol College, Oxford; substantial business interests in banking and Indian trade; first mayor of Kensington (1900); MP (C), Hull (1885–1911); KCIE.

JOHN HENDLEY KIRKWOOD (1877–1924); lieutenant in the 7th Dragoon Guards, and Royal North Devon Yeomanry; served in South African war (1899–1902); MP (C), Southeast Essex (1910–12); accepted Chiltern Hundreds (1912).

CHARLES HENRY WYNDHAM, 3d Baron LECONFIELD (1872–1952); succeeded father (1901); nephew of 5th Earl of Rosebery; married daughter of Col. R. H. Rawson and granddaughter of the 2nd Earl of Lichfield; lieutenant (1892–98), lieutenant-colonel commandant. (1901–8) and major and hon. colonel from 1914; associated with his father-in-law with the National party.

OLIVER STILLINGFLEET LOCKER-LAMPSON (1880–1954); Eton and Trinity College, Cambridge; called to the Bar; lieutenant commander, Royal Navy (1914); served in France, Belgium, Russia, Turkey, Persia, Romania, and Austria (1914–18), CMG, DSO; MP (C), North Huntingdonshire (1910–22), Handsworth Division of Birmingham (1922–45); parliamentary private secretary to Austen Chamberlain (1919–21); listed his recreation as "refusing honours."

WILLIAM FRANCIS HENRY DENISON, 2d Earl of LONDESBOROUGH (1864–1917); succeeded father (1900); grandson of 7th Duke of Beaufort; married daughter of 12th Earl of Westmorland; lieutenant, Yorkshire Hussars and hon. colonel in the 2d Volunteer Battalion of the East Yorkshire Regiment; owned 52,700 acres.

SIR HALFORD JOHN MACKINDER (1861–1947); Christ Church, Oxford; called to the Bar; reader in geography, Oxford; professor of geography, University of London (1900–1925); principal, University College, Reading; director, London School of Economics (1903–08); unsuccessful contests (1899, 1909); MP (C), Camlachie (1910–22); British high commissioner for South Russia (1919–20); chairman, Imperial Shipping Committee; author, *Britain and British Seas;* Kt, PC.

JAMES EDWARD HARRIS, 5th Earl of MALMESBURY. See Appendix 1.

LEOPOLD MAXSE. See Appendix 1.

G. V. A. MONKTON-ARUNDEL; candidate for Scarborough (1910).

SIR WILLIAM ARTHUR MOUNT (1866–1930), Bt (1922); Eton, and New College, Oxford; called to the Bar; parliamentary private secretary to Sir Michael Hicks-Beach (1902–5); MP (C), Newbury division of Berkshire (1900–1906, 1910–22); CBE.

LT.-COL. SIR JOHN NORTON-GRIFFITHS (1871–1930), Bt (1922); engineer and public works contractor; served in the Matabele and South African wars (dispatches, two medals with clasps); lieutenant colonel, 1914–18 (dispatches, DSO); served special missions to Romania (additional honors from King of Romania); MP (C), Wednesbury (1910–18), Central Wandsworth where he defeated "coupon" Liberal (1918–24); committed suicide in 1930; closely associated Empire Industries Association; KCB.

SIR BASIL PETO (1862–1945), Bt (1927); Harrow; interests in building, contracting, manufacturing, commerce, and mining enterprises; MP (C), Devizes division of Wiltshire (1910–18), Barnstaple division of Devon (1922–23, 1924–35); closely associated with Empire Industries Association.

SIR JOHN F. L. ROLLESTON. See Appendix 1.

SIR EDMUND ROYDS (1860–1946); Haileybury College; solicitor and financier; major, Lincolnshire Yeomanry, as lieutenant colonel and county commandant in Lincolnshire Volunteer Force; MP (C), Sleaford division of Lincolnshire (1910–22); OBE, Kt.

EDWARD GOULDING, Baron WARGRAVE. See Appendix 1.

VAUGHN WILLIAMS; candidate in South Shields (1910).

RICHARD GREVILLE VERNEY, 19th Baron WILLOUGHBY DE BROKE (1869–1923); succeeded father (1902); Eton and New College, Oxford; MP (C), Warwickshire (1895–1900); owned 6,000 acres; lieutenant-colonel, Warwickshire Yeomanry (1914–18).

SIR LESLIE ORME WILSON (1876–1955); captain, South African war (dispatches, wounded, Queen's medal with five clasps, DSO; lieutenant-colonel, Gallipol and France (dispatches, wounded, CMG); two unsuccessful contests (1910); MP (C), Reading (1913–22), South Portsmouth (1922–23); parliamentary assistant secretary

Appendix 2: Membership of Reveille

to the War Cabinet (1918); chairman of the National Maritime Board (1919); parliamentary secretary to the ministry of Shipping (1919); parliamentary secretary to the Treasury and chief Whip (1921–23); governor of Bombay (1923–28) and governor of Queensland (1932–46); GCIE, GCSI, GCMG, PC.

SIR LAMING WORTHINGTON-EVANS (1868–1931), Bt (1916); assumed prefix surname of Worthington by royal license (1916); solicitor; captain, 2nd Middlesex Volunteer Artillery; editor-in-chief, *Financial News;* MP (C), Colchester (1910–1918), Essex (1918–29), St. George's division of Westminster (1929–31); parliamentary private secretary to H. W. Forster (1915–16); controller for Foreign Trade Department of the Foreign Office (1916); parliamentary and financial secretary to ministry of Munitions (1916–18); minister of Blockade and parliamentary undersecretary in Foreign Office (1918–19); minister of Pensions (1919–20), minister without Portfolio (1920–21); secretary of State for War (1921–22, 1924–29) and postmaster general (1923–24); associated with Empire Industries Association; CBE, PC.

Appendix 3:
Manifesto of the Unionist Reveille (1910)

The leaders of the Unionist Reveille have issued a programme for the guidance of their speakers in the country. In certain quarters this has been represented as an act of rebellion within the Unionist Party. In other quarters the programme has been criticized as lacking in originality. As a fact, every point of it is the outcome of the policies of Lord Salisbury and Lord Beaconsfield, and has been urged time and again by Mr. Balfour himself.

The significance of the Reveille programme lies in the fact that from beginning to end it concentrates attention on the constructive side of Unionism. In ordinary times it is no doubt the first duty of an Opposition to oppose. But these are not ordinary times. The pact on the Constitutional issue renders it difficult for the leaders of the Unionist Party to be effective in criticism. There is, however, a more essential reason why it is necessary at this juncture to urge an alternative policy rather than to find the joints in the Radical armour. A wave of vague but none the less real and bitter discontent is sweeping through the popular mind, both of this country and the Continent. The revolutionary movement will generally fail, but it will none the less widely unsettle opinions. Inevitably there must be a fresh balancing of popular forces, which will determine political tendencies probably for some years to come. In the moment of disillusionment, when the bankruptcy of Radicalism is evident and Socialism has failed to bring relief, it is of the first importance to remind the electors that Unionism is not, as its opponents would have it, merely negative and obstructive. The Unionist Party is a great democratic party of some three million electors, and it stands for a scheme of constructive statesmanship, full of hope because essentially practical.

The Reveille programme contains five heads. It is, however, no Newcastle list of disjointed items, but a coherent and united plan of action. In a single word it may be described as a national policy. Tariff Reform is an essential element of that policy, but it is far from the whole of it, although our recent history has made the tariff the gage of battle between the parties. Tariff Reform is only a means to an end, and that end is the promotion of national security and prosperity.

It will be noted that the Reveille programme makes no distinction between foreign and home politics. A national policy regards them as inseparable. You cannot divide the health of the skin from that of the internal organs. In

Appendix 3: Manifesto of the Unionist Reveille (1910)

sharp contradistinction is the Cobdenite idea that you can maintain national armaments and yet internationalise the resources which are their sinews. As well might you internationalise the commissariats of two opposing armies. It is not the fault of Britain that other countries have preferred the rigour of the national game. Dislike the professional as you will, it is futile for the amateur of equal calibre to contend with him. Notwithstanding pious wishes, there never was a time when nationality was more firmly established than the present. Even the conscript armies of the Continent have withstood the general strike.

The national policy may be compared to a dock. If the water is to stand deep in the dock the gates must be kept in repair. The gates of our national dock must be our Navy and our tariff. The deep water within, held apart from the ebb and flow without, represent a steady national prosperity. A mere rill of social reform would raise the level of the water in such a national dock, whereas a full stream of radical change will escape with little benefit to the nation through the existing tidal harbour. Industrial insurance cannot cope with the chronic causes of unemployment. Limit these causes by the reform of the tariff, and insurance becomes an effective aid for the national well-being.

The Reveille programme places first the maintenance of the supremacy of the Navy—and of such military forces as are necessary to liberate the Navy—even at the cost, if need be, of a great loan. Britain goes naked into the diplomatic contest when tariff bargains are being struck. We have only our naval power to throw into the scales. Not only are our food supplies dependent upon that power, but also the markets of our industries. This is no time for a diplomatic silence on this point. The markets of Free-trade Lancashire are, in fact, protected at a great cost by the British Fleet. By the Japanese Alliance, by the Indian Empire, by the Egyptian occupation, by support of the Monroe Doctrine, British sea power has repeatedly in the last few years guaranteed the wages of Lancashire. As the result of our Cobdenite policy, it is to-day only behind our Fleet that we can erect the more peaceful defence of a tariff or broaden the base of our national existence by negotiating trade preference with the other parts of the Empire.

Second of the five heads stands the reform of our trade system by the construction of scientific tariff behind which industrial insurances may give security to our people. Without a tariff the enactment of schemes of insurance is equivalent to throwing upon Britain the weight of the economic flywheel of the world. Either our plans for insurance must be confined in their scope, and inapplicable to large sections of the population, or else they must tempt some of those who emigrate to stay at home. In the latter case the wages of nine men in Britain will be shared among ten.

With Tariff Reform to induce the greater investment of capital here, insurance and other measures of social reform become practical under the conditions of a rising market for labour. By insurance and by the increase of the number of small owners of the land the ends which the Socialists have in view will be attained by practical instead of fatal methods. Destitution will gradually be abolished, but without the loss of individual initiative and without the undue increase of officialdom. State credit and the great existing friendly societies will be used to assist insurance. So shall we avoid the ruin inherent in a Right to Work Bill. State credit will assist in the purchase of land by smaller owners. So shall we avoid the risks of State ownership of the land.

For the time being, however, it is recognized that the Poor Law, essentially socialistic and degrading in its operation, must be continued in some form. The regime of unlimited competition through which we have passed has left us a legacy of human scrapheaps in our great cities. Pending the gradual operation of the national policy exceptional measures are needed to heal the disease. Urgent though may be the reform of the Poor Law, it is of a less ultimate importance than the other elements of the programme. The more reason why minority and majority reports should not be allowed to become the standards of opposing parties! The dust of such a conflict would tend to prevent the clear vision of deeper issues, nor would it promote the early adoption of measures in regard to the Poor Law itself.

Small ownership of the land and the reform of the Poor Law are the third and fourth items of the Reveille programme. Finally—beyond and, as it were, around the national policy—is the Imperial policy, the fifth item. When all has been done that is possible to develop the force and security of our island people there remains the fact that only by gathering together the several nations of the Empire can we cope in the international balance of power with the newly-organized Continental States. The Navies of the King's Dominions will co-operate so long as the Empire pursues a common foreign policy, but there can be such a united policy only if our commercial interests are locked together. There is no scope to-day for short views in these matters. Great nations now upbuild their structures by capital investments. By sinking a hundred millions sterling in a Panama Canal the United States seeks to combine the interests of San Francisco and New York. By directing into Imperial channels the investments of our peoples we shall build together East and West and North and South in the world-wide British Realm.

The first and last items in the Reveille programme are the Navy and Colonial Preference, the vital securities on the one hand of the immediate, and on the other hand of the further future. In neither case is there a year to lose. The British Empire is at the parting of the ways. From one foreign State comes against Britain a bid for naval supremacy. From another comes to Canada the offer of reciprocity. If the gates of our dock be swept away the water within—the social prosperity of our people—must inevitably sink.

Appendix 4:
Members of the Imperial Mission (1911–1913)

Lord Abinger
Sir Max Aitken, MP
W. S. Allfrey
L. S. Amery, MP
Lord Ampthill
Lord and Lady Ancaster
Major William Archer-Shee, MP
Duke of Argyll, Hon. President, Executive Council
Lord Balcarres
J. A. Beattie Bell
H. D. Bell, New Zealand
Arthur Shirley Benn, MP
Ion Hamilton Benn, MP
Hon. Margaret Best
Hon. Mrs. Yorke Bevan
George Tate Blackstock, KC, president of Canadian (Toronto) branch
Dean of Bloenfontein
Sir John Bonham
Lady Borwick
Capt. R. B. Brassey
Charles Bright
Henry Brock, Canada
G. A. M. Buckley
Alan Burgoyne, MP
Colonel Burn, MP
Alan Campbell
Hon. Colin Campbell
J. A. Campbell of Craigie
Colonel Fred Cardew
J. J. Carrick, MP (Canada)
W. C. Cartwright
Col. Richard Chaloner, MP
Stuart A. Coates
W. F. Cockshutt, member, Ontario Legislative Assembly
Lewis Cohen, mayor of Adelaide
Capt. Muirhead Collins
Lord and Lady Ninian Crichton-Stuart
Guy Croft, secretary, Imperial Mission
Henry Page Croft, MP

Maj. Richard Page Croft
Mr. Crooks, MP
H. L. de Mel, Ceylon
Earl of Denbigh
Sir George Denton
Lord Desborough
Lady Des Voeux
Sir George Doughty, MP
Adm. Sir Archibald Douglas
Nicholas Grattan Doyle
Hon. J. J. Duncan
Earl of Dundonald
Col. Eastwood
Lord Ebury
Lady Eden
Lady Emmott, agent-general for British Columbia, New South Wales, and Ontario
Sir John Findlay, minister of Justice and attorney-general, New Zealand; president, New Zealand (Wellington) branch
Mrs. Claire Fitz-Gibbon, niece of Sir John Macdonald, Canada
E. A. Fitzroy
Sir Fortescue Flannery
Sir F. Fleming
J. S. Fletcher, MP
Sir Charles Follett
Sir John Forrest, president, West Australia branch
Hon. George E. Foster, Canadian minister of Trade
Frank Fox, executive council
Admiral Sir Edmund and Hon. Lady Fremantle
Moreton Frewen, MP
Col. Sir William Garstin, London branch
W. K. George, former president of Canadian Mfrs. Association
Hon. G. Godfrey
George Gould
Mrs. John Haldane
A. W. Hall
S. G. Hammersley, MP
Patrick J. Hannon, executive council
Earl and Countess Hardwicke
F. J. Hartnell
Dr. Alfred Hillier, MP
G. L. Hoare
Samuel J. G. Hoare, MP
R. Martin Holland, CB
Lt.-Col. Holland
John Holmes, former trade commissioner in New Zealand
Sir William Horne, MP
Rowland Hunt, MP
Sir W. Hyndman-Jones
Sir Leander Starr Jameson
Hon. J. G. Jenkins, executive council

Appendix 4: Members of the Imperial Mission (1911–1913)

Capt. H. M. Jessel
Maj. Frank Johnson, executive council
Rev. A. J. Jones
Lieut. R. W. Kiddle, RN
Sir Henry Kimble
Lady Kirkpatrick
Sir E. Durning Lawrence
Sir Joseph Lawrence
Lord Leith of Fvyie
Sir Walter and Lady Lewis
George Lloyd
Capt. Hon. Bowes Lyon
Alfred Lyttelton, KC, MP
Baroness Macdonald of Earnscliffe (widow of Sir John Macdonald), Canada
C. D. Mackellar
Hon. T. MacKenzie, high commissioner for New Zealand
Hon. Donald MacKinnon, MP-Victoria, Australia
Sir Philip Magnus, MP
H. Mallaby-Deeley, MP
Earl and Countess of Malmesbury
Admiral Sir Albert Hastings Markham
Duke of Marlborough
Sir Spencer Maryon-Wilson, executive council
James F. Mason, MP
Leopold Maxse
Hon. P. McBride, agent-general for Victoria
Hon. John McCall
Colonel Hon. James Whiteside McCoy, director of Military Intelligence, Australia
J.A. McLean
Ronald McNeill, MP
Colonel Sir Howard Meliss
Sir Lyman Melvin-Jones
Viscount Milner, vice president
Earl of Minto
Sir Newton Moore, agent-general for Western Australia
Capt. J. A. Morrison, MP
Sir Charles Morrison-Bell
Lord Morton
Lord Northcote
Major John Norton-Griffiths, MP
Daniel O'Connor, former postmaster-general, New South Wales
Lady Orr-Ewing
Sir Charles J. Owens
Almeric Paget, MP
Sir Gilbert Parker, MP
Miss Ethel Peel
Hon. William Peel, MP
Lt. Col. P. Pelletier
W. F. Pepper
Basil Peto, MP

Lord and Lady Portman
E. Pounds
Captain Hely Pounds
Sir John Pringle
Hon. Sir John Quick, former postmaster-general, Australia,
J. W. Raymond, New Zealand
Sir J. D. Rees
Sir George Reid
Lt.-Col. Renouf
Arthur E. G. Rhodes
Harold Ashton Richardson, Canada
Sir. T. B. Robinson, agent-general for Queensland
Hon. R. P. Roblin, former premier of Manitoba
Sir John Rolleston, MP
Lord Ronaldshay, MP
Hon. James Round
Sir William R. Russell, former leader of Opposition Party, New Zealand; executive council
Frederick Salter
E. Samuelson
George Sandys, MP
Major Schofield
Earl of Selborne
Hon. Clifford Sifton
Lt. Col. Snow
Sir Edward Solomon
Richard Solomon, high commissioner for South Africa
Duke and Duchess of Somerset
E. J. Spencer-Churchill
Col. Sprot
Earl Stanhope
Maj. W. Stebart
Lt. Col. Swain
Sir Charles Taring
Sir John Tavernier
Sir William Taylor
F. W. Templer, New Zealand
Lord Tennyson
P. A. Thompson
Sir T. Troubridge
Sir Charles Tupper
Sir Joseph Ward, prime minister of New Zealand
Major W. W. Warner
Hon. W. A. Watt, premier, Victoria, Australia
Duke of Wellington
R. B. Whiteside, Executive Council
Lord Willoughby de Broke
Arthur Wilson, New Zealand
Sir W. Grey Wilson
Marquess and Marchioness of Winchester

Appendix 4: Members of the Imperial Mission (1911–1913)

Hon. Bernhard Wise
Lord Wolverton
Major H. H. Woolbright
Laming Worthington-Evans, MP
Lord and Lady Wynford
Sir James Young

Notes

INTRODUCTION

1. The event was kindly recounted by Croft's nephew, Richard Page Croft, Round House, Ware, Hertfordshire (February 1991).
2. Maxton to Croft, 14 May 1940, CAC, Croft Papers, CRFT 1/16 MA/32.
3. Cutting, 13 December 1947, Croft Papers, CRFT 3/20.
4. "Mr. Amery's Tribute. Lord Croft," *The Times,* 10 December 1947.
5. *Bournemouth Daily Echo,* 9 December 1947.
6. Ibid.
7. Law to Lady Croft, 9 December 1947, Croft Papers, CRFT 3/21.
8. *Western Mail,* 8 December 1949.
9. Baron [Richard Austen] Butler of Saffron Walden, *Art of the Possible* (London: Hamilton, 1971), 30.
10. Lord Leconfield to Lady Croft, 14 December 1947, Croft Papers, CRFT 3/21.
11. "Imperial Pioneers," *Morning Post,* 11 June 1910.
12. Scholarly discussion of Croft is scarce, usually limited to a mention of the National party. Shortly after the end of the second world war, Croft drafted a brief story of his life, which was published after his death. Croft, *My Life of Strife* (London: Hutchinson, 1948). Generally historians have been introduced to Croft by W. D. Rubenstein's article, "Henry Page Croft and the National Party," *Journal of Contemporary History,* 9:1 (1974), 129–42. This article, severely limited by the lack of sources and scope, has failed to provoke much historical curiosity. See C. Wrigley, "'In the Excess of Their Patriotism': The National Party and Threats of Subversion," in Wrigley (ed.), *Warfare, Diplomacy and Politics: Essays in Honour of A.J.P. Taylor* (London: Hamish Hamilton, 1986), 93–119.
13. E. H. H. Green, 'The Strange Death of Tory England,' *Twentieth-Century British History* 2:1 (1991), 68.
14. Examination of Edwardian Conservatives began with A. M. Gollin, *Balfour's Burden: Arthur Balfour and Imperial Preference* (London: A. Bland, 1965) and R. Rempel, *Unionists Divided: Arthur Balfour, Joseph Chamberlain and the Unionist Free Traders* (Hampden, Conn.: Archon Books, 1972). It continued with G. D. Phillips, *The Diehards: Aristocratic Society and Politics in Edwardian England* (Cambridge, Mass.: Harvard University Press, 1979) and A. Sykes, *Tariff Reform in British Politics, 1903–1913* (Oxford: Clarendon Press, 1979). More recently we have seen J. A. Thompson and A. Meiji (eds.), *Edwardian Conservatism: Five Studies in Adaptation* (London: Croam Helm, 1988); F. Coetzee, *For Party or Country: Nationalism and the Dilemmas of Popular Conservatism in Edwardian England* (Oxford: Oxford University Press, 1990); R. Williams, *Defending the Empire: The Conservative Party and British Defence Policy, 1899–1915* (New Haven: Yale University Press, 1991); D. Dutton, *His Majesty's Loyal Opposition: The Unionist Party in Opposition, 1905–1915* (Liverpool: Liverpool University Press, 1992); E. H. H. Green, *The Crisis of Conservatism: The Politics, Economics and Ideology of the*

British Conservative Party, 1880–1914 (London: Routledge, 1995); G. D. Phillips, "Lord Willoughby de Broke and the Politics of Radical Toryism, 1909–1914," *Journal of British Studies* 20:1 (1980), 206–24; A. Sykes, "The Radical Right and the Crisis of Conservatism Before the World War," *Historical Journal* 26:3 (1983), 661–76; idem., "The Confederacy and the Purge of the Unionist Free Traders, 1906–1910," *Historical Journal* 18 (1975), 349–66; G. R. Searle, "Critics of Edwardian Society: The Case of the Radical Right," in A. O'Day (ed.), *The Edwardian Age: Conflict and Stability, 1900–1914* (Hamden, Conn.: Archon Books, 1979); idem., "The Revolt from the Right in Edwardian Britain," in P. Kennedy and A. Nicholls (eds.), *Nationalist and Racialist Movements in Britain and Germany Before 1914* (London: Macmillan, 1981); and E. H. H. Green, "Radical Conservatism: The Electoral Genesis of Tariff Reform," *Historical Journal*, 28:3 (1985), 667–92.

15. Green, 'Strange Death of Tory England,' 69.

CHAPTER 1. BIRTH OF AN IMPERIALIST

1. Croft, *My Life of Strife, 24;* also see J. C. Wedgwood, *The History of Parliament: Biographies of the Members of the House of Commons, 1438–1509* (London: HMSO, 1936).

2. O. G. S. Croft, *The House of Croft of Croft Castle* (Hereford: E. J. Thurston, 1949).

3. Croft (letter), *The Times,* 18 July 1901.

4. Croft, *My Life of Strife,* 37.

5. Julian Amery, *Joseph Chamberlain and the Tariff Reform Campaign,* v, *The Life of Joseph Chamberlain* (London: Macmillan, 1969), 27.

6. *The Times,* 17 May 1902; Amery, *Chamberlain and the Tariff Reform Campaign,* v, 16.

7. *The Times,* 17 May 1902.

8. Croft, *My Life of Strife,* 41.

9. H. P. Croft, *The Path of Empire* (London: J. Murray, 1912), 7.

10. Max [Lord] Egremont, *Balfour: A Life of Arthur James Balfour* (London: Collins, 1980), 147.

11. In addition to Amery's seminal study, *Chamberlain and the Tariff Reform Campaign,* see Gollin, *Balfour's Burden;* Rempel, *Unionists Divided;* and Sykes, *Tariff Reform in British Politics.*

12. Amery, *Chamberlain and the Tariff Reform Campaign,* v, 30–32.

13. *The Times,* 16 May 1903.

14. Amery, *Chamberlain and the Tariff Reform Campaign,* v, 192.

15. E. Halévy, *Halévy's History of the English People: Imperialism and the Rise of Labour* (New York: Barnes and Noble, 1961), 324.

16. L. S. Amery, *My Political Life: England Before the Storm, 1896–1914* (London: Hutchinson, 1953), i, 236.

17. *The Times,* 16 May 1903.

18. Ibid.

19. Ibid.

20. Amery, *Chamberlain and the Tariff Reform Campaign,* v, 284.

21. For a sample of the editorial policy in opposition to Chamberlain, see the leading articles in *Hertfordshire Mercury,* 30 May, 20 June, 18 July, and 1 August 1903. Also see "Unionist Gathering at Woodhall Park. A. H. Smith on Free Trade," 11 July; and "Mr. Abel Smith and Birmingham Tactics," 25 July 1903.

22. *Daily Mail,* 18 July 1903; Ware Unionist and Conservative Association, Minute Books, 1898–1924, Herts RO, D/EX 274.Z1.

23. Croft, *My Life of Strife,* 41; "A Rising Politician," *Whitehall Review,* 25 January 1908.
24. H.P.C., "Considerations for Working Men," *Hertfordshire Mercury,* 31 October 1903.
25. Gollin, *Balfour's Burden,* 200.
26. Amery, *Chamberlain and the Tariff Reform Campaign,* vi, 794.
27. Henry Chaplin (1840–1923), 1st Viscount Chaplin (cr. 1916); married to the daughter of the 3rd Duke of Sutherland; his daughter married the son of the Marquess of Londonderry; MP (C), mid-Lincolnshire (1868–85), Sleaford division of Lincolnshire (1885–1906), Wimbledon division of Surrey (1907–16); represented agricultural interests.
28. J. Chamberlain to Chaplin, 5 August 1903, in Amery, *Chamberlain and the Tariff Reform Campaign,* v, 314; Edith Londonderry, *Henry Chaplin: A Memoir* (London: Macmillan, 1926), 180–83.
29. Croft, *My Life of Strife,* 42.
30. H. P. C., "Considerations for the Working Man," *Hertfordshire Mercury,* 15 August 1903.
31. Ibid.
32. H. P. C., "More Considerations for the Working Men," *Hertfordshire Mercury,* 29 August 1903.
33. H. P. C., "Considerations for the Working Man," *Hertfordshire Mercury,* 12 September 1903.
34. H. P. C., "Considerations for the Working Men," *Hertfordshire Mercury,* 31 October 1903.
35. C. Boyd (ed.), *Mr. Chamberlain's Speeches* (London: Constable, 1914), ii, 164–63.
36. Amery, *England Before the Storm,* i, 308.
37. Croft, *My Life of Strife,* 41–42.
38. "Tariff Reform Meeting at Ware," *Hertfordshire Mercury,* 19 December; "Mr. Chaplin at Ware," *The Times,* 16 December; "Mr. Chaplin at Ware,' *Daily Chronicle,* 15 December; "Threatening the Duke: Mr. Chaplin at Ware, and the Recent Letter," *Westminster Gazette,* 15 December 1903.
39. "The By-Elections: Duke of Devonshire's Advice: Give No Vote to Chamberlain Sympathisers," *Daily Chronicle,* 12 December 1903.
40. "The By-Elections," *Daily Chronicle,* 15 December 1903.
41. "By-Elections," *Daily Chronicle,* 14 December; "The Breakup of Unionism. Duke of Devonshire's Advice: No Support to Tariff Reformers," *Westminster Gazette,* 12 December 1903.
42. *Daily Chronicle,* 15 December 1903.
43. *Hertfordshire Mercury,* 19 December 1903.
44. Ibid.
45. Ibid.
46. *The Times,* 16 December; *Hertfordshire Mercury,* 19 December 1903.
47. Chaplin to Croft, 19 December 1903, Croft Papers, CRFT 3/1; J. Chamberlain to Croft, 15 December 1903, CRFT 3/1.

Chapter 2. A Crack Begins to Show

1. Mid Devon, Norwich, Gateshead, Ayr, and Mid Hertfordshire. "Victor of Mid Herts", *Daily Chronicle,* 15 February 1904.
2. "Chaplin at St. Albans. Lord Verulam for Tariff Reform," *The Times,* 2 Feb-

Notes to Chapter 2

ruary; "Pending By-Election in St. Albans Division," *Hertfordshire Mercury*, 23 January 1904.

3. *The Times*, 6 February 1904.

4. "Mr. A. H. Smith on Free Trade, 11 July 1903; "Mr. A. H. Smith, M.P., and Birmingham Tactics," 25 July 1904; Mr. A. H. Smith's Declaration on Tariff Reform," 23 January 1905; and "Free Trade Speech by Mr. A. H. Smith," 30 January 1905, *Hertfordshire Mercury*.

5. "Recent Tariff Reform Meeting at Bishop's Stortford," 26 March; "Tariff Reform Meeting (East Herts)," 16 April; "Free Trade vs. Protection," 14 May; and "The Recent Tariff Reform at Hoddesdon," *Hertfordshire Mercury*, 25 June 1904.

6. Ware Unionist Association Minute Books, Herts RO, D/EX 274.Z1.

7. "Mr. A. H. Smith and His Constituents and Vote of Confidence Passed," *Hertfordshire Mercury*, 12 March 1904.

8. Executive Committee Report 1904, Ware Unionist Association Minute Books, D/EX 274.Z1.

9. Croft, *My Life of Strife*, 42.

10. Ibid., 42–43.

11. J. Chamberlain to Croft, 12 July 1904, Croft Papers, CRFT 1/6 CH/16.

12. *Parliamentary Debates*, 4th ser., vol. 139 (4 August 1904), c. 284–85.

13. Hugh Cecil (1869–1956), Baron Quickswood (cr. 1941); youngest son of the 3rd Marquess of Salisbury; MP (C), Greenwich (1895–1906), Oxford University (1910–37); devoted to the church and religious matters.

14. *Parl. Deb.*, vol. 139, c. 334.

15. Ibid.

16. *The Times*, 3 August 1904. See also "The Vote of Censure on the Government. Mr. A. H. Smith and the Fiscal Reformer," *Hertfordshire Mercury*, 6 August 1904.

17. Memorandum by Hugh Cecil. Private and Confidential, n.d., Hatfd Hse, Quickswood Papers, QUI 3/115.

18. H. Cecil to John Humphreys, 13 February 1905, Quickswood Papers, QUI 3/25.

19. James Smith to H. Cecil, 7 July 1904, Quickswood Papers, QUI 2/68; 16 July 1904, QUI 2/73; and 21 July 1904, QUI 2/75.

20. R. Cecil to Lady Robert, 7 July 1904, Hatfd Hse, Chelwood Papers, CHE 4/17

21. R. Cecil to Lady Robert, 12 July 1904, Chelwood Papers, 12 July, CHE 4/18; 14 July, CHE 4/20; 19 July, CHE 4/26; 24 July, CHE 4/32.

22. *Parl. Deb.*, vol. 139, c. 340.

23. *The Times*, 6 August 1904.

24. G. Rowland Hill, Greenwich Unionist Association, to Unionist electors of Borough of Greenwich, 3 April 1905, Quickswood Papers, QUI 3/91.

25. *Parl. Deb.*, vol. 139, c. 340–41.

26. J. Chamberlain to Croft, 8 August 1904, Croft Papers, CRFT 1/6 CH/17.

27. "Tariff Reform Meeting at Thunbridge. Speech by H. P. Croft," 27 August; "Tariff Reform Meeting at Hertford. Speeches by Mr. J. Ratcliffe Cousins, C.E. Wodehouse, H.P. Croft," *Hertfordshire Mercury*, 22 October 1904.

28. Croft (letter), "Liberal Meeting at Hertford," *Hertfordshire Mercury*, 17 December 1904.

29. "Unionist Split in East Herts," 5 November; "Abel Smith, M.P. and the Unionists," *Hertfordshire Mercury*, 17 December 1904.

30. Amery, *Chamberlain and the Tariff Reform Campaign*, vi, 610–40.

31. "Dissolution. Early Appeal to Electors Expected," *Daily Chronicle*, 11 January 1905.

32. "Ready for Dissolution. Mr. Chamberlain's Men Busy at Headquarters," *Daily Chronicle,* 18 January 1905.
33. Garvin to Maxse, 30 April 1905, WSRO, Maxse Papers, MSS/453.
34. "Tariff Reform Meeting at Ware. Speeches by Mr. R. B. Croft, Mr. H. P. Croft, and Mr. C. E. Wodehouse. Lively Proceedings," *Hertfordshire Mercury,* 11 February 1905.
35. "Split in Unionist Party at Ware. Threatened Three-Cornered Fight in East Herts," *Hertfordshire Mercury,* 14 January 1905, Croft Papers, CRFT 3/1.
36. Ibid.
37. Ibid.
38. "East Herts.", *Morning Post,* 16 January; "Election Intelligence," *The Times,* 16 January 1905.
39. "Election Intelligence," *The Times,* 17 January 1905.
40. *Daily Chronicle,* 17 January 1905.
41. "Election Intelligence," *The Times,* 19 January 1905.
42. Amery, *Chamberlain and the Tariff Reform Campaign,* vi, 636.
43. "Mr. A. H. Smith, M.P., and the Representation at East Herts," *Hertfordshire Mercury,* 21 January 1905.
44. "Tariff Reform. Mr. H. P. Croft Supports Mr. Smith. Meeting of Tariff Reform League," *Hertfordshire Mercury,* 11 February 1905.
45. Ibid. Also see "Tariff Reform Meeting at Ware," *Hertfordshire Mercury,* 11 February 1905.
46. "A. H. Smith at the Century Hall," 28 January; "East Herts. Conservative Association," *Hertfordshire Mercury,* 25 February 1905.
47. "Tariff Reform Meeting at Wormley. Mr. H. P. Croft's Warning to Mr. A. H. Smith, M.P.," *Hertfordshire Mercury,* 1 April 1905.
48. Croft, *My Life of Strife,* 43.
49. "Prospective Conservative Candidate for Lincoln," 26 January; "Chamberlain at Gainsborough. Welcomed by 7,000 Workers," *Sheffield Daily Telegraph,* 2 February; "Tariff Reform League," *Cambridge Chronicle,* 3 February 1905.
50. Croft, *My Life of Strife,* 70.
51. Ibid. Also see Rempel, *Unionists Divided,* 152, fn. 1.
52. *The Times,* 13 January 1904.
53. R. Cecil, "Memorandum on The Attack on Unionist Free Trade Seats," 18 February 1905, BL, Balfour Papers, Add. MSS 49737, fos. 129–32.
54. Balfour to H. Cecil, 19 July 1905, Quickswood Papers, QUI 4/12.
55. "Lincoln and Tariff Reform. Mr. Page Croft's Introductory Speech," *Lincolnshire Echo,* 15 March 1905.
56. "Representation of Lincoln. Speech by Mr. H. P. Croft," *Lincolnshire Chronicle,* 18 March 1905.
57. Ibid.
58. Ibid.
59. "Politics in Lincoln. Mr. H. P. Croft's Candidature," *Lincolnshire Echo,* 13 April; "Political Situation at Lincoln. Interesting Correspondence," *Sheffield Daily Telegraph,* 15 April 1905.
60. "Unionist Demonstration at Lincoln. Radical Misrepresentations Nailed," *Lincolnshire Echo,* 13 June 1905.
61. Col. Arthur Haig to Croft, 10 January 1906, "Official Adoption by Sir A. Acland Hood, *Lincolnshire Echo,* 11 January 1906; Croft, *My Life of Strife,* 45.
62. John Boraston to Dr. Mansel-Sympson, "Representation of Lincoln," *Nottingham Daily Guardian,* 28 June; "Lincoln and the Liberal Unionist Council," *Lincolnshire Echo,* 27 June; *The Times,* 29 June 1905.

Notes to Chapter 2

63. Croft, *My Life of Strife*, 44; F. Mabel Sympson, Ruling Councillor of the Primrose League, to Lane Fox, 17 November; "The Rules of the Primrose League," *Lincolnshire Echo*, 20 November 1905.
64. *Lincolnshire Echo*, 6 January 1906.
65. Croft, *My Life of Strife*, 44.
66. J. Chamberlain to Leverton Harris, 3 July 1905, in Amery, *Chamberlain and the Tariff Reform Campaign*, vi, 721.
67. "Tariff Reform Victory," *Daily Mail*, 5 July 1905.
68. J. Chamberlain to Croft, 5 January 1906, "Fiscal Battle at Lincoln," *Sheffield Telegraph*, 5 January; "Campaign in Lincolnshire," *Yorkshire Post*, 8 January; "Encouraging Letter from Mr. Chamberlain," *Lincolnshire Echo*, 9 January 1906.
69. "Hampstead By-Election," *Hampstead and Kilburn Echo*, 1 November 1905.
70. Ratcliffe Cousins to Croft, 18 December 1905, Croft Papers, CRFT 3/1.
71. "Ware," *Hertfordshire Mercury*, 11 November; "Mr. Henry Page Croft and the North Herts Vacancy," *Lincolnshire Chronicle*, 4 November 1905.
72. J. Chamberlain to Croft, 17 November 1905, Croft Papers, CRFT 1/6 CH/18.
73. Croft to J. Chamberlain, n.d., Croft Papers, CRFT 1/6 CH/19.
74. "Politics in Lincoln Parliamentary Borough," *Lincolnshire Echo*, 5 May 1905.
75. "Tariff Reform. Speech by Mr. Page Croft at Lincoln," *Nottingham Daily Guardian*, 28 June 1905.
76. "Tariff Reform" (letter from H. P. Croft), *Lincolnshire Echo*, 28 August 1905.
77. "Representation of Lincoln. The Case for Tariff Reform," *Lincolnshire Chronicle*, 15 September 1905.
78. "Tariff Reform Meeting at Lincoln. Speech by Mr. Page Croft," *Sheffield Telegraph*, 28 September 1905.
79. "Mr. Henry Page Croft at Washingborough," *Lincolnshire Echo*, 6 November 1905.
80. "Tariff Reform Problem. Mass Meeting at Lincoln. Address by Sir Gilbert Parker," *Lincolnshire Echo*, 2 December 1905.
81. "Mr. Croft Wants Freer Trade," *Lincolnshire Echo*, 4 January 1906.
82. "Mr. Croft at Stamp End Works," *Lincolnshire Echo*, 8 January 1906.
83. "Mr. Croft at the Blenkin Memorial," *Lincolnshire Echo*, 9 January 1906; "Mr. Page Croft and Lincoln's Attacked Industry," *Lincolnshire Echo*, 10 January 1906.
84. Croft, *My Life of Strife*, 44.
85. "Workmen's Hostility to Mr. Page Croft," *Yorkshire Post*, 9 January; "Regrettable Outburst in the Constitutional Club," *Lincolnshire Chronicle*, 12 January; "Rowdy Unionists. Scenes at the Lincoln Club," *Nottingham Express*, 8 January; "Seelyites and Crofters at the Constitutional Club," 6 January and "Rowdy Meeting at Lincoln Constitutional Club," *Lincolnshire Echo*, 8 January 1906.
86. "Lincoln. To-Day's Interesting Encounter," *Yorkshire Post*, 15 January 1906.
87. "Mr. Croft at the Church House," *Nottingham Daily Guardian*, 3 January 1906.
88. C. H. Roberts—5,110 (51.2 percent); C.H. Seely—3,718 (37.2 percent); and H.P. Croft—1,162 (11.6 percent).
89. "Politics in Lincoln Parliamentary Borough," *Lincolnshire Echo*, 5 May 1905.
90. J. Chamberlain to Croft, 5 January 1906, "Fiscal Battle at Lincoln," *Sheffield Telegraph*, 5 January 1906.
91. J. Chamberlain to James Parker Smith, 17 January 1906, in Amery, *Chamberlain and the Tariff Reform Campaign*, vi, 793.
92. Croft, *My Life of Strife*, 45.
93. "After the Lincoln Election," *Lincolnshire Echo*, 22 March 1906.

94. J. Ramsden, *The Age of Balfour and Baldwin, 1902–1940* (London: Longman, 1978), 23–24.
95. *Nottingham Daily Guardian,* 3 January 1906.

Chapter 3. From Lincoln to the Confederacy

1. Free Trade or Tariff Reform: Is It Free," 10 February; "II: Who Pays the Tax?" 17 February; "III: British Employment vs. Foreign Cheapness," 24 February; "IV: Imports and Exports," 3 March; "V: If You Are Attacked Defend Yourself," 10 March; "VI: The Necessity for Change," 17 March; "VII: The 'Big Loaf' Bogey Exposed," 24 March; "VIII: Food Taxes," 31 March; and "IX: Commercial Union of the Empire," 7 April 1906, *Hertfordshire Mercury.*
2. General Annual Meeting, 2 March 1906, Ware Unionist Association Minute Books, Herts RO, D/EX 274.Z1.
3. "Lincoln Conservatives and Unionists. An Amalgamation of Forces," *Lincolnshire Echo,* 14 April 1906.
4. Croft, *My Life of Strife,* 45.
5. Croft to Dr. Mansel Sympson, 17 April 1907, "The Representation of Lincoln. Mr. H. Page Croft Withdraws His Candidature," *Nottingham Evening Post,* 6 May 1907.
6. "Tariff Reform League. [1906] Annual Meeting of the Hertford Branch," *Hertfordshire Mercury* cutting, in Croft Papers, CRFT 3/1; "Tariff Reform Meeting in Lincoln. Speech by Mr. Page Croft", *Lincolnshire Echo,* July 1906.
7. "Tariff Reform. Meeting at St. Albans," *St. Albans Times,* 26 January 1907.
8. "Tariff Reform League. Formation of a branch for Hoddesdon," *Hertfordshire Mercury,* 5 January 1907.
9. "Mr. A. H. Smith, MP, and Tariff Reformers. Mr. H. P. Croft Criticises the Member's Action," *Hertfordshire Mercury,* 2 March 1907.
10. "Tariff Reform at Chatham," *Chatham, Rochester & Gillingham News,* 30 March 1907.
11. Croft, *My Life of Strife,* 45; "Tariff Reform Revival. Lively Proceedings at Gillingham. Attempt to Wreck a Meeting. Struggle on the Platform," *Chatham, Rochester & Gillingham News,* 23 March 1907.
12. Croft, *My Life of Strife,* 45.
13. "The Christchurch Parliamentary Division. Adoption of a Prospective Unionist Candidate. Speech by Major Balfour's Successor," *Bournemouth Guardian,* 5 May; "Mr. H. Page Croft Adopted Conservative Candidate for Christchurch," *Bournemouth Visitor's Directory,* 5 May; "Borough Conservative Candidate. Adopted by the Association," *Bournemouth Observer and Chronicle,* 4 May; Croft, "Free Trade or Tariff Reform: British Employment v. Foreign Cheapness," *Bournemouth Graphic,* 30 May; Croft, "Free Trade or Tariff Reform?: If You Are Attacked, Defend Yourselves!" *Bournemouth Graphic,* 13 June; "Free Trade or Tariff Reform: The Necessity of Change," 20 June, and "Imports and Exports," 27 June 1907, *Bournemouth Graphic.*
14. "Conservatism in the Christchurch Division. Addresses by the Prospective Unionist Candidate. Mr. Page Croft's Enthusiastic Receptions," *Bournemouth Observer and Chronicle,* 8 June 1907.
15. *Bournemouth Graphic,* 19 May 1907.
16. *The Times,* 30 January 1906, suggest there were 109 tariff reformers, 32 Balfourites, 11 free fooders (and 5 unclassified). The duke of Devonshire lists 102 tariff reformers, 36 Balfourites, 16 free fooders, and 3 unclassified. *Annual Register 1906,*

12. More recent calculations reduce the "whole hoggers" to 79 and increase Balfourites to as high as 49. See Rempel, *Unionists Divided,* 116; Sykes, *Tariff Reform in British Politics,* 100–101; and N. Blewett, "Free Fooders, Balfourites, Whole Hoggers: Factionalism Within the Unionist Party, 1906–10," *Historical Journal* 11:1 (1968), 95–124.

17. Blewett, "Factionalism within the Unionist Party," *Historical Journal,* 95.

18. R. Blake, *The Conservative Party from Peel to Thatcher* (London: Methuen, 1985), 18.

19. H. Cecil to Balfour, 4 May 1907, BL, Balfour Papers, Add MSS 49759, fos. 185–98.

20. Chaplin to J. Chamberlain, 1 February 1906, in Amery, *Joseph Chamberlain and the Tariff Reform Campaign,* vi, 810.

21. Dugdale, *Arthur James Balfour,* ii, 21.

22. R. Cecil to Balfour, 25 January 1906, Balfour Papers, Add MSS 49737, fo. 42.

23. Ridley to J. Chamberlain, 22 January 1906, in Amery, *Joseph Chamberlain and the Tariff Reform Campaign,* vi, 798.

24. Ibid. Balfour to J. Chamberlain, 14 February 1906, vi, 846–7.

25. Ibid. J. Chamberlain to Balfour, 14 February 1906, 847.

26. *National Review* (February 1906), 954–55.

27. Ibid., 972–73.

28. Garvin to Maxse, 14 March 1906, UTL, Garvin Papers.

29. Arnold-Forster to Bonar Law, 24 April 1906, HLRO, Bonar Law Papers, BL/18/2/16.

30. Amery, *Joseph Chamberlain and the Tariff Reform Campaign,* vi, 913.

31. Garvin to J. Chamberlain, 24 September 1906, UBL, Chamberlain Papers, AC/8/2/44; Garvin to Maxse, 27 September 1906, WSRO, Maxse Papers, MSS 456/s382; Garvin to Maxse, "Sunday" [4 November 1906], Maxse Papers, MSS 456/s447.

32. "Episodes," *National Review* (November 1906), 373.

33. "Episodes," *National Review* (January 1907), 759.

34. Maxse to Bonar Law, 2 January 1907, Bonar Law Papers, BL/18/3/28.

35. Garvin to Maxse, 4 December 1906, Maxse Papers, MSS 456/428.

36. Garvin to Maxse, 7 January 1907, Maxse Papers, MSS 457/466.

37. Although it is clear that one of Croft's principal accomplices was Thomas Comyn Platt, it has generally been thought that the other was Viscount Turnour, later Earl Winterton, principally because of his close friendship with Comyn Platt and subsequent association with Croft. Earl Winterton, *Pre-War* (London: Cassell, 1932), 98. The only relevant reference in Winterton's diaries is for 27 November 1906, where he notes traveling with Croft to Hitchin in East Hertfordshire. Yet he does not identify any Confederate activities until spring 1907. Winterton Diaries, 27 November 1906, Bodl Lib, Winterton MSS, c. 5. From 5 December 1906 to 12 March 1907, Winterton was abroad. It is clear that upon his return in spring 1907, he began a very active role as a Confederate. As early as February 1906, Winterton was demonstrably dissatisfied with Balfour's leadership and particularly Balfour's disdain for tariff reform. This postelection discontent precipitated an early version of the Confederacy when several advanced whole-hoggers, including Sir Gilbert Parker, F. E. Smith, and Winterton, met to consider a "revolt." Nearly fifty whole-hoggers signed a petition designed to frighten Balfour into action. The Valentine pact extinguished any uprising. Winterton, *Pre-War,* 22–23. Yet it would be inaccurate to identify him as one of the three founders. Based on significant correspondence detailing the earliest activities, it seems clear that Croft's associates were Comyn Platt and the mysterious Bernhard Wise. See Wise to Steel-Maitland, 12 December 1906, SRO, Steel-Maitland Papers, GD 193/133/427; Wise to Mary Endicott Chamberlain,

27 December 1906, Chamberlain Papers, AC/4/11/23; Comyn Platt to Garvin, 1 Feb 1907, Garvin Papers; Croft, My Life of Strife, 75–76.

38. A Confederate, "The Confederacy," *National Review* (January 1909), 741–47.
39. Croft, *My Life of Strife,* 43.
40. *National Review* (January 1909), 742; Croft, *My Life of Strife,* 43.
41. Comyn Platt to Garvin, n.d. [1909], Garvin Papers.
42. Wise to Steel-Maitland, 12 December 1906, SRO, Steel-Maitland Papers, GD 193/133/427.
43. Wise to Mary Endicott Chamberlain, 27 December 1906, Chamberlain Papers, AC/4/11/23.
44. Croft, *My Life of Strife,* 43.
45. Unionist, "Tariff Reform Methods," *Contemporary Review* (February 1908), 133.
46. Maxse to Croft, 7 February 1908, Croft Papers, CRFT 1/6 MA/23.
47. Fortunately much of the spade work has been undertaken by A. Sykes, "The Confederacy and the Purge of the Unionist Free Traders, 1906–1910," *Historical Journal* 18:3 (1975), 349–66.
48. Croft, *My Life of Strife,* 43–44.
49. Winterton, *Pre-War,* 229.
50. "The Confederates. Formation of a New Political League," *Daily Mail,* 22 February 1907.
51. "Mysterious 'Confederacy,'" *Daily Mail,* 25 February 1907.
52. Croft, *My Life of Strife,* 43.
53. "The Confederacy," *Daily Mail,* 25 January 1908.
54. "Notes and Comments," *Yorkshire Post,* 25 January 1908.
55. Henry Lygon (letter), *The Times,* 23 January 1908.
56. "Conservative or Protectionist? The Party Position Explained. Who the Confederates Are. The Secret Party Revealed," *Daily Graphic,* 21 January 1909.
57. Winterton Diaries, 1907–1908, Winterton MSS, c. 6–7.
58. *Nation,* 18 January 1908.
59. Comyn Platt to Steel-Maitland, Friday [1907], SRO, Steel-Maitland Papers, GD 193/135/52.
60. Comyn Platt to Steel-Maitland, n.d., Steel-Maitland Papers, GD 193/135/51.
61. Sykes, "The Confederacy," *Historical Journal,* 354; "Platt's Book" (December 1907), Steel-Maitland Papers, GD/193/79/9.
62. "List of Contributors," Steel-Maitland Papers, GD 193/136.
63. Comyn Platt to Garvin, 1 February, 6 August 1907, and 1 January 1909, Garvin Papers.
64. Winterton to Garvin, 22 August, 28 October 1907, and 29 October 1907; Comyn Platt to Garvin, n.d. [1907], Garvin Papers.
65. James Louis Garvin (1868–1947), born in Ireland; editor of Outlook (1905–6), Pall Mall Gazette (1912–15), The Observer (1908–42).
66. Comyn Platt to Garvin, 1 January 1909, Garvin Papers.
67. Garvin to Comyn Platt, 10 February 1909, Garvin Papers.
68. Comyn Platt to Garvin, 11 February 1909, Garvin Papers.
69. Comyn Platt to Garvin, n.d. [February1909], Garvin Papers.
70. Edward George Brunker (1871–1951), born in County Cork; Trinity College, Dublin; director and general secretary of the Free Trade Union; close association with the Cecils.
71. E. G. Brunker to R. Cecil, 6 January 1908, BL, Robert Cecil Papers, Add MSS 51072, fo. 159.
72. John Satterfield Sandars (1853–1934); Magdalen College, Oxford; called to

the Bar; private secretary to the secretary of state for home department (1886–92); private secretary to Balfour (1892–1905).

73. Sandars to Wilfrid Short, 28 October 1907, Balfour Papers, Add MSS 49765, fos. 76–77.

74. Brunker to R. Cecil, 9 January 1908, Cecil Papers, Add MSS 51072, fos. 152–54, fos. 161–63; also see Comyn Platt to Garvin, 1 February 1907, Garvin Papers.

75. G. S. Bowles to R. Cecil, 10 January 1908, Robert Cecil Papers, Add MSS 51072, fo. 127.

76. R. Cecil to Balfour, 13 January 1908, Balfour Papers, Add MSS 49737, fos. 84–85.

77. Brunker to R. Cecil, 8 January 1908, Robert Cecil Papers, Add MSS 51158, fo. 167.

78. Croft to Bonar Law, Saturday, n.d., Bonar Law Papers, BL/18/7/214; W. Long to Bonar Law (with copies of correspondence with Comyn Platt), 20 and 21 June 1912, BL/26/4/29 and BL/26/4/33; Croft, Peto, and Ronald McNeill to Bonar Law, Thursday, n.d., BL/33/2/20.

79. *Parl. Deb.*, 5th ser., vol. 1 (18 February 1909), c. 265. Hill was also mentioned by Chaplin to J. Chamberlain, 18 February 1909, Chamberlain Papers, JC/22/33.

80. Amery, *My Political Life,* i, 273–74.

81. J. Chamberlain to Lloyd, 3 December 1903, CAC, Lloyd Papers, GLLD 18/14.

82. J. Barnes (ed.), *The Leo Amery Diaries: Volume One, 1896–1929* (London: Hutchinson, 1980), 57 (15 December 1906). Lloyd and Croft had been at Eton and Trinity together and were both rowers. See J. Charmley, *Lord Lloyd and the Decline of the British Empire* (London: Weidenfeld and Nicolson, 1987), 14–28.

83. See, 15 February 1909, in Barnes (ed.), *The Leo Amery Diaries,* i, 63–64.

84. Blewett, "Factionalism Within the Unionist Party," *Historical Journal,* 117–18, fn. 103.

85. Wise to Bonar Law, 12 November 1911, Bonar Law Papers, BL/24/3/16.

86. Winterton Diaries, 1907–1908, Winterton MSS, c. 6–7.

87. Croft, *My Life of Strife,* 43.

88. Ibid.

89. Ibid., 44.

90. "The Confederacy," *Morning Post,* 27 January 1908.

Chapter 4. Croft, the Confederates, and the Balfour Question

1. Maxse to Garvin, 15 February 1907, Garvin Papers.

2. J. Hutcheson, *Leopold Maxse and the National Review, 1893–1914: A Study of Unionist Journalism and Politics* (New York: Garland, 1989), 285.

3. Maxse to Bonar Law, 2 January 1907, Bonar Law Papers, BL/18/3/28.

4. Ibid.

5. *Outlook,* 5 January 1907.

6. Sandars to Balfour, 22 January 1907, Balfour Papers, Add MSS 49765, fos. 11–16; also see Dugdale, *Arthur James Balfour,* ii, 43–44; and K. Young, *Arthur James Balfour: The Happy Life of the Politician, Prime Minister, Statesman and Philosopher, 1848–1930* (London: G. Bell, 1963), 262–64.

7. Ridley to A. Chamberlain, 15 January 1907, Chamberlain Papers, AC/7/6/2.

8. Acland Hood to Wilfred Short [Balfour's personal secretary], 14 January 1907, Balfour Papers, Add MSS 49771, fos. 166–67.

9. Edgar Algernon Robert Gascoyne-Cecil (1864–1958), Viscount Cecil of Chelwood (cr. 1923); 3d son of 3rd Marquess of Salisbury; married daughter of 2d Earl of Lambton; Eton, University College, Oxford; called to the Bar, QC; MP (C), East Marylebone (1906–10); Hitchin (November 1911–23); unsuccessfully contested Blackburn (January 1910), Wisbech division of Cambridgeshire (December 1910); undersecretary, foreign affairs (1915–18); minister of blockade (1916–18); assistant secretary of state, foreign affairs (1918–19); British delegate to League of Nations Commission Peace Conference; South African delegate to League of Nations; disarmament commissions (1926, 1927, 1929–31); Nobel peace prize (1937).

10. R. Cecil to Balfour, 17 January 1907, Balfour Papers, Add MSS 49737, fos. 62–63.

11. Balfour to Sandars, 24 January 1907, Balfour Papers, Add MSS 49765, fos. 23–25.

12. *The Times,* 2 February 1907.

13. "The Fiscal Truce? Protests from Tariff Reformers," *Daily Graphic,* 17 January; "Unionists & Tariff Reform. Attack on Mr. Balfour. Mr. H. P. Croft on a So-Called Fiscal Truce," *Lincolnshire Echo,* 17 January; "The Future of the Unionist Party. Fiscal Truce Criticisms," *Yorkshire Post,* 18 January 1907.

14. "Unionists and Mr. Balfour," *The Times,* 17 January 1907.

15. "Socialists Attacked. Hitchin Tariff Reformers. Mr. Page Croft and Mr. Priestley," *North Hertfordshire Mail,* 7 February 1907.

16. "Mr. Austen Chamberlain and the Unionist Policy," 25 January; "Unionists and Fiscal Reform," 28 January; "Mr. Chamberlain in East Worcester," 8 February; "Lyttelton on Fiscal Policy," 1 February; and "Mr. Austen Chamberlain on Unionist Policy," 5 February 1907, *The Times.*

17. W. A. S. Hewins, *The Apologia of an Imperialist: Forty Years of Empire Policy* (London: Constable & Co., 1930), i, 185–86, 189–95.

18. Ibid.

19. *Parl. Deb.,* 4th ser., vol. 169 (19 February 1907), c. 723–32; (Bonar Law), c. 794–804; (Chamberlain): c. 906–20; and (Balfour), c. 864–76.

20. "Fiscal Debate," *Spectator,* 23 February 1907.

21. Hewins, *Apologia of an Imperialist,* i, 193–96; A. Chamberlain, *Politics from Inside: An Epistolary Chronicle, 1906–1914* (New Haven: Yale University Press, 1937), 48–53.

22. Cf. Sykes, "The Confederacy," 355, 358.

23. Winterton, *Pre-War,* 39.

24. See "Tariff Reform v. Free Trade. Debate by Mr. E. B. Barnard, MP, Mr. H. P. Croft and Colonel Boyle," *Essex and Hertfordshire Observer,* 16 February; and "Ware Working Men's Unionist Club. Annual Dinner. Amusing Speeches," *Hertfordshire Mercury,* 23 February 1907.

25. [Leader], *Daily Telegraph,* 21 February 1907.

26. "Mr. Balfour and the Confederates," *The Globe,* 21 February 1907.

27. "Mr. Balfour at Hull. Re-declaration of Fiscal Policy," *The Times,* 2 February 1907; "Dinner to Mr. Balfour," *The Times,* 16 February 1907.

28. "Ware Working Men's Unionist Club," *Hertfordshire Mercury,* 23 February 1907.

29. "Mr. A. H. Smith and Tariff Reformers," *Hertfordshire Mercury,* 2 March 1907.

30. Croft to Garvin, 18 February 1907, Garvin Papers.

31. "Tariff Reform Again Baulked. Meeting of the United Club. The Difficulties of Unionism," *Westminster Gazette,* 8 March 1907.

32. Croft, "The United Club. Mr. Balfour and Tariff Reform," *Morning Post,* 11 March 1907.
33. "Mr. A. H. Smith, MP, and Tariff Reformers. Mr. H. P. Croft Criticizes the Member's Action," *Hertfordshire Mercury,* 2 March 1907.
34. Edward Goulding, "United Club," *Morning Post,* 11 March 1907.
35. "United Club," *Morning Post,* 11 March 1907.
36. *Westminster Gazette,* 8 March 1907.
37. Ibid.
38. "Mr. Balfour and Tariff Reform" [leader], *Morning Post,* 11 March 1907.
39. Croft, *My Life of Strife,* 43.
40. *Parl. Deb.* vol. 153 (12 March 1906), c. 1036–48.
41. R. Cecil to Clarke, 29 May 1906, Robert Cecil Papers, Add MSS 51159, fo. 78; also see Sir E. Clarke, *The Story of My Life* (London: J. Murray, 1918), 388; Lawrence to Balfour, 24 March 1906, Balfour Papers, Add MSS 49791, fos. 188–97; and Balfour to Herbert Gibbs, 22 March 1906, Add MSS 49858, fo. 199.
42. Blewett, "Factionalism Within the Unionist Party," *Historical Journal,* 116.
43. R. Cecil to Balfour, 24 May 1906, Balfour Papers, Add MSS 49737, fos. 51–52.
44. *Spectator,* 27 April 1907, 659.
45. Sandars to Balfour, 2 April 1907, Balfour Papers, Add MSS 49765, fos. 34–38.
46. Steel-Maitland to Ridley, 26 April 1907, Steel-Maitland Papers, GD 193/135.
47. Austen to J. Chamberlain, 6 May 1907, in *Politics from the Inside,* 82–83.
48. Ibid., 9 May 1907, 84.
49. J. Chamberlain to Chaplin, 25 May 1907, in Amery, *Joseph Chamberlain and the Tariff Reform Campaign,* vi, 919.
50. Winterton Diaries, 20 June 1907, Winterton MSS, c. 7.
51. George Frederic Stewart Bowles (1877–1955); Royal Navy; called to the Bar; MP (C), Norwood division of Lambeth (1906–10); unsuccessfully contested Blackburn (1910).
52. R. Cecil to Lady Robert, 16 June 1907, Hatfd Hse, Chelwood Papers, CHE 4/92.
53. R. Cecil to Balfour, 17 July 1907, Robert Cecil Papers, Add MSS 51071A, fo. 5; Cecil to Balfour, 9 July 1907, Chelwood Papers, CHE 92/95.
54. Balfour to Norwood Association, July 1907, Robert Cecil Papers, Add MSS 51071A, fo. 6
55. R. Cecil, "Confidential. Notes of My Conversation with Bonar Law on Tuesday, July 16, 1907," Chelwood Papers, CHE 71/1; also see *The Times,* 17 July 1907; *Parl. Deb.* 4th ser (17 July 1907), c. 363–70.
56. H. Cecil to Balfour, 27 July 1907, Balfour Papers, Add MSS 49759, fos. 210–17.
57. "Unionist Free Traders and the Fiscal Debate," *Spectator,* 20 July 1907, 76–77; Hugh Cecil [letter], *The Times,* 17 July 1907.
58. *Norwood Observer,* 12 August; *Spectator,* 24 August 1907.
59. "Bournemouth East Conservative Club. Welcome to Mr. Page Croft," *Bournemouth Observer and Chronicle,* 5 October 1907.
60. "Unionist Meeting. Speech by Mr. Page Croft," *Bournemouth Visitors' Directory,* 26 October 1907.
61. "Mr. Page Croft and Current Political Questions," *Bournemouth Observer and Chronicle,* 23 November 1907.
62. "Mr. Page Croft at Burton and Mudeford," *Bournemouth Observer and Chronicle,* 7 December 1907.
63. "Mr. Bonar Law, MP, on the Political Situation," *Bournemouth Observer and Chronicle,* 7 March 1908.

64. "Tariff Reform. Great Meeting at Ware," *Hertfordshire News,* 13 March 1908.
65. "Henry Page Croft at New Barnet. Mid Herts Conservative and Unionist Association," 3 February 1908, Croft Papers, CRFT 3/1 p. 175.
66. Ibid.
67. "Mr. Page Croft at Westbourne," *Bournemouth Observer & Chronicle,* 22 February 1908.
68. "Mr. Page Croft at Holdenhurst," *Bournemouth Observer and Chronicle,* 6 March 1908.
69. Brewery Allied Trades," *Morning Advertiser,* 10 March 1908; also see "Agriculturalists' Protest," *Morning Advertiser,* 27 April 1908.
70. Croft, "Licensing Bill," *Morning Post,* 5 March; H. Beckwith, "The Licensing Bill," *Bournemouth Observer and Chronicle,* 10 March; Croft, "The Licensing Bill. Mr. Page Croft Replies to Criticism," *Bournemouth Observer and Chronicle,* 17 March 1908.
71. "Demonstration Against Licensing Bill," *Hertfordshire Mercury,* 4 April 1908.
72. "Bournemouth Protests Against the Licensing Bill," *Bournemouth Observer and Chronicle,* 11 April 1908.
73. "The Licensing Bill. Demonstration in Hyde Park," *The Times,* 28 September 1908.
74. "Licensing Bill Protest. Demonstration in Hyde Park. Speech by Mr. H. P. Croft," *Hertfordshire Mercury,* 3 October; "Unionism in Hants and Dorset. Important Speeches by Mr. Page Croft. *Bournemouth Observer and Chronicle,* 17 October; "Enthusiastic Reception of Mr. Page Croft. Fighting Speeches," 21 November 1908.
75. Bonar Law to Croft, 31 October 1907, Croft Papers, CRFT 1/5 BO/1. Remnant served as Croft's righthand man in Bournemouth, which precipitated the following ditty: "Oh, Mr. P.C. / I think you'll agree / There is room for a Tariff Reformer; / And we all plainly see / Mr. Remnant, M. P. / In the Commons will find you a 'corn'—er." *Bournemouth Graphic.* 5 December 1907.
76. Winterton, *Pre-War,* 76–77.
77. Bentinck to Portland (copy), 11 October 1907, Balfour Papers, Add MSS 49736, fo. 40.
78. Portland to Balfour, 20 October 1907, Balfour Papers, Add MSS 49859, fos. 177–82.
79. Balfour to A. Chamberlain, 23 October 1907, Chamberlain Papers, AC/17/3/19, and Balfour Papers, Add MSS 49736, fos. 18–20.
80. Sandars to Short, 28 October 1907, Balfour Papers, Add MSS 49765, fos. 74–77.
81. A. Chamberlain to Balfour, 24 October 1907, Chamberlain Papers, AC/17/3/23, and Balfour Papers, Add MSS 49736, fos. 21–32.
82. Ibid.
83. Ibid.
84. Matthew W. Ridley (1874–1916), 2nd Viscount Ridley, 3rd Baron Wensleydale; succeeded father in 1904; grandson of 1st Lord Tweedmouth; MP (C), Stalybridge (1900–1904); officer, Tariff Reform League.
85. Ridley to Balfour, 1 November 1907, Balfour Papers, Add MSS 49859, fos. 190–93.
86. Balfour to Ridley, 2 November 1907, Balfour Papers, Add MSS 49859, fo. 194.
87. Winterton, *Pre-War,* 76.
88. *The Times,* 15 November 1907.

89. Croft, "Loyalty of Unionists," *Morning Post*, 18 November 1907.
90. *Morning Post*, 20 November 1907.
91. "The Confederacy," *Morning Post*, 15 January 1907.

Chapter 5. Croft, the Confederates, and Political Cannibalism

1. "The Confederacy," 15 January; and "Free Trade Unionists," *The Globe*, 17 January 1908; Bentinck to R. Cecil, 8 January 1908, Robert Cecil Papers, Add MSS 51158, fo. 167.

2. Rempel, *Unionists Divided*, 181; "Free Trade Unionists as Parliamentary Candidates. The Confederacy and Lord H. Bentinck," *Morning Post*, 17 January 1908. After losing in 1906 when he was sympathetic to free trade, Bentinck won (6,434–6,052) in January 1910 as an adherent of the Birmingham program.

3. *Morning Post*, 17 January 1908. In January 1910 a converted Morrison regained the Nottingham East seat for the Conservatives (5,872–5,725).

4. "Confederacy and Free Traders," *Morning Post*, 18 January 1908.

5. E. G. Brunker to R. Cecil, 9 January 1908, Robert Cecil Papers, Add MSS 51072, fos. 161–63. Brunker claimed the origin of the report was the secretary of the TRL.

6. Walter Hume Long (1854–1924), 1st Viscount Long of Wraxall (cr. 1921); married daughter of 9th Earl of Cork and Orrery; colonel, Royal Wilts Imperial Yeomanry; MP (C), North Wilts (1880–85), Devizes (1885–92), West Derby (1892–1900), South Bristol (1900–1906), South Dublin (1906–10), Strand (1910), St. George-Westminster (1910–21); president, board of Agriculture (1895–1900), president, Local Government Board (1900–1905, 1915–16), chief secretary for Ireland (1905–1906), secretary of state for the Colonies (1916–18), first lord of the Admiralty (1919–21).

7. R. Cecil to Long, 14 January 1908, Robert Cecil Papers, Add MSS 51072, fos. 52–53; Cecil to Long, 31 January 1908, Add MSS 51072, fos. 59–60.

8. Long to R. Cecil, 18 January 1908, Robert Cecil Papers, Add MSS 51072, fos. 55–56.

9. Long to R. Cecil, 23 January 1908, Robert Cecil Papers, Add MSS 51072, fo. 57.

10. G. S. Bowles to R. Cecil, 13 December 1907, Robert Cecil Papers, Add MSS 51072, fo. 103; Bowles to Acland Hood, 17 December, Add MSS 51072, fo. 104; Acland Hood to Bowles, 23 December, Add MSS 51072, fo. 108.

11. Acland Hood to Sandars, 11 January 1908, Balfour Papers, Add MSS 49771, fo. 17.

12. R. Cecil to Balfour, 19 January 1908, Balfour Papers, Add MSS 49737, fos. 86–87; also see Campbell, chairman, Norwood branch of the TRL to Bowles, 3 January, 8 January, 10 January 1908, Robert Cecil Papers, Add MSS 51072, fos. 117–18, 126, 131; Bowles to Cecil, 6 January 1908, Add MSS 51072, fo. 120.

13. "Mr. Stewart Bowles and the Confederacy," *Morning Post*, 18 January 1908.

14. "The First Constructive Policy. London Unionists' Sweeping Resolution. The Confederacy Justified," *Morning Post*, 2 February 1908; R. Cecil to Long, 31 January 1908, Robert Cecil Papers, Add MSS 51072, fos. 59–60.

15. Long to R. Cecil, 2 February 1908, Robert Cecil Papers, Add MSS 51072, fos. 62–64.

16. R. Cecil to Balfour, 13 January 1908, Robert Cecil Papers, Add MSS 51072, fos. 84–85.

17. Goulding to J. Chamberlain, 25 March 1908, Chamberlain Papers, JC/22/80.

Money was also available from Austen Chamberlain for use against the free traders. J. Chamberlain to Goulding, 27 July 1909, HLRO, Wargrave Papers, MSS A/3/2.

18. E. G. Brunker to Walter Elliot, 16 January 1908; and Cromer to Elliot, 10 January 1908, NLS, Elliot Papers, MS 4246/15/F.100.

19. "A Centre Party," *Spectator,* 25 January 1908; St. Loe Strachey to R. Cecil, 5 March 1908, Robert Cecil Papers, Add MSS 51072, fos. 194–95.

20. "Memorandum (on the Possible Consequence of the Formation of a Centre Party)," n.d. 1908, Quickswood Papers, QUI 9/43. It proposed a coalition of Lord Balfour of Burleigh, Hugh Cecil, Lord George Hamilton and the 'Roseberyites.' Harold Cox to H. Cecil, 19 May 1908, Quickswood Papers, QUI 9/101; St. Loe Strachey to R. Cecil, 5 March 1908, Robert Cecil Papers, Add MSS 51158, fo. 194; "A Centre Party," *Spectator,* 7 March 1908; and "Alarms of Lord Rosebery," *Daily Chronicle,* 3 March 1908.

21. Brunker to R. Cecil, 17 February 1908, Robert Cecil Papers, Add MSS 51072, fo. 181; Sykes, *Tariff Reform in British Politics,* 162; "The United Unionists," *Daily Chronicle,* 10 January 1908.

22. R. Cecil to Balfour, 16 March 1908, Balfour Papers, Add MSS 49737, fos. 90–91. A few days later, Goulding informed the elder Chamberlain that "you will have seen we are active at Marylebone." Goulding to J. Chamberlain, 25 March 1908, Chamberlain Papers, JC/22/80. There was an overexaggerated fear within the free trade forces that although the TRL sent only a few candidates into by-elections before 1906, they were expected to raise hundreds of candidates for the next election. G. Wallace Carter, general secretary, Confidential Memorandum of Free Trade Union, n.d., Quickswood Papers, QUI 9/51.

23. H. Cecil, "The Unionist Party," *The Times,* 19 March 1908.

24. H. P. Croft (letter), *The Times,* 20 March 1908.

25. "The Unionist Party," *The Times,* 20 March 1908.

26. R. Cecil to Balfour, 16 March 1908, Balfour Papers, Add MSS 49737, fos. 90–91.

27. William Waldegrave Palmer (1859–1942), 2d earl of Selborne; succeeded father in 1895; married daughter of 3rd marquess of Salisbury; MP (L), East Hampshire (1885–86); (LU) East Hampshire (1886–92); West Edinburgh (1892–95); undersecretary for Colonies (1895–1900); first lord of the Admiralty (1900–1905); governor of Transvaal and high commissioner for South Africa (1905–10); president, board of Agriculture (1915–16). Roundell Cecil Palmer (1887–1971), styled Viscount Wolmer; succeeded father as 3d earl of Selborne (1942); married daughter of Viscount Ridley; MP (C), Newton (1910–18), Aldershot (1918–40).

28. Balfour to Selborne, 6 March 1908, Bodl Lib, MS Selborne, c. 1/68–79.

29. R. Cecil to Balfour, 4 March 1908, Balfour Papers, Add MSS, 49737, fos. 88–89; Goulding and Winterton, *Parl. Deb.,* 4th ser., vol. 185 (4 March 1908), c. 786–97.

30. E. Tootal Broadhurst to St. Loe Strachey, 4 March 1908, Robert Cecil Papers, Add MSS 51158, fos. 196–97.

31. W. Short to R. Cecil, 20 March 1908, Robert Cecil Papers, Add MSS 51071, fo. 7; Maj. L. Darwen to R. Cecil, n.d. March 1908, Add MSS 51158, fo. 223.

32. R. Cecil to Balfour, 16 March 1908, Balfour Papers, Add MSS 49737, fos. 90–91.

33. "Election Intelligence," *The Times,* 16 April 1908.

34. Ibid.

35. R. Cecil to Long, n.d. [March 1908], Robert Cecil Papers, Add MSS 51072, fo. 68.

36. "The Confederacy. Its Aims and Methods. Interview with a Confederate," *Morning Post,* 25 January 1908.
37. "War Declared on Free Trade Tories. Tariff Reformer's Plans for Purging the Party," *Daily Chronicle,* 8 February 1908.
38. "Tariff Reform. The Position in East Herts. Unionist Party and Fiscal Reform," *Hertfordshire and Essex Observer,* 25 January 1908.
39. "Tariff Reform Meeting at Hertford. Challenge to the Member for East Herts," *Hertfordshire Mercury,* 8 February 1908.
40. Henry Abel Smith (1862–1930); wealthy banking family; grandson of 3d Earl of Chichester; married daughter of Lord Lurgan; MP (C), Christchurch (1892–1900), East Hertfordshire (1900–1910); father also represented Hertfordshire (1854–57, 1859–65, 1866–98); private secretary to Walter Long, board of Agriculture.
41. P. F. Clarke, "British Politics and Blackburn Politics, 1900–1910," *Historical Journal,* 12:2 (1969), 302–27; Rempel, *Unionists Divided;* Gollin, *Balfour's Burden;* Sykes, *Tariff Reform in British Politics.*
42. Blewett, "Factionalism with the Unionist Party," *Historical Journal,* 118.
43. Sykes, "The Confederacy," 363.
44. Long to Selborne, 25 November 1907, MS Selborne, c.73/57–68.
45. "Bishop's Stortford," *Hertfordshire Mercury,* 4 April 1908.
46. "Tariff Reformers and Mr. A. H. Smith, MP Dissatisfaction with the Member," *Hertfordshire Mercury,* 18 April 1908.
47. "Mr. Abel Smith, MP, and the Unionists," *Hertfordshire Mercury,* 18 April 1908.
48. Sir George Faudel-Phillips (1840–1922), Bt (1897); son of Sir Benjamin Phillips, alderman and lord mayor of London; married sister of 1st Lord Burnham; sheriff of London and Middlesex, alderman of Ward of Farringdon, high sheriff of County of London; lord mayor of London; high sheriff of Hertford.
49. Memorandum. East Herts. Secret, n.d., Balfour Papers, Add MSS 49860, fos. 138–46; "East Herts Conservative and Liberal Unionist Association," *Hertfordshire News,* 25 April 1908.
50. "Hertford Tariff Reformers. A Prospective Candidate," 9 May; "Tariff Reform and East Herts," 16 May; "Representation of the East Herts Division," *Hertfordshire Mercury,* 18 July 1908.
51. "Tariff Reform Demonstration at Theobald's Park," *Hertfordshire Mercury,* 4 July 1908.
52. R. Cecil to Lady Robert, 3 November 1908, Chelwood Papers, CHE 4/126.
53. R. Cecil to Lady Robert, 23 November 1908, Chelwood Papers, CHE 4/132.
54. R. Cecil to Acland Hood, 14 November 1908, Robert Cecil Papers, Add MSS 51158, fos. 270–74.
55. Acland Hood to R. Cecil, 17 November 1908, Robert Cecil Papers, Add MSS 51158, fos. 275–76.
56. R. Cecil to Acland Hood, 19 November 1908, Robert Cecil Papers, Add MSS 51158, fos. 278–80.
57. "The Representation of the East Herts Division. Mr. Abel H. Smith and the Tariff Reformers," *Hertfordshire Mercury,* 21 November 1908.
58. *The Times,* 18 November 1908.
59. "Herts," *The Times,* 11 November 1908.
60. Ware Unionist and Conservative Association, Minute Book, 23 November 1908, D/EX 274.Z1; "East Herts Politics," *Hertfordshire News,* 27 November; *The Times,* 21 November 1908.
61. "Unionist Free Fooders," *Morning Post,* 30 November; "Tariff Reformers at Ware. Position of H. P. Croft," *Hertfordshire News,* 27 November 1908.

62. Ibid.
63. J. Chamberlain to Croft, 15 December 1908, Croft Papers, CRFT 1/6 CH/23.
64. Goulding to Croft, n.d., Croft Papers, CRFT 1/20 WA/2.
65. "Herts," *The Times*, 23 December; "Mr. A. H. Smith, MP, and the Tariff Reformers. Unionist Meeting at Hertford," *Hertfordshire Mercury*, 26 December 1908.
66. "Herts," *The Times*, 8 December 1908.
67. Ibid., 15 December 1908.
68. Ibid., 17 December 1908.
69. Ibid., 24 December 1908.
70. Ibid., 23 December; "Mr. A. H. Smith, MP, and the Tariff Reformers. Unionist Meeting at Hertford," *Hertfordshire Mercury*, 26 December 1908.
71. Alfred Baker (letter), *Hertfordshire Mercury*, 9 Jan 1909. Croft responded on 16 January 1909.
72. "Free Fooders and General Election. Position in East Herts. Mr. Abel Smith and His Constituents," *Morning Post*, 21 January 1909.
73. "Sub Rosa," *Morning Leader*, 7 December 1908.
74. "The Policy of the Unionist Party," *The Times*, 20 January 1909.
75. *Daily Mail*, 19 January 1909.
76. "The Political Situation in East Herts," *Hertfordshire Mercury*, 23 January 1909. Throughout January and February, the *Westminster Gazette* ran a regular series on "The Confederates v. the Free Fooders."
77. "Proprietor," *Hertfordshire Mercury*, 23 January 1909.
78. [Leader], *Hertfordshire Mercury*, 23 January 1909.
79. *The Times*, 28 January; "Lord Ridley and the Confederacy," *The Times*, 29 January 1909.
80. "Lord R. Cecil and the Confederates," *The Times*, 29 January 1909.
81. *The Times*, 22 January 1909.
82. "Lord Hugh Cecil and the 'Confederacy,'" *The Times*, 23 January 1909.
83. "Free Fooders and The General Election. Position in East Herts. Mr. Abel Smith and His Constituents," *Morning Post*, 21 January; "Confederates v. Free Fooders IV. Abel Smith, MP, and Mr. Balfour's Undefined Policy. A Special Interview," *Westminster Gazette*, 22 January 1909.
84. "Mr. Abel Smith and His Constituents. Failure of Negotiations," *Morning Post*, 1 February; "Serious Position in East Herts. Mr. Abel Smith's Attitude," *Standard*, 1 February 1909.
85. Croft to J. Chamberlain, 25 January 1909, Croft Papers, CRFT 1/6 CH/24.
86. J. Chamberlain to Croft, 26 January 1909, Croft Papers, CRFT 1/6 CH/25.
87. Smith to R. Cecil, 25 January 1909, Robert Cecil Papers, Add MSS 51159, fos. 19–20.
88. [Leader], *Hertfordshire Mercury*, 30 January 1909.
89. "Unionist Split in East Herts. Mr. A. H. Smith, MP, and Executive Committee. Adverse Vote," *Hertfordshire Mercury*, 6 February 1909.
90. *Morning Post*, 1 February; *Standard*, 1 February 1909.
91. "Election Intelligence. Herts," *The Times*, 3 February; "The Unionist Split in East Herts," *Hertfordshire Mercury*, 6 February 1909.
92. Ibid.
93. R. Cecil to Asquith, 21 January 1909, Chelwood Papers, CHE 93/309–11; Cromer to R. Cecil, 29 January 1909, Robert Cecil Papers, Add MSS 51072, fo. 33; Rempel, *Unionists Divided*, 189.
94. Smith to R. Cecil, 2 February 1909, Robert Cecil Papers, Add MSS 51159, fo. 44.

95. "Confederates v. Free Fooders. East Herts Executive Throw Over Mr. Abel Smith," *Westminster Gazette,* 3 February; "East Herts Politics Resignation of Officials," *Hertfordshire News,* 26 February; "Unionist Split in East Herts," *Hertfordshire Mercury,* 27 February; *The Times,* 25 February 1909.

96. Salisbury to Sir George Faudel-Phillips, 22 February 1909, in "Herts and Mr. Abel Smith," *Standard,* 11 March; "Lord Salisbury Resigns Presidency of the Association," *Hertfordshire Mercury,* 13 March 1909.

97. "East Herts Politics. Mr. H. P. Croft and Lord Salisbury," *Hertfordshire News,* 19 March 1909.

98. A. Smith, "Policy of the Unionist Party," *The Times,* 11 February 1909.

99. St. Loe Strachey to R. Cecil, 3 February 1909, Robert Cecil Papers, Add MSS 51159, fo. 47.

100. Brunker to R. Cecil, 16 March 1909, Robert Cecil Papers, Add MSS 51072, fo. 192; 17 Mar, 1909, Add MSS 51072, fo. 194; 18 March 1909, Add MSS 51072, fo. 196; 16 April 1909, Add MSS 51072, fo. 200.

101. Ware Unionist Association, Minute Book, 4 March 1909, D/EX 274.Z1; "Ware Conservative Association Annual Meeting. A Call for Candidates," *Hertfordshire Mercury,* 5 March 1909.

102. "East Herts. Mr. Smith and His Supporters," *Hertfordshire News,* 12 March; "Election Intelligence. East Herts," *The Times,* 8 March; "Political Situation in East Herts," *Hertfordshire Mercury,* 3 March 1909; Brunker to R. Cecil, 9 March 1909, Robert Cecil Papers, Add MSS 51072, fo. 192.

103. Smith to R. Cecil, 11 March 1909, Robert Cecil Papers, Add MSS 51159, fos. 122–24.

104. Smith to H. Cecil, 14 March, Quickswood Papers, QUI 11/118, 17 March 1909, QUI 11/124; H. Cecil to R. Cecil, 13 March, Chelwood Papers, CHE 112/69; H. Cecil to R. Cecil, 16 April 1909, CHE 112/61.

105. Smith to H. Cecil, 19 March 1909, Quickswood Papers, QUI 11/125.

106. Smith to R. Cecil, 21 March 1909, Robert Cecil Papers, Add MSS 51159, fos. 129–30.

107. "Election Intelligence," *The Times,* 18 March 1909.

108. "Hertford Conservative Association. Annual Meeting. A Vote of Confidence in Mr. A. H. Smith," *Hertfordshire Mercury,* 20 March 1909; "Hertford Conservative Association," *Hertfordshire News,* 19 March 1909.

109. "Tariff Reform in Herts," *The Times,* 26 March 1909.

110. "Tariff Reform League. Herts Federation. Mass Meeting," *Hertfordshire Mercury,* 27 March 1909. The federation was composed of fifteen branches and 3,114 members. "Hertford Tariff Reformers. Criticism of Mr. Abel Henry Smith," *Standard,* 27 March 1909.

111. "Debate on Tariff Reform," *Hertfordshire Mercury,* 3 April 1909.

112. "Meetings in the Different Polling Districts," *Hertfordshire Mercury,* 27 March 1909.

113. Smith to R. Cecil, 7 April 1909, Robert Cecil Papers, Add MSS 51159, fos. 160–61.

114. "Chaos in East Herts. Mr. Abel Smith's Narrow Victory Grave Position," *Standard,* 7 April; "East Herts Politics. Important Meeting at Hertford," *Hertfordshire News,* 9 April; "Politics in East Herts. Mr. Smith's Supporters Recapture the Association," *Hertfordshire Mercury,* 10 April 1909.

115. "The Methods of the Free Fooders," *Morning Post,* 8 April 1909.

116. "Politics in East Herts," *Hertfordshire Mercury,* 10 April 1909.

117. Ibid.

118. Ware Unionist Association, Minute Book, 15 April 1909, D/EX 274.Z1.

119. "Politics in East Herts. Mr. Mortimer Selected as Tariff Reform Candidate," *Hertfordshire Mercury,* 22 May 1909.

120. Mortimer, educated at Harrow and Corpus Christi, Cambridge, and a barrister, was associated with the malting industry, which provided the contact with Croft. "The Unionists Split in East Herts. Tariff Reformers Start a New Association. Mr. Reginald Mortimer to Be Their Candidate," *Hertfordshire Mercury,* 24 April; "East Herts Politics. Tariff Reformers Move. New Association Formed. A Prospective Candidate," *Hertfordshire News,* 23 April 1909.

121. Ware Unionist Association, Minute Book, 30 June 1909, D/EX 274.Z1.

122. *Bournemouth Visitors' Directory,* 7 May 1909.

123. Croft, "Unionist Party Loyalty," *Morning Post,* 7 May; R. Cecil, 8 May; Croft, 9 May 1909.

124. "Tariff Reform at East Herts. Garden Party at Fanham's Hall, Ware. Speeches by Viscount Ridley, Mr. Reginald Mortimer, and Mr. Henry Page Croft," *Hertfordshire and Essex Observer,* 10 July 1909.

125. "Mr. Abel Smith and Tariff Reform," *Times,* 8 June 1909.

126. Smith to Salisbury, 26 June 1909, Hatfd Hse, Salisbury Papers, 4M/65/115.

127. Acland Hood to Salisbury, 12 July 1909, Salisbury Papers, 4M/65/134; Salisbury to Acland Hood, 23 July 1909, 4M/65/150; Acland Hood to Salisbury, 27 July 1909, 4M/65/154a.

128. Acland Hood to Salisbury, 29 July 1909, Salisbury Papers, 4M/65/154b.

129. Salisbury to Balfour, 7 August 1909, Salisbury Papers, 4M/66/6.

130. Acland Hood to Balfour, 10 August 1909, Salisbury Papers, 4M/66/9–10. An extensive report on the circumstances of the new East Hertfordshire association was put together for Balfour by Percival Hughes, Acland Hood's assistant. He was required to address a series of specific questions: Was the decision taken by the old Association in favor of the sitting member the act of the general body or of the council? Is the Unionist Association a body elected on the modern model or is it a largely nominated body? To what extent has its members been depleted by the withdrawal of Tariff Reformers? Has the new Association been fully constituted? Is it of the modern and democratic model? Is it of substantial proportion, and how does it compare in numbers with the old Association? Has it spread or is it spreading throughout the constituency? Is it affiliated to the National Union, or if not, does it propose to apply for affiliation? What steps has it taken (a) to define its objects? (b) to secure a candidate? (c) to impose a test on any candidate chose by it? P. Hughes, East Herts Memorandum, 17 August 1909, Balfour Papers, Add MSS 49860, fos. 136–37.

131. Smith to Salisbury, 16 August 1909, Salisbury Papers, 4M/66/14–15.

132. "East Herts Politics. Mr. A. H. Smith at Hoddesdon. A Plea for an Understanding," *Hertfordshire News,* 23 July 1909.

133. Smith to Salisbury, 22 August 1909, Salisbury Papers, 4M/66/17–18.

134. C. E. Longmore to Salisbury, 22 August 1909, Salisbury Papers, 4M/66/19–20.

135. Balfour to Salisbury, n.d. [August] 1909, Salisbury Papers, 4M/66/1.

136. Smith to Salisbury, 29 August 1909, Salisbury Papers, 4M/66/24–25; Smith to Salisbury, 14 October 1909, Salisbury Papers, 4M/66/56–57.

137. H. Cecil to R. Cecil, 6 May 1909, Chelwood Papers, CHE 112/79.

138. "Mr. R. B. Mortimer at Ware," *Hertfordshire News,* 24 September 1909.

139. *Standard,* 9 September 1909; Brunker to R. Cecil, 1 September 1909, Robert Cecil Papers, Add MSS 51072, fo. 211; "Plain Tory," *Morning Post,* 13 September 1909.

140. "Tariff Reformers Compromise with Unionist Free Fooders," *Hertfordshire Mercury*, 11 September 1909.
141. *The Times*, 16 September 1909.
142. "Politics in East Herts," *Hertfordshire Mercury*, 18 September 1909.
143. "Mr. R. B. Mortimer at Ware. Authoritative Statement about the Truce," *Hertfordshire News*, 24 September; "Tariff Reform Meeting at Ware. Speeches by Mr. Mortimer and Mr. H. P. Croft," *Hertfordshire Mercury*, 25 September 1909.
144. "Representation of East Herts. Important Negotiations," *Hertfordshire and Essex Observer*, 9 October 1909; "Unionist Free Traders. Decision in East Herts. An Example for Marylebone," *Morning Post*, 8 October 1909.
145. Ibid.
146. "Representation of East Herts. Important Negotiations," *Hertfordshire and Essex Observer*, 9 October 1909; "Unionist Free Traders. Decision in East Herts. An Example for Marylebone," *Morning Post*, 8 October 1909.
147. "The East Herts Withdrawals," *Morning Post*, 19 October 1909.
148. "Peace in East Herts. Both Unionists to Retire," *Standard*, 16 October 1909; Acland Hood to Sandars, 12 October 1909, Balfour Papers, Add MSS 49771, fos. 181–82.
149. Croft to chairman of the council, 18 October, in "The Unionist Split in East Herts Healed. Both Unionist Candidates Retire. Surrender to the Tariff Reformers," *Hertfordshire Mercury*, 23 October 1909.
150. R. B. Croft to Salisbury, 14 October 1909, Salisbury Papers, 4M/66/55; Smith to Salisbury, 14 October 1909, 4M/66/56–57; C. E. Longmore to Salisbury, 14 October 1909, 4M/66/58.
151. "The Political Situation in East Herts. Selection of a Unionist Candidate," *Hertfordshire Mercury*, 6 November; "Unionist Meeting at Ware. Speeches by Sir John Rolleston, Mr. H. P. Croft and Mr. Reginald Mortimer," *Hertfordshire Mercury*, 13 November 1909; Rolleston to Salisbury, 6 December 1909, Salisbury Papers, 4M/66/148.
152. Elliot to Cromer, 17 July 1909, PRO, Cromer Papers, FO 633/18, quoted in Green, *The Crisis of Conservatism*, 371, fn. 213.

Chapter 6. Imperial Mission, Reveille, and the Call to Action

1. *Parl. Deb.* (Lords), 5th ser., vol. 4 (30 November 1909), c. 1342–46.
2. "Unionist Meeting at Highcliffe," *Bournemouth Echo*, 16 October 1909.
3. "Conservative Meeting at Westbourne," 20 October; "Mr. Page Croft at Southbourne," 21 October; "Conservative Meeting at Burton," *Bournemouth Echo*, 22 October 1909.
4. "Lord Milner at Poole. Speeches by Lord Milner and Mr. Page Croft," *Bournemouth Echo*, 17 November 1909.
5. "The Hanley Division. Mr. Rittner's Candidature. Speech by Mr. Page Croft," *Staffordshire Sentinel*, 22 December 1909.
6. "Unionist Meeting at Branksome," Bournemouth Echo, 12 January 1910. Also see "Why Mr. Croft Will Win," *Daily Express* [Bournemouth Special Edition], 10 January 1910.
7. Croft, "The Food of the People. Only One Way to Ensure Its Cheapness. Preference," *Daily Express*, 10 January 1910.
8. "Christchurch Election," *Bournemouth Echo*, 18 January 1910.

9. A. Chamberlain to Balfour, 29 January 1910, in Chamberlain, *Politics from Inside*, 196–97.
10. "United Herts. A Great Unionist Celebration. Electoral Triumphs," *The Standard*, 5 March 1910.
11. Although Hugh Cecil returned with a seat for Oxford University, those within the Confederacy no longer regarded him as an "obstruction . . . he has warmly played the game throughout the general election by warmly supporting tariff reformers." "Episodes," *National Review* (March 1910), 4; R. Rempel, "Lord Hugh Cecil's Parliamentary Career, 1900–1914," *Journal of British Studies* 11:2 (1972), 127.
12. *Bournemouth Echo*, 24 February 1910.
13. *Parl. Deb.*, vol. 14 (24 February 1910), c. 437–40.
14. A. Chamberlain, 24 February 1910, *Politics from Inside*, 204.
15. "Episodes," *National Review* (April 1910), 180.
16. Garvin to Croft, 4 November 1911, Croft Papers, CRFT 1/12 GA/4.
17. P. J. Hannon to Croft, 23 May [1911], Croft Papers, CRFT 1/13 HA/28.
18. *Evening News*, 4 November 1910.
19. *Daily Express*, 30 July 1910.
20. *The Standard*, 1 August 1910.
21. *Morning Post*, 6 August 1910.
22. *Parl. Deb.*, vol. 16, c. 1526–48.
23. Sykes, *Tariff Reform in British Politics*, 213.
24. A. Chamberlain, *Politics from Inside*, 226.
25. Encouraged MP, "Imperial Mission," *Morning Post*, 2 April 1910.
26. "The Imperial Mission, How It Originated. Its Aims and Objects," *The Press* [of New Zealand], 14 September 1911.
27. "Pioneers of Empire. Spellbinder to Teach Britons at Home. Blinded Hero," *Daily Express*, 2 April 1910.
28. "Imperial Pioneers," *Morning Post*, 11 June 1910.
29. *East London Advertiser*, 18 June 1910.
30. *The Press* [of New Zealand], 14 September 1911.
31. For his introduction to Aitken, see Croft, *My Life of Strife*, 78.
32. "New Organization," *The Times*, 14 June; "Imperial Mission. New Organization Formed to Advance Preference," *Daily Express*, 14 June 1910.
33. "Imperial Mission," *The Times*, 19 July 1910.
34. "Imperial Pioneers at Whitechapel," *East London Advertiser*, 18 June 1910.
35. "Imperial Preference. Mass Meeting at Bournemouth," *Bournemouth Echo*, 11 June 1910.
36. "Unionist Demonstration at Lincoln. Visit by Mr. H. Page Croft, MP. Rousing Speech on Empire," *Lincolnshire Echo*, 28 July 1910.
37. "Episodes," *National Review* (May 1910), 352–53.
38. *Lincolnshire Echo*, 28 July 1910.
39. *Bournemouth Echo*, 11 June 1910.
40. Ibid.
41. *Lincolnshire Echo*, 28 July 1910.
42. J. Ramsden (ed.), 8 June 1910, *Real Old Tory Politics: Political Diaries of Robert Sanders, Lord Bayford, 1910–1935* (London: The Historians' Press, 1984), 20; R. Jenkins, *Mr. Balfour's Poodle: Peers vs. People* (New York: Heinemann, 1954), 145–53.
43. Croft to Balfour, 3 June 1910, Bodl Lib, Sandars Papers, MSS Eng hist, c. 760, fos. 177–78.
44. Balfour to Croft, 6 June 1910, Croft Papers, CRFT 1/3 BA/19.
45. R. Cecil to Lady Robert, 12 June 1910, Chelwood Papers, CHE 5/23.

46. "Episodes," *National Review* (April 1910), 179.
47. *Parl. Deb.*, vol. 19 (30 June 1910), c. 1143 and vol. 19 (25 July 1910), c. 1767.
48. *Parl. Deb.*, vol. 19 (25 July 1910), c. 1769.
49. *Morning Advertiser,* 26 July 1910.
50. *Parl. Deb.*, vol 19, c. 1812–15.
51. Ibid., c. 1839–42.
52. "Kirkdale Election," *Morning Post,* 21 July 1910.
53. Imperial Mission. Executive Committee Meeting, 2 August 1910, Croft Papers, CRFT 1/3 BA/20/2.
54. Croft to Balfour, 2 August 1910, Croft Papers, CRFT 1/3 BA/20/1.
55. Balfour to Croft, 26 August 1910, Croft Papers, CRFT 1/3 BA/21/1.
56. Croft to Balfour, 2 August 1910, Croft Papers, CRFT 1/3 BA/20/1.
57. *Morning Post,* 1 September 1910.
58. Croft to Blumenfeld, 27 August 1910, HLRO, Blumenfeld Papers, CRO/4. Also see Croft, My Life of Strife, 54.
59. Croft, "Reveille! The Unionist Opportunity," *Morning Post,* 30 August 1910.
60. Croft to Acland Hood, 12 September 1910, Sandars Papers, MSS Eng hist, c. 761/67.
61. Maxse to Garvin, 31 August 1910, Garvin Papers.
62. Maxse to Bonar Law, 29 September 1910, Bonar Law Papers, BL/18/6/124.
63. Maxse to Goulding, 29 September 1910, Wargrave Papers, MSS 2/73.
64. Leader, *Morning Post,* 30 August 1910.
65. "Wake Up, Unionists" [leader], *Morning Advertiser,* 31 August 1910.
66. "Waiting for a Wellington" [leader], *Lancashire Daily Post,* 31 August 1910.
67. "Reveille" [leader], *Hull Daily Mail,* 1 September 1910.
68. "By a Unionist Worker. Somnolence in the Unionist Ranks. What Should the Future Be?" *Morning Post,* 1 September; Croft was featured in the 10 September 1910 issue of the *British and Tariff Reform Journal,* which applauded his call for a new Wellington.
69. "Knowle Unionist Demonstration. Mr. H. Page Croft, MP, Makes a Stirring Appeal to Patriots," *Bristol Times and Mirror,* 2 September 1910.
70. "Unionist Reveille Movement," *Daily Express,* 24 September 1910.
71. Willoughby de Broke to Maxse, 20 August 1910, Maxse Papers, MSS 462/r697; "The Coming Campaign," *National Review* (September 1910), 59–70.
72. "Episodes," *National Review* (September 1910), 21–23.
73. Ibid.
74. Willoughby de Broke, "The Coming Campaign," 59–70.
75. "Tory Discontents," 4 October; "Tory Malcontents," *Daily Chronicle,* 5 October 1910.
76. "Unionist Organization," *The Times,* 5 October 1910.
77. *Morning Post,* 5 October 1910.
78. "Episodes," *National Review* (October 1910), 213–14.
79. Ibid.
80. An Observer, "The Need for a Militant Unionist Policy," *The Times,* 13 September 1910.
81. "Unionist Open-Air Campaign," *The Times,* 13 September 1910.
82. "Unionist Autumn Campaign," *The Times,* 17 September 1910.
83. Sandars to Short, 3 October 1910, Balfour Papers, Add MSS 49767, fos. 5–6.
84. "Political Speeches. Mr. A. Chamberlain at Birmingham," *The Times,* 23 September 1910.
85. "Payment of Members," *The Times,* 27 September 1910.
86. Howell Arthur Gwynne (1865–1950); war correspondent for Reuter's (1893–

1904); editor, Standard (1904–11); Morning Post (1911–37); supported tariff reform and Croft's National party.

87. Arthur Lee (letter), *The Times,* 27 September; Maxse to Bonar Law, 29 September 1910, Bonar Law Papers, BL/18/6/124; A. Chamberlain to Bonar Law, 29 September, Bonar Law Papers, BL/18/6/25; Memorandum by H. A. Gwynne, 28 September, Bonar Law Papers, BL/20/19; F. E. Smith to Bonar Law, 29 September, Bonar Law Papers, BL/15/6/85; Gwynne to Chamberlain, 4 October, Chamberlain Papers, AC/8/6/28, and Memorandum by Gywnne, AC/8/6/29.

88. [Leader], *Morning Post,* 23 September 1910.

89. "Mr. Balfour at Edinburgh. Leader Ignores Tory Insurgents. Against Payment of Members. Bitter Attack on Trade Unions," *Daily Chronicle,* 6 October 1910; Esher to Balfour, 30 September 1910, in Oliver Viscount Esher (ed.), Journals and Letters of Reginald Viscount Esher (London: Nicholson & Watson, 1938), vol. iii, 24–25.

90. J. Vincent (ed.), 5 October 1910, in *The Journals of David Lindsay, 27th Earl of Crawford and 10th Earl of Balcarres 1871–1940)* (Manchester: Manchester University Press, 1984), 165–66.

91. "Revolt of the Wild Men," *Western Daily Press,* 5 October; "Go On Fighting. Motto of the Unionist Forwards. A Lead Wanted. A New Group Formed for Action. Complaint of Slackness in the Party," *Manchester Dispatch,* 5 October; "Unionist Rebels. Leaders of the Party Taken to Task. Programme Wanted. New Fight Organisation Formed," *Daily Sketch,* 5 October; "New Unionist Cave," *Sheffield Telegraph,* 5 October 1910.

92. *Morning Post,* 5 October 1910.

93. "Forcing a Lead," *Globe,* 5 October 1910.

94. *Manchester Courier,* 5 October 1910.

95. "The Tory Revolt. Insurgents' Manifesto Repudiated. Official Alarm," *Daily Chronicle,* 7 October 1910.

96. "Mr. Balfour in Edinburgh," *The Times,* 6 October 1910.

97. *Morning Post,* 6 October 1910.

98. "Mr. Balfour and His Critics," *Westminster Gazette,* 6 October 1910.

99. Journal, 7 October 1910, in Vincent, *The Crawford Papers,* 166.

100. Garvin to Maxse, 6 October 1910, Maxse Papers, MSS 462/r728–29.

101. A. M. Gollin, The Observer and J. L. Garvin, 1908–1914: A Study in a Great Editorship (Oxford: Oxford University Press, 1960), 204–34.

102. Maxse to Garvin, 11 October 1910, Garvin Papers.

103. Those attending included Acland Hood, the chief whip; Percival Hughes, the chief agent; the Earl of Denbigh; Viscount Hardinge; Basil Peto, MP; Alan Burgoyne, MP; Sir John Rolleston, MP; E. A. Goulding, MP; H. J. Mackinder, MP; Edmund Royds, MP; Laming Worthington Evans, MP; Maj. J. H. Kirkwood, MP; J. W. Hills, MP; Charles Goldman, MP; Sir Alfred Bird, MP; Gerald Arbuthnot; Ralph Glyn; P. J. Hannon; L. J. Maxse; Lord Willoughby de Broke; and Croft. Individuals who joined in the following weeks included Lord Londesborough; A. E. Beck; P. S. Foster, MP; Sir H. S. King, MP; Louis Stanley Johnson; Capt. H. D. Brackenbury; MP; W. A. Mount, MP; J. E. W. Galbraith; G. V. A. Monkton-Arundel; Maj. Martin Archer-Shee, MP; Hon. E. A. Fitzroy; Vaughn Williams; Hon. William Ormsby-Gore, MP; William Orde-Powlett, MP; Oliver Locker-Lampson, MP; Sir William Bull, MP; Lord Leconfield; Col. Richard Chaloner, MP; and Capt. Leslie Wilson.

104. "Unionist Reveille," *The Times;* "Unionist Forward Movement. Programme and Campaign," *Morning Post;* "National Programme. Planks in New Unionist Platform. Definite Policy for the Constituencies," *Manchester Dispatch;* "Awakening of the Tories. Programme of the Insurgents," *Daily Chronicle,* 8 October 1910.

105. *Daily Chronicle,* 7 October 1910.
106. Frederick Edwin Smith (1872–1930), 1st Earl of Birkenhead (cr. 1922); distinguished barrister; MP (C), Walton division of Liverpool (1906–18), West Derby division of Liverpool (1918–19); solictor-general (1915); attorney-general (1915–19), lord chancellor (1919–22).
107. *Daily Chronicle,* 7 October 1910.

Chapter 7. Croft, the Reveille, and the Fight against Humdrum Toryism

1. "The Forward Movement. Why Unionism Must Fight," *Morning Advertiser,* 14 October 1910.
2. "Trumpet Call to Unionists," *Morning Post,* 14 October 1910.
3. "The Reveille Movement," *Birmingham Gazette,* 14 October 1910; Reveille Manifesto (1910), Croft Papers, CRFT 3/1.
4. Maxse to Croft, 19 October 1910, Croft Papers, CRFT 1/16 MA/25.
5. Maxse to Croft, 22 October 1910, Croft Papers, CRFT 1/16 MA/26.
6. "The Reveille Movement," *The Times;* "The Reveille Movement. Committee's Manifesto. Constructive Side of Unionism," *Morning Post;* "New Tory Charter. Five Points of Forward Manifesto," *Daily Chronicle,* 19 October 1910.
7. *Daily Chronicle,* 19 October 1910.
8. *Reveille Manifesto* (1910), Croft Papers, CRFT 3/2.
9. "Confusion of Politics", *The Times,* 19 October 1910.
10. *Morning Post,* 19 October 1910.
11. "Mr. Balfour on the Navy," *Daily Chronicle,* 20 October 1910.
12. "Lord Londonderry on Unionist's Policy," *The Times,* 20 October; "Tory Prince Ruperts. Lord Londonderry Advice to Rank Young Unionists," *Daily Chronicle,* 20 October 1910.
13. "Mr. Page Croft, M.P., at Bournemouth. Young Unionist Policy Outlined," *Bournemouth Guardian,* 15 October 1910.
14. Ibid.
15. "Reveille Leaders in Hull. A Constructive and National Programme," *Hull Daily Mail,* 26 October 1910.
16. "Enthusiastic Reveille Meeting. Unionist Policy Outlined," *Derby Express,* 28 October 1910.
17. Lord Malmesbury (letter), "The Reveille Movement," *Morning Post,* 3 November. Also see "Revolting Tories. They Think the Chancellor Less Dangerous than Mr. Balfour," *Daily Chronicle,* 3 November 1910.
18. *Morning Post,* 3 November 1910.
19. Ibid.
20. "Unionist Unrest and Its Causes. Needs of the Moment. Party Reform and Reorganisation. By a Unionist M.P.", *Morning Post,* 11 November 1910.
21. Lloyd George's Memorandum on the Formation of a Coalition, 17 August 1910, in Petrie, *Austen Chamberlain,* i, 381–88.
22. Jenkins, *Balfour's Poodle,* 164–65; Gollin, *The Observer and J. L. Garvin,* 207; P. Rowland, *David Lloyd George: A Biography* (New York: Barrie and Jenkins, 1975), 239–41; J. Grigg, *Lloyd George: The People's Champion, 1902–1911* (Berkeley: University of California Press, 1978), 265–69; J. Campbell, *F. E. Smith: First Earl of Birkenhead* (London: Jonathan Cape, 1985), 220–31.
23. "The Unionist Problem and Its Solution," *The Observer,* 9 October 1910.

24. F. E. Smith to Bonar Law, 19 October 1910, Bonar Law Papers, BL/18/6/126.
25. Lloyd George to Balfour, 11 October 1910, Balfour Papers, Add MSS 49692, fos. 216–17; Chamberlain, *Politics from Inside,* 279–97.
26. F. E. Smith to Balfour, 30 October 1910, Bodl Lib, Sandars Papers, MSS Eng hist, c. 761 fo. 290.
27. Frederick Scott Oliver (1864–1934); columnist, publicist, and wealthy businessman; author, *Alexander Hamilton (1906), Federalism and Home Rule (1910), Ordeal by Battle* (1915); influenced the establishment of Croft's National party in 1917.
28. Gollin, *The Observer* and *J. L. Garvin,* 204–34.
29. Garvin to Maxse, 6 October 1910, Maxse Papers, MSS 462/729.
30. Garvin to Maxse, 10 October 1910, Maxse Papers, MSS 462/739.
31. Garvin to Balfour, 17 October 1910, Balfour Papers, Add MSS 49795, fos. 86–87.
32. *The Reveille Movement. Manifesto on Home Rule* (Ware, 1910), Croft Papers, CRFT 3/2; *Morning Post,* 4 November; *Daily Mail,* 4 November; *National Review* (December 1910).
33. Croft to Blumenfeld, 9 November 1910, HLRO, Blumenfeld Papers, CRO/6.
34. Sandars to Blumenfeld, 7 November 1910, Blumenfeld Papers, SAN/5.
35. Garvin to Maxse, 6 November 1910, Maxse Papers, MSS 462/570.
36. Maxse to Garvin, 7 November 1910, Garvin Papers.
37. Croft to Long, 13 November 1910, Croft Papers, CRFT 1/15 LO/7/1.
38. Aretas Akers-Douglas (1851–1926), Viscount Chilston (cr. 1911); barrister; MP (C), East Kent (1880–85), St. Augustine division of Kent (1885–1911); chief whip (1892–95); first commissioner of works (1895–1902); home secretary (1902–5).
39. Jenkins, *Balfour's Poodle,* 166.
40. Journal, 9 November 1910, in Esher (ed.), *Reginald Viscount Esher,* iii, 30.
41. H. Nicolson, *King George V* (London: Constable, 1952), 133.
42. Sykes, *Tariff Reform in British Politics,* 232.
43. Sandars to Garvin, 11 November 1910, Garvin Papers.
44. A. Chamberlain to J. Chamberlain, 13 November 1910, in *Politics from Inside,* 298–300.
45. A. Chamberlain to J. Chamberlain, 16 November 1910, ibid., 300–301.
46. Journal, 16 November 1910, in Vincent (ed.), *The Crawford Papers,* 167.
47. "Mr. Balfour and the Crisis. The Unionist Programme," *The Times,* 18 November 1910; National Union, *The Policy of the Unionist Party. A Speech by Rt. Hon. A.J. Balfour at Nottingham on November 17, 1910 to the 44th Annual Conference of National Union of Conservative and Constitutional Associations,* NU No. 1398 (London, 1910), 5–6; Archives of the British Conservative Party. Series I: Pamphlets and Leaflets, 1910/174; "Episodes," *National Review* (December 1910), 724–25.
48. "The Unionist Reveille. A Call to the British People," *The Times,* 25 November 1910; Croft Papers, CRFT 3/2.
49. Gollin, *The* Observer *and J. L. Garvin,* 245–68.
50. N. Blewett, *The Peers, The Parties and the People: The British General Elections of 1910* (London: Macmillan, 1972), 182.
51. Bonar Law to Balfour, 28 November 1910, Bonar Law Papers, BL/18/8/14. His new posture is very curious because a few days earlier Bonar Law, surrounded by members of the Reveille and the Confederacy, publicly pledged his unconditional support for fiscal reform. "Mr. Bonar Law's Fighting Speech. The Unionist Policy a National One. Tariff Reform and Land Reform," *Morning Post,* 15 November 1910.

Notes to Chapter 8

52. Balfour to A. Chamberlain, 28 November 1910, Chamberlain Papers, AC/8/7/1; *Politics from Inside*, 303–4.
53. A. Chamberlain to Balfour, 29 November 1910, Balfour Papers, Add MSS 49736, fos. 122–24.
54. Bonar Law to Sandars, 29 November 1910, Balfour Papers, Add MSS 49693, fos. 6–9.
55. "Mr. Balfour at the Albert Hall. Tariff Reform and the Referendum," *The Times*, 30 November 1910; National Union, *Tariff Reform and the Referendum. Speech at the Royal Albert Hall, London, November 25, 1910*, NU No. 1437 (London, 1910), 1–8; Archives of the British Conservative Party. Series I: Pamphlets and Leaflets, 1910/212.
56. H. D. Bralley, "St. Loe Strachey and the Politics of Dilemma: A Study of Political Journalism During the Edwardian Era (unpublished Ph.D. diss., University of South Carolina, 1971), 202.
57. A. Chamberlain to Lansdowne, 18 December 1910, in *Politics from Inside*, 311–12.
58. Long to Balfour, 20 January 1911, Balfour Papers, Add MSS 49777, fos. 79–81.
59. "Mr. Croft's Campaign," *Bournemouth Echo*, 29 November 1910.
60. "Conservative Mass Meeting. Lord Northcote Defends Peers. Mr. Croft Lashes Out," *Bournemouth Visitors' Directory*, 3 December 1910.
61. "The Nation's Safety. Mr. Page Croft on Meaning of the Struggle," *Evening Standard*, 17 November 1910.
62. *Bournemouth Echo*, 8 December 1910.
63. National Union, *The Official Policy of the Conservative and Unionist Party with Regard to the House of Lords*, NU No. 1388 (London, 1910), 1–8; and *The Reform of the House of Lords. Mr. Balfour's Scheme*, NU No. 1392 (London, 1910), 1–4; Archives of the British Conservative Party, 1910/164 and 1910/168.
64. "Mr. Page Croft at Westbourne," *Bournemouth Echo*, 24 November 1910.
65. *Bournemouth Vistors' Directory*, 3 December 1910.
66. "Mr. H. Page Croft, MP, Borough Member at Bournemouth," *Bournemouth Echo*, 19 November 1910.
67. Maxse to Goulding, 10 December 1910, Wargrave Papers, MSS 2/74.
68. Maxse to Bonar Law, 14 December 1910, Bonar Law Papers, BL/18/6/145.
69. Maxse to Goulding, 19 December 1910, Wargrave Papers, MSS 2/75.

Chapter 8. Croft, Conservative Party Politics, and the Balfour Question

1. "Unionist Reveille Movement," *The Times*, 22 December 1910. Croft also commented that "the Referendum, a straightforward endeavour to submit Home Rule and Tariff Reform to the electors, has been labelled as a dodge, and this most democratic offer has been rejected by that party which fears nothing more than a straight vote on a straight issue." This provoked a private protest to Lord Malmesbury from Maxse who feared that he sensed a softening in the Reveille spirits. Malmesbury persuaded him not to wage a purge against the Reveille committee, arguing that "the moral blame" was in "the rottenness of our Party Organisation." Malmesbury to Maxse, 28 December 1910, Maxse Papers, MSS 462/789–90.
2. Croft, *My Life of Strife*, 57.
3. Plain Tory, "How Unionism Can Win: I-Organisation," *Morning Post*, 27 January 1911.

Notes to Chapter 8

4. Plain Tory, "How Unionists Can Win: II-Men," *Morning Post,* 28 January 1911.

5. Ibid.

6. Plain Tory, "How Unionism Can Win: III-Tactics: Weak Leaders and Tariff Reform," *Morning Post,* 30 January 1911.

7. Ibid.

8. Plain Tory, "How Unionism Can Win: IV-Strategy: A British Policy," *Morning Post,* 3 February 1911.

9. Ibid.

10. Ibid.

11. Selborne to Balfour, 24 December 1910, in G. Boyce (ed.), *The Crisis of British Unionism: Lord Selborne's Domestic Political Papers, 1885–1922* (London: The Historians' Press, 1987), 49.

12. Amery to Bonar Law, 16 December 1910, Bonar Law Papers, BL/18/6/146.

13. Lawrence to Chamberlain, 10 December 1910, Chamberlain Papers, AC/8/7/23.

14. C. Petrie, *Walter Long and His Times* (London: Hutchinson & Co., 1936), 149–53.

15. Esher to Oliver Brett, 15 January 1911, in Esher (ed.), *Journals and Letters of Reginald Viscount Esher,* iii, 45.

16. Ramsden, *The Age of Balfour and Baldwin,* 57–58.

17. Balfour to Akers-Douglas, 17 January 1911, in 3d Viscount Chilston, *Chief Whip: The Political Life and Times of Aretas Akers-Douglas, 1st Viscount Chilston* (London: Routledge, Kegan & Paul, 1961), 347–48.

18. *The Times* and *Morning Post,* 1 February 1911.

19. "The Reveille. Rally of Unionists at Barton Hill. Mr. Page Croft and Preference," *Bristol Times,* 3 February; "The Future of Unionism. Mr. Page Croft on Organisation and Preference," *Morning Post,* 3 February 1911.

20. "Episodes," *National Review* (February 1911), 913–14.

21. Balcarres to Lady Wantage, 6 February 1911, in Vincent (ed.), *The Crawford Papers,* 175–76.

22. *Unionist Organisation Committee,* Final Report, June 1911; quoted in Ramsden, *The Age of Balfour and Baldwin,* 59–60.

23. Journals, 19 December 1910, in Vincent (ed.), *The Crawford Papers,* 170–71.

24. Ramsden, *Age of Balfour and Baldwin,* 61–62.

25. *The Times,* 26 October 1911; R. B. Jones, "Balfour's Reform of Party Reorganization," *Bulletin of the Institute for Historical Research* 38 no. 97 (May 1965), 99–101.

26. *Parl. Deb.,* vol. 21 (22 February 1911), c. 2038–42.

27. Croft, "The Constitutional Crisis," *Morning Post,* 8 March 1911.

28. *Parl. Deb.,* vol. 22 (2 March 1911), c. 681–86; vol. 25 (15 May 1911), c. 1782–86.

29. "A United Party. The Opposition and Lord's Reform. Reveille Leader's Views," *Evening Standard,* 23 March; "Primrose League. Mr. H. Page Croft on Lords' Question," *Bournemouth Echo,* 21 April; "Conservative Association," *Bournemouth Echo,* 29 April 1991; "Mr. H. Page Croft and the Preamble. His Reasons for Voting Against It," 5 May; "The Veto Bill. Speech by Mr. Page Croft, MP," 5 May; "The Veto Bill. Borough Member's Speech," *Bournemouth Echo,* 12 May 1911.

30. *Parl. Deb.,* vol. 25 (10 May 1911), c. 1304–9.

31. Long to Maxse, 22 June 1911, in Petrie, *Walter Long and His Times,* 153–54.

32. "Episodes," *National Review* (July 1911), 732–33.

33. Gollin, *The Observer and J. L. Garvin,* 336.

34. Journals, 1 July 1911, in Vincent (ed.), *The Crawford Papers*, 189.
35. Ibid., 190–92, Journals, 6 and 7 July 1911; Esher to George V, 5 July 1911, in Esher (ed.), *Reginald Viscount Esher*, iii, 54–55.
36. Frederick George Banbury (1873–1936), Baron Banbury (cr. 1924), Bt (1902); financier and stockbroker; chairman, Great Northern Rwy; MP (C), Peckham (1892–1906), City of London (1906 by election-1924).
37. "Tory MPs in Revolt. Peers Asked to Fight to the Bitter End," *Daily News*, 13 July; "Resign or Resist?" *Commentator*, 19 July 1911. Those signing the circular included Basil Peto, Archer Shee, George Sandys, A. Hammersley, George Lloyd, D. Macmaster, Alan Burgoyne, Henry Tyrell, Rupert Gwynne, Viscount Wolmer, and Henry Page Croft.
38. Asquith to Balfour, 20 July 1911, in Roy Jenkins, *Asquith* (London: Collins, 1966), 226–27.
39. George Wyndham (1863–1913); married daughter of 9th Earl of Scarborough (and widow of Earl Grosvenor); Coldstream Guards (decorated); MP (C), Dover (1889–1913); private secretary to Balfour (1887–92); parliamentary undersecretary state for War (1898–1900); chief secretary for Ireland (1900–5).
40. Journals, 21 July 1911, in Vincent (ed.), *The Crawford Papers*, 196; Dugdale, *Arthur James Balfour*, ii, 68–69.
41. Lord [Thomas Wodehouse] Newton, *Lord Lansdowne: A Biography* (London: Macmillan and Co., 1929), 421–22; Dugdale, *Arthur James Balfour*, ii, 69.
42. Maxse to Sandars, 21 July 1911, Balfour Papers, Add MSS 49861, fo. 274.
43. "Revolting Peers. Great Rally Against the Policy of Surrender," *Daily Express*, 24 July 1911.
44. Croft, "Tyranny and Revolution," *Bournemouth Visitors' Directory*, 22 July 1911; "The Political Crisis. Strong Speech by Mr. Page Croft," *Bournemouth Visitors's Directory*, 29 July 1911.
45. *Parl. Deb.*, vol. 28 (24 July 1911), c. 1467–84.
46. Journals, 24 July 1911, in Vincent (ed.), *The Crawford Papers*, 198–99.
47. "The Commons and the Veto Bill. Extraordinary and Deplorable Scenes. Prime Minister Shouted Down," *Daily Telegraph*, 25 July 1911.
48. *The Times*, 26 July 1911.
49. Dugdale, *Arthur James Balfour*, ii, 69. A most interesting examination of Balfour is given by the chief whip, Lord Balcarres. Although Balfour had been "pressed so much to give a lead that silence is no longer possible," he nevertheless was convinced "that so far as he is concerned he can only support Lansdowne. No alternative is possible—none indeed is conceivable." Journals, 25 July 1911, in Vincent (ed.), *The Crawford Papers*, 200–202.
50. Long to Halsbury, 25 July 1911, in Petrie, *Walter Long and His Times*, 159.
51. Croft, "The Crisis. The New Spirit," *Morning Post*, 9 August 1911.
52. Gollin, *The Observer and J. L. Garvin*, 339; Amery, *My Political Life*, i, 378.
53. Croft to Maxse, 12 June 1911, Maxse Papers, MSS 463/77–78.
54. "The Political Crisis," *Bournemouth Visitors' Directory*, 29 July 1911.
55. Croft, "The Political Crisis," *Standard*, 27 July 1911.
56. Croft, *Morning Post*, 9 August 1911.
57. Diaries, 6–12 August 1911, in Williamson (ed.), *Diaries and Letters of William Bridgeman*, 48–49; *Parl. Deb.*, vol. 29 (7 August 1911), c. 759.
58. *Parl. Deb.*, vol. 29 (7 August 1911), c. 918–22.
59. *Parl. Deb.* [Lords], vol. 9 (10 August 1911), c. 1073–76.
60. Diaries, 16 August 1911, in Williamson (ed.), *Diaries and Letters of William Bridgeman*, 50.
61. William Clive Bridgeman (1864–1935), Viscount Bridgeman of Leigh (cr.

1929); grandson of earl of Bradford; MP (C), Oswestry division of Shropshire (1906–29); private secretary to colonial secretary (1889–92) and to chancellor of the Exchequer (1895–99); a Conservative whip (1911); 1st lord of Admiralty (1924–29).

62. Ibid., 49–50, Diaries, 15 August 1911.

63. Ibid., 50, W. Bridgeman to C. Bridgeman, 16 August 1911.

64. Croft to Willoughby de Broke, 13 August 1911, HLRO, Willoughby de Broke Papers, MSS WB/3/24.

65. Lord Willoughby de Broke, *The Passing Years* (London: 1924), 306.

66. Willoughby de Broke to Selborne, 12 August 1911, Selborne Papers, MSS 74/176.

67. J. Barnes (ed.), *The Leo Amery Diaries, 1896–1929* (London: 1980), ii, 82.

68. "The New Unionist Leader," *Daily Chronicle,* 2 October 1911.

69. Smith to A. Chamberlain, 13 August 1911, in E. Birkenhead, *"F. E:" The Life of F. E. Smith, First Earl of Birkenhead* (London: Eyre and Spottiswoode, 1959), 167–78.

70. Wyndham to Selborne, 16 August 1911, in Boyce (ed.), *Lord Selborne's Domestic Political Papers,* 62–63.

71. "Episodes," *National Review* (September 1911), 16; also see *The Observer,* 13 August 1911.

72. B.M.G., "The Champion Scuttler," *National Review* (October 1911), 200–219.

73. "The New Spirit," *Daily Express,* 7 September 1911.

74. Wyndham to Selborne, 16 August; Willoughby de Broke to Selborne, 17 August; Wyndham to Selborne, 19 August; Selborne to Wyndham, 22 August; Wyndham to Selborne, 23 August; Selborne to A. Chamberlain, 4 September 1911 in Boyce (ed.), *Lord Selborne's Domestic Political Papers,* 61–71.

75. Ibid., 65–66, Selborne to Wyndham, 22 August 1911.

76. "Imperial Mission," *Morning Post,* 1 July 1911.

77. Steel-Maitland to Halsbury, 11 September 1911, BL, Halsbury Papers, Add MSS 56374.

78. Selborne to Halsbury, 2 October 1911, Halsbury Papers, Add MSS 56374; Willoughby de Broke to A. Chamberlain, 7 October, Chamberlain Papers, AC/9/3/8; N. Chamberlain to A. Chamberlain, 7 October 1911, in Petrie, *Life and Letters of Austen Chamberlain,* i, 293–94.

79. Sandars, "A Note on the Events Leading to Mr. Balfour's Resignation," 8 November 1911, Balfour Papers, Add MSS 49767, fos. 296–99.

80. Lord Balcarres' Journals, 30 September 1911, Vincent (ed.), *The Crawford Papers,* 224–25; Herbert Nield to Balfour, 20 October 1911, Balfour Papers, Add MSS 49861, fos. 359–60.

81. Sandars to Balfour, 14 August 1911, Balfour Papers, Add MSS 49767, fos. 155–61.

82. Malmesbury to A. Chamberlain, 11 October 1911, Chamberlain Papers, AC/9/3/40.

83. "Forward Unionist Movement," *Morning Post; The Times;* "Halsbury Club," *Daily Chronicle;* "Halsbury Club: Union of 'No Surrender' Supporters," *Daily Express,* 13 October 1911; Lord Selborne, Memorandum on "Halsbury Club" [November 1911], in Boyce (ed.), *Lord Selborne's Domestic Political Papers,* 77–78.

84. Petrie, *Life and Letters of Austen Chamberlain,* i, 294.

85. Halsbury (letter), "Unionist Leadership. The Halsbury Club," *The Times,* 18 October 1911; Petrie, *Life and Letters of Austen Chamberlain,* i, 294.

86. Diaries, 29 October 1911, in John Ramsden (ed.), *Real Old Tory Politics: The Political Diaries of Sir Robert Sanders, Lord Bayford, 1910–35* (London: The Historians' Press, 1984), 34.

87. Long to Balfour, 19 October 1911, Balfour Papers, Add MSS 49777, fos. 108–11; Long to Buckle, 23 October 1911, in Petrie, *Walter Long and His Times,* 169; Gwynne to Maxse, 23 October 1911, Maxse Papers, MSS 464/823; A. Chamberlain, *Politics from Inside,* 372; *Morning Post,* 19 October 1911.
88. *Morning Post,* 19 October 1911.
89. Maxse to Croft, 18 October 1911, Croft Papers, CRFT 1/16 MA/28/1–2.
90. Ibid.
91. Cf. Peter Fraser, "The Unionist Debacle of 1911 and Balfour's Retirement," *Journal of Modern History,* 35 no. 4 (1963), 354–65.
92. Journals, 30 September 1911, in Vincent (ed.), *The Crawford Papers,* 224–25.
93. Ibid., 228–29, Memorandum, 2 October 1911.
94. Goulding to Garvin, 10 November 1911, Garvin Papers; Gollin, *The Observer and J. L. Garvin,* 359.
95. Croft to Bonar Law, 30 November 1911, Bonar Law Papers, BL/24/4/92. On 12 November 1911, Bernhard Wise sent Bonar Law a copy of *The New Order,* which had been put together by the Confederacy in 1908. Wise to Bonar Law, BL/24/3/16.

Chapter 9. Militant Unionism or a National and Imperial Party

1. Hewins, *The Apologia of an Imperialist,* i, 266.
2. E. Ions, *James Bryce and American Democracy, 1870–1922* (London: Macmillan, 1968), 233.
3. *Parl. Deb.,* vol. 38 (6 May 1912), c. 24–25.
4. "The Reveille. Mr. Page Croft and Preference. The Canadian Danger," *Bristol Times,* 3 February 1911.
5. Ibid.
6. William Maxwell Aitken (1879–1964), Baron Beaverbrook (cr. 1916), Bt (1916); born and educated in New Brunswick, Canada; MP (C), Ashton-under-Lyne (1910–16); close associate of Bonar Law; established newspaper empire with *Daily Express, Sunday Express,* and *Evening Standard.*
7. Alfred Charles Harmsworth (1865–1922), Viscount Northcliffe (cr. Baron, 1905, Viscount 1918); established newspaper empire with *Evening News, Daily Mail, Daily Mirror,* and *The Times.*
8. Gollin, *The Observer and J. L. Garvin,* 292–93.
9. Hewins, *The Apologia of an Imperialist,* i, 269.
10. *The Times,* 3 February; "A Plea for Delay of Judgment," *Daily Mail,* 3 February 1911.
11. *The Times,* 8 February 1911. Those attending included Croft; Lord Leith of Fyvie; Lord Wolverton; Sir William R. Russell; Major Archer-Shee, MP; Basil Peto, MP; Almeric Paget, MP; Dr. Alfred Hillier, MP; and J. G. Jenkins.
12. *Parl. Deb.,* vol. 21 (8 February 1911), c. 371–78.
13. Ibid., vol. 21 (13 February 1911), c. 684; *The Times,* 9 Feb; 14 February 1911.
14. *Parl. Deb.,* vol. 21 (20 February 1911), c. 1519–22, 1695–96.
15. *Bath Chronicle,* 18 February 1911.
16. Croft, "The Imperial Preference Campaign," *The Times,* 1 March 1911.
17. "Imperial Preference. The Canadian Agreement," *Morning Advertiser,* 2 March 1911.

18. Ibid.

19. Croft, "Why I Am in Favour of Tariff Reform," *The Empire Illustrated* (May 1911), 44.

20. "Episodes," *National Review* (February 1911), 920.

21. Croft to Maxse, 2 February 1911, Maxse Papers, MSS 455/s232.

22. Sanders to Balfour, 5 January 1911, Balfour Papers, Add MSS 49767, fos. 78–79.

23. Croft, "Imperial Preference Campaign," *The Times*, 1 March 1911.

24. "Imperial Preference Campaign," *Morning Post*, 9 March; "Meaning of Imperial Preference. An Appeal to the Electors," *Morning Post*, 11 March 1911.

25. "Tariff Reform in Herts," *Morning Post*, 11 March; "Tariff Reform in Herts," *Herts and Essex Observer*, 18 March 1911.

26. Imperial Mission, *Imperial Preference Campaign. Great East and West St. Pancras Mass Meeting. Speech Delivered by Mr. Henry Page Croft, MP, at the Prince of Wales' Baths, Kentish Town, on March 28th, 1911* (London: St. Pancras Gazette, 1911), Croft Papers, CRFT 3/2.

27. Ibid.

28. Ibid. The St. Pancras meeting was followed by the first annual meeting of the Imperial Mission held 27 May under the presidency of the earl of Dundonald. The meeting reported that since its creation in February 1910 the Imperial Mission had held four hundred meetings and addressed five hundred thousand people. "Imperial Mission. Work of the Pioneers," *Morning Post*, 27 May 1911.

29. *Parl. Deb.*, vol. 26 (31 May 1911), c. 1111–19; "The Reciprocity Agreement," *The Times*, 1 June 1911.

30. Croft, "The Greatest Weapon for Peace and Justice," *Nash's Magazine*, June 1911.

31. "Imperial Mission," *Morning Post*, 1 July 1911.

32. "Empire Politics. Significant Non-Party Movement," *Standard*, 7 September 1911.

33. "Empire Unity. What the Imperial Mission Is Doing. Great Forward Movement," *Evening Standard*, 1 August 1911.

34. Ibid.

35. Capt. Sir Ion Hamilton Benn (1863–1961), Bt (1920); businessman; London local government; director, Port of London (1909–61); served in 1914–18 (despatches, DSO); MP (C), Greenwich (1910–22); CB.

36. Capt. George John Sandys (1875–1937); Pembroke College, Cambridge; served South African War (1899–1902), BEF, 1914 (wounded); MP (C), Wells divsion of Somerset (1910–18); foreign service (1921–25).

37. Arthur Shirley Benn (1858–1937), Baron Glenravel (cr. 1936), Bt (1926); substantial business interests; officer, Association of British Chambers of Commerce, Federation of Chambers of Commerce, and International Chamber of Commerce; unsuccessful contest in 1906; MP (C), Plymouth (1910–29), Park division of Sheffield (1931–35); Kt.

38. "Imperial Mission," *The Times*, 16 November 1911.

39. The Times, 16 November 1911; Duke of Marlborough to Croft, 4 November 1911, Croft Papers, CRFT 1/16 MA/18; Milner to Croft, 24 August 1911, Croft Papers, CRFT 1/16 MI/2. Croft sought to enlist Earl Grey, who had just retired as the governor-general of Canada (1904–11), as a vice president, but the latter, while flattered, asked for time to consider the request. There is no correspondence or press report indicating Grey ever subsequently joined. Grey to Croft, 11 November 1911, Croft Papers, CRFT 1/12 GR/7. Grey had served as administrator for Rhodesia (1896–97), director of the British South African Company (1898–1904), and as

governor-general for Canada (1904–11). Croft also approached Lord Roberts who had expressed interest in the work of the Imperial Mission. Roberts to Croft, 14 October 1911, Croft Papers, CRFT 1/18 RO/2.

40. Hallam Tennyson (1852–1928), 2d Baron Tennyson; Trinity College, Cambridge; hon. colonel, South Australian Artillery, 7th Victorian Light Horse; governor and commander-in-chief, South Australia (1899–1902); acting governor, Commonwealth of Australia (1902); governor-general, Australia (1902–4); GCMG, KCMG, PC.

41. Henry Stafford Northcote (1846–1911), Baron Northcote (cr. 1900); second son of Sir Stafford Northcote (earl of Iddesleigh); married daughter of Baron Mount Stephen; clerk at the Foreign Office; private secretary to Lord Salisbury at Constantinople (1876–77), to the chancellor of the exchequer (1877–80); financial secretary, war office (1885–86); governor of Bombay (1899–1903); governor-general of Australia (1903–8).

42. Alexander John Forbes-Leith (1847–1925), Baron Leith of Fyvie (cr. 1905); the son of Admiral Leith; lieutenant, RN (1860); served in New Zealand war (1864–65); associated with Croft's National party in 1917.

43. Frederic Glyn (1861–1932), 4th Baron Wolverton; succeeded brother 1888; married daughter of earl of Dudley; lord-in-waiting (1892–96); served in South Africa, Imperial Yeomanry; vice chamberlain of Royal Household (1902–5).

44. Alfred Hillier (1858–1911); physician; president of South African Medical Congress; Reform Committee, Johannesburg; Royal Colonial Institute; unsuccessful contest, 1906; MP (C), North Herts (1910–11); author, *South African Studies, The Commonwealth,* and *A Study of the Federal System of Political Economy.*

45. Almeric Hugh Paget (1861–1949), Baron Queensborough (cr. 1918); financier; officer, Tariff Reform League; unsuccessful contest (1906); MP (C), Cambridge (1910–17).

46. *Standard,* 7 September 1911.

47. Ibid.

48. W. Orsmby-Gore, "Canada and Tariff Reform," 8 November; "Imperial Preference. Unionist Members Canadian Experience," *Morning Post,* 15 November 1910.

49. Members included Lord Leith of Fyvie, Lord Wolverton; Sir Spencer Maryon-Wilson; Major Martin Archer-Shee, MP; Henry Page Croft, MP; and Almeric Paget, MP, Basil Peto, MP.

50. Members included Northcote, Tennyson, Sir William Cooper; Hon. J. G. Jenkins; Alan Burgoyne, MP; Frank Fox; J. E. Pounds; and Assheton Pownall.

51. Members included Sir William R. Russell, Dr. E. G. Levinge, G. A. McL. Buckley, Joseph Gould, and Arthur E. G. Rhodes.

52. Members included Sir Charles Tupper; Sir William Max Aitken, MP; Ion Hamilton Benn, MP; Colonel A. D. Davidson, E. W. McL. Brown; W. Foster Cockshutt; W. MacLeod; L. Winfield Malloy; Frederick C. Salter; and F. Williams Taylor.

53. Members included John Norton-Griffiths, MP; Dr. A. P. Hillier, MP; Major Frank Johnson; Martin Hall; P. J. Hannon; and C. Leonard.

54. Members included Lord Ampthill, Colonel Sir Howard Melliss, Major W. W. Warner, L. Davidson, and W. Burton Stewart. "The Imperial Mission. The Forthcoming Campaign," *Morning Post,* 14 September 1911.

55. *Standard,* 7 September 1911.

56. *Morning Post,* 14 September; "Imperial Unity Meeting," *Telegraph,* 16 September; "Imperial Mission. Arrangements for Winter Campaign," *Standard,* 22 September 1911.

57. "Reciprocity Dead. Canada Votes for Empire. Political Landslide," *Morning Post,* 23 September 1911.

58. Croft, "The Fight for Imperial Union," *Morning Post,* 23 September 1911.
59. Grey to Croft, 11 November 1911, Croft Papers, CRFT 1/12 GR/7.
60. Croft, "The Fight for Imperial Union," *Morning Post,* 23 September 1911.
61. Ibid.
62. Ibid.
63. Lord Roberts (letter), *The Times,* 9 October 1911.
64. "The Imperial Triumph in Canada," *Morning Post,* 18 October 1911.
65. Ibid.
66. Ibid.
67. Ibid.
68. Maxse to Croft, 18 October 1911, CRFT 1/16 MA/28/1–2.
69. Ibid. In the *Daily Chroncile,* Maxse's speech was attributed to Croft. See "B.M.G. Tory Speakers Attack Their Leader. Canada Meeting at Chelsea. Turns to Indignation Demonstration," 18 October; "Mr. Maxse and the *Daily Chronicle,"* 20 October; "B.M.G. Canadian on the Anti-Balfour Demonstration," *Daily Chronicle,* 21 October 1911; L. J. Maxse (letter), *The Times,* 20 October 1911; Maxse to Croft, 18 October 1911, CRFT 1/16 MA/28/1–2. At Bournemouth, Croft established a Junior Imperialist League affiliate, which he claimed had five hundred members by the end of the year. *Bournemouth Visitors' Directory,* 14 October and 13 December 1911.
70. "Political Notes," *Morning Post,* 26 October 1911.
71. Imperial Mission, *Great and Enthusiastic Demonstration at the Queen's Hall. Lord Selborne on the Destiny of the Empire. Mr. Henry Page Croft, M.P., on the Imperial Brotherhood* (London, 1911); Croft Papers (31 October 1911), CRFT 3/2; "The Imperial Mission. Lord Selborne on the Destiny of the Empire. The Dominions and World Politics," *Morning Post,* 1 November 1911.
72. Croft to Aitken, 22 September 1911, HLRO, Beaverbrook Papers, BBK C/101; Aitken to Croft, 25 September 1911, BBK C/101.
73. Imperial Mission, *Lord Selborne on the Destiny of the Empire.*
74. Ibid. The net emigration from the United Kingdom in 1910 was 241,164. D. Butler and G. Butler, *British Political Facts, 1900–1985* (New York: St. Martin's Press, 1986), 325.
75. Croft to Aitken, 1 December 1911, Beaverbrook Papers, BBK C/101.
76. *Newcastle Journal,* 6 November; *Northern Daily Mail,* 8 November; *Jarrow Express,* 11 November 1911.
77. "The Tariff Reform League. Address by Mr. Page Croft, MP," *Southern Times,* 14 October; "Conservative Club Dinner at Boscombe. Speeches by the Earl of Malmesbury and Mr. H. Page Croft, MP," *Bournemouth Visitors' Directory,* 21 October; "Primrose League Gathering. Enthusiastic Scene at Bournemouth. Address by Mr. Page Croft," *Bournemouth Visitors' Directory,* 18 November; "Work of the Imperial Mission," *Morning Post,* 29 November; "Reading Conservative Association," *Reading Mercury,* 2 December; "Richmond Park Conservatives. Speech by Mr. Page Croft, MP," *Bournemouth Visitors's Directory,* 2 December; "Imperial Mission Meeting at Branksome. Speech by Mr. Page Croft, MP," *Bournemouth Visitors' Directory,* 13 December 1911.
78. Croft to Aitken, 1 December 1911, Beaverbrook Papers, BBK C/101. See also Croft, "The Imperial Mission," *Saturday Review,* 25 November 1911.
79. Imperial Mission, *The Imperial Mission. A Meeting under the Auspices of the Imperial Mission Was Held at Caxton hall, Westminster, S.W., on Tuesday, December 12th 1911. Sir Spencer Maryon-Wilson, Bt. in the Chair. Mr. Henry Page Croft and Mrs. Claire Fitz-Gibbons on Trade Relations of the Empire* (London, 1911); Croft Papers, CRFT 3/3.

80. Ibid.
81. Croft to Bonar Law, 30 November 1911, Bonar Law Papers, BL/24/4/92.
82. Imperial Mission, *The Imperial Mission*, 14–17.

Chapter 10. Croft, Bonar Law, and the Betrayal of the Imperial Idea

1. Duncannon to Bonar Law, 7 December 1911, Bonar Law Papers, BL/24/5/119; Duncannon to Bonar Law, 11 December 1911, BL/24/5/131.
2. Croft to Bonar Law, 14 December 1911, Bonar Law Papers, BL/24/5/137.
3. Bonar Law to Croft, 15 January 1912, Croft Papers, CRFT 1/5 BO/3.
4. Croft then approached Joseph Chamberlain who supplied the preface within a few days. The book was then published in March. H. P. Croft, *The Path of Empire* (London: J. Murray, 1912).
5. *Spectator*, 3 February 1912.
6. *Parl. Deb.*, vol. 34 (22 February 1912), c. 813–20. In 1911 Britain lost 10.1 million work days to industrial disputes which itself was an unprecedented level. However, in 1912 lost work days soared to 40.9 million, which ranks only after 1921 and 1926 as the year with the highest lost work days. Butler, *British Political Facts*, 372–73.
7. *Parl. Deb.*, vol. 36 (3 April 1912), c. 1180–87.
8. See diaries of Lord Balcarres for January-April 1912, in Vincent (ed.), *Crawford Papers*, 260–74; and letters, January-April, in Chamberlain, *Politics from Inside*, 408–80.
9. Blake, *Unknown Prime Minister*, 108.
10. Salisbury to Bonar Law, 1 May 1912, Bonar Law Papers, BL/26/3/2; Derby to Bonar Law, 14 March 1912, BL/25/3/2. See generally R. S. Churchill, *Lord Derby: King of Lancashire* (New York: Putnam, 1959), 155–56, 162–63.
11. Bonar Law to Salisbury, 3 May 1912, Bonar Law Papers, BL/33/4/34.
12. Croft to Blumenfeld, 7 April 1912, Blumenfeld Papers, MSS CRO/7; Chaplin to Blumenfeld, 20 May 1912, Blumenfeld Papers, MSS CHAP/10.
13. *The Times*, 15 June 1912.
14. Croft, Peto, McNeill to Bonar Law, Thursday (20 June 1912), Bonar Law Papers, BL/33/2/20.
15. Comyn Platt to Bonar Law, Thursday (20 June 1912), Bonar Law Papers, BL/33/2/21.
16. Lawrence, "Unionism and Food Duties," *National Review* (July 1912), 844–52.
17. "Eve of the Poll in Manchester," *The Times*, 7 August 1912.
18. "Significance of the Figures. Unionist Free Traders' Choice," *The Times*, 9 August 1912.
19. Extract of Lord Derby's letter contained in a letter from Balcarres to Bonar Law, 5 September 1912, in Churchill, *Lord Derby*, 163.
20. "Future of Tariff Reform. Declaration of Lord Lansdowne. Mr. Bonar Law on Unionist Policy," *The Times*, 15 November 1912.
21. Churchill, *Lord Derby*, 163.
22. "Spirited Speech by Mr. Page Croft, MP. Unionist Policy Outlined." *Bournemouth Echo*, 21 November 1912.
23. Croft soon found himself in a statistical debate with Chiozza Money. See L. G. Chiozza Money, "Mr. Bonar Law's Readjustment of Taxation," *Westminster Gazette*, 19 November; Croft, 22 November; and Chiozza Money (rejoinder), 29

November 1912. Also see Croft, "The Dear Loaf Cry," *Globe*, 26 November; "Barum Unionists. Mr. H. P. Croft Addresses Mass Meeting," *North Devon Herald*, 4 December; Croft, "The End of the Dear Loaf Cry," *Stoke & Newington Recorder*, 13 December 1912.

24. "Great Unionist Meeting at Stockton. Speech by Mr. Page Croft, MP," *North Star*, 6 December; "Unionism at Darlaston. Straight Speaking by Mr. Page Croft, MP, on Imperialism," *Wednesbury News*, 7 December; Croft, "Some Thoughts on Canada," *Canadian News*, 7 December; "Tariff Reform Demonstration. Programme at Hull. Mr. Page Croft, MP, and Mr. Mark Sykes, MP," *Hull Daily Mail*, 7 December; "Tariff Reform in North Yorkshire. Speech by Mr. H. P. Croft," *North Star*, 9 December; "York and District Tariff Reform League. Mr. Page Croft, MP, and Radical Lies," *Yorkshire Herald*, 9 December 1912.

25. "Tariff Reform and Food Duties. Mr. Bonar Law's Policy. A Conference with the Dominions," *The Times*, 17 December. Also see "Keeping the Flag Flying. Trusting the People," *Daily Express*, 17 December 1912.

26. Bonar Law to Chaplin, 31 December 1912, Bonar Law Papers, BL/33/4/86.

27. Diary, 30 December 1912, in Williamson (ed.), *Diaries and Letters of William Bridgeman*, 65–66.

28. Chamberlain, *Politics from Inside*, 503.

29. "Mr. A. Chamberlain on Tariff Reform. The Question of Postponement," *The Times*, 17 December 1912.

30. Goulding to Garvin, 11 January 1913, Garvin Papers.

31. "Grave Tory Crisis. Party Chasm May Soon Be Unbridgeable. Leader and MPs Confer," *Daily Chronicle*, 3 January 1913.

32. "The Attitude of Lancashire. Misgivings of Unionist Free Traders," *The Times*, 18 December; "Mr. Bonar Law's Speech. Food Taxes and Unionist Policy," *The Times*, 19 December 1912.

33. A. Chamberlain to Mary Chamberlain, 7 January 1913, in *Politics from Inside*, 508.

34. Croft, "Unionist Party and Tariff Reform. Striking Letter from Member. Refuses to Be Driven from His Faith," *Bournemouth Visitors' Directory*, 4 January 1913.

35. Milner's diary, 1 January 1913, in Sykes, *Tariff Reform in British Politics*, 272.

36. Plain Tory, "Union and Empire," *Morning Post*, 2 January 1913.

37. R. McNeill, "Unionist Policy. Pleas for Unity," *The Times*, 24 December 1912.

38. Croft, "Unionist Party and Tariff Reform," *Bournemouth Visitors' Directory*, 4 January 1913.

39. J. Collings, "Unionist Policy," *The Times*, 7 January; Tory, "Liberal Opinion and Unionist Policy," *The Times*, 2 January 1913.

40. "The Debated Food Duties. Position at Westminster," *The Times*, 4 January 1913.

41. "The Tory Split. List of MPs Who Insist on Food Taxes," *Daily Chronicle*, 6 January 1913. The next day Ebenzer Parker disavowed this position, and Sir Harry Samuel declared himself in favor of the food duties. "Lost: A Hundred Die-Hards," *Daily Chronicle*, 7 January 1913.

42. Croft, *My Life of Strife*, 66; Amery, *My Political Life*, i, 415; diary, 6 January 1913, in Barnes (ed.), *The Leo Amery Diaries*, i, 91.

43. See Bonar Law Papers, BL/41/M/9 and BL/41/M/11; Chamberlain Papers, AC/9/5/46. Also see Petrie, *Life and Letters of Austen Chamberlain*, 330–32.

44. A. Chamberlain to J. Chamberlain, 8 January 1913, in *Politics from Inside*, 508–9.

45. Diary, 7 January 1913, in Barnes (ed.), *Leo Amery Diaries*, i, 91.

46. It generally has been suggested that only six MPs refused to sign. Blake, *Unknown Prime Minister,* 117. On the evening of 7 January Lord Balcarres nevertheless identifies the body of rebels who were refusing to cooperate: Amery, Astor, Croft, Hewins, Archer-Shee, Peto, Lloyd, Charles Yate, Alfred Bigland, and Rupert Gwynne. He also recorded his displeasure: "Who are they?...not one of these men has been in the H. of C. more than a couple of years! and their influence seems greater than either their ability or experience would justify." Journals, 7 January 1913, in Vincent (ed.), *The Crawford Papers,* 299. In Amery, *Joseph Chamberlain and the Tariff Reform Campaign,* vi, 983, Aitken, Amery, Chaplin, Lloyd and Croft are listed as the holdouts. However, on 10 January Balcarres lists eight abstainers: Lord Winterton, Amery, Archer-Shee, George Lloyd, Allen Bathurst, Charles Bathurst, Burdett Coutts, and Sir George Touche." Crawford Papers, 302. It should be no surpise that Robert Sanders, a party whip under Lord Balcarres, lists the same individuals. Diaries, 12 January 1913, in Ramsden (ed.), *The Political Diaries of Robert Sanders,* 59. Their reporting was surely based on the membership tally that is found in the Bonar Law papers. List of Members [n. d.], Bonar Law Papers, BL/41/M/10. I am grateful to R. J. Q. Adams for bringing this tally to my attention.

47. Gollin, *The Observer and J.L. Garvin,* 382.

48. Bonar Law to Balcarres, 13 January 1913, in "Mr. Bonar Law and His Party. Reply to Memorial. Modification of Unionist Programme," *The Times,* 15 January 1913.

49. Sykes, *Tariff Reform in British Politics,* 271; Blake, *Unknown Prime Minister,* 115–17.

50. "Unionist Tariff Policy. Mr. Bonar Law's Speech in Edinburgh," *The Times,* 25 January 1913.

51. Chaplin to T. W. A. Bagley, secretary of the TRL, in *The Times,* 8 January 1913.

52. A. Chamberlain, "The Unionist Party and Preference," *National Review* (February 1913), 915–25.

53. "Notes and News," *Bournemouth Echo,* 15 October 1913.

54. "Progress of Tariff Reform," *Morning Post,* 31 January 1914.

55. Croft, "Free Traders in the City. Mr. Page Croft's Reply to Lord Avebury," *Observer,* 26 January; "Bournemouth Unionists," *Bournemouth Echo,* 26 April; "The Borough Member. Reply to Mr. Ure on 'Lloyd George Finance,'" *Bournemouth Echo,* 17 May; "A Brilliant Attack on the Government By Mr. Page Croft, MP, and Mr. George Terrell, MP," *Devizes Gazette,* 24 July; Croft, "Free Trade vs. Protection," *Westminster Gazette,* 29 July; "Liberal Politics Criticised," *Bournemouth Echo,* 28 August; Croft, "Free Trade and Political Purity," *Daily Express,* 3 October; Croft, "Sir John Simon and Free Trade," *Morning Post,* 11 October; Croft, "The Results of Free Trade," *Morning Post,* 15 October 1913.

56. Croft, "Under False Claims. Imperial Mission Tactics," *Daily Chronicle,* 30 May 1913 (denied that the Imperial Mission was part of the Unionist party); Croft, "The Imperial Mission," *Westminster Gazette,* 11 July and "Empire Problems. Work of Imperial Mission," *Morning Post,* 4 July, and "Vitality of the Imperial Idea," *The Times,* 4 July 1913 (denied that the Imperial Mission was an adjunct of the TRL).

57. Croft, "The Working of the Imperial Mission," *Morning Post,* 3 February 1913.

58. Ibid.

59. "Inverness and Tariff Reform. Speech by Mr. Page Croft, MP," *Highland News,* 8 February 1913.

60. "Tariff Reform. The Preference Policy. Effective Food Prices," *Glasgow Herald,* 8 February 1913.

61. "Tariff Reform. Great Manchester Meeting. Important Speech by Mr. Page Croft, MP," *Hampshire Advertiser,* 15 February 1913.
62. "Tariff Reform League. Annual Meeting of the Herts Federation," *Hertfordshire Mercury,* 5 April 1913.
63. Croft, "Food Duties. Mr. Page Croft and the Edinburgh Policy," *Globe,* 5 May 1913.
64. Croft to Aitken, 28 December 1912, Beaverbrook Papers, BBK C/101.
65. "Tariff Reform. Mr. Page Croft, MP, on Town Hall Steps," *Bolton Evening Chronicle,* 11 October 1913.
66. "Tariff Reform and Farmers at York. Mr. H. Page Croft's Plain Speaking. Lloyd George Taken to Task. Tax on Foreign Barley Advocated," Yorkshire Herald, 13 October 1913; "Speeches of the Month. Mr. H. Page Croft, MP, at York, October 12th," Monthly Notes on Tariff Reform (November 1913), 307. A copy of the speech is also found in Bonar Law Papers, BL/30/4/26.
67. Ibid.
68. Duncannon to Bonar Law, 5 November 1913, Bonar Law Papers, BL/30/4/7.
69. Duncannon to Bonar Law, 11 November 1913, Bonar Law Papers, BL/30/4/25.
70. Croft to Bonar Law, 8 November 1913, Bonar Law Papers, BL/30/4/17.
71. Ibid.
72. Ibid.
73. Bonar Law to Croft, 10 November 1913, Croft Papers, CRFT 1/5 BO/4; (copy), Bonar Law Papers, BL/33/6/97.
74. Croft to Bonar Law, 11 November 1913, Bonar Law Papers, BL/30/4/26.
75. Ibid.; emphasis added.
76. Duncannon to Bonar Law, 11 November 1913, Bonar Law Papers, BL/30/4/25.
77. Pike Pease to Bonar Law, 12 November 1913, Bonar Law Papers, BL/30/4/29. Pike Pease (created Lord Daryngton in 1923) also was a Conservative whip, 1906—January 1910 and January 1911–15.
78. "Unionist Policy. Mr. Bonar Law on the Irish Crisis. Pledge to Ulster Renewed," *The Times,* 14 November 1913.
79. Duncannon to Bonar Law, 18 November 1913, Bonar Law Papers, BL/30/4/43; Duncannon to A. Chamberlain, 27 November 1913, Bonar Law Papers, BL/30/458.
80. "Mr. Law on the Ulster Problem. Labour and Tariff Reform," *The Times,* 22 November 1913.

Chapter 11. All for Naught

1. Croft, "The Imperial New Year," *The Empire Magazine* (January 1912), 549–50.
2. "The Right to Work. Growing Demand for Repeal of Trade Disputes Act," *Daily Graphic,* 28 August 1911.
3. Croft, "The Lesson of the Strike. A Tariff Essential," *Morning Post,* 22 August 1911.
4. *The Times,* 4 March 1914.
5. "Mr. Page Croft, MP, and the Women Franchise. Opposition to Conciliation

Bill. Borough Member Argues with Suffragists," *Bournemouth Guardian,* 18 March 1912.

6. Ibid.
7. Ibid.
8. Ibid.
9. "A Canvass in Hants. Anti-Suffrage Case," *Standard,* 19 March 1912. Also see "Mr. Page Croft and the Suffragists," *Bournemouth Visitors' Directory,* 26 March 1912.
10. Croft, "Citizen Army," in Lord Malmesbury (ed.), *The New Order: Studies in Unionist Policy,* 257–68.
11. Ibid.
12. "Borough Member and the Territorials," *Bournemouth Echo,* 18 July 1912.
13. *Daily Express,* 5 November 1912.
14. "National Service League. Address by Mr. H. Page Croft, MP," *Bournemouth Guardian,* 28 January 1913.
15. Croft, "Home Defence. Need for a National Army," *Standard,* 29 March 1913.
16. "Imperial Unity. Mr. Page Croft's Plea. Unionist Enthusiasm at Swansea," *South West Daily News,* 22 February 1912.
17. "Trade of the Empire. All-Red Route. State-Owned Atlantic Cable," *Telegraph,* 4 April; Croft, "Imperial Cable. What Would It Mean to Commerce and Safety," *Evening News,* 12 April 1912.
18. Croft, "The Future of the British Race," *Outlook,* 1 June 1912.
19. Ibid., 8 June 1912.
20. Ibid., 15 June 1912.
21. "Imperial Unity. Plea for Tariff Reform and Empire Defence," *Newcastle Journal,* 22 June; "Tariff Reform, Imperial Preference and Unemployment," *Newcastle Chronicle,* 26 July; "Imperial Mission," *Newcastle Journal,* 17 August; Croft, "Self-Help for Empire. Growing Enthusiasm for Preference," *Standard,* 17 August 1912.
22. Croft to F. W. Allday, secretary of Christchurch and Bournemouth Conservative Association, 24 August 1912, in *Bournemouth Vistors' Directory,* 7 September. Also see Croft to Allday, 30 August 1912, in *Bournemouth Echo,* 12 September; Croft to Allday, 6 September 1912, in *Bournemouth Echo,* 21 September 1912.
23. Croft, "Future of Canada. Hopes and Problems in the Great Dominions," *Birmingham Gazette,* 15 October; "Mr H. Page Croft, MP, on Canada," *Bournemouth Echo,* 19 October; "Imperial Mission. Inspiring Addresses in the City," *City of London Observer,* 9 November; "Mr. H. Page Croft. Interesting Impressions of Canadian Tour," *Canadian Mail,* 16 November 1912.
24. As chairman of the Imperial Mission, Croft contributed a series to the London-based *Canadian News:* "Imperial Unity," 2 November; "Empire Defence," 16 November; "Some Thoughts on Canada," 7 December; and "The Overseas Imperial Fleet," 12 April 1913.
25. *Parl. Deb.* vol. 36 (11 April 1912), c. 1399–1514.
26. R. Murphy, "Faction in the Conservative Party and the Home Rule Crisis, 1912–1914," *History* 71 no. 232 (1986), 223.
27. Blake, *Unknown Prime Minister,* 125.
28. Long to Bonar Law, 4 June 1912, Bonar Law Papers, BL/26/4/7.
29. Croft, "Home Rule Means the Economic Ruin of Ireland," *Nash's Magazine* (March 1912), 795–96.
30. Ibid.

31. "Unionist Demonstration at Bournemouth. Speeches by Mr. Worthington-Evans, MP, and Mr. Page Croft, MP," *Bournemouth Guardian,* 27 April; "Mr. Page Croft, MP, at Blandford. Policy of Conservative Party," *Bournemouth Echo,* 12 July 1912.

32. "Mr. Page Croft, MP, at Harpurhey," *Manchester Courier,* 4 May 1912.

33. *Bournemouth Guardian,* 27 April 1912.

34. "Ulster and Mr. Churchill. Some Home Truths Compiled by Mr. Page Croft, MP," *Birmingham Gazette,* 14 August 1912.

35. It passed 367 to 257. *Parl. Deb.,* vol. 46 (16 January 1913), c. 2411–18.

36. *Parl. Deb.* vol. 55 (7 July 1913), c. 136–41; "Home Rule Bill. Mr. Page Croft's Speech in Commons," *Bournemouth Echo,* 9 July 1913.

37. *Morning Post,* 19 December 1913.

38. "Unionist Mass Meeting. Home Rule Policy Condemned. Speeches by Mr. H. Chaplin, Mr. H. Page Croft, and Sir Joseph Lawrence." *Herald,* 27 December 1913.

39. G. D. Phillips, "Lord Willoughby de Broke and the Politics of Radical Toryism, 1909–1914," *Journal of British Studies* 20 no. 1 (1980), 219.

40. Willoughby de Broke to Milner, 6 January 1914, Bodl Lib, Milner Papers, MSS Eng hist, c. 680, fos. 2–4.

41. *The Times,* 11 November 1913.

42. Willoughby de Broke, "Unionists and Ulster," *The Times,* 27 May 1913.

43. *Parl. Deb.,* vol. 55 (7 July 1913), c. 168–74.

44. Murphy, "Faction and Home Rule," *History,* 227–28.

45. "Primrose League at Bournemouth. Mr. Page Croft and the Home Rule Question. His Suggestion as to a Settlement," *Bournemouth Guardian,* 22 November 1913.

46. Diaries, January 1914, in Barnes (ed.), *Leo Amery Diaries,* i, 97–99.

47. Diaries, 13 November 1913, and 13 February 1914, in Ramsden (ed.), *Political Diaries of Robert Sanders,* 66, 72.

48. *Herald,* 27 December 1913.

49. "Mr. H. Page Croft, MP, Addresses Series of Meetings," *Bournemouth Visitors' Directory,* 24 January 1914.

50. "Bullets vs. Ballots, Government, Ulster and the Army. Protest Demonstration at Bournemouth," *Bournemouth Visitors' Directory,* 2 May 1914.

51. *Parl. Deb.,* vol. 60 (27 March 1914), c. 1077–82; "Home Rule Debate in Commons. Speech by Mr. H. Page Croft, MP," *Bournemouth Echo,* 2 April 1914.

52. "Towards Settlement. Amendments Intended to Facilitate Agreement. Motions for Both Sides," *Westminster Gazette,* 2 April 1914. Croft's amendment omitted "during the next six years."

53. *Bournemouth Visitors' Directory,* 2 May 1914,

54. Croft, "The Duty of the Unionists. Mr. Page Croft and a Federal Scheme," *The Times,* 8 May 1914.

55. Ibid.

56. Croft, "Invincible Ulster," *Morning Post,* 12 June; "Mr. Page Croft and Ulster. Impression of a Visit," *Bournemouth Echo,* 1 June 1914.

57. "Mr. H. Page Croft, MP, on His Visit to Ulster," *Bournemouth Directory,* 14 July 1914; Croft, *My Life of Strife,* 82–84.

58. Croft, "Joseph Chamberlain, Imperialist," *The Lancashire and Cheshire Junior Movement: The Monthly Magazine of the Junior Unionist Federation,* 4:7 (August 1914), 97–98.

59. "Mr. Page Croft's Message to His Constituents. 'I Have No Party Till Europe Has Been Saved,'" *Bournemouth Echo,* 5 August 1914.

60. The title of a book written by Croft on his wartime experiences. H. P. Croft, *Twenty-two Months under Fire* (London: J. Murray, 1916).

Conclusion

1. Viscountess Milner, in Croft, *My Life of Strife,* ix.
2. Ibid., 130.
3. Ibid., x.

Bibliography

MANUSCRIPT SOURCES

Individuals

Balfour Papers, British Library
Balfour Papers, Whittinghame Papers, Scottish Record Office
Bayford [Robert Sanders] Papers, Bodleian Library
Beaverbrook Papers, House of Lords Record Office
Bessborough [8th Earl] Papers, held by the 10th Earl of Bessborough, West Sussex Record Office, Chichester
Bessborough [Viscount Duncannon] Papers, held by the 10th Earl of Bessborough, West Sussex Record Office, Chichester
Bonar Law Papers, House of Lords Record Office
Blumenfeld Papers, House of Lords Record Office
Bridgeman Papers, Salop and Shropshire Record Office, Shrewsbury
Robert Cecil Papers, British Library
Chamberlain [Austen] Papers, Birmingham University Library
Chamberlain [Joseph] Papers, Birmingham University Library
Chelwood [Robert Cecil] Papers, held by 6th Marquess of Salisbury, Hatfield House
Croft Papers, Churchill Archives Centre
Derby [17th Earl] Papers, Liverpool City Library Archives
Elliot [Arthur] Papers, National Library of Scotland
Garvin Papers, University of Texas Archives
Gwynne Papers, Bodleian Library
Hannon Papers, House of Lords Record Office
Hewins Papers, University of Sheffield Library
Leconfield [Charles Wyndham, 3d Baron] Papers, held by 2d Baron Egremont Petworth House, c/o West Sussex Record Office
Lloyd George Papers, House of Lords Record Office
Lloyd Papers, Churchill Archives Centre
Long Papers, British Library
Maxse Papers, West Sussex Record Office
Milner Papers, Bodleian Library
Mount Temple [Wilfrid William Ashley] Papers, University of Southampton Library
Northcliffe Papers, British Library
Oliver Papers, National Library of Scotland

Bibliography

Quickswood [Lord Hugh Cecil] Papers, held by the 6th Marquess of Salisbury, Hatfield House
Ridley [Mathew White, 2d Viscount] Papers, Northumberland Record Office
Salisbury [4th Marquess] Papers, held by 6th Marquess of Salisbury, Hatfield House
Sandars Papers, Bodleian Library
Selborne [2d Earl] Papers, Bodleian Library
Selborne [3d Earl, Viscount Wolmer] Papers, Bodleian Library
Steel-Maitland Papers, Scottish Record Office
Strachey Papers, House of Lords Record Office
Wargrave [Edward Goulding] Papers, House of Lords Record Office
Willoughby de Broke Papers, House of Lords Record Office
Winterton Papers, Bodleian Library
Worthington-Evans Papers, Bodleian Library

Organizations

Conservative and Unionist Party Papers, Bodleian Library
Conservative Party. *Archives of the British Conservative Party* (Microfilm Series):

- (a). *British General Election Campaign Guides, 1885–1950*
- (b). *Pamphlets and Leaflets of the British Conservative and Unionist Party*
- (c). *Executive Committee Minutes of the National Union of Conservative Associations, 1897–1956, Together with Central Council Minutes and Annual Reports.*
- (d). *Minutes and Reports of the Conservative Party Conferences, 1867–1946*
- (e). *National Union Gleanings and Successors, 1893–1968*

Liberal Party Papers, University of Bristol Library
National Party Papers, Bodleian Library
Primrose League Papers, Bodleian Library
Tariff Commission Papers, British Library of Political and Economic Science
Ware Unionist Association Papers, Hertfordshire Record Office

Printed Sources

Public Documents

United Kingdom. *Parliamentary Debates,* 4th Series (1903–8).
———. *Parliamentary Debates, Commons,* 5th Series (1909–14).
———. *Parliamentary Debates, Lords,* 5th Series (1909–14).

Contemporary Newspapers

Birmingham Gazette
Bolton Evening Chronicle
Bournemouth Echo
Bournemouth Graphic
Bournemouth Guardian
Bournemouth Observer and Chronicle
Bournemouth Visitors' Directory
Bristol Times
Bristol Times and Mirror
Cambridge Chronicle
Canadian Mail
Chatham, Rochester & Gillingham News
City of London Observer
Daily Chronicle
Daily Express
Daily Graphic
Daily Mail
Daily News
Daily Sketch
Daily Telegraph
Derby Express
Devizes Gazette
East London Advertiser
Essex Observer
Evening News
Evening Standard
Glasgow Herald
Globe
Hampshire Advertiser
Hampstead and Kilburn Echo
Herald
Hertfordshire and Essex Observer
Hertfordshire Express
Hertfordshire Mercury
Hertfordshire News
Hull Daily Mail
Jarrow Express
Lancashire Daily Post
Lincolnshire Chronicle
Lincolnshire Echo
Manchester Courier
Manchester Dispatch
Morning Advertiser
Morning Leader
Morning Post
Newcastle Chronicle
Newcastle Journal
North Devon Herald
Northern Daily Mail
North Hertfordshire Mail
North Star
Nottingham Daily Guardian
Nottingham Evening Post
Nottingham Express
Observer
Outlook
The Press [New Zealand]
Reading Mercury
St. Albans Times
Sheffield Daily Telegraph
Southern Times
South West Daily News
Spectator
Staffordshire Sentinel
Standard
Stoke & Newington Recorder
Yorkshire Herald
Yorkshire Post
Wednesbury News
Western Daily Press
Westminster Gazette

Journals and Magazines

British and Tariff Reform Journal
Canadian News
Contemporary Review
Edinburgh Review
Empire Illustrated
Empire Magazine
Fortnightly Review
Lancashire and Cheshire Junior Movement: The Monthy Magazine of the Junior Unionist Federation
Liberty
Monthy Notes on Tariff Reform
Nash's Magazine
Nation
National Review
Nineteenth Century and After
Quarterly Review
Primrose League Gazette
Saturday Review
Spectator
Tariff Reform League Notes for Speakers
Whitehall Review

Memoirs and Autobiographies

[Place of publication is London unless otherwise stated.]

Amery, L. S. *My Political Life,* 3 volumes (1953).
———. *Union and Strength: A Series of Papers on Imperial Questions* (1912).
Bayford [Sir Robert Sanders], Lord. *The Political Diaries of Robert Sanders, Lord Bayford, 1910–1935.* Edited by John Ramsden (1984).
Blumenfeld, R. D. *All in a Lifetime* (1931).
———. *R.D.B.'s Diary, 1887–1914* (1930).
Cecil, Lord Hugh. *Conservatism* (1912).
Cecil of Chelwood [Robert] Viscount. *A Great Experiment: An Autobiography.* Oxford (1941).
———. *All the Way* (1949).
Chamberlain, Austen. *Down the Years* (1935).
———. *Politics from Inside: An Epistolary Chronicle, 1906–1914.* New Haven (1937).
Clarke, Sir Edward. *The Story of My Life* (1918).
Committee of the Compatriots' Club. *Compatriots' Club Lectures: First Series* (1905)
Croft [Henry Page], Lord. *My Life of Strife* (1948).
———. *The Path of Empire* (1912).
———. *Twenty-Two Months under Fire* (1916).
Esher [Reginald] 2nd Viscount (ed.). *Journals and Letters of Reginald Viscount Esher.* 4 vol. (1934–38).
Fitzroy, Sir Almeric William. *Memoirs.* 2 vol. (1925).
Garvin, J. L. *Tariff or Budget* (1910).
Gore, John (ed.). *Mary Maxse (1870–1944): A Record Compiled by Her Family and Friends.* Privately published (1946).
Griffith-Boscawen, A. S. T. *Fourteen Years in Parliament* (1907).
Gwynn, Stephen (ed.). *The Anvil of War: Letters between F.S. Oliver and His Brother, 1914–1918* (1936).

Hewins, W. A. S. *The Apologia of an Imperialist: Forty Years of Empire Policy*. 2 vol. (1931–33).
Holland, Bernard. *The Life of Spencer Compton, 8th Duke of Devonshire*. 2 vol. (1911).
Lee of Fareham [Arthur] Viscount. *A Good Innings: The Private Papers of Viscount Lee of Fareham*. Edited by Alan Clark. Privately published (1974 ed.).
Long, Walter. *Memoirs* (1922).
Malmesbury [James Edward Harris], Earl (ed.). *The New Order: Studies in Unionist Policy* (1908).
Midleton [St. John], Earl. *Records and Reactions, 1856–1939* (1939).
Milner, Viscount. *The Nation and Empire* (1913).
Newton [Thomas], Lord. *Retrospection* (1941).
Riddel [George], Lord. *More Pages from My Diary, 1908–1914* (1934).
Salvidge, Stanley. *Salvidge of Liverpool: Behind the Political Scene, 1890–1928* (1934).
Selborne, [William Waldegrave Palmer], Lord. *The Crisis of British Unionism: Lord Selborne's Domestic Political Papers, 1885–1922*. Edited by George Boyce (1987).
Strachey, John St. Loe. *The Manufacturer of Paupers* (1907).
———. *The Problems and Perils of Socialism* (1908).
Wilkinson, Spenser. *Thirty-Five Years, 1874–1909* (1933).
Willoughbhy de Broke [Richard Greville Verney], Lord. *The Passing Years* (1924).
Winterton, Earl. *Pre-War* (1932).
Wyndham, Guy (ed.). *The Letters of George Wyndham*. 2 vols. (1915).

Books and Biographies

Beer, Samuel. *British Politics in the Collectivist Age*. New York (1947).
Bell, E. H. C. Moberly. *Life and Letters of C. F. Moberly Bell* (1927).
Biggs-Davison, John. *George Wyndham: A Study in Toryism* (1951).
Birkenhead [Frederick] Earl. *F.E.: The Life of F. E. Smith, First Earl of Birkenhead* (1960).
Blake, Robert. *The Conservative Party from Peel to Thatcher* (1985).
———. *The Unknown Prime Minister: The Life and Times of Andrew Bonar Law, 1858–1923* (1955).
Blewett, Neal. *The Peers, the Parties and the People: The General Elections of 1910* (1972).
Blouet, Brian. *Halford Mackinder: A Biography*. College Station, Tex. (1987).
———. *Sir Halford Mackinder, 1861–1947: Some New Perspectives*. Oxford (1975).
Blunt, W. S. *My Diaries*. 2 vol. New York (1923).
Broderick, Alan. *Near to Greatness: A Life of Earl Winterton* (1965).
Brown, B. H. *The Tariff Reform Movement in Great Britain, 1881–1898*. New York (1943).
Campbell, John. *F. E. Smith, First Earl of Birkenhead* (1983).
———. *Lloyd George: Goat in the Wilderness* (1977).
Charmley, John. *Lord Lloyd and the Decline of the British Empire* (1987).

Bibliography

Chilston [Eric Alexander] Viscount. *Chief Whip: The Political Life and Times of Aretas Akers-Douglas, 1st Viscount Chilston* (1961).

Churchill, R. S. *Lord Derby: King of Lancashire* (1959).

———. *Winston S. Churchill. Volume 2: A Young Statesman, 1900–1914*. Boston (1967).

———. *Winston S. Churchill. Companion, Part I (1901–1907), Part II (1907–1911), Part III (1911–1914)*. Boston (1969).

Coetzee, Frans. *For Party or Country: Nationalism and the Dilemmas of Popular Conservatism in Edwardian England*. Oxford (1990).

Colvin, Ian. *Carson the Statesman* (1935).

Craig, F. W. S. *Chronology of By-Elections, 1833–1987* (1987).

Cross, Colin. *The Liberals in Power, 1905–1914* (1963).

Dangerfield, George. *The Strange Death of Liberal England, 1910–1914*. New York (1961 ed).

Dark, Sidney. *The Life of Sir Arthur Pearson* (1922).

Dugdale, Blanche E. C. *Arthur James Balfour*. 2 vol. (1939).

Egremont, Max [Lord]. *Balfour: A Life of Arthur James Balfour* (1980).

Ensor, R. C. K. *England, 1870–1914*. Oxford (1936).

Farr, Barbara. *The Development and Impact of Right-Wing Politics in Great Britain, 1903–1932*. New York (1987).

Fforde, Matthew. *Conservatism and Collectivism, 1886–1914*. Edinburgh (1990).

Fraser, Peter. *Joseph Chamberlain: Radicalism and Empire, 1868–1914* (1966).

———. *Lord Esher: A Political Biography* (1973).

Garvin, J. L., and Julian Amery. *The Life of Joseph Chamberlain*. 4 vol. (1932–51).

Garvin, Katherine. *J. L. Garvin: A Memoir* (1948).

Gollin, Alfred. *Balfour's Burden: Arthur Balfour and Imperial Preference* (1965).

———. *The Observer and J. L. Garvin, 1908–1914: A Study in a Great Editorship*. Oxford (1960).

———. *Proconsul in Politics: A Study of Lord Milner in Opposition and in Power* (1964).

Green, E. H. H. *The Crisis of Conservatism: The Politics, Economics and Ideology of the British Conservative Party, 1880–1914* (1995).

Grigg, John. *Lloyd George: The People's Champion, 1902–1911* (1978).

Guttsman, W. L. *The British Political Elite*. New York (1963).

Halevy, Elie. *A History of the English People, 5, Imperialism and the Rise of Labour, 1895–1905*. New York (1961 ed.).

———. *A History of the English People, 6, The Rule of Democracy, 1905–1914*. New York (1961 ed.).

Hutcheson, John. *Leopold Maxse and the National Review, 1893–1914: Right Wing Politics and Journalism in the Edwardian Era*. New York (1989).

Hyde, H. Montgomery. *Carson: The Life of Sir Edward Carson, Lord Carson of Duncairn* (1953).

Hynes, Samuel. *The Edwardian Turn of Mind*. Princeton (1968).

Jay, Richard. *Joseph Chamberlain: A Political Study*. Oxford (1981).

Jenkins, Roy. *Asquith* (1964).

———. *Mr. Balfour's Poodle*. New York (1954).

Judd, Denis. *Balfour and the British Empire* (1968).
———. *Radical Joe: A Life of Joseph Chamberlain* (1953).
Kendle, John E. *The Colonial and Imperial Conferences, 1887–1911: A Study in Imperial Organization* (1967).
———. *The Round Table Movement and Imperial Union.* Toronto (1975).
———. *Walter Long, Ireland, and the Union, 1905–1920* (1992).
Kennedy, Paul, and Anthony Nicholls (eds.). *Nationalist and Racialist Movements in Britain and Germany Before 1914.* London (1981).
Kruse, Juanita. *John Buchan (1875–1940) and the Idea of Empire: Popular Literature and Political Ideology.* Lewiston, N.Y. (1989).
Londonderry, Marchioness of. *Henry Chaplin: A Memoir.* London (1926).
Lucas, Reginald. *Lord Glenesk and the "Morning Post."* London (1910).
Lyttelton, Edith. *Alfred Lyttelton: An Account of His Life.* London (1923).
Mackail, John William, and Guy Percy Wyndham. *The Life and Letters of George Wyndham* (1925).
Mackay, Ruddock F. *Balfour: Intellectual Statesman.* Oxford (1985).
Magnus, Philip. *King Edward VII.* 1964.
Meadowcraft, James. *Conceptualizing the State: Innovation and Dispute in British Political Thought, 1880–1914.* Oxford (1995).
Miller, J. D. B. *Richard Jebb and the Problem of Empire* (1956).
Murray, Bruce K. *The People's Budget, 1909/1910: Lloyd George and Liberal Politics* (1980).
Newton, [Thomas] Lord. *Lord Lansdowne: A Biography* (1929).
Nicolson, Harold. *King George V: His Life and Reign* (1952).
Norton, Philip, and Arthur Aughey. *Conservatives and Conservatism.* 1981.
Nowell-Smith, S. (ed.). *Edwardian England, 1901–14* (1964).
O'Day, Alan (ed.). *The Edwardian Age: Conflict and Stability, 1900–1914* (1979).
Offer, Avner, *Property and Politics, 1870–1914: Landownership, Law, Ideology and Urban Development in England.* Cambridge (1981).
Owen, Frank. *Tempestuous Journey: Lloyd George His Life and Times.* New York (1955).
Peel, Hon. George. *The Tariff Reformers* (1913).
Pelling, Henry. *Popular Politics and Society in Late Victorian Britain* (1979).
———. *Social Geography of British Elections, 1885–1910* (1967).
Petrie, Sir Charles. *The Life and Letters of the Rt. Hon. Sir Austen Chamberlain.* 2 vol. (1939).
———. *Walter Long and His Times* (1936).
Phillips, G. D. *The Diehards: Aristocratic Society and Politics in Edwardian England.* Cambridge, Mass. (1979).
Pound, Reginald, and G. Harmsworth. *Northcliffe* (1959).
Pugh, Martin. *Electoral Reform in War and Peace, 1906–1918* (1978).
———. *The Making of Modern British Politics, 1867–1939* (1982).
———. *The Tories and the People, 1880–1935.* Oxford (1985).
Ramsden, John. *The Age of Balfour and Baldwin, 1902–1940* (1978).
Rempel, Richard. *Unionists Divided: Arthur Balfour, Joseph Chamberlain, and the Unionists Free Traders.* Newton Abbot (1972).

Rose, Kenneth. *King George V* (1983).
———. *The Later Cecils* (1975).
Rowland, Peter. *David Lloyd George: A Biography* (1975).
———. *The Last Liberal Governments*. 2 vols. (1968/1972).
Rubenstein, William D. *Men of Property: The Very Wealthy in Britain since the Industrial Revolution* (1981).
Russell, A. K. *Liberal Landslide: The General Election of 1906*. Newton Abbot (1973).
Scally, R. J. *The Origins of the Lloyd George Coalition*. Princeton (1975).
Searle, G. R. *Corruption in British Politics, 1895–1930*. Oxford (1988).
———. *The Quest for National Efficiency*. Oxford (1971).
Semmel, Bernard. *Imperialism and Social Reform: English Social and Imperial Thought, 1895–1914* (1960).
Smith, Janet Adam. *John Buchan: A Biography*. Boston (1965).
Spender, J. A. *Life of Herbert Henry Asquith, Lord Oxford and Asquith*. 2 vol. (1932).
Startt, J. D. *Journalists for Empire: The Imperial Debate in the Edwardian Stately Press, 1903–1913*. New York (1991).
Stewart, A. T. Q. *The Ulster Crisis* (1967).
Sykes, Alan. *Tariff Reform in British Politics, 1903–1913*. Oxford (1979).
Taylor, A. J. P. *Beaverbrook*. New York (1972).
Thompson, J. A., and Arthur Meiji (eds.). *Edwardian Conservatism: Five Studies in Adaptation* (1988).
Thornton, A. P. *The Imperial Idea and Its Enemies* (1959).
Young, Kenneth. *Arthur James Balfour: The Happy Life of the Politician, Prime Minister, Statesman and Philosopher, 1848–1930* (1963).
Williams, Rhodri. *Defending the Empire: The Conservative Party and British Defence Policy, 1899–1915*. New Haven, 1991.

Articles

Blewett, Neal. "Free Fooders, Balfourites, Wholehoggers: Factionalism Within the Unionist Party, 1906–1910." *Historical Journal* 11 (1974), 95–124.
Bristow, E. J. "The Liberty and Property Defence League and Individualism." *Historical Journal* 18 (1975), 761–89.
Brown, K. D. "The Trade Union Tariff Reform Association." *Journal of British Studies* 9 (1970), 141–53.
Clarke, P. F. "British Politics and Blackburn Politics, 1900–1910." *Historical Journal* 14 (1971), 302–27.
Coats, A. W. "Political Economy and the Tariff Reform Campaign of 1903." *Journal of Law and Economics* 11 (1968), 181–229.
Coetzee, Frans. "Pressure Groups, Tory Businessmen and the Aura of Political Corruption Before the First World War." *Historical Journal* 29 (1986), 833–52.
———, and Marilyn Shevlin Coetzee. "Rethinking the Radical Right in Germany and Britain Before 1914." *Journal of Contemporary History* 21 (1986), 515–38.
Cornford, James. "The Transformation of Conservatism in the Late Nineteenth Century." *Victorian Studies* 7 (1963–64), 35–66.
Crouzet, Francois. "Trade and Empire: The British Experience from the Establish-

ment of Free Trade until the First World War." B. M. Ratcliffe (ed.), *Great Britain and Her World, 1750–1914: Essays in Honour of W. O. Henderson.* Manchester, 1975.

de Rosa, Peter L. "The 'Curragh Mutiny' and the House of Lords." *Éire-Ireland: A Journal of Irish Studies* 17 (1982), 104–20.

Dutton, D. J. "Lancashire and the New Unionism: The Unionist Party and the Growth of Popular Politics, 1906–1914." *Transactions of the Historical Society of Lancashire and Cheshire* 130 (1981), 131–48.

———. "The Unionist Party and Social Policy, 1906–1914." *Historical Journal* 24 (1981), 871–84.

———. "Unionist Politics and the Aftermath of the General Election of 1906: A Reassessment." *Historical Journal* 22 (1979), 861–76.

Emy, H. V. "The Impact of Financial Policy on English Party Politics Before 1914." *Historical Journal* 15 (1972), 103–31.

Fanning, Ronan. "The Unionist Party and Ireland, 1906–1910." *Irish Historical Studies* 15 (1966), 147–71.

Fraser, Peter. "Unionism and Tariff Reform: The Crisis of 1906." *Historical Journal* 5 (1962), 149–66.

———. "The Unionist Debacle of 1911 and Balfour's Retirement." *Journal of Modern History* 34 (1963), 354–65.

French, David. "The Edwardian Crisis and the Origins of the First World War." *International History Review* 4 (1982), 207–21.

Glickman, Harvey. "The Toryness of English Conservatism." *Journal of British Studies* 1 (1961–62), 111–43.

Gollin, Alfred. "Historians and the Great Crisis of 1903." *Albion* 8 (1976), 83–97.

Grainger, J. H. "England, Whose England?—Edwardian Patriotisms." *Critical Review* 20 (1978), 55–71.

Green, E. H. H. "Radical Conservatives and the Electoral Genesis of Tariff Reform." *Historical Journal* 28 (1985), 667–92.

Jones, J. R. "England." Edited by Hans Rogger and Eugen Weber. *The European Right.* Berkeley, 1966.

Jones, R. B. "Balfour's Reform of Party Organization." *Bulletin of the Institute for Historical Research* 38 (1965), 84–101.

Kendle, J. E. "The Round Table Movement and 'Home Rule All Round.'" *Historical Journal* 11 (1968), 332–53.

Klarman, Michael. "Parliamentary Reversal of the *Osborne* Judgment." *Historical Journal* 32 (1989), 893–924.

Lipset, Seymour Martin. "Sources of the Radical Right." In Daniel Bell, *The Radical Right.* New York (1963).

McCreedy, H. W. "The Revolt of the Unionist Free Traders." *Parliamentary Affairs* 16 (1963), 188–206.

Marrison, A. J. "Businessmen, Industries and Tariff Reform in Great Britain, 1903–1930." *Business History* 25 (1983), 148–78.

Mason, J. W. "Political Economy and the Response to Socialism in Britain, 1870–1914." *Historical Journal* 23 (1980), 565–87.

Murphy, Richard. "Faction and the Home Rule Crisis, 1912–1914." *History* 71 no. 232 (1986), 222–34.

Murray, Bruce. "The Politics of the People's Budget, 1909/10." *Historical Journal* 16 (1973), 555–70.

Offer, Avner. "Empire and Social Reform: British Overseas Investment and Domestic Politics, 1908–1914." *Historical Journal* 26 no. 1 (1983), 119–38.
Pelling, Henry. "The Politics of the Osborne Judgment." *Historical Journal* 25 (1982), 889–909.
Phillips, G. D. "The 'Die-Hards' and the Myth of the 'Backwoodsmen.'" *Journal of British Studies* 16 (1977), 105–20.
———. "Lord Willoughby de Broke and the Politics of Radical Toryism, 1909–1914." *Journal of British Studies* 20 (1980), 205–24.
Rempel, Richard. "Lord Hugh Cecil's Parliamentary Career, 1900–1914: Promise Unfulfilled." *Journal of British Studies* 11 no. 2 (1972), 114–30.
Ridley, Jane. "The Unionist Social Reform Committee, 1911–1914: Wets Before the Deluge." *Historical Journal* 30 (1987), 391–413.
Rodner, W. S. "Leaguers, Covenanters, Moderates: British Support for Ulster, 1913–1914." *Éire-Ireland: A Journal of Irish Studies* 17 (1982), 68–85.
Rubenstein, W. D. "Henry Page Croft and the National Party, 1917–1922." *Journal of Contemporary History* 9 (1974), 129–48.
Shields, R. A. "Imperial Policy and Canadian-American Commercial Relations, 1880–1911." *Bulletin of the Institute of Historical Research* 59 (1986), 108–21.
———. "Imperial Policy and Canadian-American Reciprocity, 1909–1911." *Journal of Imperial and Commonwealth History* 5 (1976–77), 151–71.
Startt, J. D. "Northcliffe the Imperialist: The Lesser Known Years, 1902–1914." *The Historian* 51 (1988), 19–41.
Sykes, Alan. "The Confederacy and the Purge of the Unionist Free Traders, 1906–1910." *Historical Journal* 18 (1975), 349–66.
———. "The Radical Right and the Crisis of Conservatism Before the First World War." *Historical Journal* 26 (1983), 661–76.
Weston, C. C., and P. Kevlin. "The 'Judas Group' and the Parliament Bill of 1911." *English Historical Review* (1984), 551–63.
Zebel, S. H. "Joseph Chamberlain and the Genesis of Tariff Reform." *Journal of British Studies* 7 no. 1 (1967), 131–57.

Dissertations

Bralley, Harry D. "St. Loe Strachey and the Politics of Dilemma: A Study of Political Journalism During the Edwardian Era." Ph.D. dissertation, University of South Carolina, 1971.
Bristow, Edward J. "Defense of Liberty and Property and Great Britain, 1880–1914." Ph.D. dissertation, Yale University, 1970.
Coetzee, Frans. "Conservative Pressure Groups in Edwardian England, 1894–1914." Ph.D. dissertation, University of Chicago, 1983.
Heberle, Gerald C. "The Predicament of the British Unionist Party, 1906–1914." Ph.D. dissertation, Ohio State University, 1967.
Levine, Stephen. "St. Loe Strachey and the Ideology of Free Trade." Ph.D. dissertation, City University of New York, 1975.
McEwen, J. M. "The Unionist and Conservative Members of Parliament, 1914–1939." Ph.D. dissertation, University of London, 1959.
Parisi, F. J. "From Main Street to Fleet Street: R. D. Blumenfeld and the London *Daily Express,* 1887–1932." Ph.D. dissertation, George Washington University, 1985.

Porter, Dilwyn. "The Unionist Tariff Reformers, 1903–1914." Ph.D. dissertation, University of Manchester, 1976.

Ridley, Jane. "Leadership and Management in the Conservative Party in Parliament, 1906–1914." Ph.D. dissertation, Oxford University, 1984.

Rubenstein W. D. "Henry Page Croft and the Unionist Right, 1903–1922." M.A. thesis, The Johns Hopkins University, 1969.

Stearns, Gary M. "The Edwardian Career of Lord Robert Cecil: A Study in Adaptation." Ph.D. dissertation, University of Kentucky, 1990.

Rodner, W. S. "Lord Hugh Cecil and the Unionist Opposition to the Third Irish Home Rule Bill." Ph.D. dissertation, Penn State University, 1977.

Turner, B. H. P. "Tariff Reform and the Conservative Party, 1895–1906." Ph.D. dissertation, University of London, 1967.

Index

Acland Hood, Sir Alexander, 46–47, 61, 71, 86, 91–92, 102–5, 121, 125, 132, 140, 150, 153
Agriculture, 45, 78, 118, 136, 141, 149, 190–94
Aitken, Max. *See* Beaverbrook, Lord
Akers-Douglas, Aretas, 139, 151–52, 258n
Albert Hall, 142–44, 182, 184–85
Alien Act (1905), 78, 135
Allen, Arthur Acland, 111, 143
American-Canadian relations, 114, 126, 165–69, 176
Amery, Julian, 25
Amery, Leopold, 16, 28, 64, 73, 150, 160, 171, 177, 187, 214
Annual Register, 127
Anti-Budget League, 149
Arbuthnot, Gerald, 130, 221
Archer-Shee, Maj. Martin, 130, 157, 168, 171–72, 187, 221
Argyll, Duke of, 115, 171
Armstrong, Sir George, 62, 214
army, 45, 133, 198–99, 204–5, 207
Arnold-Foster, Hugh, 59
Ashbury, Lord, 155
Ashley, Wilfred, 62–63, 217
Asquith, H. H., 110, 114, 126, 143, 155–56, 175, 196, 201, 207
Astor, Waldorf, 187
Australia, 115, 166, 172

Baker, Alfred, 94, 100
Balcarres, Lord, 128, 141, 153, 155, 157, 163
Baldwin, Stanley, 16, 18, 195, 209
Balfour, Arthur James, 18–19, 21, 27, 44, 51, 58–59, 61, 64, 69–77, 82–83, 88–89, 95, 100–3, 106, 110, 117–19, 122, 125, 127–31, 134, 136–46, 151, 153, 155–58, 161–63, 168, 175–78, 181–82, 207, 211–13

Balfour, Gerald, 51
Balfour of Burleigh, Lord, 32, 76
Banbury, Sir Frederick, 156–57, 261n
Barnard, E. B., 98
Barnes, George, 118
Bartley-Deniss, E. R., 177
Beach, Sir Michael Hicks, 26, 31, 43
Beaverbrook, Lord, 116, 166, 176, 184, 263n
Bedford, Duke of, 156, 203
Benn, Arthur Shirley, 171, 264n
Benn, Ion Hamilton, 171, 264n
Bentinck, Lord Henry, 81, 85
Beresford, Lord Charles, 113, 203
Birmingham: politics in, 35, 56, 83, 126, 192
Birmingham Party Conference, 20
Birmingham pledge, 84–85, 89, 91, 95, 104, 131
Blackstock, George Tate, 172
Blake, Lord Robert, 56
Blumenfeld, R. D., 120, 138, 155, 161, 183, 221
Borden, Sir Robert, 173, 183, 200
Borwick, George, 143
Borwick, Nancy (wife of Croft), 78
Bournemouth: and politics, 79–80, 116, 143, 184, 197
Bournemouth Daily Echo, 16
Bournemouth Graphic, 56
Bowles, George Stewart, 77–78, 83, 86–88, 90–91, 94, 100, 112, 245n
Bowles, Col. Henry, 62, 102, 214
Bracken, Brendan, 16
Bridgeman, William, 159–60, 185, 261n
British Empire Union, 173
British League for the Support of Ulster and the Union, 203–4
British Women's Emigration Association, 197
Brotherton, Sir Edward, 98
Brunker, E. G., 64, 242n

285

Buckle, G. E., 140
Buckley, G. A. M., 116, 172
Budget Protest League, 152
Burgoyne, Alan, 60, 62–63, 66–67, 130, 155, 167, 171, 214
Butler, R. A. B., 16, 209
Buxton, C. R., 40, 42

Caborne, W. F., 62, 214
Caillard, Sir Vincent, 75
Cambridge University, 23–24
Campbell-Bannerman, Sir Henry, 35–36, 38, 79
Canada: and imperial politics, 27, 114–16, 119, 126, 161, 131, 154, 165–68, 172–78, 200–201
Carlton Club, 67, 191
Carson, Sir Edward, 75, 160–61, 163, 186–87, 202, 206
Cassel, Felix, 169
Cawdor, Lord, 137
Caxton Hall, 99, 177
Cecil, Lord Hugh, 31, 38–39, 44, 57–59, 78, 87, 95, 98, 103, 106, 151, 157, 161, 188, 237n, 254n
Cecil, Lord Robert, 20, 44, 58, 63–65, 71, 76–77, 85, 87–88, 90–92, 94, 96–101, 112, 118, 161, 244n
Central Office (of the Conservative Party), 61, 63, 86, 88, 102, 104–5, 125–26, 147, 150, 162, 191
Chaloner, Richard, 152, 222
Chamberlain, Austen, 51, 65, 71, 73, 77, 82, 104, 112–13, 115, 126, 137, 140–42, 153, 155, 160, 164, 166, 185, 187–89, 195
Chamberlain, Joseph, 19, 26, 28–30, 33–34, 37–38, 42, 46–49, 51, 58–59, 61–62, 65, 70, 83, 93, 94, 96, 164, 172, 175, 187, 206, 208, 210
Chaplin, Henry, 28, 30, 33–34, 43, 50–51, 60, 62, 64–65, 83, 141, 157, 160, 185, 187, 236n
Chinese labor, 51
Christchurch: and politics, 20, 52, 55–56, 78–79, 98, 101, 111–12, 115, 143–44
Churchill, Winston, 15, 116, 137, 155, 203
Clarke, Charles C., 203
Clarke, Sir Edward, 76
Cobden, Richard, 31–32, 34

Cockshott, W. F., 115
Cohen, Lewis, 172
Collings, Jesse, 65, 187
colonial preference. *See* imperial preference
Confederacy: organization and campaign of, 18–21, 60–66, 71–78, 81–95, 102–3, 105–9, 112, 118–19, 125, 128–30, 152, 171, 182, 186, 192, 195, 206, 210–13
confederacy: membership of, 59–68, 214–20
Conservative Party, 27–28, 38–39, 52–53, 57, 100, 110, 112, 116–17, 119, 121, 124, 128–29, 133–37, 141, 144–52, 161, 170–71, 173, 177–78, 183–84, 189–97, 199, 201, 203, 205–13
Contemporary Review, 61
Cooper, Richard, 157
Courthope, George, 62–63, 66, 215
Cousins, John Ratcliffe, 62, 215
Croft Castle, 23
Croft, Henry Page: and the Army, 45, 79, 198–99, 204–5; Arthur Balfour, 35, 69–76, 83–94, 119, 125–29, 133, 138–40, 146, 150, 158, 167; Balfour's Birmingham Pledge, 83–84, 89, 91; R. D. Blumenfeld, 138; by-elections, 118, 134–35, 167; Canada, 114–19, 126, 131, 154, 165–78; Canada visit, 200–201; Caxton Hall, 99, 177; Joseph Chamberlain, 19, 26–30, 33, 37–39, 47–48, 96; Henry Chaplin, 30–33, 35, 43; Christchurch, 20, 52–56, 79–80, 111–12, 142–44, 156; Churchill Government, 15; Civil War: fear of, 202–6; Cobden: criticism of, 31, 32, 34; Confederacy: attempt to reactivate, 183, 194–95, 201; confederacy: creation and campaign of, 19, 60–63, 69–90, 106; Conservative Party, 35, 38–40, 46, 52–53, 89, 106, 117–18, 120–22, 125–33, 138, 141, 150–51, 154, 158–59, 168, 170, 178, 189–94; Conservative Party reform, 147–54; death, 15; diehards, 157–58, 161–62; East Hertfordshire, 20, 28–31, 37, 39, 41–42, 44, 50, 54–56, 69, 74–75, 87–106, 168, 210; East Hertfordshire Conservative and Unionist Association, 91–99; education of, 23–24;

INDEX

election of 1906, 49–53, 56; election of December 1910, 143–46; election of January 1910, 20, 111–12, 142–46; family history and ancestry, 23–24; free traders, 37, 57–58, 84–106; Earl Grey, 173; disruption of House of Commons, 157; House of Lords, 78, 80, 114–17, 139, 141, 143, 146, 149–50, 154–59, 167; proposal for imperial council, 199–200; imperial idea, 21, 136–38, 174–75, 190, 195, 199, 206, 208; imperial mission: organization and campaign of, 19, 115–19, 165–78, 182, 199–201; inter-war politics, 18; Ireland, 138–39, 144, 146–50, 186, 188, 194–95, 201–6; Andrew Bonar Law, 164, 177–79, 181–95, 207; Licensing Bill, 80–81; Lincoln, 30, 43–46, 49–50, 53–54, 116; Londonderry's criticism, 134; Malmesbury, Earl of, 55–56, 116, 128–29, 135; Leo Maxse, 61, 69–70, 121–32, 156, 162–63, 167–68, 175–76; Jimmy Maxton, 15; National Party, 17, 135, 175; Parliament, 38–40, 113, 117–18, 155; Peerage, 15; Reveille, organization and campaign of, 19, 110–247, 150–52, 167–68, 178, 201; Reveille manifestos, 120–21, 132–33, 137–38, 146, 226–28; rowing, 24; Lord Salisbury, 97–98, 102–5, 158; C. H. Seely, 43–48, 51, 54–55; South African War, 24–26, 31, 45, 155; speeches, 34–35, 45, 48–50, 56, 72, 76, 78–79, 99, 111–12, 135, 141, 155, 168, 191–92; socialism, 56, 68, 78–81, 111, 138, 149–50; Tariff Reform League, 29–33, 58, 90, 93, 114, 122, 134, 168, 181, 188–95; tributes to, 16–17; Ulster visit, 206; women's suffrage, 150, 197–98; working classes, 30–31, 35, 37, 41, 46–50, 111–12, 135, 141, 148, 150, 170, 173, 182, 191–93. Books: *New Order, Studies in Unionist Policy,* 63, 105, 198; *Path of Empire,* 181. Articles: "Citizen Army," 198; "Consideration for Working Men," 30–32; "Free Trade and Tariff Reform," 54; "How Unionism Can Win," 147–50; in the *Morning Post,* 147–50; in the *Outlook,* 199; "Plain Tory," 186

Croft, Richard Benyon, 37, 91, 95–96, 100–101, 105
Croft, Richard Page, 24–26, 41
Cromer, Lord, 87, 106, 142
Cross, R. B., 95
Curzon, Lord, 137, 151, 157

Daily Chronicle, 127
Daily Express, 120, 142, 161, 183
Daily Graphic, 62, 142
Daily Mail, 61–62, 94, 142
Dangerfield, George, 17
Derby, Lord, 141–42, 151, 155, 182–85
Devonshire, duke of, 32–33, 35–37, 64, 77
Dixon, Charles, 157
Doughty, Sir George, 187
Duncannon, Viscount, 62, 66, 189, 192, 194–95, 214
Dundonald, earl of, 115, 172

East Hertfordshire: and politics, 20, 25, 28–31, 34, 37–39, 41–44, 47–48, 51, 53, 55–56, 69, 74–75, 89–105, 115, 168, 191, 210–11
East Hertfordshire Conservatives, 92, 94, 97–99, 101–2
East Marylebone. *See* Marylebone
Edinburgh speech, 127–28
Education Bill, 54, 79
Edward VII, 27, 117
elections: Attercliffe-Sheffield, 101; Crewe, 184; Dulwich, 33, 36; East Finsbury, 47; Hitchin Division-Hertfordshire, 48; Kingswinford, 47; Kirkdale Division-Liverpool, 118; Manchester Northwest, 184; Lewisham, 33, 36; Newcastle, 80; St. Albans, 36–37; West Wiltshire, 167; Worcester, 87
elections, general: 1906, 20, 50–51, 54; December 1910, 143–44; January 1910, 21, 107, 111–12
Elliot, Arthur, 87, 106
empire, 15–16, 26–28, 31–32, 50, 67–68, 83, 89, 117, 120, 125, 136, 138, 141, 155, 173–76, 178, 191, 196, 198–99, 206
Empire Industries Association, 17
Esher, Lord, 140
Evening News, 113, 142

INDEX

Fair Trade, 49, 54
Fanhams Hall, 23–24, 60
Farquhar, Lord, 153
Faudel-Phillips, Sir George, 42, 91, 95, 249n
Findlay, Sir J. G., 172
Fletcher, John S., 48, 174
food duties, 21, 31, 141, 149, 190–94
Forrest, Sir John, 172
Fox, Frank, 115
free trade and free traders, 20, 26–27, 31, 40–42, 49, 54, 57–58, 61, 76–78, 84–87, 98, 100, 111, 118, 141, 145, 150, 177, 182–84, 187

Garvin, J. L., 58–59, 63–64, 113, 128, 137–40, 155, 166, 185
George V, 155, 169
George VI, 15
Germany, 49, 50, 57, 61, 67, 117, 121, 189, 207
Gibbs, Herbert, 105
Gibbs, Vicary, 36
Glasgow speech, 32
Globe, 74, 125, 142
Glyn, Maurice, 143, 152
Goldman, Charles, 167, 222
Gould, George, 116, 172
Goulding, Edward, 60, 62, 64, 72–73, 81–82, 87, 93, 122–27, 152, 157, 164, 185, 187, 192, 219
Greenwich, 44
Gretton, John, 80
Grey, Earl, 173
Grey, Sir Edward, 207
Griffith, Francis, 62
Gwynne, H. A., 126, 183

Haddock, George, 157
Halsbury, Lord, 156, 158, 160–61, 163
Halsey, Thomas, 48
Hamilton, Lord George, 32, 83
Hannon, Patrick, 113, 115, 222
Hardie, Keir, 78
Hardinge, Viscount, 62, 64, 215
Harris, Frederick Leverton, 62, 215
Harrison-Broadley, Col., 78
Harrowby, Lord, 62, 64, 215
Hastings, Admiral, 41
Hay, Claude, 62, 215
Henderson, Sir Alexander, 192
Herbert, Aubrey, 172

Herman, Mr., 64, 215
Hertfordshire Mercury, 29, 31, 54
Hertfordshire Volunteer Battalion, 25
Hewins, W. A. S., 63, 65, 72–73, 165–66, 187, 192, 215
Hickman, Col. T. E., 203
Hillier, Dr. Alfred, 172, 265
Hills, John L., 62, 64, 66, 72–73, 75, 130, 216
Hoare, Samuel, 174
home rule, 114, 138, 144, 147, 201–5
Hope, James Fitzalan, 63, 118, 167, 217
House of Lords, 78, 80, 110, 114, 117, 130, 143, 146, 149–50, 155–56, 158–59, 161, 204
Hudson, George, 48
Hughes, Percival, 125
Hull Daily Mail, 122
Hunt, Rowland, 157, 167, 187, 223
Hunter, Sir Charles, 62, 216

imperial federation, 26, 137
imperial mission: organization and campaign of, 18–19, 21, 110, 116–19, 122, 152–54, 162–63, 168–78, 182, 195, 199, 201, 210–13
imperial mission: membership of, 171–72, 174, 229–33
Imperial Pioneers, 115, 168
imperial preference, 16, 20, 26–28, 34, 40, 42, 50, 72–74, 83, 96, 118, 122, 128, 139, 149–50, 152, 166–69, 173–78, 183, 188–89, 195
Imperial Unionist Party, 54
India, 172
Ireland, 21, 112, 114, 137–39, 144, 147, 150, 153, 188, 195–96, 202–6, 212

Japan, 117
Jenkins, J. G., 172
Johnson, Stanley, 134, 223

Kebtey-Fletcher, J. R., 157
Kinloch-Cooke, Clement, 157
Kirkwood, J. H., 130, 223
Kyffin-Taylor, Col., 118

Labour party, 17, 51, 112, 118, 126, 144, 193
Lambton, Lord, 112
Lampson, Oliver Locker, 130, 187, 223

INDEX

Lancashire Daily Post, 122
Lansdowne, Lord, 137, 142, 155–57, 184, 188
Laurier, Sir Wilfrid, 173
Law, Andrew Bonar, 16, 18, 21, 59, 62, 64–65, 70, 73, 77–79, 81, 104, 118, 121, 126, 137, 141–42, 144, 153, 164, 166, 177–89, 191–96, 199, 201–2, 207, 212
Law, Andrew Bonar: memorial to, 187–88
Law, Richard, 16
Lawrence, Sir Joseph, 73, 151, 183, 192
Leconfield, Lord, 16, 223
Lee, Sir Arthur, 66, 72–73, 79, 81, 126, 216
Leith of Fyvie, Lord, 162, 265
Lewisham, Viscount, 203
Liberal party, 17, 21, 34, 40, 56, 64, 69, 78–79, 97–98, 112, 114, 134, 136, 141, 144, 154, 156, 166, 169–70, 183, 190, 197–98, 205, 207, 211
Licensing Bill, 80–81
Lincoln, 43–44, 46, 50–53, 115–16, 210
Lincolnshire Chronicle, 45, 54
Lloyd, George, 64, 66, 113, 187, 216
Lloyd George, David, 103–4, 110, 118, 128, 132, 136, 140, 143, 148, 150, 154, 189, 193
Londonderry, Marquess of, 134–35, 155, 206
Long, Walter, 86, 88, 90, 139, 142, 151–55, 164, 202, 204, 247n
Lovat, Lord, 161
Lygon, Maj. Henry, 62, 66, 216
Lyttelton, Alfred, 51, 73, 77

McKenna, Sir Reginald, 113
Mackinder, H. J., 113, 132, 166, 168, 224
Macmillan, Harold, 16, 209
McNeill, Ronald, 62–64, 75, 171, 183, 186, 188, 203, 215
Malmesbury, Earl of, 55–56, 60–63, 66, 105, 116, 128–29, 135–36, 161, 216
Manchester Courier, 113
manufacturing, 48–50, 99, 112, 141
Marks, Harry, 62, 64, 216
Marlborough, duke of, 172, 176
Marylebone, 77, 88–90, 93, 100, 104,
Marylebone pledge, 88, 93

Maryon-Wilson, Sir Spencer Pocklington Maryon, 62, 66, 219
Maxse, Leopold, 58–66, 69–70, 72, 82, 90, 116, 118, 121–28, 132, 139, 144, 156, 160–63, 168, 174–75, 216
Maxton, Jimmy, 15
Mayo, Lord, 161
Milner, Viscount, 62, 157, 161, 163, 172, 203
Milner, Viscountess, 15, 209, 213
Mitchell-Thomson, William, 62, 77, 218
Monkton-Arundel, G. V. A., 143, 224
Morning Advertiser, 122
Morning Post, 76, 84, 93–94, 113, 122–23, 126–27, 133, 136, 147, 183
Morpeth, Lord, 63, 214
Morrison, J. A., 85
Mortimer, Reginald, 90, 101, 103, 105, 252n
Mulloy, J. B., 115

National Insurance Act (1911), 196
National Review, 57, 90, 94, 113, 116, 123, 125, 183, 188
National party, 17, 135, 175
navy, 113, 116, 128, 132–33, 135, 176, 198, 200, 204–5
New Order: Studies in Unionist Policy (book), 63, 65, 105
Newton, Lord, 157
New Zealand, 115–16, 172
Northcliffe, Lord, 166, 184, 187
Northcote, Lord, 172, 265
Norton-Griffiths, John, 130, 140, 171, 224
Norwood (Lambeth): politics in, 77–78, 86, 89–91, 100, 104
Nottingham Party Conference, 141
Nottingham East: politics in, 85
Nottingham South: politics in, 81, 85

Observer, 63, 125, 137, 139, 142, 155
O'Connor, Daniel, 115
Oliver, F. S., 64, 66, 113, 258
O'Neill, Hugh, 63, 66, 217
Oranmore and Browne, Lord, 62, 217
Ormsby-Gore, William, 87, 169, 172, 223
Osborne case, 126, 135, 196
Outlook, 58, 125, 199

"Pacificus," 137
Paget, Almeric, 172, 265
Pall Mall Gazette, 125
Parker, Ebenezer, 187
Parker, Sir Gilbert, 62, 73, 167, 187, 217
Parker, Sir William, 174
Parliament Bill (1911), 154–59, 165, 168, 176, 201–3
Payment of Members Act (1912), 196
Pease, Herbert Pike, 194
Pease, Joseph (Jack), 98
Peel, Sir Robert, 140
Peel, William, 157
people's budget, 103–4, 110
Peto, Basil, 64, 143, 155, 157, 167, 171–72, 183, 203, 217, 224
Pioneers of the Empire, 115
Pitt, William, the Younger, 17
Platt, Thomas Comyn, 60, 62–64, 66, 74, 183, 203, 217
Portland, duke of, 82
Powell, Sir Francis, 78
Pretyman, E. G., 161
Primrose League, 47, 54, 147

Quick, Sir John, 172

Randles, Sir John, 184
Rea, Russell, 134
Remnant, James L., 62, 64, 73, 81, 157, 192, 218
Renton, Maj. Leslie, 80
Renwick, George, 80
Reveille: manifestos, 120–21, 132–33, 137–38, 146, 226–28; membership of, 129–30, 221–25; organization and campaign of, 18–21, 110, 120–50, 152, 160–63, 171, 173, 177, 195, 201, 206, 210–12
Rhodes, Arthur, 116, 172
Rhodes, Cecil, 34
Ridley, Viscount, 58, 60, 62, 64–65, 77, 83, 113, 246n
Ridley, Samuel, 62, 218
Ritchie, C. T., 27–28, 32
Roberts, C. H., 54
Roberts, Lord, 174
Rolleston, Sir John L., 63, 105, 218
Russell, Sir William, 116, 172

safeguarding, 75, 83, 99, 128, 141
St. Aldwyn, Lord, 142

St. Loe Strachey, John, 87, 142
Salisbury, 3d marquess of, 18, 20, 27, 34
Salisbury, 4th marquess of, 76, 87, 97, 102, 105, 142, 151, 155–58, 161, 182–83
Samuel, Harry, 157
Sandars, J. S., 64, 72, 138, 140–41, 242–43
Sanders, Robert, 204
Sandys, George, 157, 171, 264n
Sarajevo, 21, 207
Saturday Review, 125
Savidge, Archibald, 142
Scott, Leslie, 65, 218
Scottish Conservative Club, 126
Seely, Charles Hilton, 43, 45–48, 50, 54
Selborne, (2d) earl of, 62, 150, 156, 160–61, 172–73, 176, 248n
Sheffield Daily Telegraph, 45
Simon, Sir John, 134
Skeffington-Smith, Geoffrey, 62, 66, 218
Slack, John Bamford, 36
Smith, Abel Henry, 20, 29, 37–38, 42–44, 55, 74–75, 77, 88–100, 103–4, 106, 210–13, 249n
Smith, F. E., 113, 127, 129, 137, 157, 160, 164, 187, 257n
Smith, Harold, 65, 157, 218
Smith, James Parker, 51
Smith, W. F. D., 78
South Africa, 25–27, 31, 45, 54, 115, 155, 172, 198
Spectator, 94, 98
Spencer-Churchill, E. G., 62–63, 66
Standard, the 113, 125, 142
Stanhope, Lord, 174
Steel-Maitland, Arthur, 60, 62–63, 72, 77, 113, 152–53, 161, 163, 187, 218
Stewart, Vivian, 62
Strafford Club, 60
Sutherland, duke of, 29, 64, 82
Sydney Bulletin, 115

Tariff Reform League, 29, 33–35, 38, 42–44, 48, 55, 58, 61, 71–72, 77, 82–83, 86, 90, 93, 95–97, 99, 116, 148, 152, 163, 168, 181, 184, 188–90, 192, 194–97, 211
tariff reform and tariff reformers, 19, 29–33, 34–45, 43–44, 48, 54–55, 57,

/ 71–72, 74–76, 83, 86, 90, 111–14, 134, 136, 142, 149–50, 166, 168, 185, 187–88, 191–95
Temple, Michael, 62–63, 219
Tennyson, Lord, 172, 265n
Textile Mercury, 142
Thornton, Percy, 98
Times, the, 39, 87, 104, 126, 137, 140, 142, 184, 187
Trades Disputes Act (1913), 196
Tryon, Capt. George, 62, 113, 182, 218
Turnour, Lord. *See* Winterton, Lord

Ulster (see Ireland)
Union of British Empire, 174
Unionist. *See* Conservative Party
Unionist Organization Committee (UOC), 152–53
United Club, 75, 77
United Empire Club, 189
United States, 57, 67, 114, 117, 119, 126, 154, 165–66

Valentine Pact, 58, 60–61, 70, 74
Verney, Frederick, 143
Vincent, Sir Edgar, 77

Ward, Arnold, 62, 203, 219
Ward, Sir Joseph, 116

Ware (Hertfordshire), 34–37, 51, 55, 74, 93, 101
Ware Unionist Working Men's Club, 41, 98, 101
Ware, Fabian, 65, 67, 71, 147, 219
Wedgewood, Lord 23
Westgate, H. C., 80
Westminster Gazette, 127
Williams, R. Vaughn, 134, 224
Williams, Col. Robert, 78
Willoughby de Broke, Lord, 123–24, 128, 131, 133–35, 152, 156, 160–61, 163, 173–74, 177, 203–4, 224
Wilson, Leslie, 130, 143, 224
Winterton, Lord, 61–67, 73, 77, 81, 89, 219
Wise, Bernhard R., 60–61, 63–65, 220
Wolfe, Sir Henry Drummond, 111
Wolmer, Viscount, 88, 156, 248n
Wolverton, Lord, 172, 265
Women's Suffrage, 150, 197–98
World War, First, 18, 21–22, 207
Wyndham, George, 65, 153, 156, 163, 261n

xenophobia, 34, 150

Yorkshire Post, 62
Younger, George, 152